AF812482

Research Series on the Chinese Dream and China's Development Path

Project Director
Xie Shouguang, President, Social Sciences Academic Press

Series editors
Li Yang, Vice president, Chinese Academy of Social Sciences, Beijing, China
Li Peilin, Vice president, Chinese Academy of Social Sciences, Beijing, China

Academic Advisors
Cai Fang, Gao Peiyong, Li Lin, Li Qiang, Ma Huaide, Pan Jiahua, Pei Changhong, Qi Ye, Wang Lei, Wang Ming, Zhang Yuyan, Zheng Yongnian, Zhou Hong

Drawing on a large body of empirical studies done over the last two decades, this Series provides its readers with in-depth analyses of the past and present and forecasts for the future course of China's development. It contains the latest research results made by members of the Chinese Academy of Social Sciences. This series is an invaluable companion to every researcher who is trying to gain a deeper understanding of the development model, path and experience unique to China. Thanks to the adoption of Socialism with Chinese characteristics, and the implementation of comprehensive reform and opening-up, China has made tremendous achievements in areas such as political reform, economic development, and social construction, and is making great strides towards the realization of the Chinese dream of national rejuvenation. In addition to presenting a detailed account of many of these achievements, the authors also discuss what lessons other countries can learn from China's experience.

More information about this series at http://www.springer.com/series/13571

Yitao Tao · Zhiguo Lu

Special Economic Zones and China's Development Path

SSAP

Springer

Yitao Tao
Center for Special Economic
Zones Research
Shenzhen University
Shenzhen, Guangdong, China

Zhiguo Lu
College of Economics
Shenzhen University
Shenzhen, Guangdong, China

ISSN 2363-6866 ISSN 2363-6874 (electronic)
Research Series on the Chinese Dream and China's Development Path
ISBN 978-981-10-3219-6 ISBN 978-981-10-3220-2 (eBook)
https://doi.org/10.1007/978-981-10-3220-2

Jointly published with Social Sciences Academic Press, Beijing, China

The print edition is not for sale in China Mainland. Customers from China Mainland please order the print book from: Social Sciences Academic Press.

Library of Congress Control Number: 2018945448

© Social Sciences Academic Press and Springer Nature Singapore Pte Ltd. 2018
This work is subject to copyright. All rights are reserved by the Publishers, whether the whole or part of the material is concerned, specifically the rights of translation, reprinting, reuse of illustrations, recitation, broadcasting, reproduction on microfilms or in any other physical way, and transmission or information storage and retrieval, electronic adaptation, computer software, or by similar or dissimilar methodology now known or hereafter developed.
The use of general descriptive names, registered names, trademarks, service marks, etc. in this publication does not imply, even in the absence of a specific statement, that such names are exempt from the relevant protective laws and regulations and therefore free for general use.
The publishers, the authors and the editors are safe to assume that the advice and information in this book are believed to be true and accurate at the date of publication. Neither the publishers nor the authors or the editors give a warranty, express or implied, with respect to the material contained herein or for any errors or omissions that may have been made. The publishers remains neutral with regard to jurisdictional claims in published maps and institutional affiliations.

Printed on acid-free paper

This Springer imprint is published by the registered company Springer Nature Singapore Pte Ltd.
The registered company address is: 152 Beach Road, #21-01/04 Gateway East, Singapore 189721, Singapore

Series Preface

Since China's reform and opening began in 1978, the country has come a long way on the path of Socialism with Chinese Characteristics, under the leadership of the Communist Party of China. Over 30 years of reform efforts and sustained spectacular economic growth have turned China into the world's second largest economy and wrought many profound changes in the Chinese society. These historically significant developments have been garnering increasing attention from scholars, governments, and the general public alike around the world since the 1990s, when the newest wave of China studies began to gather steam. Some of the hottest topics have included the so-called "China miracle", "Chinese phenomenon", "Chinese experience", "Chinese path", and the "Chinese model". Homegrown researchers have soon followed suit. Already hugely productive, this vibrant field is putting out a large number of books each year, with Social Sciences Academic Press alone having published hundreds of titles on a wide range of subjects.

Because most of these books have been written and published in Chinese, however, readership has been limited outside China—even among many who study China—for whom English is still the lingua franca. This language barrier has been an impediment to efforts by academia, business communities, and policymakers in other countries to form a thorough understanding of contemporary China, of what is distinct about China's past and present may mean not only for her future but also for the future of the world. The need to remove such an impediment is both real and urgent, and the *Research Series on the Chinese Dream and China's Development Path* is my answer to the call.

This series features some of the most notable achievements from the last 20 years by scholars in China in a variety of research topics related to reform and opening. They include both theoretical explorations and empirical studies, and cover economy, society, politics, law, culture, and ecology, the six areas in which reform and opening policies have had the deepest impact and farthest-reaching consequences for the country. Authors for the series have also tried to articulate their visions of the "Chinese Dream" and how the country can realize it in these fields and beyond.

All of the editors and authors for the *Research Series on the Chinese Dream and China's Development Path* are both longtime students of reform and opening and recognized authorities in their respective academic fields. Their credentials and expertise lend credibility to these books, each of which having been subject to a rigorous peer review process for inclusion in the series. As part of the Reform and Development Program under the State Administration of Press, Publication, Radio, Film and Television of the People's Republic of China, the series is published by Springer, a Germany-based academic publisher of international repute, and distributed overseas. I am confident that it will help fill a lacuna in studies of China in the era of reform and opening.

Xie Shouguang

Preface

This book, *Special Economic Zones and China's Development Path*, currently available to you, is an achievement under the Major Program of the National Social Science Fund (No. 10AJL001). It took four and a half years to complete this research. Although we hope that our research achievement is a "meticulously engraved jade", it is certainly not flawless. Even when we reviewed the final draft, we believed that much could have been done better and more thoroughly. We are keenly aware that academic research is a process of sharing, thinking and contention, sparking inspiration, and brainstorming. We hope that our research will be recognized by our peers, so that we can make some self-improvement amid debates and dialogues because both recognition and criticism are of invaluable wealth for us.

Our research is based on the following considerations.

First, though China's Development Path covered in our research refers in particular to a number of policies and choices of paths since China's reform and opening up in 1978, the reform and opening up aims at making Chinese society open, prosperous, and powerful, and fundamentally, it is designed to achieve modernization in an all-round way. Therefore, the exploration and practice of China's Development Path involve a process of choosing the path towards the modernization of Chinese society; the special economic zones, on the other hand, represent a "shortcut" for accelerating that modernization against the background of an unbalanced development. Proceeding from the different choices of paths of different countries for achieving modernization, our research aims at shedding light on the distinctive characteristics of China's Development Path in a more explicit and in-depth way by comparing the paths towards transformation adopted by different countries in the course of the historical development of the world.

Second, even though the reform and opening up in Chinese society started from the establishment of the special economic zones—the special economic zones are not only the starting point of but also part of China's Development Path—theoretically, it is certainly the focus of and the difficulty in our research to give a clear picture of the inherent logical relationships between the special economic zones and China's Development Path, which also has the highest theoretical value and the greatest significance, and is the core of the whole research. In Chap. 2, based on the theories relating to developmental economics and comparative institutional economics, by using the research methods, including empirical analysis and quantitative analysis, we first of all proceeded from the historical background of China's reform and opening up to carry out the construction of the theory and the explanation of the model regarding the inherent logical relationships between the special economic zones and China's Development Path, from both historical and logical perspectives. Chapter 3 further expands—from the perspectives of political economics, institutional economics, developmental economics, and regional economics—the research discussed in Chap. 2: This chapter abstractly and critically elaborates on the special economic zones and China's Development Path under the principles of economics.

Third, Chaps. 4–7 touch upon the theoretical contributions of the special economic zones to China's market economy, their institutional contributions to China's modernization, their economic contributions to China's modernization drive and their cultural contributions to China's modernization, respectively. Such a structural arrangement was made from the following three considerations:

(1) Theoretically and practically, China's Development Path is a concept which needs to be constantly enriched, improved, and gradually made systematic. The Path has come into being, but the experimentation is still underway; the experience has been gathered, but the theories need to be further sought after. We have reviewed and analyzed the developmental process and some mature policies, thoughts, and theories developed in that process, and we will continue the review and analysis. Among a number of things which give expression to the significance of China's Development Path, some have been crystallized into Chinese characteristics, while some are being tested in practice and show considerable room for reform and experimentation, and are being put into practice to fill the theoretical gap. Therefore, we have not researched the theoretical system of China's Development Path; on the contrary, we have summarized and expounded some policies, thoughts, theories, even modes and routes which constitute China's Development Path, and have historically explained the practical process of China's Development Path, and the theories and thoughts which have taken shape during that practical process.
(2) The special economic zones are the explorers, forerunners, and practitioners of China's Development Path. First of all, implementing pilot programs in the special economic zones as the first movers to acquire experience and then universally applying the experience across the country is the basic path towards institutional change in Chinese society and the choice of a path for modernizing Chinese society. Therefore, when summarizing, reviewing, and researching China's Development Path and demonstrating the internal logic between the special economic zones and China's Development Path, we naturally give prominence to the special economic zones as the vivid examples, the experimental fields for reform, the providers of experience, the explorers, and creators of theories. In this regard, the most typical and successful, the Shenzhen Special Economic Zone, is put in the most conspicuous position.

(3) The reform and opening up in Chinese society started from the economic reform; however, if the people's minds were not emancipated and the mind-sets were not renewed and revolutionized, the practice of China's reform and opening up and the emergence of the special economic zones would be impossible. Culture and mind-set cannot directly change society, but they can change the people, and the people can bring about changes in society. Therefore, the cultural contributions of the special economic zones to China's modernization, as expounded in Chap. 7, essentially reveal the impact of the changes in the mind-set on Chinese society. The special economic zones have created numerous economic miracles for Chinese society and have changed it with the power of the mind-set, giving rise to a revolution of the mind-set sufficient to influence billions of Chinese people. The modernization of a society begins with the modernization of the people, while the modernization of the people starts from the modernization of the mind-set. Only the people are the resource-generating resources, the wealth-creating wealth, the main players of, and the motive power behind social innovations.

Dante Alighieri said, "It is love that moves the sun and the earth". In my opinion, the conscience and feelings and the sense of mission of scholars enable us not to give up thinking and experimentation. Rationality prevails at the academic level, thus scholars should be rational and passionate. This is because there is no impulsion for creation if there is no suffering in the soul. We are lucky to live in an era of change and make contributions in such an era during which thoughts are needed and generated.

Shenzhen, China
January 2016

Yitao Tao
Deputy Secretary of the Party Committee
Secretary of the Discipline Inspection Commission
of Shenzhen University, Director, Professor
China Center for Special Economic Zone Research
Shenzhen University—Humanities & Social
Science Research Based under the Ministry of Education

Acknowledgements

After a relatively short gestation period, the *Research Series on the Chinese Dream and China's Development Path* has started to bear fruits. We have, first and foremost, the books' authors and editors to thank for making this possible. And it was the hard work by many people at Social Sciences Academic Press and Springer, the two collaborating publishers, that made it a reality. We are deeply grateful to all of them.

Mr. Xie Shouguang, president of Social Sciences Academic Press (SSAP), is the mastermind behind the project. In addition to defining the key missions to be accomplished by it and setting down the basic parameters for the project's execution, as the work has unfolded, Mr. Xie has provided critical input pertaining to its every aspect and at every step of the way. Thanks to the deft coordination by Ms. Li Yanling, all the constantly moving parts of the project, especially those on the SSAP side, are securely held together, and as well synchronized as is feasible for a project of this scale. Ms. Gao Jing, unfailingly diligent and meticulous, makes sure every aspect of each Chinese manuscript meets the highest standards for both publishers, something of critical importance to all subsequent steps in the publishing process. That high-quality if also at times stylistically as well as technically challenging scholarly writing in Chinese has turned into decent, readable English that readers see on these pages is largely thanks to Ms. Liang Fan, who oversees translator recruitment and translation quality control.

Ten other members of the SSAP staff have been intimately involved, primarily in the capacity of in-house editor, in the preparation of the Chinese manuscripts. It is time-consuming work that requires attention to details, and each of them has done this and is continuing to do this with superb skills. They are, in alphabetical order: Mr. Cai Jihui, Ms. Liu Xiaojun, Mr. Ren Wenwu, Ms. Shi Xiaolin, Ms. Song Yuehua, Mr. Tong Genxing, Ms. Wu Dan, Ms. Yao Dongmei, Ms. Yun Wei, and Ms. Zhou Qiong. In addition, Xie Shouguang and Li Yanling have also taken part in this work.

Ms. Li Yanling is the SSAP in-house editor for the current volume.

Our appreciation is also owed to Ms. Li Yan, Mr. Chai Ning, Ms. Wang Lei, and Ms. Xu Yi from Springer's Beijing Representative Office. Their strong support for the SSAP team in various aspects of the project helped to make the latter's work that much easier than it would have otherwise been.

We thank Mr. Zheng Kaixiang for translating this book.

Last, but certainly not least, it must be mentioned that funding for this project comes from the Ministry of Finance of the People's Republic of China. Our profound gratitude, if we can be forgiven for a bit of apophasis, goes without saying.

Social Sciences Academic Press
Springer

Contents

Introduction

Essentially, research on the special economic zones and China's Development Path is research on the history of China's reform and opening up in the past 40 years, the path to institutional change in Chinese society and the road to achieving China's modernization. This is because the reform and opening up in Chinese society is a process of transformation from a planned economy to a market economy, from self-seclusion to policy-based and institutional opening up, from widespread poverty to common prosperity, and from the backwardness characterized by planned development, seclusion, a small-scale peasant economy under the traditional system to prosperity featuring market-based development, opening up, internationalization, and modernization.

China's Development Path mentioned here refers to the way and path adopted by China since 1978, towards achieving social transformation, economic development, and all-round modernization. Specifically, in China, a large country—with a 30-year history of a planned economy—where the planned economy is practiced, traditional ideology undoubtedly dominates, and development is severely unbalanced among regions and between the urban and rural areas, as an institutional change, the special economic zones were established to break through the traditional system, with a view to gradually transforming the whole country from a planned economy to a market economy, so that Chinese society could embark on the path of a market economy in an all-round way in a certain period of time, gradually, really turning China into an economically prosperous, institutionally advanced socialist market economy country under the rule of law.

In my opinion, compared with the Washington Consensus, China's Development Path has certain characteristics determined by the history, culture, and the nature of a particular country: First, the establishment of the special economic zones is the first—and successful—choice of a path towards institutional change; second, giving priority to economic development and starting from the reform of the economic system is the inevitable, but very correct, starting point for institutional change; third, advancing cautiously and steadily, first of all implementing pilot programs, creating experience, exploring the path, and universally applying it is an overall—and relatively sound—train of thought and practical logic for achieving institutional change; fourth, promoting the reform through opening up is a wise and basic philosophy for reducing ideological resistance during institutional change; fifth, the "whole nation system" is an efficient political resource and power with an enormous capability for mobilization during institutional change; sixth, a government committed to continuous self-reform serves as the internal motivational power and fundamental guarantee for continuing and intensifying institutional change.

Several Theoretical Issues Concerning China's Development Path

The previous research on China's Development Path, modernization, China's special economic zones and relevant issues provide us with a wealth of solid thoughts and the academic foundation for great referential significance so that we can deepen and expand our research now. However, the previous research projects were subject to a number of limitations and there are theoretical fields not covered by them due to the era, ideology, and other factors, so some issues were left out, which needed to be further explored in our current research, and they provide a possibility and room for research with theoretical value and practical significance.

First, with respect to the starting point of China's Development Path, I agree with the view that China's Development Path refers in particular to the social developmental path or developmental experience since China's reform and opening up. As mentioned by Stephen Halper, a senior research fellow at the University of Cambridge, when it came to China's Development Path, it mainly referred to the development and a series of reforms in China over the past 30 years and more. This was because China's Development Path, that we are discussing now, was a particular concept with a special historical significance against a unique background rather than a concept simply or purely involving a history or the history of the communist movement and the history of the Communist Party of China. For a century, the Chinese people have staunchly pursued the road to national independence and modernization leading to a civilized and powerful country. China's revolutionary road and road towards construction is the one full of arduous and hard struggles, regardless of the period, from the Opium War in 1840 or the founding of the P.R. of China in 1949; however, the road that China traveled throughout history is different from China's Development Path adopted by China since the reform and opening up in 1980. Therefore, China's Development Path that is mentioned here should not be broadly understood as China's modern history of nearly 120 years starting from the old democratic revolution, the new democratic revolution to the socialist revolution and construction. Furthermore, in the first 30 years after the founding of the P.R. of China, we followed the Soviet Model instead of taking our own road. The reform and opening up is based on the repudiation of the traditional planned economy typically represented by the Soviet Model, thus logically, theoretically, and practically, it is impossible to inherit or retain the repudiated things and consider the reform and innovation as the "development" of the "reformed things".

Second, the discussions regarding China's Development Path must dispense with the ultraleft mind-set and the mentality of the Cold War, especially the dogmatic train of thought which stressed a distinction between what is socialist and what is capitalist in terms of economic development. China's reform and opening up started from the emancipation of the people's minds; an important symbol of such emancipation is the historical judgment made by Deng Xiaoping: "A market economy is not equal to capitalism, and there is also a market in socialism." As shown by the historical course of China's reform and opening up, only when the contention is shelved can China's reform and opening up be carried out, can a market economy come into being, can the special economic zones be developed, and can China's Development Path take shape. In view of the ultimate goal for human development—turning it into a prosperous, civilized and free one, the road to achieving social development, and then modernization should not be prefixed by "capitalism" or "socialism". Indeed, the developmental paths may vary according to the different countries due to history, culture, value outlook, national character, and other factors; however, this is an embodiment of diversity rather than mutual negation among diverse cultures and value outlooks. Therefore, I disagree with such a judgment: There were many roads to modernization in the world in the twentieth century, and they can be summarized into two categories: (1) modernization with capitalism as the core; (2) modernization with socialism as the core. This classification is too simple and lacks inclusiveness and respect for diverse cultures and value outlooks. Moreover, it is unnecessary to gnash your teeth at "The End of History" brought forward by Francis Fukuyama and simply consider his theory as the victory of Western capitalism over socialism. The realistic basis for his theory is the collapse of the Soviet Union. Therefore, I believe that it is more objective to consider "The End of History" as the end of the era of the traditional socialist countries. We also take note of other views of Francis Fukuyama's—for example, Francis Fukuyama said that the USA cannot determine the time when and the place where democracy occurred. Specifically, if there were not a demand in a country, the outsiders cannot impose democracy on this country; the demand for democracy and reform must emerge domestically. Therefore, democratic improvement was a long process during which the time gradually became ripe, and this process relied on gradual political and economic improvement. Similarly, the development was fostered by the poor, but not given to the poor by the rich. In an interview with the *International Herald Tribune* in June, 2011, Francis Fukuyama made the following response concerning "The End of History", China's developmental model and other issues: It was necessary for the USA to learn from China. He also believed that China's Model could not be copied by the rest of the world because it originated from particular historical and cultural traditions of bureaucracy and power in China.

However, in my opinion, China is not only a large country with a traditional planned economy but also a developing country. Its transformation from a planned economy to a market economy has been a process of reform and opening up as well as one of the constructions of an emerging market economy; in particular, amidst today's economic globalization, as a developing country with an emerging market economy, China has many similarities with other developing countries and countries with an emerging market economy. For example, we have all benefitted from but are subject to economic globalization, seen population aging before we are rich enough to be ready, and seen problems with public education, public medical service, and health; all of these countries need to improve their market economic system, social laws, and regulations and learn from best practices from other countries. I believe that once the development and social issues shared by the developing countries and the emerging countries with a market economy are successfully addressed by China under the "whole nation system" to varying degrees, this will be of profound referential significance to the developing countries and the emerging countries with a market economy. This is of universal significance like the success of the Four Asian Tigers and Taiwan's land reform. The nationality of or the country-specific success in a country often is objective of worldwide significance due to the law which governs human development and the widespread problems in human development. This significance lies in providing human beings with sharable wisdom and spiritual wealth instead of setting an example for the world. As a successful transformational path, China's Development Path provides a vivid case concerning the choice of a path for the economic development and the modernization of the emerging countries with a market economy.

Moreover, the special economic zones have become the chosen path for the developing countries and the emerging countries with a market economy to seek economic development and modernization against the background of relatively widespread poverty and unbalanced economic development. With the successful experience in China's special economic zones, China will provide the above countries with invaluable experience and lessons to pursue their economic development by establishing special economic zones.

Third, with respect to the debate on whether China's Development Path exists, I am more willing to believe that there are different perspectives or approaches towards this issue. (1) The existence of China's Development Path is an indisputable and objective fact. The transformation of Chinese society from a planned economy to a market economy and from a country with widespread poverty to one with common prosperity, and China's Miracle created in nearly 40 years since the reform and opening up mirror China's Development Path. In the opinions of the scholars who assert that China's Development Path does not exist, if China's Model and China's Development Path are discussed within the theoretical framework for the building of a modern country, China's Model is nonexistent, as is China's Development Path, because the contemporary Chinese Mainland has not yet completed the building of a modern country and the currently available unique institutional combination lacks sufficient stability and extendibility.[1] In my opinion, adopting the above view to demonstrate that China's Model is unavailable makes sense; I also believe that China's Model is currently nonexistent. A model means that the institutions have been inflexible and have become a paradigm, so it is not necessarily a good thing for a country which is in the process of experimentation and development. However, it is excessively arbitrary to conclude that China's Development Path is nonexistent just because there is no model called "China's Model". If China's Model is the result of a summarization, China's Development Path is a realistic existence and a choice. The "model" has not yet taken shape and does not exist, but a path has started taking shape in an ever clearer way.

Fourth, China's Development Path and modernization. Most scholars logically associate China's Development Path with the road towards China's modernization; they even equate the former with the latter. In my view, indeed, there is a certain internal logical relationship between both, but the former is not absolutely equivalent to the latter. China's Development Path is the result of the path chosen by the Chinese people with respect to modernization; however, the road to modernization that the Chinese people have experienced is not merely the currently discussed China's Development Path because such a road includes the Soviet Model. In my opinion, the above discussion about the relationship between China's Development Path and modernization expands the significance of China's Development Path and takes the general concept of China's Development Path as China's Development Path with a particular significance. China's Development Path can be considered the path towards modernization with Chinese characteristics,[2] but it is inappropriate to consider China's modernization as China's Development Path. The Chinese people have pursued modernization for a time, much longer than the period since the current China's Development Path took shape. The success of the new democratic revolution marked the end of "the century of humiliation" for China since the Opium War in 1840; the founding of the independent P.R. of China has laid a solid foundation for China to achieve modernization; when modernization became the theme of China's social development, how to achieve China's modernization became an issue which needed to be immediately addressed. China ultimately chose the road of "pursuing modernization but rejecting westernization": adopting socialism to develop China's economy and promote China's social development and rejuvenation of the Chinese nation.[3] From this perspective, the roads adopted by the Chinese people after the success of the new democratic revolution in order to pursue industrialization, modernization, and seek prosperity are China's Development Paths—they share the same name, but they are different in essence.

---

[1] Yao Zhongqiu, "Transformation" of an Institutional Change Mode—Take China's Institutional Change in 30 Years as an Example, *A Theoretical Analysis of China's Change in 30 Years—From the Perspective of the Austrian School*, Zhejiang University Press, 2009.

[2] Zhou Feng, China's Development Path: a Modernization with Chinese Characteristics, *Theoretical Research*, 2012 (3).

[3] Mao Liyan, An Overall Understanding of China's Development Path from the Perspective of Modernization, *Economic Review*, 2010 (2).

The road to China's modernization not only attracted wide attention from scholars, but it was also the ideal to which several generations of politicians and personages of noble aspirations dedicated their whole life. We once sincerely—but hopelessly—learnt the strong points of foreigners with the aim of containing foreigners; we even had the fever of making unrealistic and awkward attempts to surpass Great Britain and catch up with the United States; however, the road to achieving goals ran counter to the goals, thus the Chinese people who had been afraid of poverty had to reflect on whether the road they had chosen was correct. After drawing comparisons about the characteristics of modernization in major countries in the nineteenth and twentieth centuries, some scholars pointed out that the capitalist road to modernization in the nineteenth century combined private property rights with market competition and naturally took shape after hundreds of years. Private ownership, market orientation, and gradual change are the basic characteristics of this model. In the twentieth century, some backward countries took the socialist road and got involved in a top-down process of compulsory industrialization guided by an aggressive political revolution, with an attempt to rapidly achieve modernization—through the Soviet Model with national plans and radical reforms—on the basis of pure public ownership. Such a model met with a crisis after a brief success.[4] China did not really embark on the road to modernization—which was proved to be correct by practice—until the 1990s. This is the road with Chinese characteristics towards socialist modernization—the establishment of the special economic zones aimed at the reform and opening up as planned by Deng Xiaoping.[5] China's Development Path that is being currently discussed refers to China's Development Path—towards modernization with Chinese characteristics—which starts from the establishment of the special economic zones towards the reform and opening up and aims at establishing a socialist market economy in the direction of an all-round reform and comprehensive development of society.

Fifth, the relationship between the special economic zones and China's Development Path. The special economic zones and China's Development Path have been much discussed, but the internal logical relationship between them has not yet been fully discussed. China's Development Path is more associated with modernization, while the special economic zones are, to a larger extent, regarded by the people as the "experimental fields" of the early stages of the reform and opening up. In my opinion, given the logical starting point of China's reform and opening up as well as China's Development Path, it is quite appropriate to think highly of the special economic zones. This is because, if the special economic zones had not been established, the following consequences would not have occurred: the reform and opening up would not have been carried out in China; a market

[4] Luo Rongqu, Retrospect of the 20th Century and Outlook for the 21st Century—From the Perspective of the World's Modernization Process, *Strategy and Management*, 1996 (3).

[5] Zhang Yanguo, A Comparative Study and Analysis of Mao Zedong and Deng Xiaoping's Thoughts Regarding Modernization, *Wuhan University Journal* (Philosophy & Social Sciences), 2004 (3).

economy could not have been established and taken shape; the mind-sets in Chinese society could not have been updated and revolutionized; the creative power of every citizen could not have been demonstrated in the Chinese society; China's Miracle, which has astonished the world, could not have been achieved; there would have been no internal driving forces for transforming the economic developmental mode; there would have been no realistic basis for the Scientific Outlook on Development, and no social material and spiritual foundation for the Chinese dream; China's Development Path, which makes hundreds of millions of people better-off, could not have taken shape. The special economic zones are the breakthroughs in China's reform and represent a shortcut for modernizing the Chinese society by means of an unbalanced development. This has been proved by the successful experience from the early special economic zones represented by Shenzhen and the birth of the emerging special economic zones represented by Kashgar, Khorgos, and Tumen River.

The establishment of China's special economic zones is a symbol of China's Development Path. It means that the Soviet Model, the planned economy, egalitarianism in the small-scale peasant economy, the balanced development, the large-scale reform, and the original system have become unfeasible. As a result, a breakthrough was made by establishing the special economic zones to bring about a top-down compulsory, progressive institutional change outside the rigid system, so that China was able to embark on China's Development Path to modernization—a unique developmental path unlike both the Soviet Model under the traditional system and the Western model in the era of capitalism.

We should proceed from the whole process of China's reform and opening up to research the irreplaceable historical status of the special economic zones, their unique roles in pushing forward China's reform and opening up and their missionary significance for modernizing the Chinese society. In my opinion, the special economic zones are neither a phenomenon nor the product of a particular stage; on the contrary, they are the entry points for carrying out the reform and opening up in Chinese society, the forerunners to intensifying the reform and opening up and the shortcut to achieving modernization. Given the whole process and the history of China's reform and opening up, the mission of the special economic zones is far from accomplished. These views are supported by the theory of unbalanced development and the theory of institutional innovation cost. The construction of the special economic zones is a practice of unbalanced development. From the perspective of institutional innovation, as the entry points for China's reform, opening up and institutional transformation, the special economic zones have greatly reduced the tangible and intangible costs of institutional change in the Chinese society against the background in which the traditional system and ideology still hold the dominant position.

Special Economic Zones and China's Development Path

As the outcome of a special policy, the special economic zones constitute the epoch-making hallmark of rationality and fever, thinking and blindness in the modern history of China. They mark the beginning of the transformation of the Chinese society from a planned economy to a market economy and the real opening of China's gateway which had been closed for 30 years. They herald the emancipation of the people's minds and the renewal of mind-sets. They indicate that a large country on the verge of economic collapse has really embarked on the path towards scientific development. Therefore, in view of the social and political background at the beginning of the reform and opening up, the special economic zones certainly represent the only road for Chinese society to transform from a planned economy to a market economy so as to initiate social transformation in an all-round way; from the perspective of experimentation regarding the road to modernization, the special economic zones undoubtedly serve as the inevitable path for thoroughly breaking away from the conflicts between the ideal and reality, in order to take the socialist road with Chinese characteristics to common prosperity; in terms of choosing the path for China's institutional change, the special economic zones are unquestionably essential for breaking the rigid traditional system and the doctrine of ideology so as to complete the institutional change of a transitional society from top to bottom in a traditional socialist country once dominated by traditional ideology; with regard to the developmental strategy, the special economic zones are surely indispensable for a country—once overwhelmed by an ultraleft ideology—to really abandon the blind developmental concepts that "man can conquer nature" and "development is fostered only for the sake of development" and thus achieve scientific development.

Emergence of the special economic zones and the formation of China's Development Path

The institutional change in Chinese society mainly highlighted by the establishment of a market economic system constitutes an arduous and glorious course of the growth and development of the special economic zones. The practice of the reform and opening up—full of twists and turns but giving birth to outstanding achievements—in China's special economic zones represented by the Shenzhen Special Economic Zone not only reveals the uniqueness, the main features and future developmental trends of China's Development Path towards modernization with distinctive characteristics, but it also vigorously stimulates the transformation and development of Chinese society on the basis of their correct choice of path and impressive development.

China's Development Path mentioned here means that the special economic zones were established in China to complete the transformation of the system and achieve economic development. More precisely, in China, a large country—with a 30-year history of a planned economy—where the planned economy is practiced and traditional ideology undoubtedly dominates, as an institutional change, the special economic zones were established to break through the traditional system, with a view to gradually transforming the whole country from a planned economy to a market economy, so that Chinese society could embark on the path towards a market economy in an all-round way in a certain period of time, gradually, really turning China into an economically prosperous, institutionally advanced socialist country with a market economy under the rule of law.

The road to China's modernization not only attracted wide attention from scholars but also was the ideal to which several generations of politicians and personages of noble aspirations dedicated their whole life. We once sincerely—but hopelessly—learnt the strong points of foreigners with the aim of containing foreigners; we even had the fever of making unrealistic and awkward attempts to surpass Great Britain and catch up with the United States; however, the road to achieving goals ran counter to goals, thus the Chinese people who had been afraid of poverty had to reflect on whether the road they had chosen was correct. Scholars widely believe that China did not really embark on the road to modernization—which was proved to be correct by practice—until the 1990s. This is the road to socialist modernization with Chinese characteristics —the establishment of the special economic zones aimed at the reform and opening up as planned by Deng Xiaoping.[6]

Historically, the reform and opening up, initiated 38 years ago (1978), started from building the oasis of a market economy amidst the vast sea of a planned economy in China. As a place with the weakest planned economy in China at that time, Shenzhen was the first to become the oasis thanks to its geographical advantages (its proximity to Hong Kong, Macau, and its remoteness from the center of the planned economy). The blind and crazy socialist practice for nearly half a century and the situation of China's social and economic development at that time clearly showed that the planned economy had become unfeasible, so had the developmental strategy for blindly catching up with and surpassing other countries, and egalitarianism in a small-scale peasant economy. In a large backward country sustained by the egalitarianism of a planned economy and plagued by widespread poverty, the only way to shake off poverty consisted in breaking the institutional mechanism leading to widespread poverty within the system and taking an unbalanced developmental road. Such a developmental road is what was advocated by Deng Xiaoping—allowing part of the people and regions to get well-off first.

As a compulsory institutional arrangement, the special economic zones were established to break the state of general equilibrium resulting in widespread poverty in the traditional system, so that the social change characterized by unbalanced development became the best road to institutional change in Chinese society, and China—a large country governed by a planned economy for half a century—could move, in a short time, from the "plan" causing widespread poverty to the "market" allowing part of the people to become prosperous first. As a formal top-down

[6] Zhang Yanguo, A Comparative Study and Analysis of Mao Zedong and Deng Xiaoping's Thoughts Regarding Modernization, *Wuhan University Journal* (Philosophy & Social Sciences), 2004 (3).

institutional arrangement, the establishment of the special economic zones not only has greatly reduced the resistance to institutional change and cut down the costs of institutional innovations, but it has also successfully prevented the reform from possibly bringing about more risks, thus the performance in institutional change could quickly emerge and fruitfully play an exemplary role nationwide within a short period of time.

China's Development Path should be a road to modernization with Chinese characteristics. "Chinese characteristics" gives expression to the aspects—country-specific, nationality-specific, historical, and international—instead of denying the essential significance of modernization and the inherent value judgment. Therefore, "Chinese characteristics" only lies in the distinctiveness of the path towards achieving goals and the choice of a path for reaching goals rather than the goals themselves. "Chinese characteristics" involves the process through which human beings recognize universal values and are anything but a denial of international conventions.

Growth of the special economic zones and characteristics of the concepts of development

In a broader sense, especially in terms of the traditional system and developmental model in the period of the planned economy, the establishment of the special economic zones was the critical choice for scientific development and opened the road to it in Chinese society. The growth and development of the Shenzhen Special Economic Zone is in fact a process of continuously adjusting the developmental strategy amidst lessons and setbacks, optimizing the industrial structure, transforming the model of development, and exploring a gradual shift from a society driven by economic growth to a welfare-oriented society with well-rounded development. The philosophy of scientific development has expanded the "outlook on development" from the transformation of the pattern of growth to social development and from the economic field to various fields of social life. The course of Shenzhen's development sheds light on China's Development Path and its significance.

The transformation from a planned economy to a market economy is none other than the transformation of Chinese society from the strategy for catching up with and overtaking other countries to the strategy for unbalanced development. Compared with the "blind developmental outlook" in the period of the planned economy, the establishment of the special economic zones doubtlessly carved out the correct road to the scientific development of Chinese society. The Scientific Outlook on Development touches upon development in essence; it is anything but a debate on whether development should be pursued; on the contrary, it stresses the scientificity and correctness of the social developmental model, method, pattern, and choice of path. It is firmly believed that only when the philosophy of scientific development has been established can China's special economic zones come into being, can hundreds of millions of people have the pursuit of common prosperity and can China's economy be brilliant for 38 years (1978–2016).

The development of the Shenzhen Special Economic Zone was a process in which the developmental strategy was continuously adjusted amidst lessons and setbacks, the industrial structure was optimized, the model of economic development was transformed and there was experimentation regarding a gradual shift from a society driven by economic growth to a welfare-oriented society with well-rounded development. The development of the Shenzhen Special Economic Zone started from processing the materials supplied by foreign clients, processing according to buyer's samples, assembling the parts supplied by foreign clients and engaging in compensation trade. The selection of such a developmental model was determined by the factor endowment available at that time. Shenzhen was just a little-known small fishing village less subject to the planned economic system at the initial stage of the reform and opening up. The comparatively advantageous production factors in Shenzhen at that time were a cheap labor force and land, while Shenzhen had a shortage of capital, technologies, and management. This coincided with the industrial upgrading and structural adjustment of Hong Kong's economy; thus guided by the policy of reform and opening up, the labor-intensive industries dominated by the processing industry appropriately settled down in Shenzhen where the manufacturing industry was urgently needed, at just the right time. The industrial transfer was accompanied by a gradual shift of capitals, technologies, management, and a modern enterprise system to growing Shenzhen. With efforts to carry forward the chain of industrial renewal from the territories and countries with a developed market economy, Shenzhen not only reduced the costs for jump-starting the economic development, but it also greatly lowered the costs for learning from the market economy, determining the basic characteristic which defines an outward-looking economy. Meanwhile, the "importation" of the processing and manufacturing industries also gave rise to derivative demand, thus stimulating the rise and development of the tertiary industry. As of 1993, 87% of Shenzhen's foreign trade has come from the net exports from Chinese-foreign joint ventures, Chinese-foreign cooperative enterprises, and the entirely foreign-owned enterprises as well as from the income from processing the materials supplied by foreign clients, processing according to buyer's samples, assembling the parts supplied by foreign clients and engaging in compensation trade; the tertiary industry accounted for 46% of Shenzhen's GDP and the labor force absorbed by the tertiary industry made up 32.2% of the employed people in Shenzhen.[7]

As Shenzhen embarked on the track of rapid economic growth, the constraints from the inherent shortage of natural resources in Shenzhen emerged soon and aroused concern from policymakers. That shortage meant that under the law of scarcity, with any choice of a pattern of growth based on consumption and use of natural resource factors, people would have to pay relatively high prices for the creation of wealth and development, so that the price for economic growth would also increase. Moreover, as an emerging city which had become the first to practice

[7]Tao Yitao, Lu Zhiguo, *China's Economic Zones: Design, Implementation, and Impact*, Beijing, Social Sciences Academic Press, August, 2008 (1), the first print, p. 99.

a market economy, Shenzhen could not repeat the developmental model and path of traditional industry and was more responsible for experimenting with and trying out a new economic growth mode and manner of creating wealth, and thus setting a good example for the whole country.

With a shift from focusing on processing the materials supplied by foreign clients, processing according to buyer's samples, assembling the parts supplied by foreign clients and engaging in compensation trade to developing the new high-tech industries as a backbone, Shenzhen chose a path towards sustainable development in due time. The leading force of the government decision-making in institutional change (the establishment of special funds and the adoption of preferential policies, etc.) addressed the gap in financing resulting from high input during the early stages and mitigated the pressure on the new high-tech enterprises for taking risks alone. With the broad mind peculiar to reformers, actions were taken to foster an institutional environment for the new high-tech enterprises to settle down, grow, develop, and innovate in Shenzhen and this attracted a large number of new, well-known domestic and foreign high-tech enterprises to Shenzhen. With the foresight and sagacity of innovators, a solid intellectual guarantee was provided for the subsequent development of the new high-tech industries; some well-known universities and a variety of scientific research institutions took root in Shenzhen.

Imitation was the main way for increasing the output value of the new and hi-tech technologies for a considerably long time. However, the real international competitiveness of a country cannot derive from a shortcut and instant benefits brought about by imitation for a long time. The creative power of industries—the original innovation capability, the integrated innovation capability, and the capability for introduction, assimilation, adoption, and re-innovation—is the fundamental source for the permanent vitality of an enterprise and the lasting competitiveness of a country. Therefore, self-dependent innovation was put forward as a strategic train of thought giving full expression to the philosophy of sustainable development.

Theoretically, self-dependent innovation is a kind of innovative activity higher than imitation. It builds a new productive function or incorporates an unprecedented "new combination" of factors of production and production system into the production process. It stresses the applications of inventions in the economic activities and delivers profits to the parties involved in production. Therefore, self-dependent innovation emphasizes self-research and development and the ownership of the core technologies, and it underscores the added value of technologies and patents in the process of the creation of value. In this sense, self-dependent innovation is the inevitable requirement for the transformation of the economic growth mode and also an important method for such transformation. This is because if self-dependent innovation features "neutral technical progress" (unchanged proportion of the factor input), "labor-saving technical progress" or "capital-saving technical progress", it increases the output on the premise of neither increasing nor decreasing the use of factors, so as to improve the efficiency of the utilization of resources. This means that we cannot be merely content with the simple "imitation" of foreign advanced technologies and cannot just rest on the mode of introducing extensive, low-level technology dominated by the importation of equipment during the early stages of the reform and opening up; on the contrary, we should rethink and determine the economic growth mode to export the "soft technologies" and increase the contribution from self-dependent innovation (creation of the core technologies) to the GDP.

The labor-intensive processing and manufacturing industry—based on processing materials supplied by foreign clients, processing according to buyer's samples, assembling the parts supplied by foreign clients and engaging in compensation trade, the capital-intensive and the technology-intensive new high-tech industry, as well as the philosophy of self-dependent innovation have taken shape in the economic field to achieve social and economic development through the transformation of the mode of economic growth. In the meantime, the philosophy of scientific development has expanded the "developmental outlook" from the transformation of the growth mode to social development and from the economic field to various fields of social life. Solving and correcting the problems of development through the cognition of scientific development and the philosophy of harmonious development—after the achievement of brilliant successes and accumulation of wealth—represents the thoughts and reflections about moving the city of Shenzhen forward.

Shenzhen has followed a track of rapid growth to bring wealth and prosperity to the striving people. As we know, the GDP is the material base for social development, but it is anything but the ultimate goal for social development. The GDP and per capita GDP growth not accompanied by an improvement in social welfare is nothing but pure material growth without soul and humanistic caring.

A labor-intensive economy has allowed Shenzhen to build competitive power with a price advantage in seizing the market as a result of low costs, while the global financial crisis has further laid bare the problems—stemming from the economic growth mode in the labor-intensive economy—concerning the low added value of capital and technologies, lack of core competitiveness; it has also seriously presented the transformation of the mode of economic development as the inevitable strategic choice for scientific development.

A comparative advantage is an important principle for seeking economic development in different countries and territories. This advantage is a comparative advantage of the factor price determined by the degree of the relative scarcity of factors. When the labor resources are relatively abundant and thus labor cost or price is relatively low in a country or territory, with an absence of capital and the disadvantages of technological factor endowment, utilizing the cheap labor peculiar to it first has become the best natural choice with the lowest developmental cost in the period of economic takeoff. The comparative advantage of the latter was exactly the main choice for economic takeoff and the initial development in Shenzhen, even in the whole country during the early stages of the reform and opening up.

Scarcity is the basic premise for and the general principle of economics. Research on economics touches upon how a society makes use of the scarce resources to produce valuable goods and services, and distributes them among different people. However, most of the economically backward developing countries are subject to resource constraints in the sense of factor structure rather than a lack of resources in terms of natural endowment. The resource constraints in the sense of factor structure mean that the structure of the factor endowment is at a low level; in other words, there is a lack of relatively high-level factors—such as capital, technology, education, management, and legal system—but a crop of uneducated or less educated ordinary labor is available during the economic development of a country or territory. Therefore, the root cause for the low economic structure lies in the structure of low factor endowment instead of in the structure itself. The low structure is not the cause for itself, but it is the result of or realistically mirrors the structure of low factor endowment. If there is only simple labor in the stock of factors in a country, a labor-intensive economy is a natural choice. The economic structure cannot be artificially changed merely by wish in any economy because changing the quality and structure of factors is the practical, logical precondition for improving the industrial structure. Nietzsche said that nothing was scarcer than sane honesty in a philosopher. The advancement of human society needs not only diligence and passion but also thinking and rationality.

Development of the special economic zones and China's modernization

When the economic value of the people is increased, our society will enjoy a number of new and better opportunities. The government should not lead the social economy with its own wishful thinking; on the contrary, it should create an institutional environment, supply public goods, and develop a social welfare mechanism while respecting the market. Development is the result of reform and also the material prerequisite for intensifying the reform, but development cannot replace reform. If there is no reform of the political system fit for the economic system, the reform of the economic system cannot become really successful. On the unique China Path to modernization and in the course of building a law-based civil society, as the city given first priority for development, Shenzhen should show a sign of hope for tomorrow.

Theodore W. Schultz believed that the impact from the long-term change of any economy on institutional change was more far-reaching than that from wages on the change of rent.[8] The improvement in the economic value of the people generates new needs for institutions, while some political and legal systems are designed to meet these needs. Human capital calls for clarifying the situation of the social institution when seeking its own right of participation, thus many institutions are created as a result of incentives for economic growth.

In the book *Development as Freedom*, Amartya Sen, with the conscience, morality, and wisdom of a scholar, answers the question about the goal for the development of human society: As it is people-centered, the highest goal and value standard for social development is freedom. Wealth, income, technical progress and

---

[8]Theodore W. Schultz, Institutions and the Rising Economic Value of Man, *American Journal of Agricultural Economics* (50), December, 1968.

social modernization, etc., are certainly the goals pursued by the people, but they ultimately fall within the scope of tools and serve the development and welfare of the people.

China's social reform has unfolded at a relatively low level of per capita income—on the one hand, a huge middle class has not yet taken shape; on the other hand, the gap between the rich and the poor is becoming increasingly salient and wide. Therefore, poverty amidst economic growth and low welfare in economic prosperity have "prematurely" become the social problems which the government must solve through institutional arrangements. Affirmatively, the government must treat the establishment of the institution of social welfare as the guarantee for achieving common prosperity rather than the result of common prosperity. In any society, the creation of wealth begets poverty and the achievement of prosperity is followed by the decreasing happiness of some people, which is more dreadful than widespread poverty. The welfare institution—a system which is not a luxury in economic development—is an important part of the development and an integral part of substantive freedom.

There is an inherent correlation between the market and the basic freedom of people. It is not impartial that the people praise the market mechanism merely from the perspective of efficiency. A market failure may become the important basis for the people to deny the market, but a market failure does not mean a negation of the market mechanism; on the contrary, it means a perseverance in the market mechanism—the market should do what it can do, while the government should do what the market fails to do, and do it well. The government's power plays an indispensable role in compulsory institutional change characterized by top-down authorization. However, subject to the law of the market, any overwhelming government power does not duly correct a market failure but destroys the law of the market. The government should refrain from leading the social economy with its own wishful thinking and should create an institutional environment, supply public goods, and develop a social welfare mechanism while respecting the market.

The reform of Chinese society started from the economic field; this undoubtedly was the best way, but quickly a number of problems surfaced—such as the absence of supporting resources in the general social environment and a lack of the effective institutional environment—and led to system and institutional bottlenecks in intensifying the reform. The institutions are always embedded within an institutional environment, while institutional change cannot be really accomplished without an institutional environment. Likewise, if there is no reform of the political system fit for the reform of the economic system, the reform of the economic system cannot become truly successful. Fundamentally, many social problems and contradictions at the present time resulted from a lagging behind of the reform of the political system.

In a transforming society, the establishment of a brand-new social operating mechanism entails the process in which the powers and vested interests of the government officials are crippled, deprived of, and even lost, and a service-oriented government forms, develops, and grows. In an institution in which the government's powers need to be removed by the powers themselves, the level of the civilization and the foresight of the government are crucial for the institutional performance of a society.

Our society will not perish just because there is a lack of miracles; however, its vitality will not endure if the line of thought which creates miracles is not available. As the special marks of miracles and miracle-creating thinking, the special economic zones not only inject infinite vitality into the Chinese society but also bring limitless hope for this nation to create miracles. They serve as the inevitable road to the modernization of the Chinese society.

Historical Contributions of the Shenzhen Special Economic Zone to China's Reform and Opening up and the Sharing of Experiences

In the history of China's reform and opening up, no city except Shenzhen—a typical special economic zone in China—emerged to herald the beginning of an era and the end of another era; no city except Shenzhen has, through its own development, shown and led the direction of institutional change in the whole country, and created a novel, fruitful social development model; no city except Shenzhen has continuously undergone changes to bring about miracles in social transformation, and has fostered new mind-sets, spirits, and philosophies while creating wealth.

Therefore, the history of the growth of Shenzhen depicts not only the development of a city but also the trajectory of experimentation regarding the path towards institutional change and development in a transition country as well as the course of a nation's efforts in seeking prosperity. With a short history, Shenzhen records the practice of a 38-year reform and opening up in China, and in the course of 38 years, it has presented a reflection on and criticism of the traditional system which has lasted for nearly half a century, and it has indicated the goal and direction for China's future development. In these 38 years, it has provided many invaluable thoughts for China regarding transition, while its powerful and challenging thoughts and mind-sets destroyed the spiritual shackles which hindered the reform and the "sacred" things which were considered as the absolute truth in the traditional system.

Thirty-five years have elapsed since the Shenzhen Special Economic Zone embarked on its splendid course. We remember and review that history not just because we have experienced the incredible times, but because that history has left a lot of wealth to us. This wealth has mixed the miracles of success with unforgettable failures and lessons. We review the past not just because we have a profound and thrilling memory, but because the spirits, feelings, and willpower we had in the past are indispensable for us now. We respect history not just because history carries much and cannot be copied, but because the character of a city forged by trailblazers should be treasured and inherited. When we endeavor to remember history, we should bear in mind the past years and, more importantly, the endearing people who created and wrote the history during the extraordinary times. This is because, for any country, the people are always the main players in history and the most powerful force is the quality of courageousness! As we eulogize the past years, it does not mean that we are intoxicated with the past glories and miracles, but it means that we should rationally, passionately look into the future. It is impossible that Shenzhen will always serve as a "wholesaler" of the experience acquired from China's reform and opening up, but Shenzhen should not and cannot, as always, lose the pioneering spirit and the innovative character which have been accompanying its emergence and growth. This is because they constitute the cornerstone of this city and are the most valuable things left to the city by the trailblazers.

Historical contributions of the Shenzhen Special Economic Zone to China's reform and opening up

As the most typical and successful special economic zone in China, Shenzhen has made four major historical contributions to China's reform and opening up.

1. It became the first to explore, demonstrate, and practice a socialist market economy, and has contributed a "brand-new institution"—the socialist market economy—to economic development in Chinese society, thus providing an institution—the basic ideological guarantee—for the reform and opening up as well as the institutional change in Chinese society.

During the transformation of Chinese society from a planned economy to a market economy, Shenzhen has commendably accomplished the historical mission entrusted to it at its inception—the forerunner in the reform, the window for opening up, and the experimental field for the market economy. The historical data reveal the great changes which took place in Shenzhen, a small fishing village. Shenzhen's GDP was only 196 million yuan in 1979 when the reform and opening up had just started, but exceeded 1.5 trillion yuan in 2014, an increase of 7653 times in 36 years. Shenzhen's per capita GDP soared from 624 yuan in 1979 to about 24,000 USD (about 150,000 yuan) in 2014, an increase of 240 times in 36 years. Shenzhen's GDP grew by about 10% in 2014, higher than the national and provincial average growth rates; in 2014, Shenzhen reached the GDP goal—1.5 trillion yuan—specified in the 12th Five-Year Plan one year ahead of schedule, and Shenzhen's per capita GDP was the highest one among the sub-provincial cities on the Chinese Mainland. In 2014, Shenzhen's imports and exports totaled 487.74 billion USD, up 9.7% after having been adjusted for financing-based trade.[9]

China's special economic zones have a dual mission: In the sense of "reform", they are functionally designed to accelerate the transformation towards a market economy and continue to serve as the vanguards and forerunners for China's reform and opening up; in the sense of "development", they functionally aim at speeding up

[9] *Shenzhen Statistical Yearbook* (2015)

the transformation of the developmental mode and building a new regional economic landscape in China, so as to provide a shortcut for achieving modernization.

2. With its own development and success, it has verified a "new path"—China's Development Path to China's modernization, so that the Chinese society can adopt the unbalanced developmental strategy to quickly shake off widespread poverty and achieve the ultimate goal of common prosperity.

China's Development Path should be a path towards modernization with Chinese characteristics. China's Development Path means a recognition of the rules universally adopted in a market economy rather than a negation of international practice. With the establishment of the emerging special economic zones including Kashgar, Khorgos, and Tumen River, the expansion from the coastal opening up to the opening up along the border has become the grand strategic line of thought for establishing and improving the market economic system across China, and the special economic zones have made a shortcut to the modernization of Chinese society against the background of unbalanced regional development.

3. The pathbreaking practice and the courage of the first mover offers a "new spirit" for promoting the reform and opening up in Chinese society—blazing new trails in a pioneering spirit, thus driving forward a revolution to renew the mind-sets of billions of people, and helping foster a mind-set and a culture of reform innovation suited to a socialist market economy.

As an immigrant city, Shenzhen has the distinctive immigrant cultural traits: encouraging innovations, tolerating failures, being down-to-earth, pursuing excellence. The most striking innovative spirit of this special economic zone lies in daring to make breakthroughs and take risks.

According to incomplete statistics, Shenzhen has created more than 500 number ones in China and more than 120 first-ever occasions in the world in the 38 years since the reform and opening up. Each reform resounded throughout the country and each breakthrough opened a rift in the planned economy, injecting the vitality of a market economy into the transforming system and mechanism.

The reform and opening up in Chinese society started from emancipating the people's minds. If the reform and opening up is considered as the path towards China's institutional change, the emancipation of the people's minds is the prerequisite for making such an institutional change. If the people's minds are not emancipated, the reform and opening up would be impossible, while the reform and opening up put into practice such emancipation.

In my opinion, further emancipating the people's minds and breaking the fetter of traditional ideology is not a thing which has been done, but is an issue which has not yet been fundamentally addressed in Chinese society at the present time. Previously, as the people's minds had not been emancipated and the planned economic system had not been broken up, nobody could benefit from the institutional innovations, so the officials were prone to criticize traditional ideology and drive forward social reform. However, 38 years later, when the personal gains from further reform are smaller than the benefits for the society, the people with vested interests may become rigid and conservative. Therefore, economic development is restricted not only by resources but also by the people's minds and outlooks which are more important than resources.

4. With the prosperity achieved first by development and the achievements in leading China's reform and opening up, it has been proved that free development of the people is part of and the goal for social development; the creative power of every citizen is the driving force for realizing both social development and the Chinese dream; intensifying the reform is the inevitable road to fulfilling China's modernization and the Chinese dream.

China's reform and opening up was initiated by emancipating the productive forces, and such emancipation is the emancipation of humanity, and the release and emancipation of the people's creative power. During the nearly 40 years from widespread poverty to common prosperity, the Chinese people have been freed from the cage of a traditional planned economy and have demonstrated the amazing, great creative power once they had the freedom and self-reliance to pursue wealth—after the farmers were granted the right to freely develop the township enterprises and rural migrant workers emerged and China's Miracle was created; after the enterprises were granted the right to freely develop, the entrepreneur came into being and China saw rapid economic growth; after the intellectuals were granted the right to enjoy freedom, the intellectuals came out and there was open and inclusive brainstorming; after the general public was granted the freedom of speech, there was civic awareness and the characteristics of a society under the rule of law, including supervision, responsibility, and obligation. The release and emancipation of the people's creative power will certainly incorporate the people's development into the social development while creating the economic miracle.

The hallmarks of the people's emancipation include not only prosperity—of course, emancipation is out of the question without prosperity—but also the rights and dignity which accompany prosperity; the aspects which mark the emancipation of the productive forces are the right to free movement, and the equitable realization of exchange under the law of the market and the foresight of the government, as well as the effective protection of the legitimate rights and interests, the equality of opportunities and equitable granting of the right to choose. If there is no equity and freedom to choose, there is no happiness and dignity of development.

Sharing the successful experience of the Shenzhen Special Economic Zone

China is a large country with a traditional planned economy, and it is also a developing country. The transformation of Chinese society from a planned economy to a market economy has been a process of reform and opening up and the construction of an emerging market economy country; in particular, amid today's economic globalization, as a developing and emerging market economy country, China shares many similarities with other developing countries and emerging market economy countries. Once the development and social issues shared by the developing countries and the emerging market economy countries have been successfully addressed by China under the "whole nation system" to varying degrees, it will be of profound significance to the developing countries and the emerging market economy countries as a point of reference. Of course, this significance lies in providing human beings with sharable wisdom and spiritual wealth instead of setting an example for the world. As a successful transformation path, China's Development Path provides a vivid case concerning the choice of a path towards the economic development and modernization of the countries with an emerging market economy.

1. The direction of a reform-focused market economy was chosen, introduced, and upheld

As early as the 1980s when the *Regulations on the Special Economic Zones* were promulgated, Guangdong Province made it clear that the special economic zones should focus on introducing foreign capital and practicing a market economy. At that time, the market economy was considered a dreadful monster and the development of a market economy was equated with capitalist restoration in China. Therefore, there were severe criticisms from the traditional ideology, and "combating peaceful evolution" became the main theme in 1982, just 2 years after the establishment of the special economic zones. Fundamentally, China had embarked on an irreversible road towards advancing the great cause of the reform and opening up as initiated in China in 1978, but China was shrouded in vast shadows of doubt. In 1992, however, Deng Xiaoping made the "South Inspection Speech" and prevailed over all dissenting views with the political wisdom, courage, and resourcefulness of a great man to reverse the situation, and ultimately determined the market economy as the direction for China's reform and opening up. He finally concluded that the market economy was not equal to capitalism and that there was also a market in socialism.

For China, a market economy gave birth to the successful special economic zones in China and also saved China.

2. The reform was promoted through opening up

China's opening up started from the establishment of the special economic zones. The reform and opening up accelerated the overall transformation of China from a traditional society to a modern society and also led to fundamental changes in its economic system. Initially, the opening up only meant the expansion of foreign trade and the introduction of technologies and equipment, etc. With the intensification of reform and opening up, the meaning of opening up was also further clarified and extended, while the substance of an all-round opening up was institutional innovation and the use of a system for reference.

As the reform and opening up in the Shenzhen Special Economic Zone originated from the geographical advantages resulting from the area's proximity to Hong Kong, Shenzhen-Hong Kong cooperation naturally became the important part of Shenzhen's reform and opening up. In a considerable sense, the introduction of capital and technologies from Hong Kong not only conformed to the fundamental direction of the reform and opening up in Chinese society, but it also helped find a shortcut towards building a modern city. Hong Kong is the unique regional factor conducive to the success of the Shenzhen Special Economic Zone.

Logically and realistically, with respect to the reform and opening up, Chinese society experienced a transformation from an outward-looking economy to an open economy and a transition from a policy-based opening up to an institutional opening up. Both reflected the logical evolution and unity in the developmental course. They were not only two aspects of one course but also the inevitable results of development in a certain course.

First, there was a development from an outward-looking economy to an open economy. An outward-looking economy is an economic operational mode with both ends of the production process on the world market; it refers in particular to the operational mode under which the raw materials are imported and processed to make products and then those products are exported. The development of China's economy from a closed one to an open one is a unique process of transformation from an inward economic development to an outward economic development. At the initial stage of the reform and opening up, the special economic zones were established, and the coastal cities were developed and opened to mainly draw on the market management experience from foreign investors and focus on utilizing foreign capital, developing foreign trade and increasing supply to address the shortage economy, so as to stimulate economic growth. The subsequent development and opening up of the Pudong New Area was also an important step towards implementing China's strategy for developing an outward-looking economy.

However, the opening up strategy for an outward-looking economy also gradually presented some inherent defects—as actions were taken to predominantly make coastal areas open to the outside world, thus the overall economic openness was not high and the targets of the opening up were excessively concentrated; the domestic interregional differences expanded; the coordinated opening up effect was low; the opening up cycle was interrupted, etc. It was objectively inevitable for an open economy with a greater amount of openness and internal and external integration to replace the strategy for developing an outward-looking economy.

An open economy refers to the economic system—with a relatively great amount of openness—supported by a well-developed operational mechanism and legal system. An open economy works in such a way that the government carries out administrative activities basically according to the mechanism and rules which govern a market economy; an open economy is regulated by a mature economic system and has a wider significance and higher degree of openness than an outward-looking economy. The development of an open economy centers on participating in international competition and international economic cooperation, maximizing the absorption of all civilization achievements created by the human society and beneficial to China's drive towards modernization.

Second, there was a shift from a policy-based opening up to an institutional opening up. The development of an open economy is a process in which the economic system for opening up progressively evolved from a policy-based opening up to an institutional opening up. The special policy system adopted when the opening up process was initiated was not of an "institutional" nature in the strict sense as it brought differential treatments and preferential measures to special areas and objects, but it was the necessary form of the broad sense of an open economic system during the initial stage. However, after the opening up and development was rapidly promoted and a series of institutional reforms were carried forward with the endogenous forces accordingly, China gradually moved towards building a well-functioning open economic system fit for the operating mechanism which governs a modern market economy, while the open economic system gradually acquired a genuine "institutional" significance. Final establishment and improvement of an "institutional" open economic system in the strict sense is precisely the main task and objective for China in the future.

The opening up and the corresponding institutional reform were initiated by special policies during the early stage, while the establishment and development of the special economic zones was a typical case of such a mode. With the successes in the special economic zones, the Central Government continued to practice the thought and mode of "giving special policies to launch the opening up" and made more areas and fields open to the outside world—such as the open coastal cities, the economic and technological development zones, the open coastal economic areas, and a strategic shift from coastal opening up to the opening up of border areas. As the opening up was initiated by special policies, some reforms and changes also took place in the domestic system accordingly to gradually establish a relatively complete operational management system for absorbing, utilizing foreign capital, and developing foreign trade.

China's accession to the WTO in 2001 marks the commencement of a gradual shift from a policy-based opening up to an institutional opening up for really starting the establishment of an open economic system with a profound "institutional" significance.

The key to shifting from a policy-based opening up to an institutional opening up lies in actively and effectively building an institutional environment. The provision of the preferential policies was changed to environmental and institutional construction; instead of utilizing the preferential policies for boosting the opening up, a good soft social environment—including infrastructure, transportation and communication, education, human capital, administrative efficiency, laws and regulations, etc.—was fostered, to promote the development of an outward-looking economy. Global competition at the current stage mainly consists of a good institutional and legal environment, thus in order to build the new advantages for international competition and cooperation, it is essential to develop a good, fair, and transparent legal and institutional environment.

3. The emancipation of the people was respected and expanded. China's reform and opening up started from emancipating the productive force, while such emancipation was, in essence, the emancipation of the people and of humanity

First, the reform and opening up has aroused the enthusiasm of the leading actors in a market economy—individuals. The ultimate actors in the society are people as "economic men" in the market economy rather than a country, cities, and units. For example, more than 95% of the migrants in Shenzhen made up the most basic element of the productive forces—free movement of the people, while the capital vigorously introduced from Hong Kong and foreign countries made up the most powerful element of the productive forces—free flow of capital. The rural migrant workers who migrated to cities as from the 1990s became the leading actors in building and serving China's special economic zones and they are also the creators of "China's Miracle".

Second, the reform and opening up has stimulated the enthusiasm of another leading actor in China's market economy—the local government. This is also an important cause for the "charm" of Chinese characteristics. Under the planned economic system, the local governments were subject to "arrangements" and were spurred to "carry out", while in the market-oriented economic environment, the local governments take the initiative to innovate due to competition. The regional competition—including inter-province, intercity, intercounty competition—constitutes a special enormous internal impetus for China's economy, which can explain much about China's Miracle. The people have been given a solemn sense of mission and have a burning desire to change their personal destiny, making governments of the special economic zones more vibrant.

However, innovations have been conducted mainly by enterprises rather than governments. A good entrepreneurial environment in the special economic zones has ultimately given birth to a number of innovative enterprises including Tencent, Huawei, ZTE, BYD, Giant, Gree, etc., and a crop of entrepreneurs behind them. The innovative enterprises have become the mainstay in the special economic zones; 90% of the output value comes from the high and new technology industry—the IT industry, turning the special economic zones into the extraordinarily important new high-tech places in China; the entrepreneurs are the soul of the market economy, while the entrepreneur stratum serves as a solid cornerstone for the free development of the special economic zones.

The emancipation of the people lies not only in the politics but also in the economy; its fundamental part is the confirmation of individual property rights. A clear definition of assets rights is a key condition for market transactions. With the reform and opening up, China has shifted from a class-based definition of rights to the institution under which the rights are defined on the basis of assets, thus miracles have happened in China. With the redefinition of property rights, the institutional operational costs under the complete public planning mode have been substantially reduced in China, thus the productive forces and the creative power of immense human resources have been emancipated to build the competitive advantages based on comprehensive costs on the global market. The reform and opening up has significantly lowered the institutional costs in China's economy, thus China has become the fastest-growing economy and China's growth has changed the pattern of the global economy.

4. Full play was given to the advantages of the "whole nation system"

China's success with building special economic zones reflects the "charm" of distinctive Chinese characteristics, of which the "whole nation system", under which the government possesses unprecedented power of mobilization and the ability to bring all available national resources to bear in pursuit of collective endeavors is the most prominent. Examples of the unmatched scale, efficiency, and effective of this system abound, including massive events such as the China New High-tech Fair and the China International Cultural Expo. Of course, I do not believe that the transition state in the process of transformation and the undertaking of these extraordinary projects represent should be normalized and become a permanent feature. Thirty-five years of brilliant achievements made in China's development of its special economic zones are testament to the correctness of this distinct developmental path for China, whose correctness consists in its being fundamentally consistent with universal values and the development logic of market economies. It is through this particular development process that what is generally true of the development of human society as a whole is rendered even more evident.

Fundamentally, China pushed ahead with a top-down compulsory institutional change, and the governments, especially the Central Government, were starter, leader or the most direct advocator of this institutional change as well as the first to "be reformed" within this change. On the one hand, the practice of the reform and opening up cannot do without the decision and authorization from the Central Government—for example, the special economic zones were the results and products of the special policies given to the local governments by the Central Government; on the other hand, the governments also experienced self-reform in which the powers of the governments were taken away by the governments themselves. The practice of the reform and opening up in China for nearly 40 years proves that, for the countries in transition, the governments certainly play a tremendous role in compulsory institutional change; furthermore, if not driven by a powerful top-down political force from the governments, the transformation from a planned economy to a market economy cannot be accomplished and the universal establishment of today's market economy and the prosperity of the social economy would even be impossible. In particular, the Central Government and the powerful "whole nation system" can efficiently concentrate resources to do great things subject to scarce or limited resources, and make decisions in an efficient way to lead the direction of the development of the social economy. However, the government functions and roles are different under the following two circumstances: The market economic system is established by a compulsory institutional change; the market economy is improved under the condition that the market economic system has been basically established. The former may have more need of a relatively strong government intervention for promoting the formation of the market economy, so as to speed up the transformation from a planned one to a market-oriented one, while the latter requires the governments, subject to respecting the market law and mechanism, to correct market failure and serve the market rather than rein and lead the market. From the perspective of a result, a powerful country and a developed market are undoubtedly alluring, but their realization entails efforts to properly handle the relationship between the country and the market or the governments and the market.

5. The people's minds were emancipated; there was the courage to innovate; failures were tolerated; a loose, inclusive, free, shared cultural environment for the reform and opening up was fostered

China's reform and opening up was launched by emancipating the minds of the people. If the reform and opening up is considered a path to an institutional change in China, the emancipation of the minds of the people is the precondition and guarantee for achieving such a path. The practice of the reform and opening up cannot take place without such emancipation, while the reform and opening up has turned such emancipation from a philosophy into a reality; the driving forces for the sustainable social and economic development in China could not have been available without an innovative spirit, while the reality of the sustainable social development in China has offered a broader and more inclusive institutional space for bold innovations; the subjective initiative of the leading actors in the social economy—the people—cannot be stimulated without a loose, inclusive, free, and shareable social environment, while the development and demonstration of the people's subjective initiative injects vitality and creative power into the loose, inclusive, free, and shareable social environment.

I agree with such a view: Our society will not wither due to lack of miracles, but it will lose vitality because of no thoughts for creating miracles.

6. The factor endowment changes were leveraged to propel the adjustment of the industrial structure and the transformation of the developmental mode

The Shenzhen Special Economic Zone kicked off its development by processing the materials supplied by clients, processing with supplied samples, assembling the parts supplied by clients and engaging in compensation trade. The selection of such a developmental mode was determined by the factor endowment available at that time. Shenzhen was only a small, little-known fishing village with a relatively weak planned economy at the early stages of the reform and opening up. The comparatively advantageous production factors in Shenzhen at that time were a cheap labor force and land, while Shenzhen fell short in capital, technologies, and management. This coincided with the industrial upgrading and structural adjustment of Hong Kong's economy, thus guided by the reform and opening up policy, the labor-intensive industries dominated by the processing industry appropriately settled down at just the right time in Shenzhen where the manufacturing industry was urgently needed, while industrial transfer was accompanied by a gradual shift of capital, technologies, management, and a modern enterprise system to growing Shenzhen. With efforts to carry forward the chain of industrial renewal from the territories and countries with a developed market economy, Shenzhen not only reduced the costs of jump-starting its economic development, but it also greatly lowered the costs of learning from the market economy, determining the basic characteristic which defines an outward-looking economy. Meanwhile, the "importation" of the processing and manufacturing industries also gave rise to a derivative demand, thus stimulating the rise and development of the tertiary industry.

As Shenzhen embarked on the road towards rapid economic growth, the constraints from the inherent shortage of natural resources in Shenzhen loomed large soon and aroused the concern of policymakers. Such a shortage means that under the law of scarcity, with any choice of growth pattern based on excessive consumption and the use of natural resource factors, the people have to pay relatively high prices for the creation of wealth and social development so that the price for economic growth will also increase with the high costs of the creation of wealth.

Shenzhen chose a path towards sustainable development in due time mainly by processing the materials supplied by clients, processing with supplied samples, assembling the parts supplied by clients and engaging in compensation trade, and then by developing the new high-tech industries as a backbone. The leading force of the government decision-making in institutional change (the establishment of special funds and the adoption of preferential policies, etc.) addressed the gap in finances that resulted from high input during the early stages and mitigated the pressure on the new high-tech enterprises for taking risks alone; with the broad mind peculiar to reformers, actions have been taken to foster an institutional environment for the new high-tech enterprises to settle, grow, develop, and innovate in Shenzhen and to attract a large number of well-known domestic and foreign new high-tech enterprises to Shenzhen. With the foresight and sagacity of innovators, a solid intellectual guarantee has been provided for the subsequent development of the new high-tech industries; some well-known universities and a variety of scientific research institutions have taken root in Shenzhen. By 2000, the output of computer magnetic heads in Shenzhen ranked No. 3 in the world, and the output of microelectronic computers, stored program control exchanges, and genetic interferon accounted for 25%, 50%, and 60% of the total national output, respectively, and Shenzhen was also the largest production base for printers, hard disk drives, and cordless telephones nationwide, and five large new high-tech pillar industries—including electronic information, biotechnology new materials, optical, mechanical and electronic integration, and lasers—had taken shape.[10]

Imitation was the main way for increasing the output value of the new and high technologies in China for a considerably long time. However, the real international competitiveness of a country cannot originate from the shortcut and instant benefits brought about by imitation for a long time. The Shenzhen Municipal Government quickly realized that the creative power of industries—the original innovation capability, the integrated innovation capability, and the capability for introduction, assimilation, absorption, and re-innovation—was the fundamental source for the permanent vitality of an enterprise and the lasting competitiveness of a country. Therefore, self-dependent innovation was put forward as a strategic line of thought, giving full expression to the philosophy of sustainable development.

The transformation of the economic developmental mode requires our society to change its previous practice of the simple use of labor and low-price consumption, and make an institutional arrangement by turning the "catastrophic" use of cheap labor into the goal-directed value-added use—increasing the economic value of

[10]Tao Yitao, Lu Zhiguo, *China's Economic Zones: Design, Implementation, and Impact*, Beijing, Social Sciences Academic Press, August, 2008 (1), the first print, p. 99.

labor and then the added value of products by means of technical training and welfare improvement.

Most of the economically backward developing countries are subject to resource constraint in the sense of factor structure rather than lack of resources in terms of natural endowment. The resource constraint in the sense of factor structure means that the factor endowment structure is at a low level; in other words, there is a lack of relatively high-level factors—such as capital, technology, education, management, and legal system—but a crop of uneducated or less educated ordinary labor is available during the economic development of a country or territory. Therefore, the root cause of the low economic structure lies in a low factor endowment structure instead of the structure itself. The low structure is not the cause in itself but it is the result of or realistically mirrors the low factor endowment structure.

7. All-around development is the inevitable road that leads to the continued development and prosperity of a society

Economic prosperity will bring about social prosperity, but prosperity itself will not automatically lead to social civilization. Economic prosperity, institutional civilization, and social prosperity will certainly make up the ultimate goal for China's institutional social change.

Theoretically and practically, the relationship between "growth" and "development" is not like the simple relationship between one Chinese name for a potato (*Tudou*) and its other Chinese name (*Malingshu*). "Economic growth" means more output, an increase in products and services of a country, or an increase in the actual per capita output; generally, it is measured by the GDP or per capita GDP. "Economic development" is economic growth along with the reforms of the economic structure, social, and political systems; it means not only a growth in the output but also output and the structure of the income changes along with an increase in the output, as well as changes in the economic system, political conditions, and cultural conditions; it means not only social affluence but also the disappearance of poverty, hunger, associated illiteracy, diseases, and early death along with social prosperity; it means not only the abundance of material wealth but also equality in people's spirit, power and opportunity, equal respect for the people, and an equal granting of powers to the people; it means not only the maximization of personal welfare but also the improvement of the overall welfare in a society, sharing equal opportunities for social surplus. The GDP is the material base for social development, but definitely not the ultimate goal for it. The growth of the GDP and per capita GDP, which is not accompanied by the improvement of social welfare, is nothing but mere material growth without soul and humanistic care.

The Scientific Outlook on Development as put forward by the Chinese Government extends a "development" from the transformation of the growth pattern to social development and from the economic field to every field of social life, and it also truly incorporates the people's development into the significance of social development. As the main players in human society, the people are bound to awaken self-respect and a demand for freedom while creating wealth because the people's emancipation does not merely mark prosperity (of course, emancipation is out of the question without prosperity), it necessarily includes an enjoyment of rights and dignity along with prosperity. The emancipation of the productive forces marks not only the obtaining of power for free movement, but also the equitable realization of exchange under the law of the market and the foresight of the government, the effective protection of the legitimate rights and interests, the factual equality of opportunities, and equal granting of the right to choose. Happiness and dignity in development do not come without equity and the freedom to choose.

China's social reforms were carried out at a relatively low per capita income level; the huge middle class has not yet come into being, and the distribution system and social security system are imperfect in a transformational society, thus poverty amidst economic growth and low welfare in economic prosperity have "prematurely" become the social problems which the government must solve through institutional arrangements. Affirmatively, the government must treat the establishment of the social welfare system as the guarantee for achieving common prosperity rather than the result of common prosperity. In any society, the creation of wealth begets poverty and the achievement of prosperity is followed by the decreasing happiness of some people, which is more dreadful than widespread poverty. Under no circumstance can social welfare be considered a luxury in economic development in our society because it is an important part of development and an integral part of substantive freedom; moreover, it also tests and proves, at the highest moral level, the overall goal for social development.

Furthermore, profound social and institutional changes are essential in order to really establish a complete and effective social welfare system which universally benefits both rural and urban areas, and to achieve the wonderful goal of "making all people get access to education when they need to learn, and payment after they provide services, support, and care when they become elderly, and housing where they can live" because this is an institutional issue rather than merely a shortage of resources and a policy issue. The traditional system is the institutional cause for the dual urban–rural structure in Chinese society. Under the traditional system, our society is inundated with the magnificent slogans about the elimination of the urban–rural gap, it is a society where the urban and rural differences are solidified by the household registration system and ownership system, the urban–rural gap is widened and the urban and rural differences become a social normalcy which farmers cannot but accept. The primary task in this institutional change is identified as follows: Really, thoroughly break the dual urban–rural structure, change that dual structure into a unitary structure with rural-urban integration, and make farmers really enjoy the citizenship and rights of urban residents rather than treating them as second-class citizens. The urban–rural gap cannot disappear if such a dual structure is not broken down, while the social well-being cannot really become widespread in both rural and urban areas if the urban–rural gap does not disappear. Farmers cannot truly enjoy the dignity, rights, and equality of citizens unless farmers historically "disappear" from the dual urban–rural structure.

Becoming prosperous and strong is the common aspiration and goal of all people around the world. Although many goals pursued by the human race are the same, there are diverse routes and ways to realizing or achieving these goals and no one-size-fits-all developmental path and mode are available. The developmental experiences of various countries can be used for reference and shared, but only the one suitable for one's own purpose is the best, the most useful, and the most fruitful.

From the Coastal Opening up to the Opening up along the Border

The course of China's reform and opening up in nearly 40 years shows that the emergence and development of the special economic zones not only is necessary from a geopolitical perspective, but it also reflects the national strategy for regional economic development. With a gradual opening up—characterized by the special economic zones, the coastal opening up, the opening up along rivers, and the opening up along the border—in Chinese society, the new landscape of China's regional economic development has gradually become clear, and the all-round, extensive, and multi-tier pattern of opening up has also progressively taken shape under the strategic arrangement from coastal opening up to opening up along the border, ushering in a new phase of regional economic development and overall coordinated economic development in Chinese society.

The course from coastal opening up to the opening up along the border
China launched the reform and opening up in four special economic zones. According to the line of thought at that time, three major economic supporting regions—the Yangtze River Delta, the Pearl River Delta, and the Circum-Bohai Sea Region—would emerge in the course of China's opening up in the future. Facts prove that it was wise and correct to establish the special economic zones; this establishment has resulted in the universal establishment of a market economic system as well as the development and prosperity of a city or region; guided by the unbalanced developmental strategy, an effective imbalance among regions has occurred—the policy differences among regions have been actively expanded to deliver potential benefits in a special region, to effectively attract capital, technologies, and management experience to the highland of economic growth built by the special policies, to enhance economic prosperity and efficiency in this region, bring about a noticeable regional imbalance and efficiency difference, and then transfer this efficiency difference inland, so as to stimulate economic development of the whole society.[11] This was the original intention for establishing the special economic zones and also an important function of those zones.

With the development of the special economic zones, the urban comprehensive reform also started in China. The first round of the urban comprehensive pilot

---

[11] Zhang Yaohui, *Regional Economic Theory and Regional Economic Development*, Beijing, China Planning Press, 1999, p. 86.

reform was initiated in 1981 when the State Council approved Shashi in Hubei Province as the pilot city. As of 1987, 72 cities had been designated by the State Council in a single batch, and approved by provinces and autonomous regions, as the pilot cities. In this period, the grand goal for the reform and opening up was established, but the reform goal of establishing a socialist market economy had not yet been specified, so the main task of the reform involved breaking up the old system and making preparations for new innovations. The strategic thought of "developing both transportation and circulation to promote the economic takeoff" in Wuhan, the thought of "impact and reflection" and "streamlining administration and delegating power to the lower levels, invigorating enterprises" in Shijiazhuang, etc., presented beneficial experimentations regarding the establishment of a socialist market economic system.

The second round of the urban comprehensive pilot reform was launched in 1992 when the State Commission for Restructuring the Economic System approved Changzhou City as the pilot city for a new round of the comprehensive reform. As of 1998, an additional 55 cities across China had been approved as the pilot cities for this comprehensive reform. During this period, the 14th National Congress of the Communist Party of China explicitly put forward the reform goal of establishing a socialist market economy; these pilot cities focused on transforming the microeconomic system, and accomplished great achievements in the enterprise reform, the development of the market system, the transformation of governmental functions, and the establishment of a new-type social security system, as well as producing a good demonstration effect to expedite the reforms in their regions and nationwide.

The third round of the urban comprehensive pilot reform started in June 2005 when the State Council approved the Pudong New Area of Shanghai as the national pilot zone for comprehensive reform. During this period, the Central Government brought forward the strategic thought of scientific development and the building of a harmonious society in response to various prominent problems including an undue emphasis on the growth rate, the extensive growth mode, and social contradictions involving the people's livelihood; this round of pilot reforms was mainly designed to address two major themes: scientific development and a harmonious society.[12]

The urban comprehensive pilot reform, national comprehensive pilot reform, and national pilot zone for comprehensive reform mark the basic establishment of a market economic system, and the formation of two great philosophies, including the intensification of the reform and all-round coordinated development. Therefore, the national pilot zone for comprehensive reform in the third round of the urban comprehensive pilot reform started in 2005 had changed in both substance and significance. The previous urban comprehensive pilot reforms aimed at breaking the fetter of the traditional system, establishing a market economic system and

---

[12] Su Dongbin, Zhong Ruoyu, *A Study of China's Special Economic Zones*, Beijing, The Commercial Press, March, 2010 (1), pp. 325–334.

promoting the universal establishment of a market economy across China, while the national pilot zone for comprehensive reform placed more emphasis on institutional innovations—the actual local developmental problems and the practical difficulties in China's reform and opening up are considered and solved at the same time, and the local advantages are utilized to break the bottlenecks in the reform and development, so as to explore a model or path, which can be applied nationwide, to improve the market economic system, address the global economic challenges, and achieve scientific development.

Since 2009 after the launch of the urban comprehensive pilot reform and national pilot zone for comprehensive reform in China, the State Council has approved a number of regional planning schemes at the national level. The national-level regional rejuvenation plans have been introduced to cover almost every economic region across China. So far, the grand pattern of overall regional development from the special economic zones, the coastal opening up, the opening up along rivers to the opening up along the border has unfolded in an all-round way.

Characteristics of the pilot zone for comprehensive reform

The pilot zone for comprehensive reform centers on "comprehensive" and aims at changing the development outlook—formed during the course of many years—concerning an undue emphasis on economic growth. The reform should be pushed forward in various respects and fields, including economic development, social construction, urban–rural relations, land development, environmental protection, and social welfare, and the effectively coordinated management system and operation mechanism should be developed to really achieve common prosperity and scientific development after allowing part of the people and regions to become rich first. Therefore, as an institutional arrangement for intensifying the reform in Chinese society, the national pilot zone for comprehensive reform presents the following four characteristics[13]:

(1) Thanks to the universal establishment of a market economic system, the material and spiritual achievements from the reform and opening up, the national pilot zone for comprehensive reform has a more explicit theme, mission, and tasks—for example, the Wuhan Metropolitan Area and the Changsha-Zhuzhou-Xiangtan City Group mainly undertake the mission of carrying out the national pilot reform in building a resource-conserving and environmentally friendly society, carrying out experimentations and innovations regarding a system and mechanism conducive to saving energy and protecting the ecological environment.
(2) The successful experience and profound lessons from the old special economic zones, especially the Shenzhen Special Economic Zone, help reduce the trial-and-error costs for China's reform and opening up. As a result, the national

[13]Hu Limin, Cui Meirong, New Developments in the Examination and Approval of the National Comprehensive Reform Pilot Areas, *China-Today Forum*, 2009 (1).

pilot zone for comprehensive reform may—and has the necessary conditions—to transform from the reform and breakthroughs in a city at the initial stage to more emphasis on promoting coordinated regional development—for example, the Pudong New Area of Shanghai, Shenzhen, the Binhai New Area of Tianjin mainly involve the pilot reform in a city or special region, while the Wuhan Metropolitan Area is a city circle with Wuhan as the core; the Changsha-Zhuzhou-Xiangtan City Group is a city circle demonstration region consisting of Changsha, Zhuzhou, and Xiangtan; Chengdu and Chongqing actually constitute the Chengdu-Chongqing Region.

(3) The grand thought of coordinated development becomes increasingly clear and the regional disparities have gradually narrowed, so the national pilot zone for comprehensive reform has been chosen by paying more attention to the basic conditions—shifting the focus from the location of a region to the pilot reform foundation of a region in terms of a market economy. The Pudong New Area of Shanghai, Shenzhen, the Binhai New Area of Tianjin have mainly benefited from the advantages of their location, while the Wuhan Metropolitan Area, the Changsha-Zhuzhou-Xiangtan City Group and the Chengdu-Chongqing Region mainly enjoy an excellent foundation for pilot reform. Of course, this is relative because the Pudong New Area of Shanghai, Shenzhen, the Binhai New Area of Tianjin enjoy not only the advantages of their location but also a terrific long-standing foundation for reform.

(4) The Central Government has transformed its governance philosophy and functions, thus the government has shifted its focus from the giving of preferential policies to the granting of autonomous rights in supporting the pilot zones for comprehensive reform—for example, previously, the government provided the reform pilot zones with preferential policies concerning fiscal revenue, taxation, and finance; now the government attaches greater importance to granting various zones the privilege of autonomous reform, and encourages the pilot zones to make bold innovations and experimentations, while the pilot plans are developed at the local level and then reported to the National Development and Reform Commission; this leaves sufficient room for the people in various zones to actively explore their developmental paths in light of the local conditions. The granting of autonomous rights and the right to choose is the most important and most fundamental prerequisite for mobilizing the enthusiasm and the creative power of the economic players, including the local governments. This is the adjustment of the government's governance philosophy and embodies the transformation and regularization of the governmental functions. Fundamentally, freedom guarantees development. Freedom is the precondition for development and is also part of development. This is because a free economic system is the soul of a market economy.

The national comprehensive reform was piloted in the cities in the developed coastal region and then pushed forward to make breakthroughs nationwide. All of the three major zones for pilot reform—Shenzhen, the Pudong New Area of Shanghai, and the Binhai New Area of Tianjin—are situated in the eastern coastal region and are mainly designed to stimulate the development of the eastern coastal region first. The supporting pilot reform zones are established in the central and western regions, and are given an explicit developmental mission; this shows that the universal establishment of a market economy makes it possible to achieve coordinated and all-round development across China, while scientific development is the all-round synchronous development in various sectors of the society and also the all-round development of China as a whole. The national comprehensive pilot zones are the expansion of the national developmental strategy towards the central and western regions, and they represent the choice of both philosophy and reality; if there is no realistic foundation—the universal establishment of a market economy, it would be impossible to expand the developmental strategy towards the central and western regions.

The significance of the expansion of the opening up strategy

The expansion from the coastal opening up to the opening up along the border is the grand strategic idea of establishing and improving the market economic system across China; it is a major measure for achieving the coordinated development of the Chinese society; it is an active exploration of the all-round opening up path; it is a great practice in scientific development; it is the overall arrangement for realizing modernization in an all-round way. It takes a strategic perspective to outlining the grand blueprint for the all-round development of Chinese society; it will also boost the rational distribution of the industrial structure among regions, and foster and effectively give play to the comparative advantages—consisting of factor endowments and other elements—among regions; it increased the influence of China's economic growth on the outside world so as to tap a broader international market; it mitigates the impact of the worldwide economic crisis on the economic growth mode dominated by an outward-looking economy, and it helps build up economic developmental strength that is stable, sustainable, and endogenous with increasing room for growth; it is conducive to forming an economic community—characterized by regional coordination and complementation—that aims at gradual balanced development and common prosperity across China. Therefore, it exerts a profound and lasting impact on China's future development; its strategic significance is far-reaching and immense.

(1) The unique political and economic characteristics peculiar to different cities or regions because of their geographical locations will be effectively utilized to shape the comparative advantages—composed of the geographical locations and factor endowments—which can jumpstart the economy in a region and also promote overall sustainable economic development—such as the *Several Opinions Concerning Supporting Fujian to Accelerate the Construction of the Economic Zones on Both Sides of the Taiwan Straits*, which advocates early and pilot efforts to enhance the communication among the people from both sides of the Taiwan Straits, and pinpoints the direction for building a new integrated opening up channel that would serve the surrounding areas and the

goal of establishing the important advanced manufacturing base and a natural and cultural center of tourism in the eastern coastal region; the *Development Plan for Liaoning's Coastal Economic Belt*, which positions the region as the national strategic inland highland for economic development and opening up and it also specifies the goal of building the national high technology industrial base for modern agriculture as well as the historical and cultural base for showcasing Chinese civilization; the *Ecological Economic Plan for Poyang Lake*, which spells out the goal of building the guarantee zone for water ecological safety in the middle and lower reaches of the Yangtze River and the platform for international ecological economic cooperation; the overall national plan converts the regional advantages and the comparative advantage resulting from factor endowment into the "innate advantages" for overall national sustainable development.

(2) The advantages due to political resources under the "whole nation system" are leveraged to effectively promote the adjustment of the industrial structure and gradual rational industrial distribution among regions. The opening up strategy marked by the regional economic development plan is expanded to solve or drive forward the ongoing process of solving the large historical problem: the dual economy and regional economic development imbalance in China. Therefore, the expansion of the opening up strategy takes the general situation into account and also fully reflects the characteristics of industrial development and the differentiated needs in different regions; it avoids both the localization of regional plans and the one-size-fits-all approach adopted in the national plan; it is more suitable to the reality of regional economic development and is also very beneficial to adjusting the industrial structure and undertaking the industrial transfer across China, especially the rational distribution among the eastern, central, and western regions. Since 2008, the growth rate in the central, western, and northeastern regions in China has exceeded that in the eastern region, which is largely attributable to the implementation and effect of the grand strategic idea concerning the expansion from coastal opening up to opening up along the border.

(3) The influence of China's economic growth on the outside world is enhanced to exploit the vaster international market so as to cushion the impact of the worldwide economic crisis on the economic growth mode dominated by an outward-looking economy. China's reform and opening up started in the southeastern coastal areas. Europe and the USA are the main consumers of China's manufacturing and the largest, most important international markets for China's foreign trade. With the impact of the global financial crisis, we have to think about the problems and embarrassments caused to our society by excessive dependence on an outward-looking economy, and the necessity for tapping the broader multilateral international market. The *Development Plan for Jiangsu's Coastal Areas*—which specifies the construction of the new Eurasian continental bridgehead as one of its main goals—and the *Plan Outline for the Cooperative Development of China's Tumen River Area*—which aims at turning this area into an important gateway to opening up towards Northeast

Asia—and the approval of Xinjiang's Kashgar Special Economic Zone—which connects eight countries through five ports and Eurasia by one road—embody the national opening up expansion strategy, address China's social and economic development, especially the improvement and rationalization of the industrial structure, they overcome the developmental predicament resulting from the disappearance of low labor costs, and achieve a win-win outcome in such a manner that China will be able to undertake the work due to the upgrading of the industrial structure in the Four Asian Tigers during the early stages of the reform and opening up in Chinese society.

(4) Stable and sustainable endogenous economic strength with an increasing amount of space will be vigorously fostered; an economic community—characterized by regional economic coordination and complementation—towards gradual balanced development and common prosperity across China will be energetically and effectively planned and developed. The core of all developmental plans is the development of the people; all economic growth aims at enhancing the people's economic value. The key to making billions of Chinese people share the achievements of the reform and opening up lies in raising the disposable income level. Therefore, the loftiest and purest goal of the reform and opening up is to make it possible for the people to be able to consume, live a decent life, and happily create wealth and value. Confucius, a famous Chinese philosopher, said that if the people became rich, a country would certainly become prosperous; if the people lived in poverty, a country cannot become prosperous. It appears that making the people rich is the eternal theme of human progress.

It should be stressed that, in an effort to achieve regional coordinated economic development and common prosperity, when striving to solve the contradictions caused by the dual urban–rural structure and mitigate the income inequality, we should, guided by the great wisdom of Deng Xiaoping that contention should be shelved, intensify the reform to complete institutional change so as to reach the ambitious goal of building an economically prosperous, institutionally advanced modern country.

Functions and comparisons of the new and old special economic zones

The establishment of the national pilot zones for comprehensive reform is a new move which grants autonomous rights to the local governments for seeking development with the aim of promoting local economic and social development under the guidance of the Scientific Outlook on Development during the new stage of economic and social development. In a sense, these pilot zones are "new special economic zones" following the "old special economic zones", including Shenzhen. As the "new special economic zones", these pilot zones have some characteristics that are different from the "old special economic zones"; these characteristics stem from the transformation of the national developmental strategy and also reflect the changes during China's reform and opening up, as well as fully demonstrating the objective need for improving the market economy and the intrinsic requirement for social institutional change.

Regarding the background and objective of their establishment, the old special economic zones were set up against the background of the planned economy and the impressive oases in the vast ocean of the planned economy. They aimed at completing a transformation from a planned economy to a market economy and exploring a feasible developmental path from widespread poverty to common prosperity. The new special economic zones were founded when the market economic system had basically already been established, and they are mainly designed to improve the market economic system through institutional innovations.

The new and old special economic zones have different tasks and means of development. The old special economic zones were mainly intended to address the issues concerning domestic reform and opening up, with the introduction of foreign capital as an important means for development. The new special economic zones are designed to comprehensively solve the contradictions in the system of economic development, with institutional innovation as an important means for development.

The new and old special economic zones differ in the choice of method. The old special economic zones focused on the coastal cities or areas where the planned economy was relatively weak—on the one hand, these cities or areas were given the priority of development at relatively low costs as they were subject to less burden from the planned economy and less fetter from traditional ideology; on the other hand, the advantages of their coastal location were utilized to introduce foreign capital and quickly open the door that had been closed for nearly half a century by means of export substitution, thus opening a window to connect the Chinese society with the outside world and building a bridge leading to the market economy and the international community in seeking national development, prosperity, and dignity. The new special economic zones mainly proceed from the overall national strategy for regional development to explore a new mode of coordinated regional development under the new historical conditions in the new process of development, so as to practice China's Development Path and verify whether it is feasible and correct.

In a sense, the Kashgar Special Economic Zone is different from the old special economic zones; it has some characteristics that are different from the national pilot zones regarding comprehensive reform. It does not have the political capital for being the first to carry out the reform and opening up like the old special economic zones. It does not enjoy the internal and external market economic environment which endows the open coastal cities with some innate advantages—for example, Shenzhen is adjacent to Hong Kong, an area with the freest market economy in the world; Shanghai was an area with a relatively high level of economic development even in the era of the planned economy. Kashgar does not have the experience of reform and the excellent foundation for social development that some cities, city circles, and regions have as the national pilot zones for comprehensive reform; that foundation includes infrastructure, education, population quality, social public facilities, and the institutional arrangement of the social welfare system as well as other social capital, resources, and institutional stock. However, as an emerging special economic zone with its own characteristics, Kashgar has unique conditions for development and much regional and constitutional room for development for undertaking the national strategic arrangements. Specifically, there are the following three characteristics:

(1) As an emerging special economic zone, Kashgar is built and developed on the shoulders of giants because it enjoys the generous policy support at the national level and receives the assistance covering the human, physical, and financial resources from the economically developed regions, provinces, and cities. All of this constitutes the developmental conditions which are not available in other cities and areas, but are peculiar to the Kashgar Special Economic Zone thanks to selfless political and policy support.
(2) The Kashgar Special Economic Zone was established under the following general background: The Chinese society had experienced the reform and opening up for nearly 40 years; a market economic system had been universally established; social rules and regulations had been gradually improved; much experience in development had been verified; some growth paths had been recognized; the area's achievements and problems, perseverance and abandonment, and directions and goals had become increasingly clear in China. Like other special economic zones or the pilot zones for comprehensive reform, it will certainly be subject to the establishment and selection of its own developmental path, mode, and route, but its takeoff and development can be based on the lessons drawn from the previous paths, the source of education from the previous developmental price, the experience and lessons from errors of selection, and the correct developmental philosophy, giving birth to successes and a good performance. Therefore, the development of the Kashgar Special Economic Zone is entirely possible, and should begin at a relatively high starting point to deliver a significant developmental outcome at relatively low trial-and-error costs.
(3) The Kashgar Special Economic Zone has this developmental characteristic: the weak spot is its space. Its natural conditions are severe; there is a lack of resources for production; the industrial foundation is relatively weak; its level of market economy is generally low; all these aspects are undoubtedly the weaknesses for the Kashgar Special Economic Zone. However, it can draw upon the well-proven national modes of development and develop its own plan for development in light of its strong and weak points, and it might even turn its weaknesses into distractive features, rationally distribute its industrial structure, thus uniquely nurture the beauty of industrial growth and development in Kashgar and make Kashgar really embark on a developmental path with its own characteristics. According to the developmental plan for the Kashgar Special Economic Zone, a nontraditional urban developmental path should be carved out for this zone; only when the traditional mode for relying on the resource input to seek new development is broken up and a low-carbon sustainable ecological developmental path is adopted can Kashgar obtain an inexhaustible endogenous power of development.

Document No. 33, released by the State Council in 2010, specifies Kashgar's positioning: First, it is necessary to give full scope to Kashgar's local advantages in opening up to turn Kashgar into China's important window for westward opening up and help shape a new pattern with equal emphasis on both the opening up of the land and the sea. Second, it is essential to attract domestic and foreign capital, technologies, and talents; undertake industrial transfer at a high starting point; promote the development of industrial agglomerations; and build a modern industrial system, converting Kashgar into a new economic growth point for Xinjiang's leapfrog development.

In my opinion, when moving towards the above developmental goals, attention should be paid to the following issues in the practical development of the Kashgar Special Economic Zone:

(1) Development and economic growth remain the priorities for the Kashgar Special Economic Zone, but the people in this Zone must meticulously learn about and bear in mind the past problems caused to our economy and society by excessive and undue emphasis on the GDP and economic growth. Development is of overriding importance, and the reform is the major premise, while institutional innovations are fundamental. Only the growth of the GDP accompanied by the people's happiness is a healthy kind of growth; only the growth rate which increases with the people's well-being is a meaningful growth rate; only economic development which can effectively conserve the environment and is environmentally friendly is a really sustainable kind of development. With the experience and lessons from the nearly 40-year-long reform and opening up in China, the takeoff and development of the Kashgar Special Economic Zone at a relatively high starting point should be achieved in a less blind and crazy but more rational, pragmatic, and scientific way.
(2) One major mission of the Kashgar Special Economic Zone is to improve the market economy and thus develop and elevate Xinjiang's economy; however, the improvement of the market economy is anything but a simple process of economic construction; it is a process of realizing social development in an all-round way. In my view, for the Kashgar Special Economic Zone, first, it is necessary to develop education and comprehensively improve the skills, knowledge reserve, and humanistic quality of the workers so as to form the potential practical human capital because this is the internal condition for ensuring the rapid growth and sustainable development of the Kashgar Special Economic Zone. This is because a modern city is impossible and modernization cannot be achieved if the people are not modernized. Second, the renewal of the mind-set is the mental prerequisite for the development of the Kashgar Special Economic Zone. The mind-set cannot directly change the society, but it can change the people, and the people can bring about changes in the society. As a renewed mind-set is an intangible productive force, it is a deep power—which transcends the material and capital—capable of driving forth economic development and social change.
(3) As Kashgar is an emerging special economic zone in an area inhabited by minority nationalities, its development must be based on respecting, retaining, and utilizing the heritage and unique charm of the ethnic culture. Modernization is certainly a process in which different cultures are modernized in different ways, but it is not a process in which different cultures are assimilated through

modernization. In my opinion, no matter what development might be, the Kashgar Special Economic Zone must and should be a special economic zone with the characteristics of its ethnic culture and distinctive national character, in which the ethnic culture shines.

(4) Assistance from the developed areas or cities is a generous policy adopted by the Central Government to distinguish the Kashgar Special Economic Zone from other special economic zones, and also provides the good condition and possibility for the Kashgar Special Economic Zone to rapidly take off and develop, and even draw on the experience acquired in other areas. Indeed, the capital and talents from the assisting cities, regions or provinces, and the well-proven advanced philosophies of management and administrative operational modes from the developed areas are delivered to Kashgar; in particular, they have an impact on the way of acting and the philosophy of governance of the local governments, and they can quicken the transformation of the governmental functions. However, fundamentally, that assistance is nothing but an external power, while the real enduring development depends upon the Kashgar Special Economic Zone, more precisely, the cognitive ability, philosophy of development, and level of governance of the local government and its foresight for abandoning the pursuit of quick success and instant benefits.

The development of China's special economic zones is crucial for the overall reform and opening up in China and also an exploration of the path towards China's regional economic development. However, there is no currently available mode of special economic zones which can be copied; moreover, the Shenzhen Special Economic Zone is not a wholesaler of experience. Regional economic development will certainly, at different levels and at different stages, show diverse developmental paths, ways, and significance. We do not intend to develop Kashgar into another Shenzhen (Shenzhen assists Kashgar in an oriented way); instead, we should turn today's Kashgar into a new modern Kashgar.

Adam Michnik, a polish intellectual, said that we strove for a bright today instead of a bright tomorrow; we strove for an imperfect society rather than a perfect society. In my view, the implementation of the grand blueprint—an expansion from the coastal opening up to the opening up along the border—will bring a prosperous and bright future for a beautiful China!

The New Mission of the Special Economic Zones

When inspecting Shenzhen in 2012, General Secretary Xi Jinping delivered an important speech, requiring Shenzhen to bear in mind its mission and act audaciously to assume responsibilities, further sharpen wits, emancipate minds, especially encouraging the cadres and masses to make bold experimentations and innovations, and gain new achievements in building a moderately affluent society in an all-around way, comprehensively intensifying the reform, governing the country under the rule of law and strengthening Party self-discipline, and to endeavor to foster new innovative advantages in the construction of the special economic zone and reach a higher level of development. He particularly pointed out that, as the forerunner in the reform, Shenzhen should continue to produce the demonstration effect and, being the first to achieve the "Four Comprehensives"—comprehensively build a moderately prosperous society, comprehensively intensify reform, comprehensively implement the rule of law and comprehensively strengthen Party discipline—it would become the new mission of the special economic zones in the new era.

Shenzhen's Sixth Congress of the CPC Representatives vowed to succeed in accomplishing this mission in response to the earnest expectation of General Secretary Xi Jinping. It specified an impressive developmental goal for Shenzhen in the next 5 years: emancipate the mind, carry out the solid work, boldly serve as the forerunner in achieving the "Four Comprehensives", endeavor to build a modern international innovative city; strive to build a special economic zone with more of a leading role in the reform and opening up, a national independent innovation demonstration zone at a higher level, a national economic central city with more power to influence and stimulate the outside world, an international city with more competitiveness and influence, and a city with a higher quality—that of making people happy.

In order to serve as the forerunner in achieving the "Four Comprehensives", Shenzhen should continue to inherit the courage and mettle of the first mover, with the forerunner's sense of mission and the sense of mission for first-ever implementation of pilot programs, to commendably accomplish the new mission of the special economic zones in the new period

Daring to make breakthroughs and blaze new trails is the unique spirit and character which defines Shenzhen, while the first-ever implementation of pilot programs is the innate character given by transformational China to the special economic zones, the policy "privilege" given by the compulsory institutional change to the special economic zones, the right to enjoy the first priority to change subject to risks and costs given by the unbalanced developmental strategy to the special economic zones, and the reason for the enduring political vitality of the special economic zones. At the early stage of the reform and opening up, the Shenzhen Special Economic Zone enjoyed the policy "privilege" for first-ever implementation of pilot programs to become the first to initiate the great and arduous practice of the market economy in China. Under the flag of first-ever implementation of pilot programs, the Shenzhen Special Economic Zone delivered the most basic concepts and practice of a market economy—the law of value, market competition, labor power as a commodity, stock dividend—to the rest of China, and it also made the earth-shattering slogan "time is money, efficiency is life" heard across China. Thirty-eight years later, with the intensification of the great cause of China's reform and opening up, the people's expectations regarding a more profound institutional change and a comprehensive intensification of reform in Chinese society confer a more profound significance and a deeper significance to the first-ever implementation of pilot programs as well as a more far-reaching mission of the first-ever implementation of pilot programs. This new far-reaching mission is to continue, with the courage, wisdom, and resourcefulness of the first mover, to be among the top across China in comprehensively exploring the social operational rules and regulations, social institutional environment, and legal safeguard mechanism fit for a market economic system; groping for the path of institutional innovation towards the reform of the political system, the government's governance system and mechanism and capacity modernization; probing the unique path towards transforming the mode of economic development, effectively achieving innovation-driven development and maintaining sustainable social and economic development; exploring how to build a moderately prosperous society in all aspects, and make the institutional arrangement for building a welfare society in which the social surplus is equitably shared, and becoming the forerunner in further improving the market economic system, promoting the all-round healthy development of Chinese society and the first to realize the "Four Comprehensives".

The first-ever implementation of pilot programs is a process of making innovations and learning from the advanced. Such first-ever implementation involves not only the economic system and mechanism but also the deeper institutional changes in various fields of the society, including the political system, the legal environment, the government's governance system and mechanism and capacity modernization as well as cultural ideology. This is the innate character of China's special economic zones and the more challenging new mission of China's free trade zones in the new era.

As a policy, the special economic zones may disappear, but as a spirit, a choice of path for China's institutional change and the great practice of China's Development Path, they will and should not disappear. Therefore, Shenzhen should fully realize, treasure, and properly utilize the political capital accumulated through China's reform and opening up in nearly 40 years and the unique and irreplaceable political and geographical advantages resulting from its proximity to Hong Kong; moreover, it should enhance the strategic awareness and the capability for identifying its own positioning and seeking development from the perspective of overall national development. Shenzhen should continue to act as the forerunner in China's efforts to intensify the reform and a modern international city with a unique institutional character and charm in South China. In my opinion, it is particularly important for Shenzhen to continue to serve as the forerunner in China's efforts to intensify the reform; if this is abandoned, such an abandonment will lead to a loss of history and the largest and most valuable political asset that is Shenzhen. In this regard, the institutions prevail over technologies, even thoughts surpass actions. I want to quote the view of Hayek to further clarify my standpoint: From a long-term perspective, the mind-set and the people who communicated the mind-set dominated the historical developmental process. The practice of China's reform and opening up in nearly 40 years also proves another view of Hayek's: the transformation of the mind-set and the willpower of the people shaped today's world. It is impossible—and not necessary—for Shenzhen to act as the "wholesaler" of the experience from China's reform and opening up; however, it is entirely possible for Shenzhen to do that, and Shenzhen should become a city which is the most courageous in reform and the most innovative in China. This is the character which was once possessed by Shenzhen and can and should never be lost or discarded.

If there are not the first-ever implementation of pilot programs and the spirit and courage of the first mover, Shenzhen's development, Shenzhen's miracle, even a brighter tomorrow will be impossible. Shenzhen should be bold in serving as the forerunner in achieving the "Four Comprehensives" and write, with the spirit of the time, Shenzhen's character on the flag of development.

In order to boldly serve as the forerunner in realizing the "Four Comprehensives", our government should have not only foresight and wisdom but also the spirit of assuming responsibilities, the courage and mettle to revolutionize by itself. For a transformational society, only when the government is brave in reform can the society persevere in reform; only when the government's governing capacity is modernized can social development be modernized; only when the government becomes open-minded can the society become institutionally civilized

Chinese society has been experiencing top-down compulsory institutional change, while the governments, especially the Central Government, are the initiators, leaders or the most immediate advocators of this institutional change, and are also the first to be reformed in the change. If there is no decision-making and authorization from the Central Government, the practice of the reform and opening up is impossible—for example, the establishment of the special economic zones and the free trade zones is the result of the special policies given to the local governments by the Central Government and also the outcome of the overall strategic arrangement of development made by the Central Government.

The constitutional change in Chinese society follows a pragmatic path. In spite of this, it will not naturally occur just because of the potential profit-making opportunities like induced institutional change. This is because compulsory institutional change often alters the distribution of interests among the original social groups, even some people will lose their interests—in particular, the government officials as the main reformers and implementers of the reform will lose their interests—while other people will obtain interests because of it. Therefore, in principle, in a market economy under development, a protective government can make great contributions to cultivating and supporting the internal institutions. The government's functions and roles can produce the effect of a "scale economy" during restriction and transformation. However, the failure of the government's policies will also reduce or hinder the effectiveness and process of the institutional change, thus increasing the costs of social reform. In a general sense, both the maintenance of an ineffective institutional arrangement and the government's failure to take actions to eliminate the institutional imbalance are policy failures.

What the government looks like determines the institutional arrangement; the government's civilization is the precondition and guarantee for institutional civilization. Meanwhile, the government's cognitive ability also largely determines the costs and effectiveness of the reform. Therefore, remolding the government, transforming the government's functions, enhancing the cognitive ability, and the governing capacity of the government officials are the internal logical requirements for intensifying the reform and modernizing the government's governance system, mechanism, and governing capacity. China's free trade zones, following the special economic zones, undertake the mission of intensifying the reform.

The work we have constantly carried out in transforming the government's functions during the reform and opening up in nearly 40 years have mainly focused on transforming the centralized government closely associated with the planned economy under the traditional system to a service-oriented government fit for a market economy. The establishment of the government's governance system and mechanism in the process of comprehensively intensifying the reform and the modernization of the governing capacity focus on further revolutionizing the government, reshaping the system and mechanism of a modern government, and really establishing the rules of a law-based government as well as solidly pushing forward the reform of China's political system.

In my view, with respect to the government's governance system and mechanism as well as the modernization of the governing capacity, the professional views in the book *Reinventing Government: How the Entrepreneurial Spirit Is Transforming the Public Sector*, written by the American administrative science scholars David Osborne and Ted Gaebler, are very useful to us.[14] David Osborne and Ted Gaebler first affirmed that what we faced was anything but the gradual withering away of the State; on the contrary, we needed a vibrant, powerful, and very active government. We are confident in the government because we believe that if there is not an effective government, a civilized society cannot effectively operate. The government is a mechanism by which we make public decisions—for example, we need to decide on the places where the roads are to be built, how to deal with the homeless people, and what kind of education for our children; the government is a way of providing us with beneficial services covering national defense, environmental protection, police protection, roads, dams, water supply, and drainage system; the government is a way for us to solve the common problems such as drug-taking, crime, poverty, illiteracy, discharge of toxic wastes, global climate warming, and skyrocketing medical and healthcare expenses, which call for collective actions, while the collective actions cannot be taken unless the government gets involved. We believe that the problem lies in the system in which the government officials work rather than the government officials themselves. However, fundamentally, the government should operate the rudder instead of paddling. Any move designed to massively associate governance with "solid work" will severely cripple the actual policymaking capacity. Any move aimed at forcing

[14](US) David Osborne and Ted Gaebler, trans. by Zhou Dunren et al, *Reinventing Government: How the Entrepreneurial Spirit Is Transforming the Public Sector*, Shanghai, Shanghai Translation Publishing House, 1996, pp. 25–32.

the policymaking body to carry out "solid work" means that our government laboriously commits a folly. This is because the policymaking body is unable to do so, in essence, that falls outside the scope of its work. We need a powerful government which confines itself to policymaking and guidance and assigns "solid work" to others.

Instead of simply collecting the service objects to tirelessly provide services, a real efficient modern government should empower the society and the people to a greater extent. Empowerment—which is not a simple service—is precisely the creative way to fully develop our society, and utilize the enthusiasm of social organizations and the self-confidence and capability of the citizens.

A government with a modern outlook towards governance should be a government with a sense of mission. In order to enhance the governing capacity of the government, first, it is necessary to change the governmental organization that is just aware of going by the book, and turning it into a governmental organization with a sense of mission. This is because a governmental organization with a sense of mission is more efficient, effective, innovative, flexible, and energetic than a government which just knows how to go by the book. This has also been proved by the successful practice of China's reform to varying degrees. The government should foster and develop the culture of mission.

A government with a modern governing capacity should be a government with the ability to foresee rather than one which knows how to cure. In a sense, the more important function of the government lies in solving problems instead of providing services. E. F. Schumacher, a British economist, reputed as the prophet of sustainable development, said that a wise man solved problems, while a gifted man avoided problems. It is easier and more inexpensive to prevent than cure a disease. Likewise, it is easier and more inexpensive to prevent than handle a crime. Amid the debate on a high road maintenance budget, a senior mayor in the USA said that if we did not take actions right now, we would not be able to afford to do that in the future, so we decided to either correctly maintain roads or let the road system collapse; it was clear that if we did not spend money right now, we would go broke in the future.

The view of Alvin Toffler, the author of the well-known book *The Third Wave*, may be in a better position to explain the necessity for or inevitability of reforming the government: I can't understand why we had a technological revolution, a social revolution, an information revolution, and a revolution of morality and epistemology but no governmental revolution; the government should convey the best idea to our society instead of hindering our creative power, self-confidence, our desire, and ability to create a good life.[15]

---

[15](US) Alvin Toffler, trans. by Huang Mingjian, *The Third Wave*, Beijing, China Citic Press, 2006, pp.204–205.

In order to courageously serve as the forerunner in realizing the "Four Comprehensives", our society must explicitly incorporate the free development of the people and universal improvement of the social welfare into social development. The realization of the "Four Comprehensives" should and must aim at emancipating humanity and be a process of free development of the people and equalization of social welfare

China's reform and opening up started from emancipating the productive forces. The emancipation of the productive forces is the emancipation of humanity, the release and emancipation of the people's creative power.

"The first premise of all human history is, of course, the existence of living human individuals." "Man is man's highest essence." "For man, the root is man himself."[16] Marxist classic writers always considered the high development of the productive forces as merely the condition and foundation for an all-round development of the human being. The realization of an all-round and free development of the human being was always the lofty ideal of Marxist-Leninists. Karl Marx and Frederick Engels regarded the all-round and free development of the human being as the "basic principle" of the new "social form" which replaced capitalism and the "basic thought" of the future society. Karl Marx attributed the historical trend of capitalistic production to the following: It itself, with the necessity that it dominated the changes in nature, gave rise to its own negation; Karl Marx added that it itself had created a new factor in the economic system, and it also gave a tremendous boost to the all-round development of the social labor force and all individual producers, ultimately guaranteeing the economic form—all-round development of the human being—while ensuring the extremely high development of the social labor force.[17]

Some people asked, "What on earth is an international modern metropolis?" Now, many original sufferings have gone, so the original word—happiness—becomes increasingly vague. This forces us to trace the most basic value in life, that is, only in the metropolis which can, to a larger extent, concentrate the social resources and rationally allocate them, everyone—regardless of man or woman, the strong or the weak—may share the same dream and the same world. As a matter of fact, there is only one goal of happiness—living a better life. This is exactly the goal of our reform and the significance of the pursuit of the scientific spirit and humanity. I hold that this is also the significance of building a modern international and innovative city.

[16] *Karl Marx and Frederick Engels* (Vol.1), Beijing, People's Publishing House, 1956, pp. 460–461.

[17] *Selections of Karl Marx and Frederick Engels* (Vol.3), Beijing, People's Publishing House, 1995, pp. 339–342.

Qianhai: Another Hong Kong

Twenty-eight years ago, on June 3, 1988, when meeting with the representatives of the 1990s China and World Conference, Deng Xiaoping, the chief architect of China's reform and opening up, stressed that we would further build several Hong Kongs on the Chinese Mainland. In May 1989, Deng Xiaoping reaffirmed, before the then leaders of the Central Committee, that in the past he vowed to further build several Hong Kongs. As the State Council approved the *Overall Development Plan for Shenzhen-Hong Kong Cooperation in the Modern Service Industry in Qianhai*, submitted by Shenzhen, the great conception of Deng Xiaoping, a great man, about "further building several Hong Kongs" has been put into grand practice in the beautiful blueprint in Shenzhen, on which Deng Xiaoping placed a great hope. Such a grand practice means not only the emergence of a new economic cooperation zone but also a gradual intensification of China's reform and opening up on the basis of a power of institutional innovation. From a long-term perspective, the establishment of the Qianhai Shekou Free Trade Zone will give birth to another Hong Kong.

The establishment of the Shenzhen Special Economic Zone in 1978 aimed at gradually transforming the economy from a planned one into a market one across China by means of unbalanced development. The Qianhai Economic Cooperation Zone, guided by direct Shenzhen-Hong Kong cooperation, has been established in Shenzhen where the market economy has developed considerably; fundamentally, this cooperation zone is designed to further improve the market economic system through institutional innovations, learning, fostering, and creating an institutional environment suitable to the growth of the market economy so as to really bring about a great institutional change in Chinese society. Thirty-five years ago, when the Shenzhen Special Economic Zone was established, Shenzhen served as the window for China's reform and opening up; however, under the general background of globalization in which China and the outside world interact with each other, the Qianhai Economic Cooperation Zone guided by direct Shenzhen-Hong Kong cooperation will become a more extensive platform for opening up and a modern world-class metropolitan area with an international vision and competitiveness.

With the planned land covering an area of 15 km^2, situated on the east bank of the Pearl River Estuary and the west side of the Shenzhen Nanshan Peninsula, the Qianhai Economic Cooperation Zone will certainly become a vibrant economic entity with boundless creative power. Innovative financing; modern logistics; a headquarters economy; science, technology, and professional services; communication and media services; and high-end commercial services are listed as industrial priorities of this cooperation. However, its functional positioning—the forerunner zone for Shenzhen-Hong Kong cooperation, the zone for system and mechanism innovation, the zone for modern service industry clusters, and the leading zone for structural adjustment—shows the demonstration effect of the Qianhai Economic Cooperation Zone on a deeper institutional change in transformational China: It represents a kind of economic cooperation and institutional innovation; it heralds an industrial cluster and an institutional change; it creates a number of opportunities and ideas; it makes the economy prosperous and the society civilized. The innovations to the system and mechanism as well as a deeper institutional change are the preconditions for and the significance of its establishment, and they constitute the basic institutional guarantee for its survival, development, and demonstration.

Therefore, the Qianhai Economic Cooperation Zone is anything but a simple economic entity and a simple industrial cluster; instead, it should be a loose, inclusive, and efficient institutional environment which encourages innovations, and a paradise where entrepreneurs can realize their personal ideals; it should be an elegant and warm soil which nurtures civic awareness and spirit, and a beautiful and civilized harbor which reflects globalization and economic integration. Therefore, the statement made by Deng Xiaoping that "we will further build several Hong Kongs" by no means implies that we will further build several skyscrapers and simply copy the prosperity of a commercial society; instead, we will ensure that the mature market economic system which guarantees the continued prosperity of Hong Kong's society, the well-functioning social operational rules and the civilized institutional environment beneficial to social development and progress will become the more extensive consensus and the more universal social operational system and mechanism, and will exert a far-reaching impact on improving the market economic system in Guangdong Province, Hong Kong, even nationwide.

The institutional advantages of Hong Kong are utilized to ensure that international practice really becomes the institutional power for participating in international competition

The objective of the Qianhai Shenzhen-Hong Kong Cooperation Zone is to make use of Hong Kong's institutional advantages and give play to the advantages and roles of Hong Kong as the international economic center to deepen the cooperation between Guangdong Province and Hong Kong and shape a new pattern of China's reform and opening up.

In nearly 40 years since the reform and opening up, Hong Kong has always been the most direct and convenient place for the Chinese Mainland to understand the outside world, learn about the market economy, and become part of the international community. The governments (mainly the governments of the Chinese Mainland) have provided policies; encouraging free movement of private capital is the universal cooperational model between Hong Kong and Shenzhen, Guangdong Province even the whole Chinese Mainland, and the introduction of Hong Kong's capital, the establishment of joint ventures with Hong Kong investors, and the sole proprietorship of Hong Kong investors have constituted the most basic and uppermost mode of cooperation between the Chinese Mainland and Shenzhen in a considerably long time. CEPA's implementation is mainly designed to open the market of the Chinese Mainland to Hong Kong and adopt the preferential policies to permit and encourage Hong Kong's capital to compete on the market of the Chinese Mainland. Affirmatively, the cross-border movement of Hong Kong's capital, materials, goods, technologies, talents, and other economic factors has driven the reform and opening up forward on the Chinese Mainland, especially

Shenzhen and Guangdong Province; such movement has speeded up the transformation from a planned economy to a market economy and has brought forth the competition and prosperity sufficient to change the social operational system and common development based on common values. Meanwhile, Hong Kong's system and institutional resources are, to a large extent, only the exogenous variables of the economic growth for influencing our life and choices rather than the endogenous factors of social development for changing our ways of acting, our mind-sets, decision-making procedure, and modes. The establishment of a direct Shenzhen-Hong Kong cooperation zone under the "one country, two systems" policy turns the philosophy of drawing on Hong Kong's institutional advantages into the introductory factor for seeking further development and the realistic choice for achieving common prosperity. Therefore, we definitely do not simply understand the market economy as science and technology, tools, and means; fundamentally, the market economy is defined by institutions, mechanisms, cultures, and civilizations.

Hong Kong's society showcases to us an excellent framework for government management and a number of administrative operational procedures which have been tested in practice, well proven, corrected, and improved through trial and error. Hong Kong is a very valuable source of learning for the Shenzhen Municipal Government born from the reform and opening up in terms of the functions and efficiency of social management, the government's decision-making philosophy and procedure, the officials' service awareness and legal sense, the value orientation of democracy, and equity in the political life of Hong Kong.

Hong Kong's institutional advantages are invaluable resources. Learning the advanced institutions is helpful for the government of a transformational society in overcoming and avoiding its conservative line of thought and low efficiency resulting from its own limitations—for example, the vested interest and traditional ideology within the original system will directly affect the officials' choice of preference during the institutional change, while the advanced systems can produce a demonstration effect to quickly free the people from the fetter of the traditional ideology in a short time, and prevent the individual rationality constraints so as to enhance the ability to understand the institutional change. For another example, the institutional change in a transformational society is often accompanied by this kind of a situation: Even if the government is confident in making the new institutional arrangement to return to a balance from an imbalance, the government cannot make a correct institutional arrangement due to a shortage of social science knowledge. As a result, the short-term efforts in maximizing the profits will lead to the pursuit of the continuously ineffective activities (in the case of given system restrictions), and even though they pursue the productive activities, there may be an unforeseeable result. Learning about the advanced institutions can remove the lagging behind in institutional change, lower the costs of institutional change, and reduce the intangible losses—including psychological and affective losses—during the institutional change; such learning can also enable the government to become mature and rational, and develop a sense of responsibility and the value orientation of professionals regarding serving the society and the people during institutional change.

The Shenzhen-Hong Kong Cooperation Zone epitomizes the economic globalization and integration in China. Drawing on Hong Kong's institutional advantages means that we must learn to act according to the international rules under the framework of "one country, two systems". The uniqueness of Chinese characteristics lies in the path to realizing the goals and the choice of path for such realization rather than the goals themselves.

The policy "privilege" in first-ever implementation of pilot programs continues to be exercised to intensify the reform

The Qianhai Shenzhen-Hong Kong Cooperation Zone is entrusted with a new historical mission: It becomes the first to implement pilot programs to explore the path towards institutional change leading to the innovative development of the modern service industry, so as to stimulate innovations in the operational systems and mechanisms which govern the whole society, and set a good example for the whole country with an excellent performance in institutional innovations, moving forward the great cause of the reform and opening up in Chinese society.

The first-ever implementation of pilot programs is the "innate" character given by transformational China to the special economic zones and the policy "privilege" given by the compulsory institutional change to the special economic zones. Such first-ever implementation is the right—to enjoy the first priority to change subject to risks and costs—given by the unbalanced developmental strategy to the special economic zones and the reason for the enduring political vitality of the special economic zones. In an exclusive interview conducted by the journalists of the *Shenzhen Special Economic Zone Daily* on the eve of the 30th anniversary of the establishment of the Shenzhen Special Economic Zone, Mr. Donald Tsang, former Chief Executive of the Hong Kong Special Administrative Region, said that they hoped to introduce Hong Kong's service industry to Qianhai in an all-round way, and the cooperation with Shenzhen would be carried out through Hong Kong's strong points; that they wanted to build a base in the Pearl River Delta for first-ever implementation of pilot programs, the best base would be Shenzhen, while the best place for pilot efforts in Shenzhen would be Qianhai. With respect to the development of the Qianhai Shenzhen-Hong Kong Cooperation Zone, Mr. Donald Tsang also stressed that the most important foundation for Shenzhen-Hong Kong cooperation was that the "one country, two systems" policy should connect both sides. Originally, some things could not be done by Hong Kong, but this connection made things possible. Likewise, Shenzhen was not able, by itself, to do a good job in some respects, especially regarding financial services, but Hong Kong's participation could help them do better. Therefore, the "one country, two systems" policy is one of the roads to success.

Hong Kong is a developed market economy region that is full-fledged, well-enhanced, and highly internationalized, while it is a city with relatively high levels of both market economic development and degree of internationalization on the Chinese Mainland. Fundamentally, Qianhai Shenzhen-Hong Kong cooperation is a natural combination derived from market economic development and the inexorable outcome of the common choice. As if the farm output quotas were fixed on the household basis in the past, the cooperation zone was approved by the Central Government, but its creative power comes from the grassroots. Hence, we are fully confident that Qianhai is not merely an economic platform for direct cooperation between Shenzhen and Hong Kong, and Qianhai, with its practice in institutional innovations and its experience in the first-ever implementation of pilot programs, is bound to intensify the reform and opening up, in Chinese society, towards fostering a loose, open, inclusive, and civilized international life circle. Thirty-eight years ago, the proximity to Hong Kong enabled us to quickly learn about the market economy, while the current Shenzhen-Hong Kong direct cooperation zone will make it more straightforward and urgent for improving the social operational mechanism and for innovating the management system. As a well-functioning society, Hong Kong demonstrates to us a high degree of work efficiency of the service-oriented government, a democratic and transparent order for discussing official business and handling affairs, an open and competitive market order, and a well-developed, universal social security mechanism, as well as a highly developed and robust social emergency system, which are good sources of learning for Shenzhen.

The first-ever implementation of pilot programs is a process of carrying out innovations and learning from the advanced. Such first-ever implementation covers not only the economic system and mechanism but also institutional change in the political system, the administrative management system, and the social and cultural systems. This is the character and new mission of the special economic zones.

A service-oriented government is built to foster a good institutional environment as the core guarantee for the growth of the productive forces

The leading role of the government in making policies is brought into full play to create an excellent policy, institutional environment, and legal environment for the development of an agglomeration of the modern service industry in the Qianhai Zone, which is the basic guarantee for the steady growth of the Qianhai Shenzhen-Hong Kong Cooperation Zone.

The Qianhai Shenzhen-Hong Kong Cooperation Zone creates and opens a brand-new—and challenging—mode for Shenzhen-Hong Kong cooperation. Previous Shenzhen-Hong Kong cooperation mainly involved the circulation and movement of factors, while this cooperation zone will switch the cooperation from the field of pure factor circulation to the institutional level which determines the flow of factors. This cooperation zone tests our management instead of merely our entrepreneurs. The direct cooperation between Shenzhen and Hong Kong is a process of learning the modern enterprise system and moving towards a modern service-oriented government. The economic activities—especially the activities in the market economy—cannot be carried out in an institutional and legal vacuum. On the contrary, the really guaranteed individual freedom and private property rights, a sound orientation system and effective public services are exactly the prerequisites for the existence and development of a market economy. Therefore, the primary task of the government is to provide an institutional guarantee of security so that every worker can enjoy the fruits of their labor and are motivated to work in an honest and efficient way.

The government is the sole provider of the institutional environment. For a transformational society, the government plays its roles in compulsory institutional change mainly by creating, revising, and improving the basic institutional arrangement in order to foster an institutional environment beneficial to reforms and innovations. Theoretically and logically, a particular institutional environment is a legal—moral space for operating a particular institutional system and also the core guarantee for the growth of the social productive forces.

George Joseph Stigler said that the State may be either a resource or a threat to every industry in a society. Richard A. Epstein held that any political party which realized that fewer government actions would lead to more achievements would enjoy the huge and gratifying developmental opportunities in the political arena. According to Walter Eucken, the interdependence between political procedure and economic procedure forces us to address both at the same time; both are part of the whole procedure. If there is not a competitive procedure, a capable government will be unavailable, while there will be no competitive procedure if such a government is nonexistent.

For a transformational society, the establishment of a service-oriented government is a process in which the functions are transformed and the powers are delegated to lower levels. If there is not an institutional guarantee for a government, there will be no market procedure or prosperity; however, if a government acts beyond its authority and concentrates all its powers, it will do harm to the market and economic growth. In the process of transforming from a traditional investment-oriented government and an order-focused government to a service-oriented government, we should carefully learn the experience and lessons concerning Japan's Disease in the period of the 1980s-1990s, during which the Japanese Government excessively loosened control over the financial market, land prices, and large-scale infrastructure, plunging Japan's economy into stagnation.

We must be keenly aware that, in a market economy, the government is the supporting actor, while the leading actor cannot be anything but companies (enterprises). Market failure makes it possible for the government to intervene, but the roles of the market cannot be replaced by that of a government. Only when such a philosophy is developed can Qianhai become a real market—which shines with the great brilliancy of nationality, economically flourishes, and advocates fair competition—and thus embrace Hong Kong.

From the Special Economic Zones to the Free Trade Zones: The Special Mission of China's Free Trade Zones

The establishment of the Shenzhen Special Economic Zone 38 years ago was a great earth-shaking event in the history of new China—it marked the end of an era and the beginning of another era. The establishment of the China (Shanghai) Pilot Free

Trade Zone in September 2013 was an important milestone which is comparable to the establishment of the special economic zone in the history of new China's reform and opening up—it marked the deepening of the reform and opening up of Chinese society, a transformation from an outward-looking economy to an open economy and the launch of a new round of deeper institutional opening up; it means that the socialist market economic system which, under the rule of law, centers on defining the government powers is being improved in a very profound way.

In April 2015 after the China (Shanghai) Pilot Free Trade Zone was successfully built, the State Council officially approved the China (Guangdong) Pilot Free Trade Zone, the China (Fujian) Pilot Free Trade Zone and the China (Tianjin) Pilot Free Trade Zone, among which the China (Guangdong) Pilot Free Trade Zone covers the Guangzhou Nansha Free Trade Zone, the Shenzhen Qianhai Shekou Free Trade Zone and the Zhuhai Hengqin Free Trade Zone. As if the previous "5 + 2" traditional special economic zones—Shenzhen, Zhuhai, Shantou, Xiamen, Hainan, Pudong of Shanghai, and Binhai of Tianjin—led the direction of China's reform and opening up with their practice in the first-ever implementation of pilot programs, today's free trade zones represent a new form of China's special economic zones under the new historical conditions, and will continue, with practice in the first-ever implementation of pilot programs and the new functions given by the times, to undertake the mission of the times for intensifying the reform and boosting the institutional opening up in Chinese society.

China's special economic zones are not a simple economic concept; likewise, China's free trade zones are not a pure economic concept, but they are the outcome of economic globalization and regional economic integration as well as the intensification of reform in Chinese society. In a deeper sense, like the previous special economic zones, they shoulder the reform mission that is much heavier than their pure economic mission

Conceptually, China's free trade zones refer to the multifunctional special economic zones which were established outside the customs district within China's territory, and adopt the preferential tax and special customs supervision policies as the main means, and mainly aim at trade liberalization and facilitation. They center on creating a good international business environment which accords with international practice and enjoys international competitiveness for both domestic and foreign capital. However, the current free trade zones in China do not really represent the internationally accepted FTA (Free Trade Area) concept and the FTZ (Free Trade Zone) concept; instead, they make up a concept of a free trade zone with Chinese characteristics which functionally transcends the FTZ and is different from the FTA in terms of rules.

The FTA originates from the WTO rules concerning a free trade area and was included in the text of the *General Agreement on Tariffs and Trade 1947* at the earliest. Subparagraph (b), Paragraph 8, Article 24 of this Agreement makes a special explanation about the concepts of the customs union and the free trade area: A free trade area shall be understood to mean a group of two or more customs territories in which the duties and other restrictive regulations of commerce are eliminated on substantially all the trade between the constituent territories in products originating in such territories. Its characteristics are the following: It is established by a number of sovereign states or territories and is a block consisting of two or more economies; it covers two or more customs territories; with respect to the internationally accepted practice, the WTO rules are observed; the core policy emphasizes the trade openness and removal of tariff barriers among the members of a free trade area, but maintains the preservation of respective independent foreign trade policies; with regard to the legal basis, a bilateral or multilateral agreement is observed. Currently, the EU, the North American Free Trade Area, and the ASEAN-China Free Trade Area are typical FTAs around the world.

FTZ comes from the rules concerning free zones. According to the *Kyoto Convention* signed by the Customs Cooperation Council in 1973, the FTZ is part of the territories of the contracting parties, and any goods which enter this zone are generally considered to be outside the customs territory with respect to the import tariff. Its characteristics are the following: It is established by a single sovereign state or territory and its establishment is the act of a single sovereign state or territory; it is a small area within a customs territory; when it comes to the internationally accepted practice, the WCO (World Customs Organization) rules are observed; the core policy underscores "under bond" and tax exemption as the main policies, supplemented by such investment policies as income tax preference; with respect to the legal basis, the laws are made within a sovereign state, and it is not bound by a multilateral agreement. Of course, both the FTA and the FTZ are designed to reduce the international trade costs and promote the development of foreign trade and international commerce. In essence, they are, to a larger extent or mainly, economic communities or economic regions.

Developing the economy is the logical starting point of the reform of Chinese society and is also the entry point of China's institutional change. Thirty-eight years ago, under the strategic guidance of Deng Xiaoping's idea that "development is the absolute principle" and the slogan that "let some people become prosperous first", the special economic zones successfully sought out a path towards institutional change from widespread poverty to common prosperity, and also impressively accomplished the mission of the experimental fields for transforming from a planned economy to a market economy. Reform is always the most fundamental mission of China's special economic zones, while deepening the reform is undoubtedly the most fundamental mission of the current free trade zones in China.

Like the past special economic zones, China's free trade zones make up a community of mission (reform) and development (promotion of economic globalization, trade liberalization), and an experimental field for innovations to the system and mechanism and institutional innovations—for example, the overall requirement for the China (Shanghai) Pilot Free Trade Zone is as follows: The pilot free trade zone should undertake the important mission of accelerating the transformation of governmental functions, actively exploring the innovations in the management mode, and boosting trade and investment facilitation to probe a new path and acquire new experience for the intensification of the reform and expanding the opening up in China in the new period.[18] The overall requirement for the China (Tianjin) Pilot Free Trade Zone is specified here: This pilot free trade zone should, in light of the national strategy, drive forward reform, development, and transformation through opening up, focus on the institutional innovations, give play to the role of the market in determining the resource allocation, and explore a new path to transforming the government's functions and a new mode for expanding the opening up, thus groping for a new path and new experience for comprehensively intensifying the reform and opening up in China, and actively producing a demonstration effect to stimulate and serve the development of the whole country.[19] The strategic positioning of the China (Guangdong) Pilot Free Trade Zone is identified as follows: This pilot free trade zone should serve as the forerunner in reform and opening up as well as innovative development, it should focus on institutional innovations, carry out the One Belt and One Road initiative and other national strategies, and become the first to tap the reform potential and overcome the reform difficulties in building a new system for an open economy, exploring a new mode of economic cooperation between Guangdong Province, Hong Kong, and Macao and fostering a business environment under the rule of law; it is necessary to actively explore the management mode of the pre-establishment national treatment and a negative list for foreign investments, intensify the innovations in the administrative management system and enhance the efficiency of administrative management, elevate the capacity and level of in-process and postmortem supervision.[20] The overall requirement for the China (Fujian) Pilot Free Trade Zone is specified here: This pilot trade zone should, based on the national strategy, focus on intensifying the economic cooperation between both sides of the Taiwan Straits, innovating the system and mechanism, and further probing a new mode for such economic cooperation, as well as expanding a new path to reinforcing the communication and cooperation with the countries and territories along the 21st Century Maritime Silk Road.[21]

In my opinion, the special economic zones are no longer a temporary economic phenomenon, an outcome of a particular stage or a makeshift in policies; instead, they serve as the experimental fields for carrying out the all-directional reform in China and the effective choice of a path for accomplishing social transformation and institutional change, and they constitute a "shortcut" for accelerating the modernization drive in a large country where economic development is unbalanced. Given

[18] Overall Plan for the China (Shanghai) Pilot Free Trade Zone

[19] Overall Plan for the China (Tianjin) Pilot Free Trade Zone

[20] Overall Plan for the China (Guangdong) Pilot Free Trade Zone

[21] Overall Plan for the China (Fujian) Pilot Free Trade Zone

the whole process of China's reform and from the perspective of China's reform and opening up, the mission of the special economic zones is far from being accomplished. This is evidenced by the successful experience of the early special economic zones represented by Shenzhen, and by the establishment of the emerging special economic zones, including Kashgar, Khorgos, and Tumen River, and today's free trade zones. As the upgraded version of the special economic zones in assuming a more profound reform mission, China's free trade zones will certainly continue to carry forward the character and practice of the first mover to theoretically, practically enrich the essence and significance of China's Development Path.

The first-ever implementation of pilot programs for exploring the path and road, and for providing the successful experience which can be drawn on and copied for the reform in Chinese society is the unique choice of a path for institutional change in Chinese society. The correctness of this unique choice of path has been verified by the 38-year success in China's reform and opening up and evidenced by China's Miracle created by billions of Chinese people, the successful experience and the lasting vitality of China's special economic zones. Therefore, in the sense of the choice of a path for China's reform and opening up, the first-ever implementation of pilot programs is currently the "Chinese characteristic" which distinguishes China's free trade zones from the FTA and the FTZ, as if the first-ever implementation of pilot programs was the important function of China's special economic zones in the past.
As a formal top-down institutional arrangement, the special economic zones have produced the demonstration effect through the first-ever implementation of pilot programs to greatly reduce the resistance from the system during the institutional change under the condition that the traditional ideology dominates, and to lower the ideological and social costs for institutional innovations and successfully avoid more potential risks from the reform, so that the excellent performance in institutional change can quickly become visible in a short time and effectively set a good example for the whole country. Therefore, fundamentally, the first-ever implementation of pilot programs is a process of making innovations and learning from the advanced; such first-ever implementation involves deeper institutional changes in various fields of the society, including the political system, the legal environment, the government's system and mechanism of governance and capacity modernization as well as cultural ideology. This is the innate character of China's special economic zones and the more challenging new mission of China's free trade zones in the new era.

In a sense, the free trade zones are the special economic zones entrusted with a new mission under the new historical conditions and developmental background. The historical mission of the free trade zones remains the following: The first-ever implementation of pilot programs is enabled to offer the experience which can be copied and popularized for the reform in Chinese society, thus carrying forward the reform in Chinese society. For example, the Central Government requires the China (Shanghai) Pilot Free Trade Zone to follow the national strategy and further emancipate the mind, persevere in first-ever implementation of pilot programs, and drive forward reform and development through opening up, become the first to develop a cross-border investment and trade rule system under the rule of law from an international perspective, so that the pilot free trade zone becomes the important carrier for further integrating China into economic globalization. Specifically, on the premise that the risks are controllable, actions could be taken to create the conditions for piloting the Renminbi capital account conversion, interest rate liberalization and Renminbi cross-border use in the pilot free trade zone; measures should be taken to promote the development of the transshipment cargo consolidation business, and allow the non-five-star-flag ships owned or controlled by Chinese-funded companies, on a pilot basis, to undertake the coastal cargo transport through the import and export containers between domestic coastal ports and the Port of Shanghai.[22] The China (Guangdong) Pilot Free Trade Zone is required to make bold experimentations regarding institutional construction for opening wider to the outside world, take actions for first-ever implementation in this regard, and more quickly shape a high-standard investment and trade rule system.[23] The China (Tianjin) Pilot Free Trade Zone is required to pilot Renminbi cross-border use, cross-border investment and financing facilitation and capital account conversion; partner with well-known domestic and foreign equity investment institutions to establish venture capital funds on a pilot basis.[24] The China (Fujian) Pilot Free Trade Zone is required to make pilot efforts to promote financial cooperation between both sides of the Taiwan Straits.[25]

The first-ever implementation of pilot programs is the function of China's special economic zones and the unique part of China's Development Path; such first-ever implementation is also bound to be the unique function and mission of China's free trade zones. In this sense, the special economic zones and free trade zones are part and embodiment of China's Development Path as well as the expansion of China's Development Path with the times. Stephen Halper, a senior research fellow at the University of Cambridge, said that when it came to China's Development Path, it mainly referred to development and a series of reforms in China over the past 30 years and more.[26] In my view, China's Development Path is a very broad concept covering diverse aspects, but in terms of the internal logic of China's reform and opening up, China's Development Path can be described as follows: It starts from establishing the special economic zones, and adopts the path which is first-ever implementation of pilot programs, and aims at carrying out

[22] Overall Plan for China (Shanghai) Pilot Free Trade Zone

[23] Overall Plan for China (Guangdong) Pilot Free Trade Zone

[24] Overall Plan for China (Tianjin) Pilot Free Trade Zone

[25] Overall Plan for China (Fujian) Pilot Free Trade Zone

[26] Wei Xiaowen, Liu Zhili, "Recent Foreign Studies on China's Model, Their Trends, Dilemmas and Inspirations", *Theoretical Horizon*, 2010 (10).

reform and opening up, and establishing a socialist market economy under the rule of law, in order to achieve comprehensive reform and all-round development of the society, which is the path with Chinese characteristics to modernization. As the institutional arrangements at different historical periods, the special economic zones and free trade zones constitute the choice of a path with Chinese characteristics for achieving modernization.

The establishment of the special economic zones 38 years ago aimed at completing the transformation from a planned economy to a market economy, establishing the socialist market economic system and bringing about a change from self-seclusion to opening up, so that the innovations in institutional social arrangements were made to generate an internal impetus to push ahead with the transformation of the government's functions. China's free trade zones at the present time are designed to further improve the market economic system and enable a transformation from an outward-looking economy to an open economy, so as to stimulate and urge the Chinese society to switch from the policy-based opening up to an institutional opening up, transform our government from an omnipotent one to a service-oriented one, from a service-oriented one to a delegation-oriented one, really make institutional arrangements for transforming the governmental functions rather than merely stressing the philosophy of such transformation, gradually accomplishing the arduous mission of comprehensively intensifying the reform in Chinese society
Both special economic zones and free trade zones are the outcomes of the top-down compulsory institutional change; all of them are part of the overall national strategy and undertake different missions during different historical periods of the reform and opening up in Chinese society. Meanwhile, driving forward the reform through opening up represents their common logical starting point. As the 5 + 2 traditional special economic zones in the past can exert an influence at the regional level, China's free trade zones at the present time have the important function of reshaping and enhancing the regional landscape of China's economic development, and will become the powerful supporting points and engines for coordinated regional development. For example, the China (Guangdong) Pilot Free Trade Zone is intended to boost the long-term economic cooperation between the Chinese Mainland and Hong Kong, Macao to form the Pan-Pearl River Delta Economic Circle with mutual benefits, reciprocity, and shared prosperity, and become the important hub for the 21st Century Maritime Silk Road. The China (Tianjin) Pilot Free Trade Zone will serve as the locomotive for the coordinated regional integrated development of Beijing, Tianjin, and Hebei Province. The China (Fujian) Pilot Free Trade Zone places emphasis on the cooperation between both sides of the Taiwan Straits, and opens a new path to enhancing communication with the countries and territories along the 21st Century Maritime Silk Road. As the traditional special economic zones in the past were bound to explore the ways to transform the government's functions and reform the government, China's free trade zones at the present time continue, at a more profound level, this difficult exploration that has a vital bearing on the success of the reform in Chinese society. In the compulsory

institutional change in which the government's powers need to be dismantled by the government itself, the cognitive ability of the government is undoubtedly crucial.

What the government looks like determines the institutional arrangement; the government's civilization is the precondition and guarantee for institutional civilization. Meanwhile, the government's cognitive ability also largely determines the costs and effectiveness of the reform. Therefore, remolding the government, transforming the government's functions, enhancing the cognitive ability and the governing capacity of the government officials are the internal logical requirements for intensifying the reform and modernizing the governance system of the government and its mechanism and governing capacity. According to Walter Eucken, an American economist, the interdependence between the political order and the economic order forces us to address both at the same time; both are part of the entire order. If there is no competitive order, a capable government will be unavailable, while there will be no competitive procedure if such a government is nonexistent. Making the institutional arrangement for transforming the government's functions instead of merely focusing on the philosophy of such a transformation is a process of building a government under the rule of law. The significance of a government under the rule of law means that the government governs the country according to laws, and more importantly, the government is bound by those laws. China's free trade zones, following the special economic zones, undertake this more profound and arduous mission.

Becoming prosperous and strong is the common aspiration and goal of almost all of the people around the world. Although many goals pursued by the human race are the same ones, there are diverse routes and ways to realizing or achieving these goals and no one-size-fits-all developmental path and mode are available. The developmental experiences of the various countries can be used for reference and shared, but only the one suitable for one's own purpose is the best, most useful, and most fruitful. China should not be caught in the line of thinking that only unlimited economic growth is healthy; China may rationally adjust its direction and shift from the unlimited output growth to the improvement of the people's social welfare. In this regard, we may suffer from the ordeal from the conflict between the ideal and the reality; however, it is certain that the future is immensely bright. China's free trade zones, full of vitality, herald a bright and brilliant future.

Positioning and Responsibilities of a Law-based Government

The key to a law-based governance of a country is the transformation of the government's governance mode, while the key to such transformation lies in identifying relevant government functions in a standardized way and transforming the corresponding functions. In a sense, for transformational China, only when the government is reformed can the rational goal—which arouses the enthusiasm for reform—of building a society under the rule of law be achieved.

Which functions really need to be undertaken by the government? Basically, this is a fundamental issue concerning value judgment. Thus, it, to some extent, depends on the philosophy of a design of the social system and the cognitive ability and the level of a government. According to the experience in the development of the human society, the provision of public goods, the correction of market failure and the establishment of a social security system which universally covers all of the people are the important responsibilities of a government; however, fundamentally, protection is a function which basically positions a government under the rule of law and is the core responsibility of a government under the rule of law.

The protective function of the government means that the government utilizes the power of laws to preserve the social order, guarantees the rights that every citizen should enjoy and protects these rights against infringement by anybody. The economic life is unquestionably the most important part of the human societal activities, so it is an important responsibility of the government for protecting the way of resource allocation and the economic operational model chosen by a society; property rights and private autonomous rights are the indispensable prerequisites for the normal operation of a market economy, thus protecting property rights and private autonomous rights is undoubtedly the primary responsibility—with the significance of building—of the government in a transformational society. The government is a group of particular professional people and the government functions are performed by the governments at various levels and the government officials, so the government must assume the responsibility of self-learning and self-cultivation in the process of building a government under the rule of law, which is the fundamental guarantee for governing the country according to laws.

The government is the largest provider of public goods in the market and the most powerful preserver and protector of the market system and order. A well-developed legal system is the internal institutional guarantee for a full-fledged market economic system, while the market economy is certainly an economy under the rule of law, even the market system can be considered a legal system. This is because the mechanism on which the effective operation of the market economy depends is bound to be the power of making equal treatment without discrimination before laws rather than lucky speculation, the result of plans, and an arbitrary decision of a power. A government under the rule of law is the guardian which ensures selflessness and justice in such an institutional environment with equal treatment without discrimination.

The extent to which the institution and the laws of a country help meet the economic goals of the economic growth rate and members of an economic community greatly varies with the type of such institution and the degree of perfection of the laws, resulting in a significant gap in the social welfare. The neoclassical growth theory only identifies the most direct growth conditions such as capital accumulation and technological change, while in order to explain why the people save, invest, acquire, and gather the useful knowledge, we must focus on various institutional systems and value systems behind economic success. For any society, a full-fledged legal system is the original principle followed in the above systems and also the guarantee for the effectiveness of these systems. The protective function of the government can enhance the social order, and make it easier for individuals, private manufacturers, and nongovernmental organizations to make coordination in face of ignorance and thus build up confidence in the social institution. Under many circumstances, the protective function of the government cannot be performed unless the laws and regulations are made. Famous economist Milton Friedman gave his standardized answer about the core responsibilities of the government in the market economy: The government should preserve law and order, define property rights, act as the tool for us to revise the property rights and other economic game rules, adjudicate the disputes arising out of the explanation rules, compulsorily execute deeds and promote competition...In the *Centesimus Annus* in 1991, Pope John Paul II stressed that the economic activities—especially the activities in the market economy—cannot be carried out in an institutional, judicial, and legal vacuum. On the contrary, it is conditional upon the really guaranteed individual freedom and private property rights, a stable currency and the effective public services. Therefore, the primary task of a country is to provide such security so that all of the people engaged in work and production can enjoy the fruits of their labor and are motivated to work in an honest and efficient way. For a country with an emerging market economy, the most striking protective function of the government lies in building and preserving a fair and equitable market order, guaranteeing free competition, protecting all citizens against coercion, and maintaining economic and social order. Theoretically, the undertaking of the protective function by the government in a market economy is equivalent to the conclusion of a "disarmament pact" among all of the citizens. Our society will pay extremely high exclusion costs and compulsory execution costs if it becomes anarchic, and compulsion is restricted only relying on the "violence potential" of the parties, and all members of the society must resist others by themselves to protect their own property. Anarchic self-protection will inhibit much favorable labor division and greatly hinder social prosperity. Therefore, the government is "employed" as an agent by the people and is also entrusted with the mission of protecting individual freedom, and safeguarding social and economic order, justice, and equity. In a market economic system in which the government can correctly undertake the above protective functions, the state of the market—free competition—can be protected and healthily exist. This is because a world with personalized micro-relationships always thrives amidst increasing improvement and expansion of a competitive market order.

Today's Chinese society is in the state of the "semi-market-oriented" "semi-traditional" mixed economic system led by the government. On the one hand, a well-developed market economic system has not yet really taken shape; on the other hand, the legal system has not yet become full-fledged. The underdevelopment of both systems increases the costs for the operation of the market economy and institutionally subjects the law of the market to the administrative order, thus institutionally making administrative power stronger than the strength of the legal system. When the market has to yield to the administrative order, the original functions of the market mechanism cannot work; when the power is stronger than the strength of the legal system, the laws are nothing but the tools of power.

In my opinion, with respect to the protective function of the government, the government should build a well-developed market system by improving the legal system, and ensure that every citizen can participate in the market in a fair, orderly, protected, and equal way, as well as restrict its own powers and its power in the economic life by the coercive force of laws. In the framework of compulsory institutional change in which the government's powers need to be deprived of by themselves, an important goal of transforming the government's functions is to reduce the intervention of power in the market and inhibit the infringement of the citizens' interests and the interests of the general public by power. Therefore, the primary premises for the government to perform and realize the corrective protective function are self-discipline, self-restraint, self-regulating delegation of powers and rational self-"weakening" subject to meta rules, really transforming the government from an authority-oriented one to a service-oriented one.

From the perspective of the market economy, a great defect in China's current economic system is that the property rights institutional foundation of the market is unclear; in particular, the land property rights institution is severely defective. A lack of a property rights institution is a fatal damage to the market economy. This is because the market economy is conditional upon a clear definition of property rights and the autonomous right to conclude deeds. The government not only is the sole provider of the institutional arrangement of the property rights, but it also necessarily performs the function of legal protection and compulsory execution of property rights. This can be considered the important and conventional social responsibility of a market-friendly government.

The market economy is based on establishing and protecting the exclusive institution of private property rights, while such property rights are the prerequisite for deed-based voluntary transactions. Well-defined and protected property rights are essential for inspiring the people to make efforts. Once this condition is available, the people will make efforts of their own free will. These efforts can function as the "invisible hand", which always objectively benefits others, while the strivers often do not know these beneficiaries. The property rights are not an abstract concept which merely influences large enterprises or the intangible financial market. They are closely related to everyone's daily life. They have a direct bearing on employment, consumers' choices and the motivational power for everyone to learn. They are vital for the living opportunities of the ordinary citizens, especially the people who are not born with a silver spoon in their mouths.

Generally, the property rights are defined as a combination of rights of individuals and organizations to be protected. They can enable the owner to hold or dispose of assets by purchasing, using, mortgaging, and transferring those assets, and possess the benefits generated from operation of those assets. Of course, they also include the negative benefits—losses. Therefore, property rights determine the responsibilities and benefits in the operation of properties. Property rights include, but are not equal to, ownership, so someone cannot confuse property rights with his/her own articles. Private property rights always establish a relationship between a particular individual and a particular asset. This asset may be a material product, a thought or a human body. Where property rights are fully respected and well protected, "economic freedom" can be deemed available. As an institutional arrangement, property rights—being universal—form an integral part of social justice. Such universality is that the institution shall not have differential treatments towards individuals without a definite reason; no one can be above the law; therefore, it means equal procedure for everyone. On the contrary, where property rights are unclear and uncertain, many favorable property uses may disappear due to less protection of property rights.

There is another concept—private autonomous rights—which is related to property rights and merits our attention. Private autonomous rights mean that the rights of the property owner with respect to the use of the properties are not restricted by a private person or the government. Once an individual enjoys the autonomous right to use personal private properties—including his own knowledge and labor—, he enjoys the right to economic freedom. When the property owner is subject to excessive restrictions, his autonomous right will also be infringed. When such intervention becomes legitimated by virtue of political actions, this will increase the information and transaction costs for the operation of the society, and incur losses to the society. The right of economic freedom to own and use the private properties constitutes the essence of civil liberty and the freedom of choice. It makes it possible for every citizen to use his own material means to safeguard his own rights without others' prior consent.

The nonpublic sectors of the economy have become an important part of China's basic economic system since the 15th National Congress of the Communist Party of China, and serve as the foundation for building and governing the country together with the public sector of the economy; however, the class worship of the public ownership and the ideological discrimination against private ownership have affected the real establishment and improvement of the property rights institution during the building of the market economy, and have exerted an impact on the level of the people's cognition of property rights, private autonomous rights, and the sense of reverence in the legal sense—sacred and inviolable. Even with the shadow cost from the "natural" superiority of public ownership from an ideological perspective, the infringement of private rights by public rights becomes justified and appears to have the innate justice and legitimacy to overstep laws. However, the supervision over public rights is very weak; subject to the inertial thinking under the traditional system that "public" means "shared by all the people", it is difficult to supervise public rights and such supervision seems to be unjustifiable and an offense or a challenge against one idea by another one.

Numerous successful cases in the market economy prove that when the institutional arrangement of property rights makes the people feel it is worthwhile to engage in production activities, there will be continued socioeconomic growth. We should not ignore property rights when respecting the market, and should not restrict private autonomous rights while pursuing economic growth because one thing cannot exist without its fundamental basis.

The constitution is the fundamental law of a country; however, the conventional thinking of acting according to the official documents has taken shape and continued since the period of the planned economy—on the one hand, Chinese people are unfamiliar with the constitutional articles; on the other hand, the performance of the officials is evaluated mainly by the extent to which the indicators assigned by the departments at higher levels are accomplished, rather than the standard that they shall act according to laws, so the constitution is essentially shelved. This is one of the important reasons why it is difficult to really and fundamentally promote law-based governance in China. The building of a government under the rule of law is anything but a manifestation of an authority-oriented government but is bound to give expression to a service-oriented government; it is anything but an intervention in the market by the power, but it is certainly a protection of rights by laws; it is anything but the monopolization of "something scarce" by the privilege, but it is necessarily the reverence of fairness for justice and equality. Self-learning and self-cultivation of a government under the rule of law is the fundamental premise for building a society under the rule of law

William Niskanen said that the objective of the constitution was to define the island of the government's power in the vast ocean of individual rights. Hayek held that protecting individual freedom was the ultimate function of the constitution and a standardized test of the constitution. The constitution refers to a number of high-level institutions. They establish a set of "meta rules", while these rules become the general principles which result in and regulate more specific external institutions. The constitution contains two basic parts: First, specifying the people's rights; second, defining the limits of the government's functions and powers. The former protects the people's rights and interests from being infringed, while the latter ensures that the State apparatus in the hands of the government is only used to protect the people's constitutional rights, but it cannot, and it refrains from being used to infringe on the people's basic rights. An analysis of the economic consequences of various constitutions is part of the research regarding constitutional economics. The basic premise for constitutional economics is the individuals who act in light of their own interests rather than the people's class or group. Therefore, an analysis of constitutional economics focuses on various rules which guide the individual choices and resorts to various individual values—autonomous economic rights of private individuals.

The constitution contains a number of high-level institutions, while they cannot be easily changed like the low-level institutions, so they offer a framework involving continuity and foreseeability for the unavoidable regulation of the low-level institutions. The constitution contains the affirmation of the basic and inalienable individual rights. These rights should be negated by the low-level institutions, the private strong forces or government bodies. The most fundamental logic for protecting personal properties as enshrined in the constitution is that personal properties provide the material foundation for individual autonomy.

The principles and institutions discussed under the constitution are the high-level and universal constraints on public policy. They help supervise the abuse of the official powers. They are designed to restrict the collective authority, protect the free domain of individuals, and contain the opportunistic and rent-seeking activities of the government as the agent. In other words, the principles and institutions under the constitution are established to restrict the political powers which make differential treatments. These principles and institutions are always incorporated into the political charter and the economic charter: The overarching principles will not be rocked in case of revolutionary change. Only when we understand the importance of the order can we agree to build a protective mechanism to resist opportunism.

Under no circumstance can we simply understand the constitution as the means for Western countries to govern the countries, while the constitution should also be adopted in socialism to govern the socialist countries. The fundamental guarantee for building a society under the rule of law consists in upholding the authority of the constitution, developing the reverence for laws and fostering a legal culture of abiding by laws. Meanwhile, it is particularly necessary for our officials to learn to subject the mentality of leading officials to rules and submit rules to laws; our government should also first learn to replace policies—especially the policies of handling special cases with special methods—with rules, replace administrative orders with laws, and incorporate or make policies and administrative orders into legal constraints, instead of replacing the fait juridique to dominate the operation of the society. The political order of a country should be established under the constitutional framework: The administrative powers are restricted and thus are not abused. Political democracy should be achieved under the meta rules of the constitution: Every citizen can rationally and lawfully exercise their rights to participate in administering the country. Human dignity should be realized under the protection of the constitution: Every citizen enjoys the freedom given by laws so that everybody is equal before the law.

A society under the rule of law is first of all a civil society since a civil society is the soil for a society under the rule of law. Civil liberty refers to that state of a person: He is protected by laws and civil institutions and can independently use all of his strength for the sake of his welfare. We consider happiness as the outcome of freedom and freedom as the fruit of courage, while laws serve as the guarantee for both things for which we yearn. Laws are relentlessly rational (Aristotle). We are slaves to laws, so we are free (Marcus Tullius Cicero).

Putting people first is anything but a top-down political slogan showing solicitude for the people; instead, it is a developmental philosophy focusing on free development of the human being and also the core of the Scientific Outlook on Development (*Report to the 18th National Congress of the People's Republic of China*). The people are not only the power which creates wealth but also the power which enjoys the life that they have the reason to treasure. If we measure the social development only by GDP, we will deviate from the real goal; likewise, if we merely treat the people as the "productive force", this implies that we replace the real major players with other major players. The establishment of a correct developmental outlook is a process of using mind-sets to conquer mind-sets and also a process in which the government's understanding is deepened. When human economic value increases, our society will usher in some new, better fields of opportunity. Human development is not only a part and the goal of social development but also the outcome and fruit of social development; meanwhile, human development is also the prerequisite and guarantee for making human society really civilized and free. The decision to begin the reform and opening up is vital to the destiny of contemporary China; the reform and opening up is the only road towards developing socialism with Chinese characteristics and rejuvenating the Chinese nation; only socialism can save China and only the reform and opening up can develop China, socialism, and Marxism (*Report to the 18th National Congress of the People's Republic of China*). We neither replace the reform with development nor stick to the way or mode of a particular stage during the reform as the ultimate goal. Seeking development through the reform and pushing forward the reform through opening up remains the developmental path that must be followed in Chinese society.

Victor Hugo said that freedom begins where ignorance ends. Once a nation moves from ignorance, conservativeness, and seclusion towards self-consciousness, change, and opening up, it gains a strong institutional force to achieve free development. This institutional force is the charm of the socialist system shown to the people in the *Report to the 18th National Congress of the People's Republic of China*.

January 2016

Yitao Tao
Deputy Secretary of the Party Committee
the Secretary of the Discipline Inspection
Commission of Shenzhen University
Director, Professor at the China Center
for Special Economic Zone Research
Shenzhen University—Humanities & Social Science
Research Based under the Ministry of Education

Chapter 1
Different Paths to Modernization

Modernization is a process of all-round development, covering all the aspects in the economic, social, political and cultural fields, which expresses a dynamic process of balanced development. First, modernization is an economic concept—the advanced technologies are adopted in the economic activities to achieve an economic leap on the basis of new technologies and to improve social productivity; second, modernization is a political concept and calls for building and developing a rational political institution and an effective governance system; third, modernization is a cultural concept and reflects the changes and renewal of the people's social values; finally, modernization is also a concept of social change and means that the composition of the social structure and the people's social life will change with the drive towards economic modernization, while social modernization is the foundation for and the outcome of continued modernization.

From the perspective of historical development in various countries, different types of countries share some similarities against a certain background of the times during modernization and they also present the unique characteristics of their paths towards modernization on different endowment foundations. With the first mover advantage, the Western countries developed the strength for expansion through the Industrial Revolution, and then established the capitalism-led modern world system by means of colonialism. In the early 20th century, the developed capitalist countries experienced a severe economic crisis, and various countries made a number of adjustments in their economic policies to address the crisis, so that a new mode in which the state regulated capitalism took shape and they adopted different developmental paths—the experimentation of the Soviet socialist path towards modernization offered some experience and lessons for human beings to choose the non-capitalist developmental model; the national liberation movement disintegrated the imperialist colonial system, and the developing countries which gained national independence (the emerging market countries) practiced several modernization models with national characteristics while they were choosing their own paths towards development.

© Social Sciences Academic Press and Springer Nature Singapore Pte Ltd. 2018

Y. Tao and Z. Lu, *Special Economic Zones and China's Development Path*,
Research Series on the Chinese Dream and China's Development Path,
https://doi.org/10.1007/978-981-10-3220-2_1

China's modernization is part of worldwide modernization. China needs to critically inherit the developmental models of the developed countries and the emerging market countries and draw on their experience and lessons in order to go forward on a path towards modernization that is consistent with China's national conditions.

1.1 The Paths Towards Modernization of Major Developed Countries

Many developing countries proceed with modernization by catching up with and learning from major developed countries. Therefore, in its search for a path towards modernization, China cannot ignore the experience and successful practice of major developed countries in their different stages of modernization. Reviewing and reflecting on the paths towards modernization and the developmental models adopted by major developed countries is of very important referential significance for evaluating and reexamining the current paths towards modernization and the developmental models of the emerging countries.

I. **The Paths Towards Modernization of Major Developed Countries**

(I) **The United Kingdom**

The UK is the first modern country. The UK's process of modernization features a clear curve: on the verge of world civilization, it followed the rise of Western Europe to develop into a European power and a world power, and then returned to Europe as a regional country. As the pioneer in the era of global capitalism, the UK has successfully retained and continued its traditional cultural and social structure, and has succeeded in introducing a market economy into the original social structure, thus entering a period of benign rapid development, which marks the fundamental shift towards a new human civilization.

The UK has taken a peaceful, progressive and reform path to modernization. The UK's process of modernization has the following prominent features:

1. Its institutional innovations led the tide of the world's modernization. The institutional innovations in the UK's process of modernization mainly refer to the innovations in political institutions, which aimed at adapting to the developmental changes in the UK's society, adjusting the contradictions among social strata and rationally allocating social interests, thus achieving a continued stable and harmonious development of the whole society. The institutional innovations guaranteed a smooth process of modernization in the UK and offered a successful reference for the democratic institutions and reforms in the Western capitalist countries. Afterwards, the European countries and the USA drew on the experience of the UK in their political, economic and democratic reforms, and developed political institutions fit for their national conditions to push forward their own modernization.

2. The Industrial Revolution and scientific and technological progress were the propellers of the UK's modernization. The Industrial Revolution opened a new chapter in human history so that human beings were able to enter the modern era of industrial civilization from the traditional agricultural civilization. The Industrial Revolution created huge productive social forces, making the UK the world's factory. The Industrial Revolution brought about great changes in the UK's method of production, class structure, lifestyle and values. The Industrial Revolution shaped a world pattern in which the West became advanced but the East remained backward. Overall, the Industrial Revolution promoted the rapid development of the UK's process of modernization in various respects, leading the world's modernization for 200 years.
3. The UK's modernization largely depended on colonies which were the UK's lifeline. As one of the countries with overseas colonial activities at an early stage, the UK formally established maritime hegemony and drastically expanded its overseas market in the 19th century. With the accelerated primitive accumulation of capital, the original method of production in handicraft workshops failed to meet the market demand, giving rise to the Industrial Revolution and the world's factory in the UK. The colonies became the areas for producing raw materials, the commodity markets, the capital importers and the destinations for the migration of the population for the UK, injecting unceasing impetus into the UK's capitalist development. The UK became the largest capital exporter in the world in the period of the second Industrial Revolution. As the colonies delivered enormous profits to the UK, the UK was less motivated to make technical innovations, and experienced slow economic development; consequently, it was surpassed by the USA and Germany, and declined.
4. A long-term stable political situation was the vigorous guarantee for a smooth process of modernization in the UK. The UK's modernization has been a process full of contradictions and conflicts; however, unlike other countries, the UK is a country where both parties involved in conflicts meet each other halfway and go together instead of one party engulfing or collapsing the other party. In the contradictions between the emerging industrial bourgeoisie and the landed aristocrats or the conflicts between the proletariat and the bourgeoisie, the conservative and steady British have always found a point of balance of interests acceptable to both sides through reforms in order to achieve a new social harmony.

(II) **The United States**

The USA is one of the most developed modern countries in today's world. With several hundred years of development, the USA has basically developed a developmental model of modernization dominated by a free market economy and democratic politics, and has set a good example for many late-mover countries.

With a short history of just 200–300 years, the USA has no specific concept of nationality. Compared with other Western countries, the USA presents very unique and distinctive characteristics in its formation and rise among the modern countries. As the USA was never fettered by the feudal system, the factors which hindered the start and development of modernization in the USA occurred in small quantities, and it was also easy for the democratic republican system to take root. With respect to its path towards modernization, the modernization of the USA started with a breakthrough in the political field; an early and good launch of political modernization offered a good political environment and institutional guarantee for the USA to achieve all-round modernization. During the process of economic modernization, along with its transformation from an agricultural country to an industrial country, the USA transformed from a closed natural economy to a market with free competition, from 1776 when it was founded to the 1990s. From the late 19th century to the early 20th century, the US market economy changed from free competition to monopoly, thus the government started an appropriate control over the economy; with adjustments during a century, the USA ultimately adopted its unique market economy mode.[1] The modernization of political institutions and economic institutions is important support for the modernization of the USA. The USA's path towards modernization has the following characteristics:

1. There was an outstanding capability for innovating political practices. The *Declaration of Independence* affirmed, in the form of a governmental document for the first time in human history, the principles of equality, freedom and human rights put forward by the enlightenment intellectuals; these principles governed the practice of building up the USA after the victory in the War of Independence; the USA stood out in institutional creation among the modern countries though it was a latecomer in this regard. The *United States Constitution*, established and promulgated in 1787, successfully practiced the philosophy of modern democracy proposed by the French enlightenment intellectuals, giving birth to the democratic republican regime, the most advanced political institution in the late 18th century, which made great contributions to the modernization movements throughout the world. As a macroeconomic means of regulation and control by which the power of the State intervened in the market economy, Roosevelt's New Deal, adopted in the USA amidst the world's economic crisis, was universally emulated by the Western countries after the Second World War.
2. The democratic revolution and the Industrial Revolution promoted each other. The USA waged the War of Independence to break away from British colonial rule, established a federal system, founded a democratic republic, and maintained long-term political stability, thus creating the conditions for the USA's Industrial Revolution. This is comparable to the French Revolution and France's process of modernization. As the Industrial Revolution unfolded and the regional economic development became unbalanced in the USA, the contradictions between two economic Institutions in the north and the south escalated, triggering the American Civil War. Ultimately, this war led to the abolition of the slavery system in the USA, removing the obstacles to modernization and laying a foundation for the rapid rise of the USA in the second revolution.

[1]Peng Sen, An International Comparison and Experience of the Reform of China's Economic System (M), People's Publishing House, February, 2007 (1), pp. 115–116.

3. A leapfrog development was achieved in the economic field. The USA's Industrial Revolution started from the transatlantic dissemination of the textile technology from the UK in the 1890s. The USA rose from the second revolution, consolidated its international position in the Second World War, and ultimately established its position as a world power. In the early 20th century, the USA's industrial output ranked No. 1 in the world, making it the No. 1 industrialized country in the world, and the USA created an economic developmental miracle characterized by a rapid transition from an agricultural society to an industrial society. After the two World Wars in the 20th century, the USA hurtled from an industrial world power to a world superpower.
4. The scientific and technological innovations boosted modernization. In the two scientific and technological revolutions in the 19th century, the USA developed into a leader by catching up with the other countries. In the second scientific and technological revolution, science and technology developed by leaps and bounds, the country took the leading position in the world in terms of the number of scientific and technological inventions, and became the frontrunner in the world's industrial development. During the 1940s, the USA was the forerunner in the information revolution, stimulating the transformation of human beings from the era of industrial civilization to the era of information civilization. The USA experienced rapid development in the high-tech industry, making it the country with the highest level of modernization in the world.

The United States' path towards modernization has distinctive characteristics and has generated a smashing success. It is believed that the process of modernization in the United States has basically incorporated the merits of the processes of modernization in all Western countries: aggressive democratic politics, constitutionalism and capitalism characterized by state monopoly; furthermore, the USA assimilated the economic achievements made during the Industrial Revolution and was also the source of the information revolution. In addition, the spirit of equality and freedom also played an important role in its modernization.

(III) **France**

France's outstanding contribution to the world's modernization was the French Revolution. This revolution initiated the rising political democratization around the world, so it is regarded as the epoch-making milestone in the history of the world's political development. The French Enlightenment Movement developed, popularized the tenets of the bourgeoisie—freedom, equality and human rights—and established them as the universal ethics, turned them into the legal cornerstones for modern democratic societies, countries and politics, and made them widely recognized. The unequalled mass strength mobilized during this revolution led to the affirmation of these universal ethics as the source of legitimacy and a benchmark for all political institutions.

Compared with the USA's and the UK's processes of modernization, France's process was prominently characterized by political democratization amidst a changing political situation and developmental lag in industrialization. Its intellectual revolution started the tide of worldwide political democratization.

1. Political democratization took place as the political situation changed. The French Revolution unfolded with great momentum, ups and downs. It underwent a number of severe tests, including the restoration of the old dynasties and an autocratic monarchy; France's democratic regime experienced twists and turns, even over a very long period of time after the French Revolution, and a stable free constitutional system was not established in France. For example, France enacted 14 constitutions in 86 years after this revolution in 1789 and hovered between a monarchical dictatorship and a republic; the republic was not established until the constitution was promulgated in 1875; afterwards, France embarked on a path towards political modernization.
2. Industrialization was relatively slow. France is a large country which was the first to initiate the Industrial Revolution on continental Europe. As early as the last stage of the Bourbon Dynasty, France introduced the new industrial technologies from the UK. France's Industrial Revolution was not finished until the 1870s. It should be noted that France's strength in financial capital much surpassed that of the industrial capital in the economic field, thus it was labeled as "usurious imperialism". This is an important striking characteristic of France's industralization and process of modernization, and it also made way for France's functions, position and roles in the two World Wars.
3. The intellectual revolution gave an impetus to the political revolution. The thoughts—natural rights, separation of the three powers, freedom, equality, democracy and the rule of law—advocated in France's Enlightenment Movement fundamentally rocked the ideological foundation of the feudal rule, providing the theoretical basis for the French Revolution. The development of the Enlightenment Movement was a process of mobilization of public opinion, which objectively popularized and practiced the political conception that the bourgeoisie obtained the dominant position and developed the capitalist system. During the French Revolution, democracy became a universally applicable value outlook, a philosophy capable of carrying out popular sovereignty, and put into practice the principles of equality and freedom. Since then, the thoughts of the bourgeoisie—freedom, democracy and equality—have been widely recognized and diffused, kicking off the surging tide of political democratization around the world.

(IV) **Germany**

Capitalism developed rapidly in Europe in the 19th century, but Germany fell apart politically without national reunification. This was the cause of a more tortuous and complicated situation in Germany's process of modernization than those in the UK and France. Two reunifications of Germany promoted Germany's modernization and also exerted a far-reaching impact on the development of human civilization.

Germany's path towards modernization shared some common characteristics with that of other Western developed countries and also had its own unique features, mainly including:

1. The political process and the economic process coincided. Germany's modernization was a process of national reunification and national rejuvenation, and

secession and reunification alternately occurred during this process. This is one of the important characteristics of Germany's process of modernization. The "blood and iron" philosophy prevailed during the entire process. The "guns before butter" policy adopted during the Second World War inherited this philosophy. Therefore, there was an extremely strong unity between economic development and the political process in Germany.

2. Economic modernization and political modernization were unbalanced. Germany saw great industrial achievements and an astonishingly rapid economic growth, but its political democratization severely lagged behind. Germany became the source of the two World Wars, causing a great catastrophe to the world, while the German nation also took a heavy toll due to both World Wars. It took only about 30 years for Germany to finish industrialization after its reunification, making Germany one of the modern developed countries. However, the autocratic monarchy was retained, hindering the bourgeois democratic reform. Driven by Prussia's militaristic tradition and national chauvinism, Germany used its tremendous strength developed during the period of its industrialization to struggle for supremacy in Europe and in the world. In just 20 years, Germany provoked the two World Wars, greatly devastating human civilization; Germany was split into two countries after the Second World War.
3. Two reunifications had a profound impact on the development of human civilization. The first reunification of Germany ended the long-term political secession and vigorously promoted the development of capitalism. After reunification, Germany had a strong sense of militarism. Germany triggered the two World Wars in the first 50 years of the 20th century, wreaking havoc on human civilization. After the reunification of East Germany with West Germany, its GDP much exceeded that of the UK and France, and its international political status greatly improved, intensifying European integration, thus promoting the development of the contemporary worldwide pattern of moving towards multi-polarization.

(V) **Japan**

Japan is the country which was the first Asian country to complete industrialization and modernization. Japan is a late-mover outward-looking country; the colonial threat and the Western world's demonstration of civilization are the essential key factors for initiating Japan's modernization. Japan has had an extremely good ability to learn from the advanced civilizations since ancient times and Japan's traditional social structure was, to some extent, the same as that of Western Europe, which helped enhance the efficiency of its modernization. The Meiji Restoration was the starting point in Japan's process of modernization. With the national policy of departing from Asia for Europe, Japan comprehensively reformed the traditional society, and actively learnt about modern industrial civilization from the Western world. In less than half a century, Japan successfully transformed itself from a traditional society to a modern society. This prevented it from being colonized by the Western world and prompted Japan to become one of the world powers. Japan is a good example of an Asian country that successfully achieved transformation by learning from modern

Western civilization. Japan's path towards modernization can serve as an important reference for studying the path towards modernization of the emerging countries.

Japan's modernization process has the following characteristics:

1. Its development was unbalanced. The imbalance in Japan's process of modernization first occurred among the economic, cultural, social and political subsystems. Unlike the European countries and the USA, as a late mover, Japan witnessed very efficient dissemination of modernization in its economic system; moreover, the Japanese were accustomed to adopting and carrying forward its industries as cultures; this was a collective consciousness, and the government also provided vigorous guidance and impetus, thus economic modernization started at the earliest and became the most perfect; however, the modernization of the political system was inefficiently disseminated and was not easily accepted by the general public, and the government restricted its development; as a result, the level of political modernization was not high in Japan before the Second World War; it did not rapidly develop until the reform stage after the Second World War[2]; there were similar problems in the modernization of the social and cultural systems. After the Second World War, Japan made tremendous achievements in its economic, cultural, social and political reforms, but many pre-modern factors were still retained, so there was an imbalance in the modern structure of Japan's national society.
2. "Government substitution" played an important role in Japan's economic development. "Government substitution" played the leading part in Japan's economic development during the process of modernization from the Meiji Restoration to the Second World War. Likewise, "government substitution" also played an important role in Japan's postwar economic development—in the period from the end of the Second World War to the extensive industrialization in the 1980s, the specified goals were not achieved by the spontaneous function of the complete market mechanism in Japan; instead, the Japanese Government, rationally and to different degrees, replaced the undeveloped or incomplete part of the market mechanism by distorting the relative market prices and market information to rapidly cultivate a number of the leading industrial sectors and their corresponding enterprise organizations to shoulder the heavy responsibilities, as planned by the government, for economic growth and industrialization, so as to smoothly and swiftly achieve both economic growth and industrialization.
3. Japan was good at absorbing the modernization achievements from the developed countries. Japan attached great importance to drawing on the Western developed countries' achievements in modernization during its own process of modernization. In the early postwar period, in order to reverse the economic and technological backwardness and rapidly reach the world's advanced level, Japan chose an "absorption strategy" for actively introducing new technologies from foreign countries, extensively applying the existing advanced scientific and technological achievements in the world to push forward the technical revolution in its

[2]Ding Jing, The Process of Japan's Modernization and Its Revelation to China's Modernization, *Value Engineering*, pp. 328–329.

domestic economy and narrow the technical gap with major European developed countries and the USA at a relatively high rate and lower prices. With extensive utilization of the existing advanced scientific and technological achievements from various countries, Japan saved the research expenses and valuable time in catching up with and overtaking the world's advanced level, removed the technical gap more quickly and at lower prices, greatly quickening the process of modernization; as a result, Japan caught up with the developed European countries and the USA at an extraordinarily high rate and became an economic giant with highly developed industrial technologies.

II. **Experience and Lessons**

With many years of evolution, the major developed countries, including the UK, France and Germany, have developed a method of modernization which combines a market economy with democratic politics. This method has given birth to the first—and the only—"first-mover modernization" method in the world. Its main characteristics are illustrated as follows: Modernization evolves nationally in a down-top manner; industrialization is carried out mainly by private enterprises; economic operations are mainly regulated by the market; there is less direct political intervention; the State provides the institutional guarantee for the macroeconomic operations and development by legislative and compulsory means.

The practices and experiences of modernization from the Western developed countries have much referential value for the current process of modernization in China:

1. It is necessary to establish and improve the model of a market economy with China's own characteristics.

The economic modernization of the developed countries is closely related to the modernization of the market economy. With several hundred years of development, the developed countries have established a full-fledged market economic system. Practice has proven that the mature market system of the developed countries has contributed to optimizing the allocation of resources and enhancing the efficiency of economic operations so as to drive economic modernization forward. Meanwhile, the models of a market economy vary with the different developed countries—they adopt the models with their respective characteristics, subject to maintaining the overall characteristics of a market economy. Typically, there are four basic models: (1) the UK's "free market economy" model; (2) the USA's "regulating market economy" model; (3) Germany's "social market economy" model; (4) France's "planned market economy" model.

It is necessary for China, during the process of modernization, to draw on the experience of the developed countries, and establish a well-developed market economic system consistent with China's own developmental characteristics, give play to the role of the market mechanism in determining the allocation of resources, ensure that the production factors can flow freely, that all economic activities and economic relationships are arranged and regulated by laws and regulations, that there is a complete range of market types and forms, and that the transaction mode has been modernized. Meanwhile, the government should also properly exercise and fulfill the power and obligation of market regulation, scientifically and effectively perform macroeconomic management, guarantee the operational order and efficiency of the market economic system.

2. Industrialization, urbanization and all-round modernization should be promoted at the same time.

The modernization of major developed countries has been broadly driven by endogenous factors and exogenous factors.[3] The modernization of Western European countries which entered the process of modernization at the earliest has been driven by the former, while that of the USA and Japan has been driven by the latter. The driving forces for modernization were different among the developed Western countries, but all of their industrialization and modernization started from the light and textile industries and followed the trajectory of the light and textile industries—the heavy and chemical industries—the hi-tech industry: there was a gradual upgrading from the labor-intensive industry, the capital-intensive industry to the technology-intensive industry; the industrial structure gradually unfolded along with the process of industrialization—the proportion of the primary industry rapidly decreased, while that of the secondary industry soared; when industrialization was preliminarily completed and there was a development towards a high level, the proportion of the primary industry was stable at a very low level, and that of the secondary industry declined to some extent, while that of the tertiary industry increased very quickly, approaching and exceeding that of the secondary industry.

The modernization and industrialization of major developed countries were closely related to urbanization. With the intensification of modernization and industrialization, agricultural labor productivity substantially improved, and the agricultural surplus labor massively flocked to the industries from agriculture; consequently, with the aggregation effect, the industrial cities gradually took shape and rapidly expanded—urbanization. Urbanization almost synchronized with industrialization: the higher the degree of modernization and industrialization, the higher the rate of urbanization. Gradual economic modernization was accompanied by great changes in political, social, cultural and other fields; overall, politics was increasingly democratized and institutionalized, while culture became diverse and was more accessible to the general public.

The efforts to concurrently promote industrialization, urbanization and modernization, and the political democratization and cultural diversification during the modernization of major developed countries highly tally with the economic, social and cultural reality of China in the current process of its modernization; their practices and experiences serve as the inspirations and reference for us.

3. A modernization strategy needs to be developed and implemented to move modernization forward.

The process of modernization of the developed countries is closely related to the roles of the market mechanism. However, the market is not omnipotent; the State

[3]Xu Dongqing, The Modernization Experience from the Developed Countries in the World and Its Revelation, *Forum of World Economics & Politics*, November, 2012 (6).

still plays the irreplaceable role of guiding and planning social and economic development; it is still necessary to proceed from the national conditions to develop the developmental goals, policies and plans which are not fully subject to the market—the strategy of development.

For example, the USA can be considered a country where various aspects of modernization have developed in a relatively synchronous and harmonious way; it finished its process of industrialization to become an industrial power in the world in the late 19th century. Since the 20th century, the USA has gradually entered the developmental stage of modernization. The U.S. economic status peaked in the early 1950s, but the U.S. economy was caught in stagflation in the 1970s; in the 1980s, it remained sluggish though there was an improvement. In order to stop and reverse this situation, the Reagan Administration introduced a number of policies for revitalizing the U.S. economy—essentially, reindustrialization—focusing on thoroughly transforming the economic structure, and actively developing the emerging industries while intensifying the traditional industries. In essence, reindustrialization was the United States' medium and long-term developmental strategy.

Japan can be considered a country where excellent modernization strategies were developed in various periods and they produced remarkable effects. As early as the period of the Meiji Restoration, Japan outlined the overall strategy for learning from Europe and the USA to rapidly develop capitalism. This strategy enabled Japan to become one of the economically powerful capitalist countries in the early 20th century. After the Second World War, Japan released a plan called *Basic Issues Concerning the Reconstruction of Japan's Economy* in 1946. This plan was actually the first strategic conception for the postwar development of Japan's national economy, and it played an important role in restructuring and getting the economy to recover. In the mid-1950s, Japan put forward a new strategic goal for modernizing the national economy through extensive growth. Before the 1970s, the core of its strategic measures consisted in basing the country's development on trade. It basically achieved modernization in the early 1970s, with the strategic measures centering on basing the country's development on technology and moving towards all-round modernization—the famous *Maekawa Report*, the *Basic Strategy for the 21st Century* and other documents were the outcome of this strategy.

Other developed countries also attached great importance to and developed their modernization strategies in the process of modernization.

As a developing country, China should draw on others' extensive successful experience and formulate its own feasible scientific modernization strategy in light of the national conditions, and articulate the inclusive, systematic and resilient steps, measures, construction scale and speed for achieving the strategic goals; moreover, China should, while actively promoting economic growth, properly deal with the relationships between economic development and cultural construction, between economic development and political change, between economic growth and ecological protection, between economic growth and human development, production, life, the gap of wealth, and it should pay attention to the long-term coordinated development of the society.

4. The significant opportunities from the scientific and technical revolutions should be grasped.

The scientific and technical revolution presented the opportunities for pushing modernization forward by leaps and bounds. In the mid and late 18th century, the invention of the textile machine and steam engine brought about the first Industrial Revolution and boosted the astonishingly vigorous development of the productive forces in the UK, with a transition from the handicraft workshop to the large factory production based on machines in the UK. In the middle of the 19th century, the UK accomplished a transformation from the traditional agricultural society to a modern industrial society. From the late 18th century to the early 19th century, with the influence from the UK's Industrial Revolution, the Western European countries, including France, Belgium, the Netherlands and Germany started the process of modernization. From the second half of the 19th century to the early 20th century, the second industrial revolution characterized by electrification thoroughly changed the world's economic landscape. The USA, Germany, Italy and other countries seized the opportunities and achieved success. In the middle of the 20th century, with a large number of hi-tech inventions—including electronic computers, semiconductors and nuclear energy applications, and television broadcasting—and the huge demand generated by the damage from the Second World War, the major developed countries grabbed the golden opportunity from the third industrial revolution to develop their production in a hi-tech, professional and diverse way and increase the level of economic modernization.

The new technological revolution represented by information and biological science and technology is swiftly progressing. We must seize this great historical opportunity for achieving a great leap forward in modernization, and make arrangements beforehand to occupy the commanding height of the new scientific and technological revolution and accelerate the rejuvenation of the Chinese nation.

1.2 The Paths Towards Modernization of the Emerging Market Countries

The emerging markets broadly refer to some countries and territories under development, such as India, South Korea, Brazil, South Africa and China. Some countries and territories generally enjoy low labor costs and abound in natural resources, thus the production lines are generally shifted from the developed countries and territories to the emerging markets to enhance competitiveness through low labor costs; meanwhile, the inexpensive raw materials are purchased from the countries and territories with abundant natural resources by the developed countries and territories. The developing countries and territories can, through such purchases, obtain advanced production technologies, increase their income, improve their consumption ability and stimulate their economic development. These emerging market countries have adopted paths towards development that are greatly different from those of the Western developed countries while they were exploring paths towards modernization.

I. The Paths Towards Modernization of the Emerging Market Countries

(I) India's Path Towards Modernization

India is a large developing country with a several-thousand-year history of development of civilization. After India gained political independence in the 1940s, India was dedicated to developing its national economy. As a member of the British Commonwealth and the BRICS countries, India is one of the fast-growing countries in the world with an impressive economic growth. With great efforts for half a century, India has achieved a transition from an underdeveloped market economy to a relatively developed market economy. In a sense, India is the typical example of modernization among the emerging market countries.

The overall historical process of India's modernization started in the period of British colonial rule in the middle of the 19th century. British colonial rule kicked off India's modernization. This modernization triggered a profound social change in the Indian society and put India on the track towards modernization though this was a passive modernization for India. India broke away from British colonial rule to gain independence in 1947, creating the conditions for pursuing modernization in an independent way. However, the overall level of the productive forces was relatively low in India at that time; the choice of the path towards development and modernization cannot be separated from the reality of the country's productive forces. At that time, there were two developmental models in the world—the capitalist market economy and the Soviet planned economy under the central command. India acted in a way that was unlike most of the developing countries which refused to take the Western path and copied the Soviet Model. Nehru, the first Prime Minister of India, attempted to take the "third path" with the aim of building an independent quasi-socialist country where both public and private sectors of the economy coexisted. In 1948, the government, formed by the Indian National Congress, issued an industrial policy decision according to a planned economy and a mixed economic policy, laying the foundation for India's method of modernization. With three five-year plans, the Nehru Government repealed the intermediary tax system—the Zamindar system—in India's rural areas, promoting the development of agricultural capitalist factors. The government's industrialization strategy for expanding the public sector of the economy yielded some preliminary results, the basic industry rapidly developed, and a relatively powerful state-run economic system took shape.

After Nehru passed away, the mixed economic model adopted by Nehru was retained in India, but India started stressing the role of the market and relying on science and technology to develop the economy. India continued the cause of modernization pursued by Nehru and made some progress in this period, but generally, the achievements were not ideal. In the early 1990s, India gradually moved out of the old model taken in the Nehru era since its independence, and changed towards a mixed liberalist model. During this transformation, the Indian Government canceled most of industrial permit systems to provide a level playing field for enterprises; it revised the monopoly law and greatly narrowed the business scope of the enterprises run by the government, introduced the mechanism of free competition, expanded the scope of private enterprises, vigorously carried out the opening up to gradually turn the economy from an inward-looking one to an outward-looking one, reformed and adjusted the foreign trade policy and system to increase the level of internationalization of India's economy. From the late 20th century to the early 21st century, India caught up with the tide of the knowledge economy around the world, saw a robust development of the new economy led by the information industry, and became one of the fastest-growing countries in the world.

(II) South Korea's Path Towards Modernization

In modern history, South Korea has been invaded and plundered by Japan for a long time, the foundation for economic development has been weak and the distribution of the industrial structure in various areas has been extremely irrational in South Korea. Since the 1960s, South Korea has adopted the export-oriented economic developmental strategy, impelling rapid economic development and helping create the amazing Miracle on the Han River in South Korea.

The year 1961 was a milestone and symbolic year for initiating South Korea's modernization since this country started the implementation of the *Five-Year Economic Development Plan*. The key to the first five-year plan was that the free enterprises served as the foundation, and the government directly participated in and provided an input to stimulate the key industrial fields. With foreign capital and the government's input, this plan successfully quickened economic development. South Korea's refined oil, cement, chemical fertilizers, electronic products and drugs became available on the domestic market. The industrial products brought about an astonishing growth rate in exports. During the period of the second five-year plan, South Korea's export growth rate dramatically increased, attracting the world's attention. During the period of the third five-year plan, the world's economic crisis broke out, posing grave challenges to South Korea's economic development. The South Korean Government used the long-term loans to purchase the much-needed advanced machines and equipments, while the resulting huge productive forces quickly offset the loan debts. As the Asian countries endured the sharp pain from the oil crisis, the aggressive economic strategy adopted by South Korea led its economy to advance admirably. The fourth five-year plan centered on relying on the heavy, chemical and electronic industries to expand the country's exportations. For this purpose, the South Korean Government advocated the localization of the industrial machinery in South Korea—improving the status of South Korean products in international competition by the quality of its products. These four five-year plans gave birth to the Miracle on the Han River in South Korea, making the poor and weak country become one of the Four Asian Tigers in only 20 years.

South Korea experienced two leading stages of economic system changes in its process of modernization:

First, there was a change from a laissez-faire market economic system to a government-led market economic system. This was mainly reflected in the five five-year plans, which rigorously stipulated that the government should regulate and impose constraints on the market economic system, and preserve a good market order for economic development and a good financial order for the development of the industries and new-type industries. South Korea established and improved a unified examination and verification system for the introduction of technical support and the financial supervision of capital, and set up a special body designed to provide fast, prompt and accurate information and consulting services for that introduction. The government performs the functions of technology introduction, capital supervision, collection and processing of relevant information, with the purpose of preventing blind and repeated introduction, excessive high introduction costs during the early stages of social and economic development while providing a good financial order to ensure healthy and effective economic development. Besides the industries, the South Korean Government also made relevant policies for its agricultural economy—for example, the grain purchase price was increased; other industries provided more jobs for farmers; the government gave more subsidies to farmers—to safeguard the long-term rights and interests of farmers and increase the farmers' income.

Second, there was a change from a government-led market economic system to a market economic system led by the neoliberalist economic model. With long-term economic development, South Korea has become one of the emerging industrialized countries and has actively participated in economic globalization. In the meantime, the South Korean Government has realized that, amidst economic globalization, the government departments should reduce their intervention in the economic activities of the market players, and practice a market economic system according to the international rules under the multilateral trade system to achieve free development of the market economic system within the general environment. In view of this, the South Korean Government has surrendered more economic regulatory functions to the market mechanism, and has established an economic order and industrial structure with free competition. South Korea's "something-led" system has effectively promoted sustained rapid economic development and enhanced the comprehensive strength of South Korea.

After the 1990s, in South Korea, with the adjustment of the industrial structure, on the one hand, the industries and sectors with a great number of advanced technologies and hi-tech personnel developed more quickly; on the other hand, the competitive conditions of small and medium-sized, large enterprises increasingly improved. Thanks to the adjustment of the industrial structure, South Korean enterprises accumulated more capital and intensified their technological development, and there was a transformation from high fixed capital industries to the hi-tech and information industries so that South Korea was upgraded to an emerging industrialized country.

(III) **Brazil's Path Towards Modernization**

Brazil's process of modernization started from the abolition of the slavery system and the collapse of the monarchy in the late 1880s. The period from the late 1880s to the 1930s was a period of the Westernization movement. This movement mainly covered the following four aspects: First, with the *United States Constitution* as the chief source, Brazil established and promulgated its *1891 New Constitution*, and set up the federal republic system; second, Brazil pursued economic liberalism, and quickened the operations of the primary product export model; third, Brazil emulated the industrialization in Europe and the USA to develop a Western industrial style; fourth, Brazil vigorously encouraged European immigration. This movement was an effort made by Brazil to put Brazil onto the capitalist track by emulating the political and economic institutions of the Western countries, including the UK, France and the USA, so as to industrialize Brazil. It accelerated Brazil's modernization.

Brazil really became an emerging industrialized country during the 1960s–1970s, during which the Brazilian soldiers launched a military coup d'état to overthrow the radical Goulart Government and establish a military regime. When military officers were in power, Brazil held high the banner of "development" with the main objective of achieving economic modernization, and put forward the slogan of "high investment, high growth" and "export as the way out", carrying forward Brazil's modernization in a higher and more profound way by relying on the foundation built during the Westernization movement. Economically, Brazil practiced technocracy, and continued the path towards industrialization via import substitution to conduct a complicated substitution of the durable consumer goods, intermediate products and production materials, and paid attention to the external market; thus Brazil saw great economic growth and an Economic Miracle. Politically, Brazil established high centralization of authority to create a relatively stable political and social environment for modernization. Its social policies aimed at improving the residents' living standard by adopting the price index, regularly adjusting the minimum wage system and introducing other social welfare policies. Diplomatically, Brazil continued to pursue its traditional diplomatic policy of automatic alignment with the United States, and gradually developed a diversified kind of diplomacy. During this period, the Westernization movement advanced by leaps and bounds—the average annual GDP growth rate exceeded 10% during the period 1968–1973, higher than Brazil's annual average growth record and the rate of development in other countries around the world. This was hailed as Brazil's Miracle.

In the late 1980s, Brazil's new constitution was promulgated, establishing a democratic institution with the equitable social policy as the strategic priority for governing the country; Brazil stepped up efforts to solve the problems including unfair domestic distribution of income and violent crimes; the Real Plan greatly improved the severe inflation and reduced the peak value of the Gini coefficient in Brazil, gradually building an olive-shaped society dominated by the middle class, and laying a solid foundation for Brazil's becoming one of the BRICS countries. Brazil also attached great importance to the development of and input into biotechnology and new-energy science and technology; moreover, it paid attention to consolidating the South Common Market and reinforced the economic and trade relations with China, Russia and India. A number of factors contributed to the good situation of Brazil's modernization. After 2011, Brazil's GDP aggregate surpassed that of Russia, making Brazil the seventh largest economy in the world, an emerging global economy and one of the fastest-growing countries in the world.

(IV) South Africa's Path Towards Modernization

South Africa's modernization started during the period of the 1860s–1880s and had lasted for 130–140 years at the beginning of this century; as a result, South Africa has become the most economically developed country on the African Continent.

South Africa's modernization was driven by its mineral resources. South Africa's industrialization started from the discovery and exploitation of diamonds and gold in the second half of the 19th century. With the exploitation and exportation of the important mineral resources, including diamonds and gold, South Africa enjoyed a certain primitive accumulation of capital and technical strength, gradually carrying out industrialization and all-round modernization.

During the Second World War, in order to meet the needs of the Allied Forces, the South African Government energetically developed its military industries, stimulating the development of the civil fields including building materials, chemicals, machinery, electric appliances and textiles. After the Second World War, South Africa's manufacturing industry continued to maintain rapid development. The output value of South Africa's manufacturing industry grew annually by 9.1% on average during the period 1945–1949. By 1960, the proportion of the output value of the manufacturing industry in GDP increased to 21%. After the 1960s, South Africa focused on developing the heavy and chemical industries including automobile manufacturing, oil refining, mining equipment, mechanical manufacturing and armaments, with additional considerations given to such hi-tech industries as computers, electronics and atomic energy. The second strategic adjustment in South Africa's industrialization had kicked off, so South Africa entered a period of focus on the heavy and chemical industries. In the mid-1970s, South Africa's industrial technical equipment—including the technical equipment involving engineering, mining, the electronic industry, the petroleum and the chemical industries—which had mainly been imported in the past – were homemade and exported, and the industrial output value made up more than 36% of the GDP; moreover, a relatively developed modern industrial system took shape; the basic industries and the tertiary industries were relatively complete, reaching the level of development of the moderately developed countries in the world.

In the 1980s, South Africa's economy stagnated and declined due to a number of internal and external factors, including the dual economic system (the white people's modern industrial economy and the black people's backward agricultural and husbandry economy) and the increasingly severe international sanctions caused by the longstanding apartheid policy designed to preserve that dual economy.

In the mid-1990s, the founding of new South Africa was an important historic node in South Africa's process of modernization. With the founding of new South Africa, the international community removed the economic sanctions against South Africa, and the confrontations between South Africa and the southern African countries disappeared; and South Africa is increasingly emerging as a market which has drawn wide attention from the international community. In order to revitalize the economy, the President of South Africa, Nelson Mandela, and his successors have carried out the international developmental strategy for keeping a foothold in Africa and quickly becoming part of the international community—the Butterfly Strategy. Under the guidance of this strategy, South Africa built and advocated the New Partnership for Africa's Development (NEPAD) through the Southern African Development Community to push forward its cooperation with the southern African countries, and even the whole African Continent in such fields as infrastructure; South Africa has increased its presence in Africa's financial service industry, the mining industry and other fields through investments made by its financial institutions and mining giants, actively fueling Africa's development.[4] In recent years, South Africa has seen low economic growth, high employment, a huge gap in wealth, an imbalance in the labor supply and demand structure, an unbalanced development of the industrial structure, and an irrational foreign capital structure underpinning the current account deficit, as well as the need for economic and social transformation. However, in general, in 20 years of South Africa's political change, the macro economy grew steadily, structural social and economic progress was made, and South Africa successfully became one of the BRICS countries, enjoyed an important status in the world economy and an increasingly important standing in the international community.

II. Experience in and Inspirations Regarding the Path Towards Modernization from the Emerging Market Countries

The paths towards modernization in India, South Korea, Brazil and South Africa are four typical models of late-mover countries for achieving modernization. The experience and lessons from these countries during their experimentation with modernization offer inspirations for China's modernization:

1. The Late-Mover Advantages are Strengthened and the Late-Mover Disadvantages are Overcome in Order to Promote the Take-off of Economic Modernization

The late-mover advantages mean that the late-mover countries can have advantages over the first-mover countries and will also develop at a greatly increased speed in achieving modernization thanks to the "demonstration effect" of successful experience seen in the first-mover kind of modernization, the scientific and technological achievements and management experience of the first-mover countries which the late-mover countries can draw on. Practice has proved that the four major emerging market countries seized, in due time, the opportunity for achieving modernization and fully leveraged their own late-mover advantages while overcoming the late-mover disadvantages to boost the take-off of economic modernization. Meanwhile, the four major emerging market countries showed different characteristics during the utilization of the late-mover advantages: based on Nehru's socialist ideology, India experienced three stages of modernization, and saw accelerated liberalization of the economy and quickened reform of the public sector as well as continued development of the private economy; South Korea stressed the central position of the economy in national development and believed that putting the economy first was the highest

[4] Yang Lihua, South Africa's Economy—Seeking Development across Africa, *West Asia and Africa*, 2005 (6).

principle for the economic construction in many East Asian countries and territories, and also guaranteed South Korea's trajectory of a leap in modernization; Brazil underwent a dynamic process from the self-seclusion of the traditional society to opening up to an attachment to the Western developing countries and then development amidst such attachment, ultimately development through autonomous opening up; South Africa transformed from attachment to autonomous development during modernization, while South Korea's process of development was greatly related to its own factor endowment and cultural characteristics.

China is the largest developing country in the world. Since the reform and opening up, China has correctly brought into play its late-mover advantages and has created excellent conditions for turning its potential capability into practical advantages, thus tremendous achievements have been made in China's modernization. At present, China has entered a stage of modernization at which important strategic opportunities and salient contradictions interweave; China is seeing the erosion, to varying degrees, of its late-mover advantages and is being subjected to new potential challenges due to a particular stage of modernization, changing the external environment and realistic problems. Converting these potential challenges into the advantages conducive to further development in the future is a significant issue for China's modernization. At this stage, it is still of great importance to fully draw on the experience from the developed and developing countries and continue to make good use of its late-mover advantages.

2. **Both Domestic and International Markets and Resources are Fully Utilized to Promote Joint Modernization of Both a National Economy and an Outward-Looking Economy**

The key for the four major emerging countries to make great economic progress lies in tapping and utilizing their own potential resources and international resources, and gradually relying on capital and technologies to use the world's natural resources. In the process of modernization, they have been good at taking full advantage of both domestic and international markets and resources, and refraining from, as far as possible, fully relying on their own natural resources to utilize the international capital.

The four major emerging countries have also paid great attention to joint modernization of both a national economy and an outward-looking economy. The modernization of the national economy is the backbone of a country and a territory. In the increasingly volatile environment of international economic modernization, there is no development in the modernization of a national economy and the developmental foundation for the endogenous economic modernization of a country or a territory if there is no powerful modernization of the national economy. If there is no opening up, the advanced foreign technologies and equipment will not be introduced, the foreign capital will not be utilized, and it is impossible to achieve rapid growth in the modernization of the national economy, and this is also not beneficial for realizing the powerful modernization of the national economy.

We must draw on the experience from the four major emerging countries, properly handle the relationships between domestic and international markets, capitalize on both domestic and international resources, and subject ourselves to self-independence, closely follow the development of the times to reinforce international open cooperation so as to rapidly move China's modernization forward.

3. **There is a Scientific and Rational Government Intervention in the Process of Modernization**

The four emerging countries have attached importance to the roles of the government in modernization, and have strengthened and optimized the planning of and guidance for the whole process of national modernization, provided through the economic function of government intervention. For example, the Indian Government set up the State planning commission in 1950 and carried out the first five-year plan for economic and social development as from 1951. In each five-year plan, the Indian Government specified the basic goals for economic and social development and the specific indicators concerning economic development. In order to ensure the realization of the economic and social developmental goals and the economic growth indicators, the Indian Government implemented directive plans for the public sector of the economy and guidance plans for the organized private sectors of the economy, and allowed other private sectors of the economy to be regulated by the market. In order to achieve the basic goals for economic and social development, the Indian Government also exercised a relatively strict control over economic development. South Korea developed, as from the 1950s, the developmental plans covering different periods; South Korea spelled out the sectors defined as developmental priorities and stated the investment directions for guiding the private capital in different periods. In the early 1960s, South Korea specified the goals for industrialization and carried out the strategy of "putting exports first". In the 1970s, South Korea implemented, step by step, the strategy for the industrialization of the heavy industry in light of the changing situation. Brazil also worked out the five-year plans, developmental outlines and plans for industrial development.

The governments of the four major emerging countries guided the allocation of resources by various policy means. These governments adopted clear industrial policies to guide the direction of resource allocation, regulated and guaranteed the existing developmental mode by other macroeconomic policy means, laws and decrees. For example, after East Asia's economy became export-oriented in the 1960s, the South Korean Government provided preferential credit and taxes for the enterprises which produced exported commodities, stimulated exports through the adjustment of the exchange rate, and safeguarded normal market operations through small and medium-sized enterprise laws, monopoly restriction laws, foreign exchange administration laws, foreign capital introduction laws and other laws. Brazil adopted the protective tariffs and foreign exchange administration policy to restrict the importation of foreign products which competed with domestic products, and introduced special preferential policies and an import exchange rate to encourage the import substitution sectors to import raw materials, fuels and intermediate products.

As shown by the growth and development of the emerging market countries, all of the countries which have become relatively successful during economic modernization and have avoided detours, have promoted developmental plans suitable for their national conditions. Likewise, in order to achieve the modernization goals, China, as a developing country, must work out scientific developmental plans, consistent with the national conditions, for the various stages of modernization in order to accomplish the historical mission of modernization on a staged, step-by-step basis. Meanwhile, it is necessary to optimize the government's intervention in modernization, properly handle the relations between the government and enterprises, between the government and the market, between the government and society, transform the government's functions, earnestly cultivate and develop the market, really give play to the roles of the market in resource allocation, and actively push forward the upgrading of the industrial structure. The government's intervention in non-economic factors should focus on the key fields and objects, the major issues having a vital bearing on the overall situation and long-term development, especially the educational, scientific and technological development, the national innovative line of thinking and capability to carry out innovation. It is essential to strengthen the capacity building of the government to create an incorrupt and fair environment for economic development so as to promote sustainable social development.

4. **The Active Role of Traditional Culture in Modernization is Brought into Play**

In the process of modernization in India, South Korea, Brazil and South Africa, the traditional cultures have exerted a profound impact on those countries' paths towards modernization. India, South Korea, Brazil and South Africa are part of the following cultural circles, respectively: the typical Buddhist subculture circle in Asia, the typical Confucian subculture circle in Asia, the typical Christian subculture circle in Latin America and the African cultural circle highly influenced by Western culture. These four countries are part of different cultural circles, but the cultural backgrounds have similar influences on the development of the emerging countries. First, ethicality: The family ethical norms are extended to the political and economic fields so that the rights, powers, responsibilities and obligations are turned, in the traditional cultures, into common norms which govern social relationships. These ethical norms are beneficial to social harmony and stability. Second, diversity: These four countries have their own religious beliefs and cultural traditions, which helps choose the methods of modernization which accord with the national conditions. Third, inclusiveness: The cultures of these four countries are highly inclusive; each invasion by external nationalities has brought different elements to the cultures of these four countries; the external cultures have become part of and have enriched and innovated the local cultures.

Chinese traditional culture has played an active role in China's modernization. The thoughts—in Chinese traditional culture—of placing equal emphasis on both law and discipline rites and putting people before policies, coincide with the policies, advocated by us, of governing the country according to the laws and increasing the moral level of the nationals. This plays an important role in stabilizing the social order and promoting social development. Moreover, Chinese traditional culture is hardly matched by any other culture in terms of cohesive force. The ethical outlooks—humanity, justice, propriety, wisdom and trustworthiness—in Chinese traditional culture are conducive to harmonious interpersonal relationships and social relations, and serve as the spiritual bond for maintaining national unity and ethnic solidarity. In addition, a combination of the excellent elements of Chinese traditional culture and those of the advanced cultures will effectively arouse national vitality and creative power, making the traditional culture become the basic strength for promoting China's modernization.

1.3 Exploration and Selection of the Paths Towards Modernization of the Countries in Transition

The countries in transition, mentioned here, refer to the countries which had practiced a planned economic system and have finished their transformation towards or are transforming towards a market economic system; these countries mainly include the former Soviet Union, Eastern Europe and the Chinese Mainland. In this section, we will explain the formation and characteristics of the planned economic system in these countries and the main differences among their methods of economic transformation. In short, the different national conditions and historical conditions of the former Soviet Union, Eastern Europe and the Chinese Mainland led to differences in their planned economic systems, thus they ultimately took different paths towards transformation.

I. **Exploration and Selection of the Paths Towards Modernization of the Countries in Transition. One: Industrialization and Planned Economy**

In the first half of the 20th century, some socialist countries were established in some parts of the world, mainly in Eastern Europe and Asia. The socialist political power, built at the earliest, was the former Soviet Union, while most of the other socialist countries were established after the Second World War, and their establishment resulted, more or less, from the influence of or inspirations from the former Soviet Union. With the impact of the Soviet Model, these countries adopted a planned economic system for a certain period of time after their establishment, but most of them, except a few special cases such as North Korea, advanced further to transform their economic system into a market system. Therefore, we call these countries "countries in transition".

Historically, the market economy is generally the result of a gradual institutional evolution and can be regarded as a high-level commodity economic system which naturally comes into being along with economic development. In striking contrast to the market economic system, the planned economic system in countries in transition is generally not the result of a gradual institutional evolution in the countries; on the contrary, it is an economic system which was compulsively realized by political intervention after the socialist political power was established through violent revolution or external intervention. The former Soviet Union and other countries in transition chose the central planned economic system for the following reasons: On the one hand, theoretically, the Marxist theory on which the political power of these countries relies predicts that socialism will replace capitalism and the planned economy will supersede the market economy; on the other hand, practically, repeated economic crises and the World Wars further reinforced the judgment of the leaders of the countries in transition that capitalism and the accompanying market system had declined.

Regarding the economic form, most of the countries in transition were in an agricultural society immediately after socialist political power was established—agriculture made up the largest proportion of the national economy and there was no full industrialization. Therefore, after socialist political power was set up, the governments of those countries found that the excessively weak industrial foundation was not beneficial to developing the economy and executing a central planned economic system. As a result, in parallel with the establishment of a planned economic system, economically, those countries in transition generally took compulsory industrialization measures to quicken their industrial development. Those measures enabled many countries in transition to greatly enhance their industrial foundation in a very short time and laid a solid foundation for the survival and development of those countries and their political power; however, to some extent, it harmed the agriculture in those countries; for example, adverse consequences, such as famine, occurred in some countries.

Overall, the establishment of the socialist system can simply be considered a political revolution and an economically compulsory execution of industrialization and the planning system. The economic systems varied in the countries in transition; they were planned economic systems based on Stalin's Model. Their basic characteristics were the same.

First, the social planner (the central government) played a crucial role in the national economic activities. Other economic entities, such as individuals and enterprises, carried out the economic activities under the command of the social planner.

Second, the countries in transition were mainly governed by public ownerships, while other ownerships made up a very small proportion. The public sector of the economy was dominated by the state-owned enterprises, while there were some economic players under a collective ownership in rural areas.

Third, with respect to resource allocation, top-down plans and commands were generally used to coordinate the economic activities, and the economic decision-making power was highly centralized. Meanwhile, the roles of the market and prices in allocating resources were obviously suppressed.

Fourth, the distribution of the income was conducted mainly by means of distribution based on work, supplemented by other manners of distribution. Compared with the manner of distribution of the traditional market, the incomes (including profits, interests, land rent) from capital and resources were subject to great restrictions.

The planned economic system was originally designed to overcome some latent drawbacks in the market economy—such as, a large gap of wealth and the cyclical economic crises resulting from excessive decentralization of production. At particular historical stages—for instance, when the socialist countries, including the former Soviet Union, Eastern Europe and China—were established, the planned economic system was helpful to those countries in fully mobilizing and consolidating manpower and material resources, and realizing rapid industrial and economic accumulation in a short period of time. However, there were some severe drawbacks in the planned economic system, mainly:

First, the plans were complicated and unfeasible. Every manufacturer and consumer in the market economy respectively determined the quantity of production and consumption. The production and distribution of commodities were regulated by prices. The preliminary concept of the planned economic system was that the production and distribution in the economy—the manufacturer of each commodity, its production quantity, the quantity of productive factors consumed in production, the quantity of products distributed to each consumer, the price of each product and the wages of each worker—were determined by the central plans. However, the total quantity of commodities in a country was very large, and the production and distribution of commodities and production factors were coordinated in a holistic way; it was very complicated, even impossible, to fully rely on plans to conduct production and distribution. Furthermore, given the complexity of the plans, in case of an external shock, it was difficult for the planned economy to make quick adjustments, and it was slow to re-formulate the plans for production and distribution.

Second, there was a lack of an adequate incentive mechanism. One problem—a frequent target of criticism—in the market economy was that it often led to a large gap of wealth, while one characteristic of the planned economic system with regard to income distribution was that there was a small gap of wealth. However, such apparent equity was acquired at a very heavy price: an excessively even level of income would severely undermine personal motivation for progress; there was no adequate mechanism for stimulating the people to create wealth. As a result, labor productivity, individual investments and innovations were at relatively low levels in the planned economy, economic vitality and efficiency would be hit hard, and economic development would be hindered.

Third, under the planned economic system, it was difficult to effectively allocate the resources and it was easy to cause an imbalance between supply and demand, especially a shortage. Theoretically, both market and plan are a means to allocating resources, including production factors and products. The market allocates the resources according to prices; every economic entity determines, based on the given prices, the quantity of the production factors and products to be purchased or supplied. Under the planning system, the resources are regulated and controlled by commands, and the government adopts plans to determine the quantity of the production factors and products owned by each enterprise, and the consumption quantity of each household. As a manner of resource allocation, the market is generally effective. Under the market system, even if there is a temporary local imbalance between supply and demand—commonly, the demand is generally insufficient or excess products occur amidst an economic crisis, the equilibrium of demand and supply and the rational allocation of the resources can be achieved again through rapid price adjustments. However, as a method of resource allocation, the plan is prone to causing an imbalance between supply and demand, especially the excess of product output over demand—shortage. An example of shortage was that commodity quota purchase vouchers, such as food coupons, were commonly used in China before the reform and opening up.

Finally, the planned economy gave rise to a situation in which there was not a variety of products. One characteristic of a market economy is the full market competition in which one kind of product is generally made by many different manufacturers. In order to avoid excessively tense competition, these manufacturers will make efforts to set their products apart with distinctive features, thus diversifying the products, expanding the range of choices for consumers and increasing the consumers' level of welfare. Under a planned economic system, manufacturers only made certain products according to orders and were less motivated to develop distinctive products because those products often fell short of demand. Therefore, there was not so much of a variety of commodities in the planned economy.

II. **Exploration and Selection of the Paths Towards Modernization of the Countries in Transition. Two: Institutional Change and Transformation of the System Model**

From the 1980s, the traditional socialist countries carried out transformations of and changes in the economic and political systems. We can explain such transformations and changes from internal and external perspectives. Within those countries, the drawbacks of the planned economic system increasingly loomed large, with a gradual accumulation of economic problems, thus the people became more and more skeptical of the sluggish planned economic system. Externally, with comparisons of the speed and quality of the economic development between Western and Eastern countries, the people became increasingly aware that the market economy enjoyed huge institutional advantages over the planned economy, the socialist countries were in a disadvantageous position in international competition and the gap gradually widened. Under the domestic and foreign pressure, the governments of those countries ultimately launched large-scale economic reforms, and pressed ahead with political reforms amidst resistance to reforms on the part of the political institutions.

Different countries in transition shared similarities in the basic direction of their economic transformation—all of them aimed at transforming towards a market economy by replacing the original planned economic system. However, different countries in transition were greatly different in their guiding theories for reforms, the transformation strategy and the path towards development. We can broadly divide the manners of transformation of the countries in transition into two categories: the shock therapy represented by the former Soviet Union and most of the Eastern European countries, and the gradual reform represented by China. From the perspective of institutional economics, these two methods can be understood as a compulsory institutional change and an induced institutional change. How can these different transformation methods be evaluated? Currently, the mainstream views in the academic circles hold that the economic performance of the shock therapy was not ideal, as it caused a long-term or short-term economic retrogression to varying degrees in the countries in transition. The cause for such failure may be that the designer of the shock therapy did not really understand the social operational institution of the

Soviet Union and Eastern Europe, and did not realize the environmental and institutional conditions for the operation of an economic institution, as well as a failure to be fully aware of the social unrest caused by the drastic transformation and the difficulties in taking countermeasures. On the contrary, the gradual reform represented by China became greatly successful, mainly because the gradual reform can, to a greater extent, proceed from the actual national conditions and start from the areas with minimal resistance to reforms and from the easiest-to-reform institutions; moreover, it is easy to make partial adjustments in a gradual reform in the face of difficulties and mistakes.

However, this does not mean that such countries as Russia could simply duplicate China's success. In fact, the Soviet Union carried out a gradual economic reform from 1985 to 1991, but failed. Similar reform measures were successful in China, but unsuccessful in the Soviet Union, which is possibly attributable to the differences in the national conditions between the two countries. The socialist political institution and the planned economic institution in the Soviet Union were relatively developed and stable; as defined according to the game theory, the Soviet Union was in a state of relatively stable equilibrium, so a partial reform would meet with great obstructions, and only a holistic reform similar to the shock therapy could rock the existing institutions. The political organizational structure and the economic operational institution in China were less stable and systematic due to the impact of political movements such as the Cultural Revolution. There were sufficient ideological needs for reforms after the Cultural Revolution, so it was easier to accept a gradual change.

Chapter 2
Theory Construction Concerning the Special Economic Zones and China's Development Path

The Third Plenary Session of the 11th Central Committee of the Communist Party of China initiated China's Development Path towards modernization in the new period. For more than 30 years, China has made tremendous achievements in political, economic, cultural and social construction, and China's economic aggregate has exceeded that of the UK, France, Germany and Japan, making China the new engine for the world's economic development and the second largest economy in the world. These great achievements reflect the superiority of China's development path towards development and prove that the path to China's development is correct, its theories are scientific and its institutions are rational. This is China's greatest confidence in its path in more than 30 years. In this regard, the *Report to the 18th National Congress of the Communist Party of China* states that we should have confidence in the path, theories and institutions under socialism with Chinese characteristics, and this requires us to enhance the theoretical self-consciousness and the theoretical innovations on the basis of this confidence. The special economic zones are the starting point and touchstone for China's Development Path, thus how to lay the theoretical foundation for China's Development Path, build the theoretical framework for it, and propose the corresponding explanation of the model on the basis of the practice in the special economic zones is of very important significance; moreover, it is the inevitable requirement for building up confidence in China's Development Path and theories as well as a theoretical self-consciousness.

2.1 The Special Economic Zones and China's Development Path: Theoretical Foundation

Regarding the theoretical foundation, the most important characteristic of China's Development Path is that the path is unbalanced, and the modernization goals are systematic and do not merely focus on the modernization of economic development.

© Social Sciences Academic Press and Springer Nature Singapore Pte Ltd. 2018

Y. Tao and Z. Lu, *Special Economic Zones and China's Development Path*,
Research Series on the Chinese Dream and China's Development Path,
https://doi.org/10.1007/978-981-10-3220-2_2

Therefore, in order to better explain China's Development Path and build the theoretical paradigm of it, it is essential to seek a theoretical foundation according to the theory of unbalanced development, the theory of point-axis development and growth pole, the theory of circular cumulative cause and effect and the accidental historical event, the theory of economic agglomeration and diffusion, the theory of plan-market relationship and the theory of institutional change and market formation.

2.1.1 The Theory of Unbalanced Development and Its Explanation of China's Development Path

"Equilibrium" originates from the concept of "balance" in physics; in particular, it means that the joint force applied to a certain system by various mutually contradictory forces is zero, and the system is in a stable state that the original movement does not change. Fan Gang (1991) believed that the Walrasian Equilibrium referred, in particular, to the market equilibrium achieved by the spontaneous actions of the contradictory market forces (without the third-party actor) under conditions of perfect competition, and that meant that there was a quantitative equality among the contradictory forces and no force had the motive or ability to change the status quo so that the behavior was optimal or certain. With the Keynesian Revolution and the emergence of the planned economy in the socialist countries, the concept of equilibrium dispensed with the assumptions of "perfect market competition" and even "market economy", and it referred in particular to a description of the "difference" or "equality" in the acting force—intervention or plan—applied on the market players by the "third party"—the government, such as "balanced fiscal policy", "balanced investment strategy", and "unbalanced reform path" for a transition economy.

In the academic circles, there were different views about whether to adopt the balanced developmental strategy or the unbalanced developmental strategy. Based on the complementarity and correlation among the economic entities, Rosenstein-Rodan (1943), Nurkse (1953) and Scitovsky (1954) believed that various sectors and regions should develop together. Murphy, Shleifer and Vishny (1989) further proved that the unbalanced growth was inefficient where investments were fixed. Hirschman (1958) held that the developing countries had no adequate resources to make massive investments, so they would first concentrate their investments on some advantageous sectors. A "transition economy" has different attributes and missions from those in a "developmental" economy. Luo Haiping and Zhong Jian (2009) thought that China's Development Path was designed, under the institutional background of a planned economy, to complete, in a relatively short time, the process of marketization which took several hundred years for the Western developed countries to experience. Regarding this aspect, in a reform period without mature and independent leading players in the market economy, the reform method of the third party—the government—becomes the important factor affecting the performance of the reform. The most prominent feature of China's reform is "unbalanced" rather than "gradual" and "dual". China's Development Path is the uppermost form of the unbalanced spatial reform path. Li Yining (2008) believed that, as a conscious action of the government, the special economic zones were like the large stones thrown into the stagnant lake of the planned economic system, and certainly generated spectacular ripples. A particular model explanation of the special economic zones has not yet been made in China's academic circles, while they are explained by a number of theories: Sheng Hong (1991) and Lin Yifu (1993) adopted the "authorized reform or experimentation and popularization" to explain the unbalanced marketization path of China's special economic zones; Miao Zhuang (1992), Sheng Hong (1992), Fan Gang (1993) and Lin Yifu et al. (1994) considered the special economic zones as reforms "outside of the planned economic system" or "incremental" reforms; based on the "experimentation-demonstration-popularization" analysis paradigm, Xu Xianxiang et al. (2008) believed that the special economic zones constituted the starting point for China's gradual, unbalanced reform and opening up and its transition to a market economy.

John M. Litwack and Yingyi Qian (1998) held that the success of the unbalanced developmental model in China was related to the special nature of the special economic zones. During the reform period, China had no realistic background, as defined by the theory of balanced growth, for opening up, and no full-fledged market system. The special economic zones are "outside the customs boundary within China's territory" to some extent, and are mainly designed to develop and expand the outward-looking economy; in particular, they draw on the resources from Hong Kong, Macao, Taiwan and the Chinese abroad. Contrary to the complete seclusion of the planned economy, the special economic zones do not compete with other areas on the Chinese Mainland for the limited investment resources. Overall, the following situation—a concern of Murphy, Shleifer and Vishny (1989) from the "equilibrium school"—does not occur: The developmental model of the special economic zones is so unbalanced that the special economic zones will be hindered by the development of the late-mover inland areas. On the contrary, with the advantage of an excellent location, the special economic zones first carried out pilot programs to acquire experience in the successful transformation of the whole planned economy, and they will play an increasingly apparent role in stimulating the development of the inland areas as the first-mover areas are open to the inland market. Therefore, the special economic zones serve as the catalysts for the transition on China's Development Path from a planned economy to a market economy and from a backward one to a modern one.

2.1.2 The Theory of "Point-Axis" Development and Growth Pole and Its Explanation of the Regional Developmental Mode on China's Development Path

The representative figure of the theory of "point-axis" development is the French geographer W. Christallar. The core of this theory is the theory of the central place and the theory of the growth axis. The former theory focuses on the role of "points" and holds that the markets of different hierarchical centers are different, causing the hierarchical division of work in cities. The latter theory stresses the role of the "axis" and states that, once the traffic arteries serve as the link among the central places, free movement and rational allocation of the resource factors can be promoted, and transportation and production costs may decrease, so the location with comparative advantages will come into being, and the regional economy will develop more rapidly as the "growth pole" attracts such factors as population and capital. The practical significance of the theory of "point-axis" development lies in first revealing the disequilibrium in regional economic development—the leapfrog allocation of resource factors may be achieved among points to leverage the function of the axial belt so as to stimulate the economic development of the whole region.

August-Losch put forward, in 1939 at the earliest, the thought that the regional economic activities would concentrate in growth poles. In *Economic Space: Theory and Applications* and *Note on the Concept of Developmental Poles*, etc., F. Perroux, in 1950, conducted a systematic study of the developmental pole, the growth pole and other concepts, and conceived the theory of unbalanced growth marked by the developmental pole and based on the theory of unequal power or the dominance theory. In his subsequent *Note on the Concept of Growth Poles* (1955), he asserted that growth does not occur in all places at the same time; it first, with different intensities, appears at some growth points and growth poles, and then spreads through different channels, and produces different final effects on the whole economy (Sheng Zhipeng and Mai Fu 2005). According to F. Perroux's theory, economic development is an unequal and unbalanced dynamic process in which a dominant unit plays a leading role; the dominant economic factor can produce the "push" effect—its own growth and innovations will induce and stimulate the growth of other economic factors. The push-type enterprises engage in more transactions with other enterprises relating to them by expanding their scale to increase sales. Therefore, the emergence of a push-type enterprise will result in an increase in the sales of a group of enterprises. The push effect is related to industrial relevance. The industries with strong forward, backward and lateral links have great push effects. As shown, the growth pole conceived by F. Perroux is a dominant economic factor or an enterprise with a strong push effect, rather than a spatial "pole". It is the center or pole which generates the centrifugal force and the centripetal force; each center is surrounded by many other centers, and has a sphere of action with a certain attraction and repulsive force. Apparently, F. Perroux's theory of a growth pole cannot reflect the special nature of the special economic zones well. This is because a special economic zone is a concept of a region instead of a dominant economic factor or an enterprise with a push effect.

The French professor J. Boudeville studied the growth pole by really taking it as a concept of a "space". In 1966, he proposed the concept of space about the growth center, emphasizing the regional characteristics of an economy and believed that an economic space was the operation of economic variables within or above a geographic space, and that it was more advisable to compare a growth pole, as a pole formed by the geographical agglomeration of economic activities, to a sectoral complex system. In general, a growth pole would appear as a city or a town with a conglomerate consisting of push-type enterprises. As defined by J. Boudeville, a growth pole is an industrial conglomerate which continuously expands in the urban regional allocation and guides, within the scope of its influence, the economic activities to develop further. A growth pole has two explicit definitions: (1) a push-type industry at the spatial level—a sectoral growth pole; (2) a city or a town with an agglomeration in a geographical space—a spatial growth pole or a spatial growth center. Therefore, a growth pole represents a growth in the sense of both "industrial push" and "spatial agglomeration". Obviously, a special economic zone can be explained only by a growth pole with "spatial agglomeration". This is because the most basic attribute of and requirement for a special economic zone is that the special economic zone is a city or a town with an agglomeration in a geographical space and a spatial growth center. Only when a special economic zone becomes a growth pole capable of spatial agglomeration can it play a role in a transitional economy. This is the material foundation for the special economic zones to bring about China's Development Path.

In recent years, with the development of the theory of unbalanced growth, great changes have taken place in the significance and the form of the growth pole or the way to realizing the growth pole, mainly:

(1) In terms of goal, a growth pole shifts to an innovative center (incubator). The rise and growth of new enterprises, especially small enterprises, is the important symbol of an emerging area. Small and medium-sized enterprises are less able to resist risks and make innovations; if the government can take measures—such as the establishment of business incubation centers for small enterprises—and preferential policies—such as provision of risk capital and excellent infrastructures—to create a good incubation environment and growth mechanism, they can indirectly reduce the innovation risks and the developmental costs for enterprises, and further help the emerging enterprises survive and succeed. This trend is very obvious in the special economic zones and park-type special economic zones such as the national-level high-tech parks, the economic and technological developmental zones and the functional pilot zones in other medium and large cities. In the park-type special economic zones, capital, technologies and industries are highly concentrated, and there is a different special policy support, provided by the Central Government, concerning capital, knowledge, talents and innovation.
(2) With respect to the polarization mode, the special economic zones relied on the top-down administrative force or a single external force during the early stages—for example, growth poles and growth centers were built by an excessive dependence on foreign capital or natural resource endowment; however, there has been a shift towards relying on the internal forces such as knowledge and technical innovations to develop the regional economy rather than merely building growth poles, such as the Shenzhen Special Economic Zone as a national innovative city.
(3) There has been a shift from the building of growth poles to the construction of sticky places. There are four types of sticky places: the Marshallian or Italian District, the Hub-and-Spoke District, the State-centered District and the Satellite

Platform District. A sticky place is not a spatial growth pole; it is an area, attached to a growth pole, built to avoid industrial hollowing-out caused by the outflow of capital and enterprises, brain drain from an emerging growth pole or growth center. In China, a sticky place commonly refers to a satellite town or a new developmental zone of a large city or a megacity, such as the Pudong New Area of Shanghai, the Binhai New Area of Tianjin, and various types of developmental zones attached to large cities.

(4) The developmental strategy stresses competitive advantages, cooperative advantages and localization. M. Porter divided the factors of production into basic factors—innate "hereditary" natural resources, geography, climate and population—and advanced factors—advanced talents, scientific and educational institutions, infrastructural and institutional environments which are "artificial", developed later and require long-term investments. The traditional comparative advantages are built on basic factors, while the competitive advantages are based on advanced factors. The competitive power of a country, in the final analysis, depends on the total sum of the characteristic industries with competitive advantages in various regions. Fredriksson and Lindmark believed that cooperation and competition were equally important. The appearance of the production system is a trend that goes from vertical integration to vertical disintegration, so many enterprises increasingly adopt the strategy of partial outsourcing instead of covering every aspect of a task. This calls for correctly handling two linkages—the local linkage for lowering the transaction and transport costs and the non-local linkage for reducing direct production costs—and properly dealing with the relationships between the economy of scale and the economy of scope, and realizing the external economy of scope by geographical means of specialized industrial agglomeration, thus forming a small enterprise network and a regional production agglomeration with cooperation and competition.

(5) There has been a shift from the growth pole to the network development. Economic development gives rise to growth poles (central cities and towns) and developmental axes, and the growth poles and developmental axes generate a network conducive to the flow of goods, capital, technologies, labor force and other production factors in larger regions and a transportation and communication network. The theory of network development underscores the efforts to move the diffusion of growth poles and growth axes outwards, characterized by balanced dispersion, to narrow the developmental gap among regions. On the one hand, it is necessary to transform, renew, spread and shift the existing traditional industries; on the other hand, it is essential to comprehensively develop new areas to achieve a balance in the economic layout. Generally, new developmental areas take the form of point-axis development rather than decentralized investments covering extensive fields. As the new and old points and axes gradually spread and interweave, an economic network system takes shape spatially.

Overall, the theory of the growth pole is a typical unbalanced developmental theory for regional development. It stresses centralized development, centralized investment, main construction, development of agglomerations, government intervention, diffusion, optimization of the economic structure, development of the starting-up industries, and optimization of the structure of the economic regional space for driving the development of the whole region through centers for development. In a modern sense, a spatial growth pole is an economic activity center resulting from the development of agglomerations of the enterprises which lead the industries and have the capability for innovation in a region or a large city. A center for economic activity can perform the functions of a center for production, for trade, for finance, for information, for transportation, for services and for decision-making; for example, a "magnetic field pole" can attract the external factors and exert an influence on other areas, and promote its own economic development and that of other industries and areas.

2.1.3 The Theory of Circular Cumulative Cause and Effect and the Historical Accidental Event and Its Explanation of the Special Economic Zones

In 1957, Gunnar Myrdal developed the theory of the circular cumulative cause and effect in urban growth. According to this theory, once a force, such as a new industry, triggers the growth of a city, it will push forward the growth of other relevant sectors thanks to the interrelation among industrial sectors, while the growth of these sectors gives birth to the growth of the sectors relating to them, accompanied by the entry of new industrial sectors and a new round of circulation. A city takes shape and expands in this process of continuous accumulation and circulation. This theory mainly explains the issue concerning the growth mechanism of a city which has developed to a certain stage. This theory holds that, when an industrial city develops to the extent that the local resources are almost fully utilized, the growth of the city depends on its ability to gather capital and talents.

For the developing countries in transition, the assumption that a well-developed market economic system necessary for the traditional growth poles is unavailable, thus the polarization factors become more diverse, and policies, humanity, traditions and historical events constitute the driving forces for gradual polarization through the circular cumulative causal effect. According to Paul R. Krugman, an urban location is not fully determined by the distribution of resources, while accidental historical factors and the expectation regarding self-enforcement, etc., may help to explain an urban location. When examining the reasons why Chicago could become an economic center, the historians William Cronon and Paul R. Krugman pointed out that Chicago did not have a very unique natural geographical location, and the First Nature was insufficient to bring about today's Chicago as a metropolis, while today's Chicago results from fully leveraging the self-reinforcing development of or the positive feedback loop or the circular accumulation of the Second Nature—the central market which formed later in Chicago, such as the population and product agglomeration and the establishment of a center of a transportation network. Cronon considered Chicago's phenomenon as a typical example of the Path Dependence proposed by David (1985); he believed that the historical events guided the people to develop the expectation that Chicago would serve as a "center" and turn this expectation into reality. Paul R. Krugman built a model based on this thought of Cronon's. The importance of the historical factors and expectational factors, to some extent, implies the rationality of the economic intervention, while multiple equilibria and evolution ensure that the spatial economic intervention is effective. Once a random economic event leads the economy to a particular path, this choice may be locked in but another better choice may be abandoned. For the special economic zones represented by Shenzhen in China, the whole process, from their establishment to their growth into modern metropolises, is both historically accidental and realistically inevitable, and these modern metropolises come from the circular accumulation of various favorable factors during a period of more than 30 years.

2.1.4 The Theory of Economic Agglomeration and Diffusion and Its Explanation of the Formation of the Spatial Route Involving China's Development Path

(I) **Economic Spatial Agglomeration**

Spatial agglomeration is a tendency and process of concentration of the economic activities in a geographical space. Spatial agglomeration is driven by three forces: First, the orientation of the location of the economic activities—the economic activities at the same location often tend to gather in the area, within a region, in which relevant resources and factors are concentrated; second, the internal linkage among the economic activities—for the sake of reinforcing the interrelation, some closely interlinked and highly interdependent economic activities are often intensively carried out in a proper area; third, the pursuit of the agglomeration economy by the economic activities—the agglomeration can generate the agglomeration economy, so the economic activities need to converge spatially in order to pursue the agglomeration economy. The very important aspect of the agglomeration mechanism is the self-formation and self-reinforcement mechanism of the agglomeration: Once the agglomeration process is initiated (such initiation may be attributable to the choice of the location, accidental historical events and government acts), it is easy to shape the forces for promoting agglomeration, characterized by the circular causation, so as to accelerate the agglomeration.

The agglomeration economy can deliver enormous economical benefits under the modern technical, social and economical conditions. (1) The spatial agglomeration of industries helps further deepen the work division in production and increase the degree of specialization, thus enhancing the labor productivity and greatly reducing the production costs; (2) agglomeration is conducive to lowering the costs for long-distance transportation and transfer among related products, relevant information costs, and the transportation costs; (3) agglomeration is beneficial to building efficient infrastructures and public service networks, especially the developed financial, insurance, information and consulting industries necessary for modern social and economic development, resulting in huge external economical benefits; (4) agglomeration is favorable to forming a developed labor force training program and supply market to facilitate the flow of the labor force and make the specialized technical personnel stand out; (5) agglomeration can bring about the actual vast market and the potential market, more helpful for product renewal and technical innovations. Overall, the spatial agglomeration of industries helps make improvements in production costs, collaboration costs, external economy, labor supply, market expansion and promotion of innovation.

(II) **Economic Spatial Diffusion**

Spatial diffusion is a process in which such "flowing actors" as materials, capital or information emerge at sources at a particular time and space and spread out to acceptors after a certain period of time. The Swedish scholar T. Hagerstrand put forward the spatial diffusion issue for the first time in 1953, and divided spatial diffusion into three basic types: contagious diffusion, hierarchical diffusion and relocation-type diffusion. (1) Contagious diffusion means that the diffusion from a source to an external space is a progressive and continuous process, as when a ripple occurs after a stone falls into the water. In contagious diffusion, the diffusion gradually weakens along an increasing distance due to the frictional resistance effect; (2) hierarchical diffusion mostly refers to the diffusion of humanistic phenomena and government policies relating to gradient development. In hierarchical diffusion, the geographical distance does not always exert a very great impact, while the social hierarchy, city size and the administrative level of a city play very obvious roles, and new policies, new thoughts and new technologies are often first accepted in the distant cities on an equivalent scale and then spread out to the secondary cities. Hierarchical diffusion occurs in case some new things are initially accepted at a relatively high "threshold" so that they are prevented from being rapidly disseminated and can only spread out in a gradual top-down manner; (3) relocation-type diffusion means that the number of acceptors does not increase and only the spatial displacement of the original acceptors takes place during the diffusion, such as the immigration process.

Whether spatial agglomeration or spatial diffusion is involved, the economic spatial pattern and the corresponding saturation degree are always affected by the people's cognitive or learning ability and their capacity to adapt. According to the study conducted by R. Morrill, the quantitative and temporal distribution of the acceptors of new things is a normal type of distribution; time can also produce a certain independent effect, and the proportion of the people who have doubts and cause resistance is relatively high at the initial stage of the diffusion; however, when the acceptors reach a crucial proportion, they often follow the trend or show a sheep-flock effect. Such an effect reinforces the temporal imbalance in the diffusion process. Besides anthropogenic factors, L.A. Brown believes that the sources of innovation, the selection of the diffusion center and the diffusion strategy are very important for successful diffusion. Meanwhile, both spatial economic diffusion and agglomeration are subject to certain obstacles. R. Morrill classified the obstacles into two categories according to their permeability: complete impermeable obstacles and partial permeable obstacles. The complete obstacles mean that, when a phenomenon diffuses towards an obstacle, such a phenomenon will be reflected due to impenetrability, so it is more likely that the areas surrounding the obstacle will accept the phenomenon or phenomena, and the original curve showing a decline is restored to a certain uptrend. R. Morrill used the increase in the rainfall on the windward slope in nature to explain such a phenomenon of spatial diffusion. When an obstacle becomes partially permeable, the spatial diffusion curve, which originally indicates that a phenomenon decreases with distance, will be interrupted at the time of the penetration of the obstacle, and then declines with increasing distance at a very low starting point. R. Morrill maintained that such an effect would take place where there are great differences in the economic development between two countries; for example, on the borderline or at the political boundary. Government policies are greatly different among regions in China, so the regional administrative boundaries—for example, between the special economic zones and the areas other than the special economic zones, between the bonded zones and the areas outside the bonded zones—also have a similar impact on economic spatial diffusion.

2.1.5 The Theory of Institutional Change and Market Formation and Its Explanation for the Formation of an Institutional Environment for China's Development Path

Douglass C. North thought that the market emerged from exchanges. He described the generation of exchanges as follows: My analysis started from the local exchanges within villages, or the simple exchanges in the hunting and gathering society in which women and men engaged in gathering and hunting, respectively. In that world, specialization was just elementary, and self-sufficiency was the characteristic of most of the single households. Small-scale village trade existed within a "dense" social network subject to the informal constraints, while the informal constraints promoted local trade, in which the trading costs were very low. There was an intimate relationship among people, while the violent threat was a persistent force for maintaining the order.[1] Douglass C. North also based his analysis concerning the origin of the market on his observation about the formation of the social institution and evolutionary change. In his opinion, the institutions were the game rules in a society, or more normatively, they were some constraints which were developed by people

[1](US) Douglass C. North, The Role of the Institutions in Market Economic Development, *Discussions about the Market Economy by Contemporary Foreign Economists*, Party School of the Central Committee of C.P.C Publishing House, 1994, pp. 50–51.

and governed the relationship among people, including formal constraints—such as laws and regulations—and informal constraints—such as practice, code of conduct and ethical norm—and enforcement characteristics of these constraints (Douglass C. North 1994). Douglass C. North examined the origin of the institutions and the market from the perspective of the eternal human nature in the abstract. This human nature is the assumption—the condition of cognition and self-interestedness of people—concerning the characteristics of human behavior, called by O. E. Williamson (1999) one of the key good ideas in new institutionalism. The contribution from Douglass C. North is that the institutions, as the external prerequisites for neoclassical economic analysis, were endogenized into the framework of neoclassical analysis with the cost-benefit of the self-interested individuals as the basic paradigm. The new institutionalists, including Douglass C. North, held that, in an environment with information insufficiency and information asymmetry, subject to the restrictions from the cognitive ability and driven by the desire to achieve the maximization of utility, the opportunistic behaviors such as fraud, laze and free riding often occurred during transactions, so that there were conflicts of interest and frictions among people, the transaction costs and transaction consequences became more uncertain, finally their own well-being was harmed, while the institutions were the contracts concluded by people to prevent opportunism, thus the market was based on a number of contractual arrangements.

For Douglass C. North's explanation of the market from the contractual perspective, Adrew Schotter (1981, 1983) and Robert Axelrod (1986) adopted the game theory to make further explanations. They assumed that the initial condition for human society was that it was at the "Hobbes State", which was the natural state of a prevalence of opportunism and conflicts of interest. With multiple games, people found that the institutional building—the conclusion of contracts—can generate "cooperative income" or "cooperative surplus", and this income was higher than the increase in the total income of the parties in the case of not concluding contracts. Therefore, people concluded contracts and developed the private property rights system, thus going beyond the "Hobbes State".

In the *Economy of Man*, Hungarian economist Karl Polanyi made a unique explanation of the issues concerning the exchange and the origin of the market from the perspective of economic history. Karl Polanyi gave a new significance to "transaction": If a transaction was defined in terms of its operational function, the transaction served as the indirect means adopted to acquire properties which cannot be directly acquired. Transactions were carried out according to a particular equivalent relationship, so all transactions were nothing but the particular transactions corresponding to different transaction objects. For these particular transactions, transactions first occurred in the edge area which contacted two communities. For the origin of the market, Karl Polanyi believed that the "market" was not an institution associated with a few transactions conducted or a few currencies used by primitive men within a community; instead, it gradually developed in the society at a later time. According to Karl Polanyi, the market institution came from two different sources: one outside a community, another within a community; the external development of the market was closely related to the "non-local" transactions, while the internal development of the market was closely linked to the internal supply of grain. The essence of the market was exchange and transaction, while the market economy was the highest development of the commodity exchange relationship with currency as the media. The market did not exist without the commodity exchange relationship; the accidental and partial commodity exchange was not necessarily the market economy, while the market economy was certainly characterized by commodity accumulation, and the extensive, socialized and comprehensive commodity exchange behaviors. The development of the productive forces determines the degrees of commercialization and marketization. Only when the productive forces reach high levels can the all-round, highly developed market economy come into being. Therefore, China's marketization must center on the development of the productive forces—economic construction. As long as the market transaction is taken as the objective, the choice of path regarding the development of the productive forces does not necessarily determine marketization. The emphasis on the roles of the government and reformers on China's Development Path to the formation of the market economy, especially at the early stage of the development of the special economic zones, does not run counter to the direction and goal of the market-oriented reform.

2.2 China's Development Path: Initial Conditions and Path Attributes

China's Development Path originated from the socialist planned economic system gradually established after liberation in China. As an economic form peculiar to all socialist countries at that time, China's planned economy had many salient characteristics compared with the system of a market economy. Consequently, the planned economy constituted the important initial condition for China's Development Path and determined the unique attributes of China's developmental route.

2.2.1 Initial Conditions for China's Development Path

(I) **Shortage and Shortage Economy**

János Kornai believed that the shortage economy was the epitome of a large number of phenomena in the traditional socialist economy. Shortage in a planned economy included horizontal and vertical shortages—the vertical shortage existed between the central authority responsible for material allocation and the local authorities which needed or asked for materials, and in particular, it meant that the total amount of the materials which could be allocated by the central authority failed to meet the needs of the governments or departments at lower levels, while the horizontal shortage occurred between enterprises or between the seller and the buyer, and it meant that the seller's supply could not satisfy the buyer's needs. There was a lack of necessary complementary input and production capacity, so production bottlenecks, and the shortage which restricted the production capacity of the whole society, often appeared. János Kornai thought that the primary cause for the shortage was the absorption mechanism peculiar to socialism. This absorption mechanism reinforced the general shortage caused by frictions, and a frequent and acute shortage in reproduction. Such an absorption mechanism was mainly characterized by investment hanger and expansion impulse, quantity impulse and propensity to hoard, soaring exports, and excessive demand from consumers for commodities and free services on the market. János Kornai insisted that investment hanger and expansion impulse were the primary causes for shortage, while other mechanisms were the secondary causes and additional factors (Tao Yitao 2000).

(II) **Soft Budget Constraint**

According to János Kornai, the soft budget constraint is a striking phenomenon in a socialist economy and an important cause for socialist shortage. Like the rubber band, the budget line of the socialist state-run enterprises is elastic—in case of difficulties from poor operations, enterprises always break the budget line to obtain help from the government and overcome financial distress. The budget becomes soft mainly because the government is soft in price management, taxation, subsidies, credit and other fields. It is so soft that enterprises pay little attention to sales revenue and internal fund accumulation and become less sensitive to prices, and risks are borne not by enterprises but by the government, enterprises hardly satisfy the needs of investors and fail to perform an effective demand management. Ultimately, the shortage is certainly reinforced, while the fundamental cause for being soft is the attachment of the planned economic enterprises to the government and a lack of competition among enterprises. János Kornai believed that the government (the central government) was "paternalistic" towards the state-owned enterprises (local governments) in the socialist countries. "Paternalism" meant that when enterprises or local governments faced difficulties, the central government always offered help to help them out of difficulties while they assumed no operational responsibility.

(III) **High Governmental Capacity for Accumulation and Mobilization**

Deng Xiaoping said[2] that socialism's superiority over capitalism was that socialism ensured that the all-round and coordinated arrangements could be made nationwide and various forces could be concentrated to focus on key points. The primary reason was that China still retained the traditional modes of socialist public capital accumulation during the reform period especially in the initial period, including[3]: (1) the self-deprivation type of national industrial accumulation; (2) a low-wage welfare system; (3) a price control for guaranteeing national industrial accumulation; (4) a

[2]Deng Xiaoping, Decade-long Work Was a Preparation for the Next Decade, October 14, 1982, *Selected Works of Deng Xiaoping* (Vol. 3), People's Publishing House, 1993.

[3]Wu Wenqiang, Historical Review of the Changes in the Mode of Socialist Capital Accumulation and Institutional Construction in China, a paper from the 2nd China Political Economics Annual Conference (2008).

distribution system under which property rights were owned by all and universally shared; (5) supporting control over low-cost accumulation, such as dual control over labor forces, price control, command-based purchase and sale, control over public services, and strict control over the increase in labor production and reproduction costs to ensure low labor production costs. These traditional accumulation modes rapidly concentrated resources and production factors at relatively low organizational costs during the reform period. This provided the conditions for the special economic zones to acquire resource advantages across the country and created the growth miracle in a short period of time.

(IV) Triple Attribute: A Developing Country + A Country in Transition + A Socialist Country

Chang Xiuze (2008) believed that China was not merely a country in transition from a planned economy to a market economy, and unlike such countries in transition as Russia and Eastern European countries, China had the following three attributes: a developing country, a country in transition and a socialist country. China was a developing country which remained backward at the beginning of its transition, in industrialization, urbanization and per capita income level, so compared with a high degree of industrialization in the Eastern European countries, the transition tasks for China were not only marketization, but also "development" including the intensification of industrialization and urbanization and increasing the level of per capita income. In this regard, industrialization, urbanization, marketization and internationalization would be the tasks for China during the transitional period, and the four major supporting forces for China's economic developmental model, among which marketization would be the most fundamental institutional support. Another of the biggest differences was that China's transition was based on the original political framework and ideology, and marketization meant the building up of a socialist market rather than a capitalist market. Its attribute of being socialist was the "constitutional" provision for China's marketization. As repeatedly emphasized by Wang Zhenzhong during the 2nd Political Economics Annual Conference (2008), the fundamental difference between China, Vietnam and other countries in transition was the direction of the reform instead of its speed: gradual or radical. The preservation of the socialist attribute guaranteed higher growth and welfare performance in China during marketization than such economies in a complete "capitalist" transition as the Eastern European countries and the former Soviet Union were.

(V) M-shaped Organizational Structure

Qian Yingyi et al. (1993, 1998) maintained that China's administrative governance structure was a typical M-shaped structure involving both sectors and regions; the advantages of the M-shaped structure over the U-shaped structure only involving sectors included: (1) The M-shaped structure was beneficial to fostering effective competition in reform. Each region was self-sustaining, only the authorities in the regions where the local economy developed well could enjoy and freely dispose of more fiscal revenue, so the local authorities were motivated to develop the economy; the promotional incentives for Chinese officials were prone to increasing the competition among the local officials in developing the local economy; (2) the capacity for resisting risks was high. In fact, the U-shaped organizational structure was the pure top-down sectoral type of management, but the degree of interdependence among sectors was very high; if certain sectors were subject to an external shock, the whole economy would be affected. On the contrary, the regions in an M-shaped structure were relatively independent from each other, so the shock in any or several regions would not affect the whole economy and would be limited to the particular region or regions; (3) it was convenient for learning among regions. The regions in an M-shaped organization were mutually independent and relatively autonomous, but the regions with a similar economic structure still existed. Regions can learn from each other; for example, the late-mover regions can learn from the first-mover regions, and the regions with a poor developmental performance can learn from those with an excellent performance. Under the U-shaped structure, it was very difficult for the steel sector to learn something valuable from the transportation sector; (4) it facilitated the decentralized implementation of pilot programs. For an M-shaped organization, the regions were mutually independent and had their own systems, so this helped choose the scattered points to carry out pilot programs and then popularize the experience. China's Development Path relied precisely on the fact that the M-shaped structure was easy to experiment in; (5) it can reduce the coordinational dependence on the central government. Compared with a U-shaped structure, in an M-shaped organizational structure, the local governments were mainly responsible for coordination, while the central government was less responsible for that aspect (Wang Limin 2003).

2.2.2 *The Attributes of the Path in China's Development Path*

(I) **Authorized Reform or Experimentation and Popularization**

Sheng Hong (1996) believed that authorized reform or experimentation and popularization meant that the market-oriented reform was limited to a relatively small scope, such as a region, an industry, even an enterprise, where the pilot reform was carried out to acquire reform experience, accompanied by extending this reform to a wider range. The special economic zone mode is an important form of authorized reform within a region or a space. All of the special economic zones, the Pudong New Area and the Binhai New Area, comprehensive reform pilot zones, and small function zones, such as export processing zones and bonded zones, have undergone experimentation and reforms authorized by the central government. The authorized reform is designed to produce a demonstration effect on a wider scope, and even nationwide, after success is achieved. Essentially, the authorized reform is a reformer-led process of learning about the new institutions, while the demonstration effect of a success can help persuade people and reduce the resistance to the reform. The special economic zones represented by Shenzhen are the successful examples of the authorized reform on the basis of the transformational thought of the authorized reform or experimentation.

(II) **Reform Outside a Planned Economic System**

The reform mentioned here refers to that outside of the original planned economic system. The original institutional arrangements, such as the spatial expansion of the planned economy, are fixed, so it is necessary to make the new institutional arrangements to ensure the development and self-expansion of the new economic activities. For example, the development of the township enterprises, the non-public sectors of the economy, the launch of new products and the rise of the special economic zones reflect the line of thought regarding the reform outside the planned economic system. The reform outside the planned economic system is conducted to build the market system in the original institutional "vacuum", so as to avoid the troubles which occur in the case of making new institutional arrangements based on the original system. On the one hand, it can mitigate the repulsion incurred to the new institutional arrangements by the inertia of the old planning system; on the other hand, the interest pattern developed under the established system does not exist outside a planned economic system, thus generally, nobody will be damaged by the reform and the reform will not meet with opposition. Therefore, the reform outside the planned economic system is relatively simple, practicable and low-cost. Facts have proven that such a reform is the main way to carry out reforms in order to ensure that China's market-oriented reform becomes successful.

(III) **Government-Led, Strongly Promoted Reform**

Li Yining (2008) believed that an important difference between the establishment of the special economic zones and the emergence of the rural household contracting responsibility system, the rise of the township enterprises, was that the establishment of the special economic zones was completely a conscious action of the government. Only in this way can the special economic zones such as Shenzhen emerge in China. The fact—the establishment and development of the special economic zones—more clearly showed how the planned economic system was firmly and closely connected to the administrative powers. It was assumed that the government would not take any conscious actions, it was impossible to, subject to a firm combination of the planned economic system and the administrative powers, enable a certain region to break the fetter of the planned economic system to develop its economy according to the rules of the market economy. The achievements in the construction of the special economic zones offered the following inspiration to the people: The economic and technical gap between China and the developed countries can be greatly narrowed through marketization. As long as the planned economy contracted more and market regulation improved to a higher level, economic growth would increase and the people's living standard would be substantially elevated. The success of the special economic zones was like a large stone thrown into the stagnant lake of the planned economic system to generate spectacular ripples. They broke the longstanding abnormal silence to bring about a dynamic economic landscape, so that China's economy was able to irreversibly embark on the path of reform, opening up and a market economy.

(IV) Integration of Partial Reform, Marginal Reform and Gradual Transition

Under this reform mode, the market-oriented reform is temporally and spatially divided into small units to gradually carry out spatial and temporal expansion and popularization (Hu Ruyin 1992; Miao Zhuang 1992; Lin Yifu et al. 1993 1994). The advantages of this reform mode include: First, the reform is not finished in one go, so the existing organizational resources, especially government resources, can be fully utilized to maintain a relatively stable and effective institutional linkage during institutional innovation (Lin Yifu 1993 1994). Second, the reform costs are distributed in multiple stages so as to reduce and spread out the resistance to the reform and the reform costs (Hu Ruyin 1992; Miao Zhuang 1992). Third, a comparison and judgment can be made with respect to different reforms in different fields at any time and any place; some areas with relatively low costs are chosen, while certain areas with relatively strong resistance are avoided. The constraint conditions may change with time, in which case, some areas with a relatively strong resistance at the present time may become the areas with less resistance due to other partial reforms (Miao Zhuang 1992). Fourth, the gradual partial reforms can make the transition process more controllable (Lin Yifu et al. 1993 1994). This is particularly apparent during the opening up: First, the special economic zones were established in Shenzhen, Zhuhai, Xiamen and Shantou adjacent to Hong Kong, Macao and Taiwan, and were granted special economic policies and widely open to the outside world, while the bold experimentation was made in these zones to blaze a new trail: exploring a path to economic reform and opening up. Shortly after, significant achievements were made, 14 coastal cities were open, and the whole Hainan Island was established as a special economic zone; afterwards, the development and opening up of the Pudong New Area of Shanghai, and the opening up of the areas along the border and in the Yangtze River basin was announced.

(V) Relation-Based and Rule-Based Governance Modes

Li Shuhuo (Li 2003) differentiated two governance modes[4]: relation-based governance—the relationship includes the relationship of authority of leaders and governments—and rule-based governance. Relation-based governance is self-enforced through a long-term game among the fixed players. Rule-based governance is enforced by the restraint from third-party laws and regulations. As an implicit contract, the maintenance of the relation-based contract only requires both sides to know partial information on the contract variables and have the same expectations about the results. Rule-based governance means that the relevant contract information is the public information which can be verified by the third party, and enormous set-up costs for developing rules and systems are required in the institutional infrastructure. According to Li Shuhuo, the relation-based contract is a good governance structure for the countries in transition at the initial stage of market formation; its requirements for the contractual information structure are relatively low (this can be verified without a third party), so a slew of transactions and contract sets can be carried out; it

[4]Li, S., 2003, "Relation-based versus Rule-based Governance: an Explanation of the East Asian Miracle and Asian Crisis", Review of International Economics, 11(4), 651–673.

dispenses with the set-up costs for establishing a legal institution, thus huge transaction costs can be saved. In particular, the people's attachment to and reverence for leaders or authoritative figures can significantly lower the coordination costs for leaders or authoritative figures. However, with the intensification of the reform and the expansion of the scope of the market, the governance costs for the relation-based contract will loom large because the marginal transaction cost, such as, the coordination cost for an individual will increase, while the marginal transaction cost for rule-based governance will decrease; in other words, rule-based governance has an economy of scale thanks to a massive input of set-up costs during the early stage. Li Shuhuo maintained that the members of the society and the social "organizations", such as units, were highly interconnected in the era of the planned economy before the reform. For example, "units" provide employees with the goods and services which should be made available on different specialized markets, so employees are attached to the relation-based contracts in their organizations. An important objective of a market economy is to cultivate a multitude of free microcosmic market players. The micro-mechanism of the reform consists of a transition of the governance mode from the relation-based contract with a high degree of interconnection to the rule-based contract with a low degree of interconnection. The transition between both modes entails a complicated interactive relationship. The success of the transition greatly depends on the reform mode—such as gradual reform and radical reform—and the scope of the market. The radical reform destroys the maintainability of the original self-contract, and will lead to governance failure where the labor division and the scope of the market are limited. An advantage of the gradual reform is that, where the scope of the market remains relatively small and before the contract is duly put into place and an alternative governance mechanism emerges, the initial relation-based contract still works by itself to ensure normal social and economic operations.

2.2.3 Special Economic Zones on China's Development Path: Attributes and Characteristics

China's Development Path is an important way to achieve China's unbalanced, gradual and induced opening up and formation of a market economy, and it is the developmental model, in the period of intense and progressive reform, under which the special function zones developed by special economic policies—including the special economic zones, coastal economic development zones, new development zones and comprehensive pilot zones—serve as the carriers. The special economic zones are the important carriers for China's Development Path, and have played an important role in China's transition from a planned economy to a market economy. The special economic zones constitute the "starting point" of the path to the unbalanced and gradual formation of a market economy. The formation of China's market economy contains the historical and special characteristics of a transition market as well as the general features of the original market. The internal relationship between the original market and the transformational market should be considered to clarify the nature and significance of the special economic zones, which is of great significance for correctly understanding the inherent law which governs the formation and development of the special economic zones and China's socialist market economy (Luo Haiping and Zhong Jian 2009).

(I) **Special Economic Zones as "Market Aggregators" and "Exchange Intermediaries"**

The special economic zones are special products during a period of transition away from a planned economy. After the special economic zones were separated from the planned economic community, they served as the "market aggregators" and "exchange intermediaries" between the community of the Chinese Mainland and the outside world. Marketization in the transition period is a process of gradual man-made transition from a planned economy contradictory to a market economy instead of a natural evolutionary process. Under the "artificial fast-growing market" or "external market" conditions, the formation of the market no longer involves a path of evolution from accidental physical exchange and commodity relationships and a long process from the commodity exchange to the establishment of a capitalist market economy. However, the inherent law which governed the origin of the original market also governs the formation of the market economy in a transition economy. According to Karl Marx's theory of market origin, the market starts from the exchange among different human communities (Zeng Tinggui and Sun Chaoying 2007), while marketization is a process in which the market relationships originating from the boundary or ends of different communities permeate within the human community, or a process of market internalization. On the roadmap of China's gradually induced transition and market economy, the special economic zones witnessed the birth of the "artificially chosen" market at the earliest time, and acted as the "starting point" for China's spatial unbalanced gradual marketization path—China's Development Path.

The exchange is the initial impetus for market formation and the essence of the market. Things themselves exist outside the people, so they are transferable. In order to turn a transfer into a mutual transfer, the people only need to quietly and mutually act as the private owners of the things to be transferred, so that the people become mutually opposite as independent people. However, the relationship in which the people treat each other as outsiders is nonexistent among the members of the primitive community… commodity exchange is the end of communities, and starts from the place where they contact other communities or other members. Nonetheless, once a thing externally becomes a commodity, it remains a commodity within a community due to reverse action.[5] Therefore, in order to engage in transactions and form a market within a community, it is essential to "externalize" the members of the community, while the special economic zones are part of externalization targets. After there is a separation between the special economic zones and the areas other

[5] *Karl Marx and Frederick Engels* (Vol. 23), People's Publishing House, 1972 First Edition, pp. 105–106.

than the special economic zones, an internal exchange market emerges in the special economic zones and non-special economic zone community, and the reverse action gradually gives rise to an exchange relationship and a commodity relationship among the areas other than the special economic zones in a community, and marketization. The special economic zones enjoy the policy advantage in directly developing trade contacts with the outside world, especially with Hong Kong, Macao and Taiwan, according to the international rules, so the special economic zones become the "market aggregators" and "exchange intermediaries" between the community of the Chinese Mainland and the outside world. The world market gets access to the community of the Chinese Mainland through the special economic zones, thus the "external market" is transplanted to indirectly achieve market internalization on the Chinese Mainland or induces the original market of the Chinese Mainland to realize that internalization.

(II) Special Characteristics of Both China's Development Path and the Special Economic Zones

A "transition market" is essentially different from and is special compared with the original "revolutionary market", while the market under the planned economic system has its own special features. The market economy formation route subject to the unbalanced China's Development Path is the Pareto Optimum improved from the original economic system. The formation of the transitional market has the special characteristics which are not shown in the natural evolution of the original market. First, China's original market and planned economy failed to elevate China's urbanization and industrialization to the level of a modern industrial country, so the current transition in China is a process of "time-space compression" as analyzed by David Havey. The release of the potential elastic energy developed during the process of the "time-space compression" certainly triggers contradictions and drastic deformation; second, a transition from the traditional planned economy least endowed with market factors and completely opposite to the market will certainly be subject to more obstacles including "path dependence" and "traditional influences"; second, the process of transition is led by the "central government", the highest fortress within a planned economy, and is a process of its "self-reform", so such marketization itself is a process of planning, making the market economy more affected by planning, resulting in market "deformation" and "market planning". Given the above characteristics of transition, the process of market internalization will be subject to the traditional social structure, special interest group and the cognition of the general public. Therefore, the radical market transition—the shock therapy—in China will be accompanied by strong reverberations, even an "explosion effect", from the release of potential elastic "time-space compression" energy. In view of this, the design of the path necessarily focuses on carrying out unbalanced marketization, dividing the resistance to marketization, and taking a gradual path to release the potential elastic "time-space compression" energy on a step-by-step basis. With respect to strategy, it is necessary to launch the market-oriented pilot programs in some areas which are least vulnerable to the planning system and ideology and far from the political market, but closest to the successful market economy, so that the market mechanism can function independently and the traditional system of the planned economy disturbs market experimentation less. It is necessary to reduce the opposition to and resistance from the interest groups under the planning system as much as possible, take old and new measures towards the existing and new players, respectively, and disintegrate the bureaucratic groups under the planning system, cultivate the reformers of the governments at various levels, and reinforce the reformer-led governmental authority. Regarding the target mode, it is essential to start by building a civilian society, follow the principle of personal material interests in order to develop and expand the beneficiaries on the private market, creating the conditions for the development of the individual and private economy and capital self-accumulation (Zeng Tinggui and Sun Chaoying 2007).

As the outcome of the planned economy, the special economic zones are the "variants" which combine the planned economy with the market economy. Giving priority to marketization in the special economic zones is certainly conditional to the "special political treatment". This is because, under the planned economic system, the political resources determine the allocation of the economic resources. The special preferential policies are the highly scarce resources whose allocation depends on the preference of the authority responsible for allocating the policy resources—the central government—or a game between the departments at higher and lower levels. With the implementation of the special preferential policies, on the one hand, the original system is no longer a monolithic whole, and the unbalance from the special preferential policies will quickly catalyze the destruction of the old system and the establishment of a new one. On the other hand, as discriminatory treatments, the special preferential policies are bound to an unbalanced division of economic interests. This goes against the inherent principle of the market economy—the principle of equal competition–, thus the special policies which the special economic zones enjoy are historical and will not exist permanently; with the development of the inland market, continuous progress towards a free market is inevitable.

(III) **Special Zone Method for Capital Accumulation**

Being unbalanced, gradual and making breakthroughs in part is the choice of a path for China's capital accumulation, opening up and formation of a market economy, while the special economic zones constitute the "starting point" of the spatial, unbalanced and gradual change. The evolution of the original market once existed, but was slow in China, and China was forced to accept the "external market" from the Western industrial countries before the era of the industrial market economy. Before liberation, China's market economy was a mixture of the weak original market and the external market. In the 30 years after liberation, the planned economy cut the exchange relationship, commodity relationship and the market economy as the "tails of capitalism", so the evolution, transplantation and development of the market economy were artificially interrupted. With the "preference" of ideology as the choice, the market economy tolerated by socialism is no longer the capitalist market economy "opposite" and "hostile" to the main market players; instead, it is the modern "independent" and "competitive" market economy. In the Western world, the key step of market internalization was achieved through primitive accumulation of capital, but such an accumulation was fraught with wars, bloodiness and plunder. It is impossible for China, a late-mover backward country, to follow the old path of primitive accumulation of capital. This is determined by the nature of socialism and the inherent characteristics which distinguish the transitional market from the original market. Therefore, in China, the main market players can accumulate capital only in the following ways: (1) the original main players under the planning system carry out a capital conversion towards the enterprise market—through the restructuring of the state-owned and collective enterprises and a change in the property rights; (2) the individuals are given the status of main market players and accumulate by themselves, such as individual households; (3) the government allocates the developmental opportunities in an unbalanced way to provide and create, for the following areas, the opportunities to give priority to development: the areas with great potential for developing a market economy or the areas most capable of utilizing the external market environment. Priority is given to aggregating the internal and external factors, especially the external factors, to quickly form market developmental poles and "capital bonanza"; (4) rent is set within the planning system, so that the public capital is rapidly privatized through "corruption"—the capital productivity is unchanged. Among the above schemes, Scheme (1) may involve issues of efficiency and material incentives because the state-owned and collective enterprises have a relatively strong dependence on the path; Scheme (2) falls within the scope of encouragement, but it is subject to limitations and certain developmental bottlenecks, and private capital accumulation is uncontrollable and is not beneficial to the planning within the process of marketization; Scheme (4) is prohibited by laws or is an omission in those laws; it will cause severe inequity and stronger internal repulsive forces for marketization. Only Scheme (3) is feasible: on the one hand, the process of marketization is controllable for the government; on the other hand, the unbalanced factors are absorbed—flow to the special economic zones, developmental zones and new developmental zones, so it is easy to develop "poles" in a short time, bringing about spatial institutional inducement.

China's unbalanced and spatially gradual developmental model—China's Development Path—is based on Scheme (3). Deng Xiaoping said that it was necessary to allow some areas, enterprises, workers and farmers to first receive more income and live a better life on the basis of hard work and great performance. Once some people have first lived a better life, tremendous demonstration effects would certainly be produced, influencing the neighbors and stimulating the people in other areas and other units to learn from them. Therefore, the whole national economy would continuously develop, and people of all nationalities across the country would quickly get rich.[6] This is the roadmap for China's reform and opening up and the path plan for full transition from a planned economy to a market economy. Based on this unbalanced developmental idea, the Central Government decided to launch the reform of the economic system in 1978, and the construction of the export-oriented special economic zones including Shenzhen and Zhuhai in 1979; four special economic zones

[6] *Selected Works of Deng Xiaoping* (Vol. 2), People's Publishing House, 2002 First Edition, p. 152.

were built in 1980; 14 coastal cities were open to the outside world in 1984; the coastal economic development belts took shape in 1985; Hainan Special Economic Zone was established in 1988; the Pudong New Area of Shanghai was developed and open, and a number of cities along the Yangtze River were open to form the Yangtze River open belt, led by Pudong, in 1990; since 1992, the Central Government has decided to open a number of border cities and all of the capitals of provinces and autonomous regions in the inland areas to the outside world. As a result, China has created an all-round, multi-layered and wide-ranging opening-up pattern covering the coastal areas, the areas along rivers and the border as well as the inland areas. On the roadmap for gradual spatial reform, opening up and marketization, the starting point is the special economic zones. They are the economic zones designated by the Central Government, placed at the forefront of the reform and opening up, and that deserve to enjoy the highest level of opening-up and development in China. The special economic zones are the zones that are "isolated" from the community of the Chinese Mainland and are relatively "independent", whose capital is mainly foreign capital, whose raw materials and products are mainly from and exported to foreign countries. Based on their own resource endowments, the special economic zones mainly see the development of the labor-intensive enterprises engaged in processing with supplied materials or given samples, assembling supplied components and compensation trade, with a high degree of freedom and less intervention from the government. The international market in Hong Kong and Macao is highly developed and the factor prices are greatly different, so the special economic zones have a lot of potential for undertaking an industrial transfer from the international market, and will be bound to develop rapidly once the special economic zones are open to the outside world.

(IV) The "Planning" of China's Development Path and "Experimentation" in the Special Economic Zones

The "experimentation" of the special relationships between the Central Government and the governments of the special economic zones has provided the "foresight" and experience for the Central Government to address the issues and contradictions in full transition from a planned economy to a market economy, and has created the conditions for mitigating the contradictions and dealing with the issues as planned.

No successful socialist market economy was available in the world to serve as a reference, and the longstanding institutional environment and ideology in China was incompatible with a market economy, thus the evolution of the local market and the transplantation of the external market could not become successful in old China. This could not be separated from the deep-rooted bureaucracy in traditional Chinese society and a lack of the independent stakeholders. The "Three People's Principles" advocated by Sun Yat-sen, the Mao Zedong thought that "people, only people are the motive power for creating the history of the world", the Deng Xiaoping theory that "power is decentralized and profits are surrendered" and Deng Xiaoping's "Three Favorables" criterion, Jiang Zemin's "Three Represents" and the philosophy of "putting people first" share an important thought: The prevalent Chinese traditional bureaucratic system is negated or doubted, and importance is attached to independent individuals. In order to push forward market internalization, it is imperative to shatter the bureaucratic system. However, in a clan society which has existed for several thousand years, the Chinese people put the interests of clans or small groups above everything else; in particular, the centralization of authority reached an extreme level under the highly centralized planned economic system in more than 30 years. As analyzed above, where the people's awareness and power are very weak, it is necessary to leverage particular forces to press ahead with a transition to a market economy. On the one hand, steps are taken to properly guide the "path dependence" of the old system and capitalize on the administrative planning system and ideology to ensure a relatively stable institutional environment for reform; on the other hand, the centralization of authority is used to drive marketization forward while ensuring that marketization proceeds in a planned and controllable manner.

However, the reform of the market economy is a self-reform under the traditional system rather than a reform conducted by others; the reform is greatly affected by the dependence on the path and the politicians' awareness of reform. The resulting market economy and modern market economy arising out of original natural evolution undoubtedly show certain anthropogenic deformations and distortions. For example, an important transformation from a planned economy to a market economy is that the Central Government delegates powers to the local governments and the special economic zones, but such delegation is often accompanied by the struggle for power among the governments and departments at various levels. Overall, the centralized administrative system is a double-edged sword for the formation of the market economy, and involves the North Paradox: On the one hand, it is necessary in order to achieve institutional change and social stability; as a tool for achieving stability and a compulsory "policy thrust", it must be fully controlled by the Central Government and it is necessary to strengthen the centralization of power. On the other hand, marketization requires the Central Government to delegate powers, and surrender powers to the people or the market. Therefore, the special economic zones are the special result of the reform of the Chinese-style planning system. The special economic zones were established on a pilot basis in a top-down manner, and the Central Government delegated powers to the governments of the special economic zones and granted to them the right to freely carry out pilot programs relating to the market economy, which carried out "practice" in rationalizing the relationships between the Central Government and the local governments in the market economy, and provided the first opportunity for the special economic zones to seek their own development. This helps make certain preparations and acquire experience for solving the problems in the comprehensive market-oriented reform, and it helps address a variety of issues and contradictions caused by marketization in the order of increasing difficulty in a planned way.

(V) The Public Nature of the Special Economic Zones on China's Development Path

The special economic zones have the attribute of public goods. The special economic zones are so public that they should provide the community of the Chinese Mainland with the practical experience in the formation of a market economy, and achieve rapid economic growth to become the growth poles for the induced changes. With the emergence of the "market of economic growth", both success and failure of pilot programs in the special economic zones become public goods for the Central Government and the areas other than the special economic zones. The nature of the special economic zones as public goods is mainly defined by the fact that they are experimental. Xu Xianxiang and Chen Xiaofei (2008) believed that there was a "market of economic growth" in the reform of China's economic system. At the inception of the special economic zones, the Central Government clearly positioned them as follows: making the first-ever attempt to conduct pilot programs for finding the methods and modes, which can be popularized, of reform and opening up in order to promote economic growth. However, these successful methods and modes were noncompetitive and nonexclusive, and they were public goods, while the public goods generally should be provided by the Central Government. According to Xu Xianxiang and Chen Xiaofei, the special economic zones were willing to provide public goods because a "market of economic growth" had been around in China since the reform and opening up. The Central Government was the party which had a demand for economic growth and made payments through fiscal revenue and political promotion. The local governments were the suppliers of the economic growth and got a political promotion. The market of economic growth was monopolized by the buyer, so the officials of the local governments competed for growth, and this was a championship competition. During the period of experimentation, the Central Government designated certain areas in which to establish the special economic zones, and authorized them to take the first-ever step, and separated the special economic zones from other areas on the Chinese Mainland, so the experimental result from the special economic zones was "temporarily" exclusive, and the private benefits in the results of the experiments did not greatly deviate from the social benefits. Thus the special economic zones actively carried out experimentation. Once the methods and modes of reform and opening up for promoting economic growth were found through experimentation, and the demonstrative growth performance was achieved by these methods and modes, the officials of other local governments who were competing for growth were motivated to learn the successful methods from the special economic zones in order to boost their local economic growth. Therefore, when the Central Government popularized the successful methods from the special economic zones, the officials in other areas were active in their response; ultimately, the methods and modes of reform and opening up for promoting economic growth across the country became similar. Xu Xianxiang and Chen Xiaofei (2008) maintained that this experimentation—popularization—similarity mode ensured rapid and steady economic growth in China.

The most important function of the special economic zones is experimentation, followed by their construction as the economic growth poles. How should the experiments be carried out and where should those experiments start? The cost-benefit principle and David Ricardo's comparative advantage principle must be followed. The unique location and policy advantage stimulated the special economic zones to start their experiments on the economic system from the fields where it was most necessary to introduce foreign capital—from the factor market to the product market, from partial reform to all-round reform, and gradual introduction of the market economic system. As of 1987, Shenzhen conducted reforms and experiments in the planning system, the enterprise system, the price system, the circulation system, the fiscal system, the credit system, foreign trade and the system of foreign economic management, the managerial system for foreign exchange, the labor personnel system, the wage system and the managerial system for capital construction, so that the basic framework of the market economy took shape and the market economic system was exercised in advance in Shenzhen.

The special economic zones have the attribute of being public, so the experimental results and experiences are not exclusively owned by the special economic zones, and full-scale popularization follows local experimentation, the experimental results, whether successful or unsuccessful, are noncompetitive and nonexclusive. This is because once the methods and modes of building a socialist market economy in China have been identified through experimentation in the special economic zones, these methods and modes will become part of the Government's reserve of reform knowledge, and will be ultimately popularized nationwide as decided by the Central Government and identified as a formal institution. In addition, the special economic zones also promote the development of the common market on the Chinese Mainland by means of informal institutional change—institutional penetration into inland China. As the Central Government delegates powers and surrenders profits, and gradual marketization is carried out, the non-special economic zone areas, enterprises and individuals in the inland areas of China gradually become independent interest bodies, while their interests drive them to actively seek independent cooperation with the special economic zones or work with the special economic zones on development and construction of the special economic zones in order to make the practice of the market, the concept of the market and the officials' awareness of the market more pervasive in inland China. The officials in the special economic zones invite, by means of internal linkage, the officials, department heads and company leaders from other areas in inland China to the special economic zones to learn and cooperate, immediately exerting an impact on inland China by providing those areas with valuable experience. The independent bodies which cooperate with the special economic zones, participate in developing the special economic zones and maintain business contacts with them get the first opportunity for development; they become the scattered secondary poles for induced changes after the special economic zones, making way for extensive development of the inland market.

For the special economic zones, the path to induced development of their regional economy and induced formation of the market economy requires a "high potential energy" point—an "inducing pole" or "growth pole"—for development and change. As the special economic zones serve as the starting point for the gradual spatial reform, the realization of the special economic zones' functions depends on the fact that the special economic zones really become the "growth poles" and "inducing poles". All-round efforts across the country are essential for the special economic zones to achieve rapid economic growth in a short time to become the "growth poles" for leading the development nationwide and the "inducing poles" for institutional change. Where "the Central Government gives no financial support, you must blaze new trails", the special economic zones can only rely principally on the investments from Hong Kong, Macao, Taiwan and overseas Chinese to carry out capital construction. Given this special status of the special economic zones as outward-looking areas, a win-win situation undoubtedly emerged after the inland provinces and municipalities with export and foreign exchange plans, the central departments and large state-owned enterprises cooperated with the special economic zones to attract investments. Such special economic zones as Shenzhen, Zhuhai, Shantou and Xiamen started from scratch without industry or infrastructure and with an acute shortage of capital during the early stages of special economic zone development, for which it was very difficult to attract foreign investments, while many provinces and municipalities in inland China other than the special economic zones enjoyed considerable industrial strength during the period of the planning system, thus the special economic zones circumvented the Central Government to directly work with the inland provinces, municipalities, departments and enterprises for joint development of the special economic zones during the early stages. Although this ran counter to the goal of developing an outward-looking economy in the special economic zones and was very controversial, there was acquiescence from the Central Government. This made up the "shortcut" for accelerating the development of the special economic zones, leaving more time and laying a foundation for subsequent large-scale development of an outward-looking economy.

(VI) **Reformers on China's Development Path and their Spirit**

The formation and reality of the special economic zones calls for separating reformers from the group of politicians under the old system, while the special economic zones are so experimental that there is a need for reformers and a reforming spirit: making breakthroughs and taking risks. A transition towards the market is a government-led top-down process of institutional change, and a self-reform initiated by the central group in the planned economy. This requires a separation of top-down reformers from the original bureaucratic system. The reformers and reforming spirit are conspicuous phenomena in the Chinese style of a transitional economy. The reformers are the politicians who lead the reform of the old system and are dissociated from the politicians born out of the planned economy. The reformers are pushers in the active transition from a planned economy to a market economy. In the modern market in the Western developed countries, entrepreneurs are the "kings of economic growth" (Zhang Weiying and Sheng Bin 2004), while the reformers are really the "kings of economic growth" in transitional economies like China. The special economic zone reformers played a role similar to that of a professional manager at an enterprise and undertook the dual responsibility for the experimentation and economic growth in the special economic zones. However, the nature of the special economic zones as public goods determined that the risks and costs of the construction of the special economic zones were not completely borne by the special economic zones, but were borne by the whole community of non-special economic zone areas represented by the Central Government. There were no hard constraints on the reform costs, so the special economic zones saw the act of making breakthroughs and taking risks—an act considered "bold" in other areas, even "illegal" under the planning system—during the initial stages of the construction of the special economic zones. Such an act is exactly the special economic zone spirit which the special economic zones must possess in performing their function of first-ever implementation of pilot programs. Emancipation of the people's minds, bold exploration, first-ever implementation of pilot programs, and efforts to blaze new trails with a pioneering spirit are the soul of the special economic zones for development ahead of the others. The requirement for an intensity of innovation is extraordinarily high in those zones. This is determined by the status and role of the special economic zones. This is because innovation is the historical prerequisite for the emergence of the special economic zones, and they themselves are an innovation; if there is no innovation, the special economic zones could not be established, let alone could their development occur ahead of that of the others. Therefore, the special economic zone reformers and their awareness of innovation, the background of international relations and their reserve of market knowledge become the key factors affecting the direction for and rapid development of the special economic zones, as well as the most important variables in their function of economic growth concerning the special economic zones. However, after all, the special economic zones are experimental, so the special economic zone reformers must be bold and steadfast.[7] Comrade Deng Xiaoping urged many times for the reformers to be bolder, and more courageous in experimentation, not to be timid like women with bound feet, to take bold actions to make attempts and breakthroughs once the targets were identified. He stressed that the important experience gained in Shenzhen was that the people had to be bold in making breakthroughs.[8] He said that it was necessary for us not to be afraid of making mistakes, that the special economic zones were experimental... new things, so mistakes were inevitable; we should continuously sum up our experience, lose no time in correcting our mistakes and ensure that minor mistakes did not become major ones.[9]

During the period of reform, the reformers were politicians, the development and status of the special economic zones were directly related to the political status and political potential of the special economic zone reformers, while the political prospect of the reformers was closely related to the social and economic development of the special economic zones governed by the reformers. However, the special economic zones were so experimental and politically sensitive that their reformers faced many uncertainties; in particular, with the impact of the traditional ideology, the practice and innovations in the special economic zones often met with doubts and debates; for example, the reformers were mistakenly considered capitalists, traitors and corruptionists. On the one hand, these public opinions directly affected the continued innovations made by the reformers and tested the reformist spirit; on the other hand,

---

[7] Deng Xiaoping, *Selected Works of Deng Xiaoping* (Vol. 3), People's Publishing House, 1993, p. 130.

[8] Deng Xiaoping, *Selected Works of Deng Xiaoping* (Vol. 3), People's Publishing House, 1993, p. 372.

[9] Party Literature Research Centre of the CPC Central Committee, *Excerpts of Deng Xiaoping's Exposition of the Building of Socialism with Chinese Characteristics*, Central Party Literature Press, 1992, pp. 84–85.

they affected the reexamination and review of the special economic zone reformers by the Central Government. Therefore, China's special economic zones were subject to the political business cycle. The affirmation and public support from the high-level decision-makers of the Central Government was most important for the special economic zone reformers, while correct judgment regarding the practice in the special economic zones and prompt popularization were important for the Central Government. In 1984, after Deng Xiaoping inspected the Shenzhen and Zhuhai special economic zones, he affirmed that the Zhuhai Special Economic Zone was good, and believed that Shenzhen's development and experience proved that our policy for establishing the special economic zones was correct. On the one hand, he bolstered the morale for the reform in the special economic zones; on the other hand, he affirmed the continued efforts at taking the path of unbalanced gradual opening up and gradual marketization. As a result, shortly after Deng Xiaoping inspected the special economic zones, the Central Government opened 14 coastal cities; afterwards, it designated the entire Hainan Island as a special economic zone, and announced the reform and opening up of the Pudong New Area of Shanghai, and the opening up of the areas along the border and the Yangtze River basin, so that China's Development Path to gradual, unbalanced opening up and formation of a market economy took shape. After Deng Xiaoping inspected Shenzhen and other areas for the second time, he clearly vowed to establish a socialist market economic system. The final theoretical and political preparation for fully building China's market economy had been made, and it was based on the successful practice in the special economic zones.

2.3 China's Development Path and the Special Economic Zones: Paradigm and Theoretical Framework

China's unique developmental experience and path are called differently in domestic and foreign academic circles, with common names including China's experience, China's development path, China's model and the Beijing Consensus corresponding to the Washington Consensus. There are great differences in understanding, but the essential significance is the same—all of them are used to denote China's unique path and developmental model from the traditional planned economy to the socialist market economy and from a backward country to a modern country, while the only difference lies in the discourse system. The differences in explaining China's Development Path are mainly attributable to a lack of paradigm for China's Development Path and its diversity. The construction and deconstruction of the paradigm for China's Development Path is the theoretical deconstruction and innovation of China's developmental path to the reform and opening up in a period of more than 30 years.

2.3.1 China's Development Path: The Nonexistence of a Paradigm and the Integration of Paradigms

Scholars generally believe that the market-oriented reform or transformation along China's Development Path is regarded as a "model" for the following reasons: First, historical progress has been made in China's social and economic reform; more importantly, many social contradictions and problems in China's reform have been overcome through continuous policy adjustments and institutional innovations to guarantee further reforms, so that no drastic and subversive political and social turmoil has occurred during the accelerated reform in China. Second, China's Model is independently put forward because China's economy is neither promising according to the Western theory of mainstream economics nor a new thing "foreseen" by the neoclassical research programme. As the Western theory of mainstream economics cannot explain China's Miracle or China's Model, a new research program or science will certainly come into being.

The research paradigm for China's Model is characterized by the nonexistence of a paradigm and the integration of paradigms (Lu Xinbo 2007). China's reform and development are special. The prevailing research paradigms in the Western countries, such as neoclassicism, new institutionalism and evolutionism, have been widely applied in researching China's economy in the academic circles, but these research paradigms are essentially unsuitable for researching China's Model. China is a country in transition and drives marketization forward by means of planning, and the market economy cannot be taken as the predetermined premise in the case of China, so the research paradigm—neoclassicism—fails to explain China's phenomenon. Neo-institutional economics is more able to explain a transitional market than is neoclassicism in terms of institutional formation and evolution; however, it is very difficult to incorporate the awareness of the design or the self-awareness of institutional change in China's market-oriented reform into a framework for analysis. Likewise, evolutionism or evolutionary economics seems to suit China's gradual marketization and institutional change path, but like Darwinism, evolutionism dispenses with the "self-designed" "anthropogenic" things in its research. Therefore, although the above research paradigms appear to be rational in explaining China's Model, China's reform is so complicated and special that no paradigm exists. For the disciplinary fields, given China's attributes—"developmentalism + market economy + socialism" or "developing + transitional", developmental economics, transitional economics, neoclassicism and socialist economics—planning economics—can be used to explain China's Development Path; in particular, in the research on the particular historical process of current transition and development, the research paradigms provided by transitional economics and developmental economics are the main research paradigms. For the nature of transition, the disequilibrium theory, evolutionary economics, neo-institutional economics, experimental economics and behavioral organizational economics can be considered the tools of analysis. Spatial economics and regional economics are also essential tools for analyzing China's Development Path. Therefore, the nonexistence of a paradigm actually means the integration of paradigms. However, the integration of paradigms does not mean a new paradigm and research program.

In order to understand China's Development Path or build a research program or paradigm for China's Model, it is necessary to figure out the characteristics and special nature of China's Development Path. The current widely-recognized "China Path" is the Beijing Consensus coined by Joshua Cooper Ramo, Senior Advisor to the well-known US investment bank Goldman Sachs. Joshua Cooper Ramo pointed out that[10] the Beijing Consensus was characterized by hard work, a ruthless willingness to innovate and experiment (e.g. the establishment of the special economic zones), a lively defense of national borders and interests (e.g. handling of the Taiwan Issue), gradual advancement (e.g. "groping for stones to cross the river"), the increasingly thoughtful accumulation of tools of asymmetric power projection. It focused not only on economic development, but also on social changes. It also involved politics, the quality of life, the global balance of power and other aspects. It reflected a developmental path for seeking equitable and high-quality growth. Joshua Cooper Ramo believed that China's experience based on the Beijing Consensus[11] had universal value, much of which could serve as a reference for other developing countries, it could be considered a model for some backward countries in pursuing economic growth and improving the lives of the people. Joshua Cooper Ramo thought that China's Model was a developmental path which adapted itself to China's national conditions and social needs, and sought an equitable and high-quality type of growth; moreover, he maintained that the Beijing Consensus was more able to explain China's Miracle than the Washington Consensus.[12]

---

[10]The Beijing Consensus Brings Hopes to the World, *Reference News*, June 10, 2004.

[11]The Beijing Consensus is defined by hard work, a ruthless willingness to innovate and experiment, a lively defense of national borders and interests, gradual advancement, the increasingly thoughtful accumulation of tools of asymmetric power projection. Innovation and experimentation is its soul; it is both pragmatic and ideological. It is flexible in solving problems in light of circumstances without imposition of a unified solution. It focuses on both economic development and social changes. It stresses that social improvement is made through economic development and perfect management.

[12]The Washington Consensus: In 1989, the Latin American countries caught in the debt crisis had an urgent need for carrying out domestic economic reform. The U.S. Institute for International Economics invited the research fellows from the International Monetary Fund, the World Bank, the Inter-American Development Bank and the U.S. Treasury Department, and the representatives of the Latin American countries to convene at a seminar in Washington, with the purpose of providing solutions and countermeasures for the economic reform in countermeasures. John Williamson from the U.S. Institute for International Economics presented ten policy measures for the domestic economic reform in the Latin American countries, on which a consensus had been reached together with the above institutions, which was called the Washington Consensus. This consensus included the following ten recommendations: (1) Fiscal discipline, with actions to reduce the fiscal deficit, decrease the inflation rate and stabilize the macroeconomic situation; (2) Redirection of public spending towards the fields with high economic benefits and those beneficial to improving the income distribution, such as culture, education, health and infrastructure; (3) Tax reform, broadening the tax base and adopting moderate marginal tax rates; (4) Interest rate liberalization; (5) Competitive exchange rates; (6) Trade liberalization, opening the market; (7) Liberalization of inward foreign direct investment; (8) Privatization of state enterprises; (9) Deregulation; (10) Legal security for property rights.

Unlike the research paradigms in traditional Western economics, the first characteristic of China's Development Path was the "endogeneity" of the market economic system and market economic awareness, as well as a combination of "endogeneity" and "transplantability". Such a combination is achieved by an institutional adaptability experiment based on learning. Adam Ferguson said that nations or countries were accidentally formed, but their institutions were really the result of the people's actions instead of anthropogenic design. The social and economic institutions of a country resulted from the long-term evolution and changes of the distinctive features of the country and nations, and these institutions embodied the "endogeneity"; meanwhile, they also absorbed the civilizations, cultures, policies and rules of the human society, which was manifested as the "transplantability" of market institutions in the developing countries or the countries in transition. For institutional reform, "endogeneity" means that the evolution of a new institution towards a market economy mainly relies on the national conditions, and the policies, rules and modes developed during reform, rather than on the "introduction" of the existing policies, institutions and rules from the outside world (the Western countries). "Transplantability" mainly stresses that the rules, policies and (formal) institutions of the mature market economy countries are transplanted into an immature market economy country in transition. However, the "endogenesis" and "transplantation" of the market is not an isolated process since the formation of new institutions is hardly separated from the national tradition and historical inertia of a country. The mature institutions and rules transplanted from the developed market economy countries to the developing countries, especially the countries in transition, are prone to becoming very "immature" in terms of their adaptability, for example, they are hardly accepted; the interest pattern is readjusted; the problems and difficulties impossibly arising out of the mature market economy occur; the due institutional advantages cannot be leveraged. Therefore, continuous correction and adaptive training are necessary for the "external" institutions. Institutional adjustment and adaptation is a process of making institutions endogenous. Thus, Tian Chunsheng (2005) held that China's institutional transformation was characterized by "endogeneity" as compared with the "transplantability" of Russia's policy and institutional arrangements.

Another important characteristic of China's Development Path is political unity, the leading role of the Central Government and the resulting high state capacity. This characteristic is mainly derived from the centralization of authority under the original planning system. When it comes to this attribute, Thomas Heberer (2005) believed that China was a developmental state where the Central Government had a fairly strong developmental purposiveness, a strong determination and willpower to develop. The Chinese Government, especially the Central Government, had a high capacity for development and energy to carry it out, it was a strong government with "state capacity" and could adeptly leverage the political power to actively and effectively serve economic development and social transformation. Thomas Heberer explained the state capacity of the Chinese Government in the following ways: First, it had the ability to ensure that the original political system was legitimate and acceptable to its residents. The original planning system economically underperformed in China, but the socialist political system under which the people were the masters of the country was still supported by the people, so that China was among the few countries in transition where the original administrative system and social ideology were retained, and the transition costs decreased; second, it has the capability for social regulation and control; the party and government organizations, administrative organizations, various mass organizations and social groups attached to the party and government ensured that the government could effectively control and regulate the social affairs during the period of transition; third, it was able to compulsorily allocate resources. China's Development Path required unbalanced allocation of resources and developmental opportunities, so the Central Government had to have the means and ability to compulsorily allocate resources; fourth, it had a consultation ability—an ability to consult with the emerging social groups, associations and organizations during cooperation, and strike a balance among different exclusive conflicts of interest. For China's Development Path, this mainly involved the ability of the Central Government to coordinate the relationships between the special economic zones or all regions or sectors where special policies were implemented and non-special areas and sectors; fifth, it had the ability to learn; the ability to learn in the transitional period was the important embodiment of the spirit of the government reformers. The ability to learn meant the ability to learn from mistakes and failures, and the government's ability to choose the way towards institutional learning. China's Development Path was an important way of learning for China in transition and reflected the state capacity of the Central Government.

An additional very important characteristic of China's Development Path is shown in the path of marketization and reform. China's Development Path features the following characteristic: The first-ever implementation of pilot programs, subsequent standardization or affirmation of institutions—market conduct—is accompanied by the promulgation of institutions. During the initial stages of the reform, the institutional changes first came from nongovernmental, private changes, and the changes outside the planned economic system and plan, and most of these changes were the earlier changes in the informal rules, such as folk customs and value outlooks; they tally with the inherent law which governs the evolution of the original market and the market economy, so that full play is given to the autonomy of the participants in the reform. The special economic zones are the important forms of China's unbalanced regional developmental path. The path to unbalanced market formation and opening up from the outward-looking areas to inland China, including the special economic zones, coastal developmental zones and the open cities along rivers, follows the law of spatial gradient diffusion of the market factors and factors, so that the allocation of policies and factors is smooth to some extent, not merely unbalanced and compulsory.

Overall, the most important characteristic which distinguishes China's Development Path from the transition of other socialist countries, except Vietnam, is that the attribute of socialism is retained. So "socialism + market economy" is the hard core of China's transition and developmental model, and the most fundamental, as well as irrefutable, prerequisite. Cai Tuo (2005) held that China's Model was a social developmental model of transition from a planned economy to a market economy. The socialist nature is retained, so the original administrative system—the governmental organization in transition, organizational form and rules—remains unchanged, and the high concentration of power in the Central Government is emphasized. This ensures that the transition is controllable, and prevents political secession and unrest. Furthermore, the planned economy is stripped of its essential attribute—socialism, and it is defined as a tool, so in the process of marketization, the government still regulates and controls the macro economy and works out the "plan" for transition and development, and this creates the conditions for achieving a balance between both. All this is determined by the hard core of China's Model. Meanwhile, the "plan" stripped of its attribute of socialism and the "market" identified as the transition goal jointly determine the characteristic of transition during the whole stage: "plan + market".

2.3.2 Special Economic Zones and China's Development Path: Theoretical Framework

The special economic zones constitute the important way and main carrier to realizing an unbalanced China's Development Path; they are the important embodiments and important part of China's Model. Christopher Francis Patten, former Governor of Hong Kong, said that the frightening thing from China was the new developmental model provided to the world by China rather than its hard power, and the special economic zone model deserved to be popularized worldwide.[13] As an important part of China's Development Path, the special economic zones have placed more emphasis on the institutional "transplantability" and experimentation in the formation of the system of a market economy. Su Dongbin (2008) maintained that the establishment and development of China's special economic zones aimed at probing the mode of transition from a planned economy to a market economy. This was because the special economic zones were the experimental fields for the "transplanted" institutions and the starting point for institutional learning. The "transplantability" in the special economic zones has offered the conditions for "endogeneity" in the formation of the whole modern institution in China. In the case of separately researching the special economic zones, institutional "transplantability" is the first characteristic of the special economic zones on China's Development Path; experimentation and learnability are two of the main functions of the special economic zones. The experimentation in those zones suggests a tool for learning, while learnability embodies the goal.

Besides the general attributes of China's Development Path, the special economic zones have their own unique paradigms and theoretical attributes. The special economic zones are the areas where special policies are implemented; likewise, the special economic zones are the areas where special economic policies are carried out, thus the hard core of the special economic zones lies in the power of and force to execute special policy advantages, or the disequilibrium policy. The Central Government has a very high state capacity, so it is possible and realistic for putting

[13]The Special Economic Zone Mode Deserves to Be Applied Worldwide, *Nanfang Metropolis Daily*, December 12, 2008.

the special regional policies into practice. This attribute comes from the attribute of socialism in the hard core—"socialism + market economy"—of China as a transition economy, that is, as emphasized many times by Deng Xiaoping, socialism's superiority over capitalism[14] is that the all-round and coordinated arrangements can be made nationwide and various forces can be concentrated to focus on key points. The special economic zones are the outcome of the above-mentioned arrangements under socialism. This mobilization of efforts across the country in the construction of the special economic zones ensured that the special economic zones rapidly grew at the outset of the reform and the "polarization" function of the special economic zones as the "inducing poles" was realized. As the policies and resources accumulated in the special economic zones, the special economic zones were at the forefront of the whole country regarding economic growth, opening up and innovation in the system of a market economy, creating the conditions for the special economic zones to further "induce" the changes in the economic institution in other areas.

The hard core of the special economic zones determines the possibility of special policy implementation, and more importantly, indicates its inevitability. Such inevitability consists of the situation in which the regional economic bodies during the reform and development under China's Model do not have the ability to independently self-reform and develop—the ability of regional self-survival, self-reform and self-development, called "autorotation ability"—under the planned economic system. This is an important hypothesis for explaining China's Model and an important implicit premise for the hard core of the special economic zones. When explaining China's economic miracle—building China's Model—Lin Yifu et al. challenged, at the enterprise level, the hypothesis, implied in the system of the theory of neoclassical economics, that enterprises had viability. He found that the enterprises in the countries in transition, including China and many other developing countries, did not have viability.[15] The Central Government had long-term planned control over and restrictions on regions in China during transition and development, so the regional economic bodies were "planned" and "organized" all the time, and the local authorities lacked independent financial and administrative powers as well as the right to make laws and rules. The regional bodies did not have the ability for self-determination with respect to major issues affecting the regional economic development, including the time, the direction and the method of reform, so the regional economic bodies did not have the autorotation ability and were attached to the Central Government in the reform. Thus, it was necessary for the Central Government to vigorously develop the ability for self-reform—the autorotation ability—of the regional bodies, such as the special economic zones, by delegating powers and surrendering profits with a strong political guarantee. The special policies which the special economic zones

[14]Deng Xiaoping, Decade-long Work Was a Preparation for the Next Decade, October 14, 1982, *Selected Works of Deng Xiaoping* (Vol. 3).

[15]Lin Yifu defines the concept of an enterprise's "viability" as follows: In an open, competitive market, as long as there is normal management, the enterprise is expected to obtain an acceptable normal profit rate on the market without the support of or protection from the government or other external forces; see Lin Yifu, The Challenge to Modern Economics of China's Economic Transition, *Studies on China's Special Economic Zones*, 2008 (1), Social Sciences Academic Press, 2008, p. 6.

enjoyed were based on strong political power, so the reformers on China's Development Path—the special economic zone reformers—had the status of "political man" beyond the "special economic zones".

Fan Gang (2009) held that[16] the institutional information was incomplete, the process of understanding—correction—establishment of transition goals was not completely known and there were uncertainties during China's transition, or during the formation of the market economy. The significance of the special economic zones as pilot zones was that, under the condition of incomplete information, certain reform policies were piloted within a smaller scope and the overall "information cost" was saved by local incoordination costs. In order to overcome the incoordination caused by incomplete information under the new institutions in the special economic zones as regional pilot zones for all-round reform, the key was that the special economic zones had the autonomous right to reform, namely, the autonomous right to make decisions and local legislative power. This was the essence which distinguished the special economic zones from the partial experimentation—pilot implementation—of a certain special policy. Relative to the behavioral hypothesis about the reform bodies under China's Development Path, as far as the special economic zones were concerned, as the "learning objects" were identified, the "orientation" and "incomplete information" of the reform was turned into "information guidance" and "available sources of learning"—the objects directly available for learning, such as Hong Kong, available resources, such as foreign capital. The special economic zones were the "experimental fields" designated by the Central Government to carry out pilot programs relating to the market, so, as regional bodies, the special economic zones had the right to shift risks to others, and make mistakes in a limited way or enjoy immunity in the case of making mistakes—they were not responsible for all of the consequences of failure, namely, they are experimental. With such a "tendency towards opportunism" and the "trial-and-error right", the "special economic zone people" represented by the reformers of the special economic zone governments first had the natural instincts of an "economist". This was because the market institution was first practiced in the special economic zones, and then popularized and disseminated. However, the difference with the hypothesis of the neoclassical economist was that the natural instincts of an economist—earlier expanding inner impulsion, inflated desire and pursuit of maximization—were supported by and conditional upon political power. Political backing is the precondition for the special economic zones being experimental and taking risks borne by others. Since its inception, the program for China's Development Path has been a temporary one; relevant hypotheses about China's Development Path suggest that the special economic zones are temporary, not permanent and eternal. The special economic zones do not need to pay the complete cost for development; however, from a dynamic perspective, the priority right which the special economic zones enjoy means a necessity to pay the future costs. It is necessary for the special economic zones to pay the costs for helping the areas other than the special economic zones in the future. Therefore, in a sense, the right to

[16]Fan Gang, *A Study of China's Special Economic Zones-Yesterday and Tomorrow's Theory and Practice*, China Economic Publishing House, 2009. p. 14.

experimentation and the right to priority for the special economic zones overdraw on the future. This overdraft is accompanied by return risks, but the risks of experimentation for the special economic zones are actually assumed by the Central Government or the whole country rather than the "special economic zone people"—the special economic zones can enjoy the shift of risks to others (political backing). As the payment for assuming risks, the returns from the special economic zones, including the reform experience, are shared or controlled by the Central Government. The Central Government applies the reform experience from the experimentation in the special economic zones to the communities of areas other than the special economic zones. This is the important channel for the community to freely acquire the knowledge acquired by reform.

Chapter 3
Practice in the Special Economic Zones and Formation of China's Development Path

Since the reform and opening up, the special economic zones represented by Shenzhen have always been served as the experimental fields for China's opening up and economic development, among which Shenzhen has been among the top across the country in various aspects and has led China's Development Path. Since the establishment of the special economic zones, Shenzhen's GDP has grown annually by an average of nearly 30%; when Shenzhen was a border town, its GDP was less than 200 million yuan, but it soared to 1,450,023 million yuan in 2013, 8055 times what it was before 1980, when it was established. At present, Shenzhen has developed into a modern megalopolis which is ranked No. 1 in terms of per capita GDP, GDP per sq. km of land area, exports, No. 2 in total industrial output value, No. 3 in local fiscal revenue and No. 4 in the GDP of China. Earth-shaking changes have also taken place nationwide, with the GDP hitting 56,884.5 billion yuan in 2013, 125 times the GDP in 1980. The successful practice in the special economic zones is an important part of the success of China's Development Path, and the success of China's Development Path is an important guarantee for the success of the special economic zones.

3.1 Choice and Functional Orientation of the Special Economic Zones on China's Development Path

The most important role of the special economic zones in the induced unbalanced formation of China's Development Path lies in forming the spatial poles of economic growth and institutional inducement—growth poles and inducing poles. The growth poles are divided into industrial and regional growth poles; the industrial growth poles refer to the production operation units with comparative advantages, competitive advantages, relatively strong relevancy, broad market prospects and high innovation capacity. The development of the industrial growth poles stimulates the development of relevant industries. The spatial growth poles refer to those cities or

© Social Sciences Academic Press and Springer Nature Singapore Pte Ltd. 2018
Y. Tao and Z. Lu, *Special Economic Zones and China's Development Path*,
Research Series on the Chinese Dream and China's Development Path,
https://doi.org/10.1007/978-981-10-3220-2_3

city groups with location advantages, resource advantages and market advantages, the attraction, aggregation and polarization effects on the production factors and a radiation and transmission/diffusion economy which can promote regional economic development (Xu Zhiyao 2007). China's comprehensive special economic zones are regional as growth poles or inducing poles, they are not industrial growth poles, while the derivatives—as poles—of the special economic zones, such as the export processing zones and hi-tech parks, show industrial characteristics. Regarding the attributes of the growth poles, they are characterized by continual growth, a large economic scale, a large market scale and an innovation center, and they have the functions of capital transfer, knowledge and technology spillover, and welfare compensation in the regions that have been relatively developed (An Huisen 2007). These characteristics and functions were unavailable in five major comprehensive special economic zones in China during the early stages of their establishment or development, when they did not necessarily have the attributes of growth poles. However, the circular cumulative causation among the economic growth rate, capital concentration, market scale, innovation center and economic growth rate remains the mechanism for forming the regional growth poles in a transitional economy. Thus the initial selection principle for the special economic zones was not based on the selection criteria for the inducing poles, especially the growth poles. The establishment of China's special economic zones was first based on a partial regional breakthrough in the traditional planned economy. For the selection and positioning of the special economic zones, a successful breakthrough was first made in the inducing poles, followed by giving them their functions and realizing them.

The inducing poles or the growth poles within which the special economic zones have grown are not the result of natural selection under the market mechanism and circular accumulation; on the contrary, they were built by the people with the initiation by and great impetus from the Central Government or the core layer of power. According to the new regional economic theory developed by Paul R. Krugman,[1] they result from a historical accident. The formation of the inducing poles or the growth poles is attributable to the establishment of the special economic zones—a historical accident, suggesting that if Deng Xiaoping had not designated Shenzhen as a special economic zone, Shenzhen would not have become an important growth pole in the Pearl River Delta and an inducing pole as a model for national institutional reform. Therefore, the special economic zones, including Shenzhen, were a choice made by the people as a result of a historical accident rather than the result of natural selection. Paul R. Krugman classified the initial location, the natural resources and endowment of a region into the First Nature for city development, and held that the First Nature was insufficient to turn a city into an economic center or a growth pole, and only the Second Nature, for city development, formed by the self-reinforcing historical accident—historical choice—based on the First Nature can make a city grow into a center. For five major comprehensive special economic zones, the First Nature—proximity to the developed overseas markets, including Hong Kong, Macao

[1]Paul R. Krugman: First Nature, Second Nature, and Metropolitan Location, NBER WORKING PAPERS SERIES, Working Paper No. 3740.

and Taiwan and numerous relatives of nationals living abroad—existed in the traditional planned economy. However, under the planning system, the First Nature was not converted into the developmental factors for Shenzhen, Zhuhai, Shantou, Xiamen and Hainan. Only after historical accidents—the collapse of the Gang of Four, Deng Xiaoping's return to power, the reform and opening up as well as the adoption of the special economic policy authorized by the Central Government—occurred could the First Nature play a role. The special status of the special economic zones, their position as the forerunners in the reform and opening up became the Second Nature for city development thanks to historical accidents.

However, the mechanism for turning the five major comprehensive special economic zones on China's Development Path into the inducing poles is special compared with that under Paul R. Krugman's theory (Table 3.1). First, in the special economic zones—as a reform mode in the planned economy—where the free choice available on the market did not exist, the Central Government adopted various "artificial" means, including economic planning, preferential policies, major investments and delegation of powers to build new institutional inducing poles or regional growth poles. This is the common characteristic of a country in the initial stages of transition. With the gradual establishment and improvement of the market mechanism and step-by-step decrease in the "artificial" factors contributing to the growth poles, the role of natural selection has gradually increased. Of course, in the "artificial" process of choosing, designating and designing the special economic zones, the First Nature factors, including the geographical location and natural environment became endogenous or were partially internalized into the human decision-making, directly or indirectly affecting the occurrence of such historical accidents, as the establishment of the special economic zones. As a result, although the factor—state involvement—played the leading role, the choice of China's special economic zones as the inducing poles still took into account two types of polarization factors. Xu Xianxiang and Li Xun (2005) used the regional economic analysis paradigm "exogenous variables → endogenous variables → economic performance" and found that the exogenous natural resources, the geographical location and the humanistic environment, determined the differences in the endogenous variables—especially endogenous institutions—in the regional economy, and further affected the regional economic performance. Therefore, the special economic zones were the result of policies and showed endogeneity, but such endogeneity was conditional upon or based on the exogenous variables, such as the geographical location, the humanistic history and other "social infrastructures". China's special economic zones are the natural location-type inducing poles or growth poles, so the examination of the attributes of the special economic zones as the inducing poles should start from the locations of the inducing poles.

The advantages of location are the important factors for the preliminary formation and distribution of the growth poles (Chen Rixin and Chen Xiangyang 2008). These growth poles take shape mainly thanks to special geographical locations, and special geographical locations provide them with an easy access to the outside world; for example, as Shenzhen and Zhuhai are adjacent to Hong Kong and Macao, respectively, they have benefited from the industrial transfer and economic diffusion from

Table 3.1 Characteristics of the location of three major coastal regional growth poles and five major special economic zones as the inducing poles

Pole	Pole type	Characteristics of the initial location
Pearl River Delta	Growth pole	Proximity to Hong Kong, Macao, overseas Chinese, excellent harbor, abundant labor force, etc.
Yangtze River Delta		Yangtze River waterway, excellent harbor, earlier rise of the modern industry, Shanghai factor
Circum-Bohai Gulf		Being surrounded by the sea, excellent harbor, key industrial base, Beijing and Tianjin factors
Shenzhen	Inducing pole	A neighbor of Hong Kong, the only land channel between Hong Kong and Chinese Mainland; a place situated on the west of Dapeng Bay, on the east of the Pearl River Estuary; a place with excellent port resources; the hometown of overseas Chinese
Zhuhai		A place contiguous to Macao; the important channel between Macao and Chinese Mainland; a place situated on the west of the Pearl River Estuary, and with excellent port resources; the hometown of overseas Chinese
Shantou		The hometown of overseas Chinese; a place with a certain industrial foundation and adjacent to the sea
Xiamen		The hometown of overseas Chinese; a place with a certain industrial foundation and adjacent to the sea, relatively close to Taiwan
Hainan		An island with tropical crops, abundant tourism and land resources; the hometown of overseas Chinese

Hong Kong and Macao as the developed market economies, transplantation of the formal institutions, including market rules and legal institutions, and permeation of informal institutions, including thoughts and ideas from Hong Kong and Macao. Regarding the four major early special economic zones, Shenzhen, Zhuhai, Shantou and Xiamen, the available special external resources—such as foreign capital, spatial proximity, hometown of overseas Chinese and frequent overseas people-to-people contacts—facilitated their opening up and the first-ever practice of new institutions, and they were prone to inducing an all-round government-led institutional change, thus helping deliver the excellent economic performance which was impossible under the old institutions. Hong Kong and Macao were the primary inducing poles for Shenzhen and Zhuhai, respectively, and the high potential energy areas for the market economy. Shenzhen and Zhuhai serve as the secondary inducing poles for non-special economic zone inland areas. Shantou and Xiamen are close to Taiwan, a developed market economy, but Taiwan is not an inducing pole with high potential energy for Shantou and Xiamen due to the political situation across the Taiwan Straits. Therefore, Shantou and Xiamen—two inducing poles—mainly rely on the intangible inducing factors—the overseas relations such as the hometown of overseas Chinese—to induce the institutional changes and generate economic radiation through circular accumulation for the nearby areas. Compared with other developmental factors, the overseas Chinese, as the inducing factors, are a combination of diverse differentiated factors (Huang Zhilian 2008). Unlike the four major comprehensive special economic zones that were the first to be established, the Hainan Special Economic zone has no conspicuous external inducing poles or inducing factors. As a special economic zone, Hainan has mainly depended on its own unique resources; the Central Government hoped that Hainan could take advantage of its excellent geographical location, abundant natural resources and preferential policies, without the support from the central finances, to rapidly enter a stage of high-speed economic development.[2] Therefore, Hainan is an inducing pole based on resource development, which is built up through major investments from the Central Government by focusing on its regional resource advantages and their comprehensive development and utilization.

The choice of the special economic zones as the inducing poles is attributable to the resistance to reform and inducements in addition to location. Fan Gang (2009) believed that the new institutions were first piloted in the areas with less resistance on the unbalanced China's Development Path. The distribution of the resistance to reform in a transition economy had the following characteristics: (a) The areas with less development of the old institutions were chosen to make breakthroughs with less resistance to reform; (b) The lower the economic income level was, the smaller the economic benefits under the old institutions were, the higher was the people's motivation to carry out reform, and less resistance there was to reform. China's special economic zones showed the above characteristics of the resistance to reform. In the 30 years immediately before the reform and opening up, for historical reasons, the coastal areas in Fujian Province and Guangdong Province were not the priorities for economic development under the planning system, and new construction projects and state-owned enterprises were not arranged in those areas. Therefore, whether in Shenzhen, Zhuhai or Hainan, at their inception as special economic zones, there was almost no state-owned industry; the number of state-owned employees was very small; the government exercised less control over the economy; the vested interests were less strong; the local economy was relatively backward; the people's income was relatively low; the motivation for seeking changes was high. With the adoption of new institutions in these areas, the resistance to reform was naturally small, while the reform incentive was great. Before Xiamen and Shantou were established as special economic zones, they were cities where the old institutions were relatively developed and there was a certain industrial foundation, so the inertia of the old institutions was relatively strong and the resistance to reform was high, the economic vitality resulting from the reform in both cities was lower compared with Shenzhen and Zhuhai, leading to less progress towards reform and performance.

A common or more essential characteristic in building China's special economic zones into growth poles is that the growth poles in which all special economic zones have developed are policy-initiated ones and are based on gradual agglomeration as

[2]Chen Xuewei, *Hainan Provincial Bureau of Statistics: A Survey of Major Events and Decisions since the Third Plenary Session of the 11th Central Committee of the Communist Party of China*, The Publishing House of Party School of the Central Committee of C.P.C, 1998. 294–295.

a result of utilizing the special preferential policies granted by the State to create a good environment for market investment and comprehensively leveraging their own developmental factors. The difference between the inducing pole attribute of the special economic zones and other theories of the economic growth pole is that the special economic zones did not, at the time of their establishment, have the complete and developed conditions of a market economy that were necessary in order to form a growth pole. The special economic zones themselves only serve as the "stones for exploring the path" to the reform and opening-up; many uncertainties still exist with respect to whether the special economic zones can become successful and ultimately grow into the poles with high potential energy or the radiation centers for inducing other areas to comprehensively establish the market economy and carry out opening-up. According to the growth pole theory developed by Francois Perroux, it is essential to have a group of innovative enterprises and entrepreneurs in order to build a growth pole. Schumpeter's innovation theory also maintains that innovation is the main impetus for economic development and social progress, and innovation is a process of efficient combination and optimal allocation of production factors and production materials, and this process is completed by high-caliber entrepreneurs, and entrepreneurs are the major motivational forces for economic growth (Liu Zhiguang 2004). However, the main actors in innovation were the reformers with an "entrepreneurial spirit" rather than the entrepreneurs defined by the traditional growth pole theory at the initial stage of the special economic zones, though all reform policies were innovative compared with the original institutions. This is because the special economic zones and the whole economic reform have been led by the reformers, and the reform and opening up, the reform path towards the market economy, the developmental strategy for the special economic zones, even the entrepreneur group, are the "output" of the reformers. This is because the market economy is endogenous in a reformational economy and is the goal set for a reformer-led reform.

3.2 Formation Mechanism for the Economic Growth Poles in the Special Economic Zones

The special economic zones, including Shenzhen, have made important contributions to China's reform and opening up and have created the miracles of industrialization, urbanization and modernization in the world. The success of the special economic zones is not historically accidental, but is attributable to a number of factors. Theoretically, those factors are mainly the policy advantage of the special economic zones in the first-ever implementation of pilot programs, the unique local advantage in external development, most importantly, the roles of the reformers and their spirit. The empirical research on the special economic zones, including Shenzhen, shows that the miracles of the special economic zones have originated from the institutional innovations and technical progress. The difference in the institutional innovations and technical progress lies in the endowment difference in the reformers and their spirit, entrepreneurs and their spirit.

3.2.1 Agglomeration Factors Under Special Policies

Roal Prebish adopted the Core and Periphery Theory to explain the imbalance in the world economy. He divided the world economy into two parts: core and periphery—the core consisted of the industrialized countries, while the periphery included all underdeveloped countries engaged in agriculture and specialized production of primary products, and the whole world economy was built on this dual structure.[3] Roal Prebish believed that the outcome of the Core and Periphery development was that the backward peripheral countries were economically attached to the developed central countries; the division in the internal structure took shape and was continuously intensified. The Core and Periphery Theory developed by Roal Prebish can be used to explain the "double-peak" potential differences from the domestic and world economy for the special economic zones. The special economic zones are part of a backward transition economy—a peripheral country—amidst the central countries and territories in the world economy, and the central countries and territories have a highly developed industry and world trade as well as a well-functioning market economic system, thus creating a high peak of institutional and economic development for the whole transitional economy including the special economic zones. The great difference in development brings forth a tremendous motivational force for the foreign capital from the central countries and territories to seek profits. The business operating in the developed capitalist Hong Kong is owned by China Merchants (Hong Kong) under the Ministry of Communications subject to the traditional planned economic system; China Merchants (Hong Kong) were the first to discover the opportunities for survival and development behind the huge difference in developmental potential. Therefore, the embryonic form of the special economic zones started with the establishment of the Shekou Industrial Zone in Shenzhen's Shekou Peninsula by China Merchants (Hong Kong). The developed foreign market and inexpensive domestic factors as well as the special policies adopted by the Central Government for first-ever reform and opening up constituted the "institutional peak", presenting huge opportunities for development that were unavailable in non-special economic zone areas to the Shekou Industrial Zone and all of the subsequent special economic zones. The huge domestic and foreign "double-peak" potential differences had created the conditions for the special economic zones to foster development through the introduction from foreign countries and domestic agglomeration. As a result, such introduction and agglomeration have become the important means for all of the special economic zones to build inducing poles and achieve the status of growth poles.

---

[3]Ye Jingyi, *Development Economics*, Peking University Press, 2007, p. 243.

The introduction from foreign countries refers, in particular, to the economic and technological cooperation between the special economic zones and Hong Kong, Macao and foreign countries, including the introduction of developmental resources and outward business such as capital, technologies, equipment, talents and management methods. The domestic agglomeration in particular means that the special economic zones serve, under the enormous institutional advantages, as the "low-lying land" to aggregate resources, including talents, technologies, capital, foreign exchanges and outward business, from the inland areas. The effect of domestic agglomeration is inseparable from the extensive and in-depth inland connections from the special economic zones in addition to the institutional advantages of the special economic zones. Such inland connections mean an alliance between the special economic zones and the inland enterprises in capital, technology, talents and resources. Fan Gang (2009) thought that introduction from foreign countries was the functional positioning of the special economic zones by the Central Government, while the inland connections were the inevitable inherent requirements for the special economic zones to be able to introduce rare resources. In the Shenzhen Special Economic Zone, foreign capital mainly focused on processing the materials supplied by foreign clients, processing according to the buyer's samples, assembling the parts supplied by foreign clients and engaging in compensation trade during the initial stage. From 1980 to late 1982, the foreign investments in such processing, assembling and compensation trade accounted for 88.41% of the total foreign investments, while the number of cases involving joint ventures, cooperation and sole proprietorship was not large. This situation persisted until the early 1990s. In 1991, as many as 8500 enterprises engaged in such processing, assembling and compensation trade in Shenzhen, constituting the main part of the introduction from foreign countries. However, the channel for international economic and technological exchanges was opened and the bridge for international economic cooperation was built through cooperation, joint venture, utilization of foreign capital and business development based on science and technology, the introduction of advanced foreign technologies and equipment as well as on management and concepts, and the above processing, assembling and compensation trade[4]; more importantly, the special economic zones shed light on the real market and the real developed market economy for the whole body in transition, helped identify the reform goal for the body in transition and created the conditions for the full learning and practice of reform.

Before 1984, the proportion of the actual foreign investments was not high, but the total fixed asset investments rapidly increased in Shenzhen, which mainly came from the ministries and commissions under the Central Government, the funds raised by and domestic loans obtained by relevant units, enterprises and public institutions in the inland provinces and municipalities. The main players that flocked to the special economic zones were not foreign investors as imagined; on the contrary, they were

[4]Wang Guanyi, A Study of the Sustainable Development Strategy for China's Five Major Special Economic Zones, Economy & Management Publishing House, 2004, p. 2.

Table 3.2 Investments in the Shenzhen Special Economic Zone during the initial stage (1980–1984)

	Unit	1980	1981	1982	1983	1984
Total investments	10,000 USD	27,122	86,360	18,028	33,451	62,604
Actual foreign investments	10,000 USD	3264	11,282	7379	14,393	21,050
Proportion of foreign investments	%	12	13	44	43	34

domestic enterprises which participated in the construction of the special economic zones through inland connections,[5] as shown in Table 3.2.

In 1980, the first year of the Shenzhen Special Economic Zone, the total investments were 271.22 million USD in the Shenzhen Special Economic Zone, but the foreign investments were only 32.64 million USD, accounting for 12% of the total investments. During the second year, the total investments grew by nearly four times, to 863.60 million USD, but the foreign investments made up 13%. Apparently, on the one hand, foreign capital was in the wait-and-see state during the initial stage of the special economic zones; on the other hand, the Shenzhen Special Economic Zone was at the stage where a massive infrastructure construction was carried out to create a better investment environment for introducing foreign capital. By 1982, foreign investments reached 73.79 million USD, accounting for nearly 44% of the total investments. In 1983, such momentum was basically maintained, with the proportion being 43%, but it decreased to 33.6% in 1984. Overall, the investments for realizing the function of polarization during the early stages of the special economic zones, especially at the time of initiating the reform and opening up, mainly came from domestic capital. However, the trend chart concerning foreign investments in actual use and total fixed asset investments in Shenzhen over the years shows that the special economic zone was obviously outward-looking (Fig. 3.1). Foreign investments in the Shenzhen Special Economic Zone rapidly grew in 30 years. The growth of foreign investments in the Shenzhen Special Economic Zone was faster than that of the total fixed asset investments in the Shenzhen Special Economic Zone from 1983 to 2004. Therefore, in general, the functional positioning of the special economic zone—introduction from foreign countries—did not deviate from the original direction as the role of inland connections was reinforced.

Inland connections have made important contributions to realizing various functions of the special economic zones. With the institutional and policy advantage differences, new institutions have been adopted to effectively allocate rare resources to form the "low-lying land for resource aggregation" in the special economic zones, making development breakthroughs and stimulating development across the country. One important role of the special economic zones led by the market system is that the new system and new development policies—the policies for foreign trade,

[5]Fan Gang, A Study of China's Special Economic Zones-Yesterday and Tomorrow's Theory and Practice, China Economic Publishing House, 2009, p. 97.

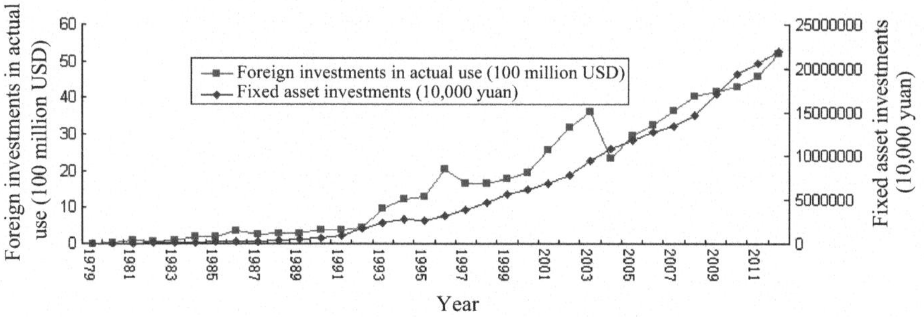

Fig. 3.1 Trend chart of foreign investments in actual use and total fixed asset investments in Shenzhen over the years

foreign exchanges, capital attraction, investment and labor employment—are used to bring about the institutional and policy differences between the special economic zones and other areas in China, so that the "low-lying land for resource aggregation" is formed to attract the excellent rare resources from the rest of the country; these resources are effectively utilized in a centralized way to the greatest extent to make a breakthrough in growth in China, a country with a shortage of both capital and talents, to spur growth across the country and do things which are hardly done in a planned economy. In this regard, during the initial stage, all other special economic zones such as the Shenzhen Special Economic Zone, mostly, attracted domestic capital rather than foreign capital, introduced domestic talents rather than foreign talents, and saw the transfer of the technologies invented but not fully utilized in the inland areas rather than foreign technologies. The role of the special economic zones consists in quickly grouping a great number of enterprises and talents from the rest of the country in the special economic zones, especially Shenzhen. The Central Government did not provide the special fiscal support to the special economic zones, but only gave policies to them; the new system and new developmental policies made the special economic zones different, thus concentrating the excellent rare resources from the rest of the country in the special economic zones. They were effectively relocated to promote the rapid economic development of the special economic zones and elevate the overall national level of economic development and the efficiency of resource utilization.

Domestic agglomeration or inland connections has or have the significance of a tool for introduction from foreign countries: More and better inland connections aim at more quickly making more and better introductions from foreign countries. The "double-peak" potential differences for the special economic zones created the conditions for the special economic zones to take advantage of introduction from foreign countries and inland connections. The climax of introduction from foreign countries and inland connections have occurred twice in more than 30 years since the establishment of the Shenzhen Special Economic Zone—one took place between 1984 and 1985, while another one occurred between 1992 and 1993. According to historical data, the total fixed asset investments and foreign capital in actual use in Shenzhen, in both periods were more than double what they were in the previous year—1983 and 1991, respectively, representing a leap. After Deng Xiaoping made the first inspection trip to south China in 1984, the special economic zones were highly commended by him. The market economy which presented the institutional advantages and the opening up which invigorated the market were widely recognized by the inland bodies in transition. As the experimental field for the market economy and the springboard for connecting the inland areas with the outside world, Shenzhen became greatly attractive. Furthermore, for the sake of domestic agglomeration, Shenzhen introduced a number of preferential policies for the enterprises with inland connections in terms of land use fees, profit sharing, registered permanent residence of the enterprise employees, taxation, product sales, importation of raw materials and equipment as well as the enterprise operation structure; consequently, the enterprises in the inland areas made investments and set up factories in Shenzhen. The enterprises with inland connections first engaged in small-scale commerce and trade, and then mainly engaged in large-scale industry; a small alliance between Shenzhen and one province, one county developed into a large systematic alliance with provinces and municipalities; the production of a single product evolved into a comprehensive type of cooperation in research, development and brand promotion; there were many production enterprises with their "body" in the inland areas, but their "head" in Shenzhen; they carried out elaborate processing and deep processing of the domestic raw materials and semi-finished products in Shenzhen, and then exported products with added value, or they researched and developed new products in Shenzhen and settled domestic famous-brand products and high-quality products in Shenzhen, took advantage of the opening up policy in Shenzhen to upgrade products and export them. Shenzhen gradually became the production base and export base for the inland areas and the national market. By 1991, more than 40 ministries, commissions and parent companies under the Central Government, the authorities of more than 30 provinces, municipalities and autonomous regions had established more than 300 offices in Shenzhen, and more than 40 large enterprises across the country had set up branches in Shenzhen, with registered capital and actual investments reaching 9.12 billion yuan and 5.4 billion yuan, respectively, and at least two million people were working in Shenzhen.

According to Fan Gang, one important reason why special economic zones have been able to gain access to some of the best resources in the country, including some that are intrinsically scarce, is the easing of institutional constraints. Under the macro background of the extensive planning system in China, the initial conditions for establishment of the Shenzhen Special Economic Zone certainly led to aggregation and expansion of such factors as population, capital and technology in Shenzhen. During the initial stage of the special economic zone, domestic rare resources were of great importance since they addressed the weak foundation and resource shortage at the initial stage. Moreover, they helped build a platform, at a higher level, for introduction from foreign countries, so that breakthroughs were made early to further develop Shenzhen. More importantly, the introduction from foreign countries and inland connections, the good interaction in inland connections quickened the building of the special economic zone as the inducing pole for a market economy, and ensured that the inland enterprises and personnel would join the special economic zone, during the stage of experimentation, to exercise the operation of market institutions. This played an important role in cultivating the excellent market forces in the inland areas, and disintegrating the forces in the traditional system. Therefore, China's market reform and experimentation is not a process of one-way inducement by the inducing poles; on the contrary, it is a process of magnetized inducement with multi-way interactions. The special economic zone, as an inducing pole, was the "field center" of the market, and it produced the multiplied radiation and diffusion effect, internally and externally, by incorporating the resource factors. The following major factors contributed to the success of inland connections and introduction from foreign countries in Shenzhen: (1) With support from the Chinese Mainland, the inland connections helped introduce a great variety of resources, offering more choices for various kinds of foreign trade; (2) with the domestic regional opening up and invigoration of the inland areas, the rural population migrated to cities and the developed areas creating an excess of population, providing almost unlimited labor resources for the special economic zone; (3) as enterprises mainly engaged in processing and the exportation of finished products rather than in import substitution, on the one hand, they were less affected by the fluctuations in the international prices of primary products; on the other hand, the pressure of competition on the domestic industry was slight and there was the composite force for outward-looking development; (4) the proximity to Hong Kong played a very important role in stimulating Shenzhen to develop foreign trade and exports. As an international market, Hong Kong has become China's entrepot trade and transfer center, and the main channel for attracting foreign capital; meanwhile, Hong Kong is also the largest overseas investor for the inland areas and the special economic zones.

3.2.2 Outward-Looking Economy in Special Economic Zones

Being "Outward-looking" is the most important attribute of all the special economic zones. It means that "both ends are in the outside world"—attraction of FDI and development of export trade. FDI and export trade have become the important forms for turning the special economic zones into inducing poles. Since the late 1980s, massive amounts of FDI have flowed into developing countries. As the first special economic zone in China, Shenzhen is one of the cities which have introduced the largest amount of FDI and have seen the most concentration of FDI, and it is also one of the cities with the fastest economic development (Chen En and Zhou Kexuan 2008). Shenzhen ranks among the top in Guangdong Province and large cities across the country in terms of cumulative number of introduced FDI projects, the total amount of FDI utilized through agreements, and the total FDI in actual use. Compared with other large and medium-sized cities with the leading position in the introduction of FDI across the country, Shenzhen ranks 5th in the total introduction of FDI, only after Shanghai, Suzhou, Beijing and Guangzhou.

In China's special economic zones and coastal development zones, industrial agglomeration has gradually taken shape by fully taking advantage of FDI. A close look at the economic development trend in the Shenzhen Special Economic Zone over the last more than 30 years since the beginning of reform and opening up reveals a high degree of correlation between FDI and economic growth in Shenzhen. There can be little doubt that as a form of direct capital input, FDI has contributed greatly to rapid economic growth in the city. In particular, during the initial stage of the special economic zone that lasted from 1979 to 1990, with capital shortage and a large foreign exchange gap, introduced foreign capital played an important role in mitigating the capital demand gap and achieving capital-driven economic growth in Shenzhen. During that period, FDI and Shenzhen's economy rapidly grew at the same time. From 1991 to 1996, as Deng Xiaoping made the South Inspection Speech, which gave a strong boost to Shenzhen's reform and development, FDI soared in Shenzhen, when the number of FDI projects surged from 757 in 1990 to 1633 in 1995 and the actual investments leaped from 0.39 billion USD in 1990 to 2.05 billion USD in 1996, an annual increase of 39.37%. Driven by rapid FDI development, Shenzhen's economy grew by an astonishing 28.61% from 1991 to 1996. With the impact of the Asian financial crisis from 1997 to 2007, Shenzhen's FDI and economic growth declined from 1997 to 1998. After a temporary decrease, with the smooth implementation of the macroeconomic regulation and control measures and the recovery of the international economy, Shenzhen's FDI showed a sustained and healthy growth, keeping Shenzhen's economic growth at a high rate of between 14 and 20%.

As foreign trade and FDI are correlated, the introduction of FDI certainly gives rise to the development of foreign trade. The special economic zones represented by Shenzhen are the important areas to which FDI is introduced and also the important export bases in China. The most direct sources of learning for China's special economic zones and coastal open cities were the newly industrialized countries and territories—including Taiwan, South Korea and Hong Kong—during the initial stage. The Shenzhen Special Economic Zone was very similar to the economic takeoff of some emerging industrialized economies in East Asia in the 1960s; for example, the export market was utilized to the greatest extent; the exportation of non-resource products was y developed principally; the labor resources were relied upon; FDI stimulated foreign trade exportation. In more than 20 years, since 1990, Shenzhen's total amount of imports and exports accounted for about 13% of that across the country, and Shenzhen was the most important export and import base in China (Table 3.3).

3.2.3 First-Ever Implementation of Pilot Programs and Catch-up Effect in the Special Economic Zones

Special economic zones have two things working in their favor at the same time, one being the so-called advantage of backwardness (i.e., late-mover advantages) and

Table 3.3 Comparisons of the total amount of imports and exports in the Shenzhen Special Economic Zone and those across the country over the years

Year	Shenzhen's total imports and exports (100 million USD)	Total national imports and exports (100 million USD)	Proportion of Shenzhen's total imports and exports in the national ones (%)
1980	0.2	381.4	0.05
1985	13.1	696	1.88
1990	157.0	1154.4	13.60
1991	194.8	1357	14.35
1992	235.8	1655.3	14.24
1993	282.0	1957	14.41
1994	349.8	2366.2	14.78
1995	387.7	2808.6	13.80
1996	390.5	2898.8	13.47
1997	450.1	3251.6	13.84
1998	452.7	3239.5	13.98
1999	504.3	3606.3	13.98
2000	639.4	4742.9	13.48
2001	686.1	5096.5	13.46
2002	872.3	6207.7	14.05
2003	1174.0	8509.9	13.80
2004	1472.8	11,545.5	12.76
2005	1828.2	14,219.1	12.86
2006	2373.9	17,604.4	13.48
2007	2875.3	21,765.7	13.21
2008	2999.5	25,632.6	11.70
2009	2701.6	22,075.4	12.24
2010	3467.5	29,740	11.66
2011	4140.9	36,418.6	11.37
2012	4668.3	38,671.2	12.07

the other the so-called first-mover advantage. The first[6] refer to the benefits and advantages countries enjoy in which the process of industrialization began relatively late. First, they can secure advanced technologies and equipment from countries that already have them through import. This is a key factor behind growth acceleration in economically backward countries in which industrialization has only recently begun. This makes possible for these countries to save on costly R & D and to avoid some of the risks involved. Secondly, not being the first allows one to learn from the experiences of those that have tried to do the same thing before them.

[6]Nie Hualin, Wang Chengyong, *The General Theory of Regional Economics*, China Social Sciences Press, 2006, p. 114.

A transition economy involves the transformation from a closed economy to an open economy, from a centralized economy to a free economy and from a planned economy to a market economy, thus the special economic zones and the whole body in transition, learning goals, learning objects and learning path are closely related to the outside world. Therefore, all external economic activities are those of learning by doing as the market economy is learned and practiced in the special economic zones, while foreign capital and foreign enterprises serve as the bond for the special economic zones to learn from. The differences in performance among different types of sectors and enterprises are the prerequisite for both transfer of resources and the spillover effect. The typical fact of China's transition is that the sectors with different types of ownership coexist and the differences in performance are maintained, while the positive spillover effect reinforces this pattern.

The learning and catch-up in the Shenzhen Special Economic Zone is a process of spillover of Hong Kong's Model. The process in which the Shenzhen Special Economic Zone learns from Hong Kong in institutional reform and transition, serves and catches up with Hong Kong in the economic development mode and the allocation of development factors is actually a process of spillover of Hong Kong's Model. The tremendous achievements made by Shenzhen in learning and catching-up during transition and development reflect the significant performance from spillover of Hong Kong's Model. Moreover, the path of the Shenzhen Special Economic Zone towards institutional transition and economic development by learning and catching up with Hong Kong's Model also makes up the complete chain of the special economic zone's transition and development from learning and catching-up to first-ever exploration and demonstration of the spillover effect. Only after the special economic zones have experienced the whole process of learning, catching-up, first-ever demonstration and spillover during institutional transition and economic development can they really serve as the windows, experimental fields and forerunners of China's progressive path towards development.

3.2.4 Roles of Self-Organization in the Special Economic Zones

In a planned economy, the planning command from the Central Government is the fundamental force for driving regional economic organization, operation and evolution. All regional economic players, whether residents, enterprises or local governments, are not fully entitled to independently pursue their own development. Their behaviors are the responses to the central planning and their own independent objective functions cannot be formed, so regional economic organization and operation in a planned economy is a typical organized one. The concept of self-organization in regions with a market economy is relative to the "organized" aspect in a planned economy.[7] Self-organization means the purposeful and active activity towards a certain goal through self-organization and coordination within a system without the effects of external factors. In a market economy, all regional economic players, whether residents, enterprises or local governments, enjoy a considerable amount of economic autonomy and can rely on the cost-benefit function to make decisions and take actions according to their own preference and utility needs. Moreover, in a market economy, the regional economic players no longer passively accept the organization and arrangements from the governments at higher levels; on the contrary, a community of interest or an organized work division takes place under common goals and interests. The interdependence, mutual promotion and self-coordination among the regional economic players in regional development amidst the relatively stable work division and cooperation under the common interests are considered regional "self-organization". The fundamental driving force for self-organization is the market mechanism. The spatial self-organization is mainly reflected in the internal driving force behind cumulative causation from the spatial behaviors of the regional players. This driving force stimulates the formation and evolution of the regional economy.[8] Regarding the regional economic players, one of the objectives of a market-oriented economic reform is to move away from being "organized" under the planning to gradually bring about regional self-organization. In a transitional economy, the regional economic self-organization and other-organizations—being organized—coexist. The self-organizing system composed of enterprises and residents follows and presents the laws and characteristics of a market economy, while the difference lies in the relations among governments, enterprises and residents. In a transitional economy, the top-down regional economic development policies developed by the governments still exert an influence, even play the leading role, in enterprise and resident self-organization. The one-way connection between the regional local governments and the self-organizing system still exists. Although it is not compulsorily and fully organized in a planned economy, the government can produce an effect on the regional self-organizing system by formulating regional economic policies, so the indirect decisive impact still exists. Furthermore, in a transitional economy, with the inertia of the planned economy, the government still directly acts upon the spatial behaviors of enterprises—mainly state-owned enterprises—and residents. However, with the gradual improvement in the market economic system, the direct connections between the government and the regional micro bodies are on the decrease and are weakening, while there are more indirect connections.

In order to expand and balance the self-organizing systems, the self-organizing systems in the special economic zones must engage in the exchange or communication of energy, materials and information within the organization to coordinate the internal organizational relationship and maintain a state of internal dynamic stability and balance. Meanwhile, self-organizing in the special economic zones must

[7]Jin Liguo, *Main Regional Players and Spatial Economic Self-organization*, Shanghai People's Publishing House, 2007, p. 133.

[8]Jin Liguo, *Main Regional Players and Spatial Economic Self-organization*, Shanghai People's Publishing House, 2007, p. 123.

continuously receive new members to expand and renew the self-organizing systems. From the perspective of the self-organization in the special economic zones, labor accumulation, capital accumulation and technical progress are not independent production factors, but are internalized in the behaviors and performance of the regional self-organization and become part of the regional development; moreover, they represent the growth mode at a higher level in the special economic zones during development. The quantitative expansion and qualitative transformation—including labor accumulation, capital accumulation and technical progress—accordingly require that the economic aggregate, industrial structure, economic efficiency and population quality adapt to them. The special economic zones still get involved in reform and reform-focused experimentation, thus with respect to self-organization in the special economic zones, the reform spirit and innovation spirit are the most important factors for economic growth and institutional reform, and they are the most central and most fundamental factors for guaranteeing the political status and performance of the economic development of the special economic zones, the common or fundamental interests of the self-organization members, and for rallying the self-organization members. Of course, the spiritual factors—including the spirit of reform and of innovation—are ultimately manifested in the expansion and accumulation of the material factors, such as capital accumulation, technical improvement and enhancement of the human capital. This is the Myrdal process of spiritual and material interaction in the self-organization in the special economic zones.

3.3 Mechanism and Path for the Formation of China's Development Path Through the Special Economic Zones

The function of the special economic zones concerning first-ever implementation of pilot programs on China's Development Path is realized through multiple channels, including diffusion of the economic development factors, popularization of the innovation system and the impact from the spirit of the special economic zones. Its fundamental goal is to ultimately facilitate the formation of China's Development Path, and guide, through first-ever demonstration, China's Development Path towards rapid development in the correct direction.

3.3.1 Induced Institutional Change Triggered by the Special Economic Zones

Institutional change is the manner under which the institutions are established, changed and broken up with time; "inducement" is a particular form of institutional change. According to a study conducted by North (1994), institutional change is a spontaneous alternate behavior of pursuing the potential profit opportunities in the case of an unbalanced system. This process is either compulsorily propelled by the government by means of laws, policies and orders, or spontaneously advocated, organized and carried out by individuals or the voluntary groups in response to the opportunities for profit (Li Yifu 1989)—there are two types of institutional change: compulsory institutional change implemented by the government through policies and decrees subject to the goal of pursuing the maximization of the rent, and induced institutional change which occurs where people seek the potential opportunities for profit in the case of an unbalanced system. Compulsory institutional change is a top-down, aggressive kind of institutional change led by the government, including the Central Government and local governments. The government has a relatively strong power in institutional arrangements, so the institutions are introduced in a short time and vigorously promoted, and the government's authority can guarantee the good operation of them. However, this institutional change is not the result of repeated games among relevant stakeholders, in which the decision-makers or the interest groups affecting the decision-making may take the opportunities from the institutional supply to seek interests for themselves, and free-riding is unavoidable in the case of information asymmetry. If the institutional arrangements made by the government are merely based on experience rather than practical needs, inefficiency may arise due to inadaptation to the institutional environment. Induced institutional change is a down-top kind of institutional change led by the microeconomic layers such as farmers, residents and enterprises. In this institutional change, the players, at the grassroots level, first have institutional needs due to the discovery of the potential opportunities for profit, and then there are or is the down-top institutional needs or recognition, until the decision-makers are influenced to make better arrangements. Therefore, induced institutional change consists of marginal revolution and incremental adjustment, and it is a process of gradual evolution in which the costs of reform are apportioned.

Institutional inducement is essentially different from the spatial transfer of industry, capital, technologies and knowledge, but the former (institutional inducement) and the latter (spatial transfer of industry, capital, technologies and knowledge) reinforce and accompany each other, especially when it comes to the change in and transplantation of social ideology, behaviors and thinking mode as informal social institutions. As the integrated transplantation and formation of an institutional environment, the market economic system is special and complex. This is because the market economic system needs to emerge and develop in a planned economy, which is opposite to a market economy in terms of behavioral pattern, concept and ideology, and it is no longer a simple reference, adaptation to and establishment of the single market rules, laws, regulations and institutions. According to the theory of institutional change developed by North, the institutional environment, institutional arrangements, institutional equilibrium and disequilibrium are very central concepts. The institutional environment refers to a series of basic political, social and legal rules which govern production, exchange and allocation. The institutional arrangements refer to the rules which govern possible manners of cooperation and competition among the economic units, while the commonly-known institutions refer to the institutional arrangements. Institutional equilibrium means the players' contentment with the existing institutional arrangements and institutional structure. The corresponding institutional disequilibrium means the players' dissatisfaction or discontentment with the existing institutional arrangements, with the desire for, but failure to, change. If an institutional arrangement is in a state of institutional disequilibrium, there is the motivation and possibility for making institutional changes. Only when the expected benefits are higher than the expected costs can the players be motivated to push forward until they ultimately realize institutional changes.

The impact of the growth poles on the surrounding areas is the trickle-down effect during the stage of polarization and the spillover effect at the stage of diffusion. An inducing pole involves two stages: the stage of pole formation and the stage of pole diffusion. In this regard, the inducement by the special economic zones, as the inducing poles, is divided into polarization inducement and diffusion inducement. Polarization inducement means the impact of the special economic zones, through the polarization of the non-special economic zone areas and the external economic activities, on the institutional change in the non-special economic zone areas during the formation of the inducing poles, such as the market inducement from inland connections during such formation. Diffusion inducement refers to the inducement of other areas made by the special economic zones through active external economic activities after the formation of the pole, for example, the investment from the special economic zones in the inland areas is a typical kind of diffusion inducement. Of course, polarization inducement and diffusion inducement are not two totally different independent processes; they are prone to advancing each other because polarization is often accompanied by diffusion. Polarization entails the inflow of factors to the special economic zones, while diffusion means the outflow of factors from the special economic zones. It is often difficult to distinguish the inflow of factors from their outflow, but both exert an inducement impact on the market economic system and ideology in the economic players and regional players which carry out the corresponding activities.

3.3.2 Impact from the Ideological Change in the Special Economic Zones

As the special economic zones had a unique status, the first-ever implementation of pilot programs first led to the ideological change peculiar to the special economic zones. Such change produced an effect on the inland areas through event diffusion and typical public praise, so China's Development Path unfolded nationwide. Even diffusion means that the ideological conflict in a certain event is expanded to affect the formation of the third-party awareness. The formation of the market economy is the formation and wide application of the market system and market operation mechanism; more importantly, such formation means that the market awareness, market thinking and the philosophy of freedom consistent with the essence of the market economy consciously replace, in the minds and behaviors of the people, the planning thought, planning awareness and bureaucracy. The special economic zones became the first to initiate the market practice, so the thoughts consistent with the market economy first came into being in the special economic zones, and were bound to severely conflict with the traditional line of thought of the planned economy in the inland areas which lagged behind in the reform. Against such a background, the Shekou Debate on ideology occurred in Shekou, the "special economic zone in the special economic zone". The Shekou Debate exerted a huge ideological impact on China at that time, it was deemed as the second great debate on a truth criterion. It was a brainstorm between the young workers at the forefront of the market economy and the most outstanding young educational experts within the fortress of the planned economy. The debate involved small issues such as whether the "gold diggers" contributed to the country and society. Yuan Geng, a prominent reformer in Shekou, said that, looking back, that debate was quite understandable; it was essentially a conflict between a planned economy and a market economy, and a conflict among different outlooks of values under two different economic systems.[9] Therefore, that was a debate, launched by Shekou's young people, which really focused on the market economy. That was because it touched upon the most central thought of Adam Smith, the father of the Western market economy,—the most central philosophy of the market economy: the invisible hand. The two contending sides did not concentrate the debate on the ideology of the market economy; however, the small-scale debate within a meeting room in the Shekou China Merchants Building, in Shenzhen, attracted wide attention from the media, triggering a confrontation between the new and old ideologies across China; as a result, the new ideology of the market economy met with wide response and was extensively diffused.

Another typical case also came from Shekou. Shenzhen's slogan that "Time is money, efficiency is life" was put forward in the Shekou Industrial Zone; the board which shows this slogan was put up at the entrance to the Shekou Industrial Zone. After 1978, although the Central Government shifted the work focus to economic construction, the people had less idea of an economic concept and a philosophy of efficiency, and were ashamed of talking about money. With his personal observation of Hong Kong, Yuan Geng, the founder of the Shekou Industrial Zone, hailed it as China's "test tube of reform", and was keenly aware of the severe harm caused by "the big pot" system in the planned economy on the Chinese Mainland which led to the fact that people did not highly value their time, and paid little attention to efficiency; the state-owned enterprises were generally inefficient; the costs were ignored in production. Yuan Geng brought forward the slogan that "Time is money, efficiency is life", with the aim of encouraging an accelerated construction of the Shekou Industrial Zone. However, that slogan immediately caused an uproar and was vehemently opposed by some people. Some people labeled it as capitalism and asserted that Yuan Geng was more ruthless than capitalists, relentlessly chasing after money by risking life. Many veteran cadres shouted: "The Five-Starred Red Flag was available, but socialism has disappeared in Shenzhen", "the special economic

[9] *Nanfang Metropolis Daily*, December 18, 2008.

zone has become capitalist rather than socialist". However, Yuan Geng, once again, prevailed over all the dissenting views and put up a huge signboard, which read "Time is money, efficiency is life", in the most conspicuous position of the Shekou Industrial Zone in 1981. On January 26, 1984, Deng Xiaoping inspected Shekou and Yuan Geng talked about that sensitive issue before Deng Xiaoping, and Deng Xiaoping immediately gave a positive reply: right. Shortly after he returned to Beijing, on February 24, Deng Xiaoping reaffirmed that slogan in a meeting: "Shenzhen's construction is quite fast… the construction in the Shekou Industrial Zone of Shenzhen is faster… their slogan is that "Time is money, efficiency is life". Several months later, in the parade celebrating the 35th anniversary of the founding of new China, the striking slogan on the float of the Shekou Industrial Zone was "Time is money, efficiency is life". So, that slogan gradually became the people's consensus and code of conduct, and was praised as the "first spring thunder which breaks the fetter of thought".

The typical public praise means that the typical successes or extraordinary deeds created under the new institutions were widely commended by the audience under the old institutions. Like the diffusion of an event, the typical public praise is conducive to expanding the institutions, new lines of thought and new behaviors concerning the market economy, and can shock the people involved in the reform by the miracles created under the institutions that were introduced, thus highly motivating the people to reform and emulate. As an inducing pole of the market economy, the Shenzhen Special Economic Zone created "Shenzhen's Speed" with the most far-reaching impact. Since its inception, the Shenzhen Special Economic Zone impressed the whole country with its extraordinary developmental speed. During 37 months, from November 1982 to December 1985, the Shenzhen International Trade Centre Building was constructed at an amazing speed of one storey in three days. That could not be seen in the rest of China at that time. That speed—Shenzhen's Speed—created in the Shenzhen Special Economic Zone, unprecedentedly shocked the slow-moving people who had gotten used to the old system. In the spring of 1992, Deng Xiaoping, at the age of 88, delivered the famous South Tour Speech at the revolving restaurant at the top of the Shenzhen International Trade Centre Building. That Building was synonymous with Shenzhen's Speed, and became the historical symbol of the special economic zone and an important sign of China's reform and opening up. Since then, the idea of speed has been more deeply rooted in the people and has profoundly changed the people's way of working and their routine of life. Of course, there are many similar typical events in the special economic zone's practice, involving various aspects of the market economic system. The column of the *Shenzhen Special Economic Zone Daily* which chose, through appraisal, the 10 most influential events in Shenzhen during the initial stage of the reform and opening up, and listed 23 events in Shenzhen, which were of great significance for the reform, opening up and the construction of the market economy across China, each of which exerted a great influence on the formation of the market economy across China.

3.3.3 Factor Spillover from the Special Economic Zones and Welfare Compensation

The spillover of factors means the outflow of capital, technologies, knowledge and talents through economic investments. The factor spillover from the special economic zones is an important mode of inducement by the special economic zones. The enterprises in the special economic zones made investments in the non-special economic zone areas, in most cases, after the special economic zones preliminarily grew into poles and the crowding effect emerged. The effect of the investments, in the inland areas, made by the enterprises in the special economic zones on the inland areas was similar to that from FDI on the special economic zones. The spillover effect, concerning institutions, technologies and capital, from the investments made by the special economic zones was more active than that from the experimentation in the special economic zones and imitation across China. This was an inducement which placed more emphasis on the technology spillover from the market economy than the inducement from the market economic system. First, investments posed competition pressure and awareness on the enterprises which "ate from the same big pot" in the planned economy. The enterprises in the inland areas were stimulated to follow the market principles learnt from the special economic zones to enhance efficiency, improving the technical efficiency of local enterprises and sharpening the overall competitive edge of relevant industries. Meanwhile, in order to exploit the inland market, the enterprises in the special economic zones had to speed up the spillover of their comparative advantages in technologies, narrowing the technical gap; as a result, continuous technical progress at the source of spillover resulted in technical improvement at places towards which spillover moved. The investments made by the special economic zones also brought about new changes in the industrial chain relating to the investments, which was beneficial to the market-oriented economic reform; for example, there was backward linkage with the upstream enterprises, including the inland suppliers or forward linkage with the downstream enterprises, including retailers, producing a linkage effect on the whole relevant industrial chain and improving the industrial structure and industrial performance. The most direct spillover through the investments from the special economic zones was training conducted by the investing enterprises; it covered production skills, methods, management skills and the quality of workers. The enterprises in the special economic zones became the first to get access to the market economy, and the special economic zones had close connections with the overseas market, so they had more advanced technologies and management experience, a more scientific financial management system, more efficient marketing and means of development than the inland enterprises under the planning system. Besides the technical improvements in the above "hardware" or "physical factors" of the market economy, the investments from the special economic zones also gave rise to the spillover of and changes in the market systems and rules. With emulation and adoption, by the inland enterprises, of the market systems observed by the enterprises in the special economic zones, including systems of contract, patented technologies, the credit system and the system for the protection of trade secrets, this was all conducive to breaking the traditional economic operational mechanism.

Unlike the knowledge spillover effect in the Center-Periphery or growth pole mode, the interregional knowledge spillover on China's Development Path is artificially controlled or guided and diverted, and largely reflects the spatial path towards the central market reform; moreover, it is the outcome of experimentation-popularization rather than the simple natural spillover. In market reform inducement from knowledge spillover, the people in the inland areas acquired not only the knowledge of the market economy from such experimental sites as the special economic zones, but also the reform knowledge of the change from a planned economy to a market economy. This knowledge needed to be adaptively corrected in guiding the reform in the inland areas; however, the knowledge spillover from the inducing poles of the special economic zones can offer the practical basis or pattern for reform in the inland areas, reduce the search costs for acquiring reform knowledge and quicken the formation of a market economy. Meanwhile, market knowledge and reform knowledge can enhance economic performance compared with the traditional knowledge of the planned economy, so the use of knowledge which is made available through spillover can compensate for the welfare loss caused by the polarization in the unbalanced reform of the "special economic zones-non-special economic zones areas".

The realization of welfare compensation is also an inducement mode. Given the priority hypothesis that a market economy can deliver a higher performance than a planned economy, all spillover or inducement behavior which can help the non-special economic zone areas acquire the reform knowledge are of the nature of welfare compensation. Such compensation may be the result of either the natural economic activities or anthropogenic factors. The compensation effect from China's Development Path led by the Central Government is special to some extent. For whatever reason, the compensation effect from the special economic zones on the non-special economic zone areas is temporal, spatial and asymmetrical. "Temporal and spatial" means that the welfare compensation from the special economic zones for the non-special economic zone areas refers to the compensation made by the Central Government for the particular areas in particular periods of time, and it is not the undifferentiated compensation for all non-special economic zone areas or the equal amount or equivalent compensation based on the contributions from various areas to the inducing poles of the special economic zones during the stage of polarization. Direct economic compensation is often made by offering more help and assistance to the backward areas, poverty-stricken areas or disaster-affected areas, such as the help from the special economic zones, coastal provinces and regions to the counties and cities severely affected by the Wenchuan earthquake. Such a function does not focus on the help-oriented inducement amidst the reform; on the contrary, it reflects the realization of welfare compensation from the function of the growth pole of the special economic zones as the inducing poles.

3.3.4 First-Ever Implementation of Pilot Programs Under the Special Policies and Popularization of the Experience

With the formation and evolution of the market economy on China's Development Path, China's special economic zones, as the inducing poles, are essentially different from the special economic zones in other countries around the world. Generally, in the special economic zones in other countries, more special preferential policies are adopted within an established, full-fledged system to deliver the local and temporary interests, while the objective of these special economic zones is by no means to popularize. China's special economic zones are experimental and exploratory, and serve as forerunners. Experimentation makes way for subsequent popularization.[10] This experimentation-popularization mode is the most typical inducement process of China's Development Path. According to Fan Gang (2009),[11] the role of the special economic zones lies in the process of first-ever opening up and first-ever access to relatively complete institutional information. This information is reflected in the process of the institutional transition with the first-ever implementation of pilot programs for being the first to make progress. The first-ever reform produces a demonstration effect across the country, while a great deal of information about institutions spills over into the country during the demonstration process; for example, it plays a role in developing the national reform policy, and spreads to other areas as the people make a tour of observation and learn from the special economic zones. The incremental information obtained by the first-ever implementation is converted into the "internal knowledge" of a country through assimilation and absorption, and it is no longer the knowledge of "foreign countries". Where the practices in foreign countries are directly learnt, the matter of opportunity arises and many things hardly tally with the domestic special reality. In learning from the special economic zones, the domestically feasible practices are learnt and the cost of incoherence is very low. The information obtained from the special economic zones is assimilated and then spread, while the incremental information becomes an important factor for pushing forward the reform and reducing the cost of incoherence as this information is easier to be accepted by other areas and across the country.

The special economic zones are the experimental sites and forerunners in practicing an outward-looking market economy. Among the five major comprehensive special economic zones in China, Shenzhen became the first in the institutional experimentation to break the traditional rigid planned economic system, shape a uniform, open, competitive and orderly market system, and give play to the basic role of the market in allocating resources. The special economic zones became the first to break the operational mode in the traditional planned economy, and pioneered in adopting the market economic principles to organize production, development and construc-

[10]Su Dongbin, A Study of the Development and Market Economy in China's Special Economic Zones, *Studies on China's Special Economic Zones*, 2008 (1).

[11]Fan Gang, A Study of China's Special Economic Zones-Yesterday and Tomorrow's Theory and Practice, China Economic Publishing House, 2009, p. 15.

tion. This includes the marketization of the construction funds of the production and sourcing of materials, and the use of human resources and product sales. In the economic construction of the special economic zones, subject to the condition that "the Central Government gives no financial support, you must blaze new trails"—the Central Government made no investments, the special economic zones became the first to follow the market principles to raise funds through multiple channels, including the attraction of foreign capital, investments made by the ministries and commissions under the Central Government, funds from provinces and municipalities as well as individual investments. During the initial stage, the special economic zones and the coastal economic development zones focused on processing the materials supplied by foreign clients, processing according to buyer's samples, assembling the parts supplied by foreign clients and engaging in compensation trade, with raw materials directly imported from foreign countries and based on some local resources; after the economic development reached a certain scale, raw materials were sourced by continuing to expand the overseas market and further extend to domestic provinces and municipalities. Therefore, the sourcing of materials basically did not rely on the allocation under the national plan. Meanwhile, the use of the labor force in the special economic zones was first free from the control by government plan targets and was fully considered by enterprises in light of the actual needs; when production developed, the number of the employees could be increased; when production became sluggish, the number of the employees could be decreased. The recruitment of a labor force was not subject to the restrictions from the household registration system and regions, with employees coming from provinces and municipalities across the country. The recruitment of the labor force was first marketized, so the special economic zones could absorb the outstanding talents from various areas under the market principles with high salaries and generous benefits; in particular, a large number of management personnel and engineering technicians from large cities, including Beijing, Tianjin and Shanghai and old industrial bases, came to the special economic zones. The products made in the coastal areas and the special economic zones were not subject to the direct purchase and direct allocation targets set by the Central Government, so the enterprises in the special economic zones marketed their products fully in light of market demand from the very beginning. As an innovative project for a system, marketization was not merely reflected in production. With respect to the performance of institutional experimentation in the special economic zones, Nan Ling, former Director of the Shenzhen Municipal Office for Institutional Reform, once made the following classic summarization by taking Shenzhen as an example: Shenzhen became the first to initiate the price reform, making the price trends determined by the market; Shenzhen became the first to launch the factor market reform, resulting in paid transfer of land use rights; the first stock was issued in Shenzhen, giving birth to the capital market; the labor resources were allocated through the talent market. Shenzhen became the first to reform the state-owned enterprises and explore the modern enterprise system for separating the ultimate property ownership rights from the property rights of the legal person. Shenzhen became the first to reform the examination and approval system, promoting adjustments of the government's functions. Shenzhen became the model to follow in order to carry out the system for old-age care and medical insurance and build up a modern safety net. Roads were carved out little by little and extended to establish the institutional framework for the socialist market economy… In 30 years, Shenzhen's GDP grew by an average of about 20%; undoubtedly, it set world records; so far, it has kept the world records.[12]

3.3.5 Exchange and Learning from the Experience of the Special Economic Zones

The process of inducement by the special economic zones was governed by action mechanisms, which were similar to those in the Center-Periphery transmission process, including product price, factor price and factor scarcity. However, these mechanisms unfolded among different systems—between the experimental market economy in the special economic zones and the planned economy in the non-special economic zone areas, so there were benefits and welfare under different systems. However, the great difference in such benefits could not directly put the new institutions into practice, but helped the sense of and became aware of the new institutions. As the inducing poles, the special economic zones became the first to carry out the mode of market-based allocation of resources, thus the special economic zones gave rise to great price scissors in product prices and factor prices compared with the prices under the planning system; consequently, the factors flowed from the non-special economic zone areas to the special economic zones, and the most central price mechanism in the market economy was transmitted to the non-special economic zone areas. With the gradual expansion of the factor flow, the pricing in the transactions within the non-special economic zone areas was gradually affected. In the factor transactions between the enterprises or sectors in the special economic zones and those in the non-special economic zone areas, the market principles learnt by the special economic zones from the international transactions were imparted to the enterprises involved in transactions through internal practice. In the planned economy, the flow of factors was completely command-driven, and the enterprises did not have the pricing power and the right to freely engage in transactions. Therefore, in the market transactions between the enterprises in the special economic zones and the non-special economic zone areas, the benefits obtained by the enterprises in the non-special economic zone areas were not more than those obtained by the enterprises in the special economic zones, and even "losses" might have incurred from the perspective of equal footing in transactions. However, the transaction factors were "public properties", so the leaders of the enterprises responsible for specific transactions were indifferent to the increase or decrease, gains or losses in the "public properties", they had the desire to become the bosses in the special economic zones. With a hope for the market, there were frustrations about their own value under the old system, and self-reflection was turned into alienation from the "planning", leading to

---

[12]Nan Ling, Practice of the Scientific Outlook on Development in Shenzhen, *Studies on China's Special Economic Zones*, Social Sciences Academic Press, 2008 (1), p. 132.

"betrayal". In this way, a market awareness arose in the enterprises with inland connections or the enterprise employees involved in inland connections. The enterprises with inland connections had business contacts mainly with the inland enterprises in the non-special economic zone areas instead of merely with enterprises in the special economic zones. With the influence of the enterprises with inland connections, other enterprises which had never had business contacts with those in the special economic zones gradually developed an awareness of the market or gained some understanding of the market. However, a certain degree of awareness and understanding does not mean that the transaction principles in the market were thus applied in the inland areas and the "community" of the planned economy. This is because that "private" inducement by the special economic zones could not be officially acknowledged and allowed unless as a means of experimentation in the special economic zones and popularization by the Central Government. However, the sporadic, "private" inducement by the special economic zones of the inland enterprises developed the driving force for the popularization by the Central Government and reduced the resistance from the old system, thus expediting the popularization by the Central Government.

The first-ever implementation of pilot programs in institutional reform and economic development occurred in the special economic zones, so there was an apparent gap between the special economic zones and the rest of the country which lagged behind in transition and development; even a duality emerged between the special economic zones and the non-special economic zone areas. The rest of the country, which was relatively backward, learnt and caught up with the special economic zones, and the demonstration mode of the special economic zones was comprehensively emulated or transplanted in terms of institutions and development, producing the spillover effect from demonstration in the special economic zones to national emulation and transplantation. This was evidenced by the fact that the people in various areas spontaneously made a tour of observation, engaged in communication, learnt from and drew on experience acquired in the special economic zones; in particular, they learnt the reformer spirit and drew on the reform experience; for example, the Party and government cadres from the inland areas received training in the special economic zones; the leaders of the ministries and commissions under the Central Government took temporary posts in the special economic zones; under the leadership of the Central Government, the leaders of various areas were exchanged with the leaders of the special economic zones; the Party and government leaders at higher levels or the reform-influencing groups inspected, visited and learnt from the special economic zones, resulting in spillover of the practical experience in a market economy from the special economic zones, inducing the leaders of other areas or the Central Government to learn or make reference to the experience from the special economic zones amidst transition and reform. The people in the foreign academic circles considered the special economic zones as "Deng Xiaoping's cadre training schools" and the ideal "training grounds" for the leading cadres to learn from the market, reform, opening up and the reform spirit. Furthermore, the contacts of the personnel between the special economic zones and the inland areas, the importation of labor services and technology exportations, the rural migrant economy and massive "immigration" aroused the spread and spillover of the market awareness and concept and their penetration into the inland areas, exerting an impact on the reform and the formation of a market economy in the inland areas. Of course, this involved a process in which the floating personnel became part of the market economy in the special economic zones—a process of brainwashing by the market. Only after the line of thought focused on a planned economy was replaced in the special economic zones could the "ancestral" market awareness from the floating personnel take shape.

3.3.6 Creation and Motivation of the Special Economic Zone Spirit

The experimentation and first-ever implementation of pilot programs in the special economic zones has instilled a spirit into the special economic zones, and this spirit can be learnt and shared. The innovative spirit of being bold in making breakthroughs and experimentations in the special economic zones is essential for the special economic zones to become the inducing poles on the path to the gradual formation of a market economy. Realizing that China's opening up and the new institutions of the market economy sparked changes in the special economic zones regarding poverty and blankness, the creation of the inducing poles was fundamentally driven at a spiritual but not a material level. Therefore, Su Dongbin (2008) believed that the greatest contribution from Shenzhen was the establishment of a new system—the socialist market system—and the formation of a new spirit—the spirit of innovation, of being brave in blazing new trails and taking risks—rather than tax revenue and assistance to the poverty-stricken areas. This was the "special economic zone spirit". This spirit was embodied in building the special economic zones into the inducing poles and the whole process of inducement. Therefore, this was the reason why the special economic zones were considered the inducing poles for transformation instead of the growth poles for China's regional economic development. In the special economic zones, spiritual motivation was more effective than material motivation. This was the reason why the special economic zones were called special economic zones rather than export processing zones, free trade zones and industrial zones as defined according to international practice.

Being courageous in making breakthroughs is not a spirit of innovation, but it is the spiritual quality necessary for institutional innovations in transformation; it has opened the door to institutional innovations, and it is the inevitable requirement for initiating reform and transformation. According to Su Dongbin, the concept of the special economic zones has been converted from a physical one to a spiritual one, while the core of this spirit is the courage to make innovations. The special economic zones no longer have the right to monopolize experimentation. The innovative spirit in transformational experimentation is more important than the transformational experience from experimentation in the special economic zones. Any experimentation has a boundary and is the result at a particular temporal and spatial level against a particular cultural background; only the innovative spirit can travel through history and into the future. Therefore, whether in the activities commemorating the 30th anniversary of the reform and opening up or the 60th anniversary of the founding of new China, the eternal theme is spirit or courage. For example, in the column "Special Planning for the 60th Anniversary of the Founding of New China: Searching for Modern China, Looking Back to Historical Moments" at Sohu.com, there was a special report, entitled "1978, Shekou People Blazed New Trails for Survival", on Yuan Geng's Shekou reform, which held this view: "The things which Chinese people were afraid of doing were done by Yuan Geng in Shekou; the things done by Yuan Geng in Shekou cannot be done today." That report affirmed Yuan Geng's courage to reform and his reformer spirit, as well as the important roles of reformers like Yuan Geng, who had enormous energy and capability, on China's Development Path.

3.4 The Special Economic Zones and the Spatial Route on China's Development Path

China's modernization accompanies the opening up, so the spatial route on China's Development Path is essentially China's opening-up path, or China's modernization path is generally based on China's opening-up path. For the significance or the objective of modernization, modernization covers both economic and institutional levels. The modernization path at the economic level is the spatial route to China's regional development, while modernization at the institutional level is mainly the establishment and improvement of the market economic system, and is the most essential requirement for realizing the economic opening up and free market economy, thus the spatial route to institutional modernization follows the spatial route to opening up. As shown, the spatial route on China's Development Path is, in essence, the opening-up path and the path of gradual strategic advancement from the eastern coastal areas to the inland areas of China. The special economic zones characterized by first-ever implementation of pilot programs, focused development and preferential development have played an important role on this path.

3.4.1 Special Economic Zones and the Path Deriving from Them

During the 11th Five-Year Plan period, China introduced a number of national strategic plans for regional development. These plans inherited and developed the developmental thoughts for China's special economic zones: designating special areas or particular areas to adopt the unbalanced regional development and opening up strategy for focused development, preferential development and model demonstration. Although these special economic zones were not called special economic zones, they developed and improved the pedigree of the special economic zones, and embodied the essential significance of the special economic zones. Compared with the traditional special economic zones, these special economic zones can be considered the emerging special economic zones. Therefore, the emerging special economic zones refer, in particular, to the economic functional zones, with the functions of experimentation and demonstration, established across China in the new period, especially the 11th Five-Year Plan period, including comprehensive reform pilot zones, economic zones for first-ever implementation of pilot programs, ecological economic zones and main functional zones.

With the intensification of the reform and opening up, the concept, significance and roles of the "special economic zones" expanded and evolved, and the special economic zones became comprehensive and diversely experimental. In January, 1979, the State Council gave an official reply to the *Report on the Establishment of an Industrial Zone in Baoan of Guangdong Province by China Merchants in Hong Kong*, permitting the allocation of the land covering an area of 2.14 km^2 on the Shekou Peninsula to China Merchants. The establishment of the Shekou Industrial Zone marked the beginning of China's Development Path. Four special economic zones, including Shenzhen, Zhuhai, Xiamen and Shantou, approved in 1980, were the first to be established; subsequently, the derivatives of the special economic zones emerged, for example, 14 coastal cities, including Dalian, Qinhuangdao, Tianjin, Yantai, Qingdao, Lianyungang and Nantong, were approved for opening up in 1984 and the national economic and technological development zones were established on the basis of these cities; the Hainan Special Economic Zone was established in 1987; the Pudong New Area of Shanghai was approved and established in 1990. After Deng Xiaoping made an inspection trip to South China in 1992, the special economic zones with opening up as their main goal were initiated in the inland areas besides those in the coastal areas. Since 1992, 34 pilot cities have been designated nationwide, with the supporting reform focusing on state-owned enterprises and an all-round exploration regarding the establishment of a market system and a social security system. Since the beginning of the new century, new regional development plans have been unveiled. The Pudong New Area of Shanghai and the Binhai New Area of Tianjin were approved as comprehensive reform pilot zones in 2005 and 2006, respectively. Chongqing and Chengdu were approved as the comprehensive reform pilot zones for a balanced urban-rural development, and Wuban and Changsha-Zhuzhou-Xiangtan were approved as the comprehensive reform pilot zones for building a resource-conserving and environmentally-friendly society in 2007. The regional development plan for the Beibu Gulf of Guangxi was upgraded to a national strategy in 2008. The regional development plans for the Western Taiwan Straits Economic Zone, the Guanzhong-Tianshui Economic Zone, the Liaoning Coastal Economic Belt and the Jiangsu Coastal Economic Belt were upgraded to a national strategy in 2009. The development plans for the Poyang Lake Ecological Economic Zone, the Yellow River Delta Efficient Ecological Economic Zone, the Yangtze River Delta, the Pearl River Delta, the Beijing-Tianjin-Hebei economic circles and the Northeast Old Industrial Base were introduced and upgraded to a national strategy in 2010. As the *National Plan for Main Functional Areas* was officially released in December, 2010, the new path to China's regional development gradually became mature. The special economic zones were turned into the areas for preferential development and focused development. Therefore, the special economic zones and the emerging special economic zones fall into the scope of four categories of main functional areas.

3.4.2 Ramifications of the Special Economic Zones and the Formation of the Spatial Route on China's Development Path

Deng Xiaoping's idea of "two overall situations" which has exerted an impact on the spatial pattern of China's institutional change is the reform-focused regional governance idea based on the level of economic development. Deng Xiaoping required that the opening up should be accelerated in the coastal areas to make those vast areas with a population of 200 million people develop quickly first, thus stimulating a better development of the inland areas; he stressed that that was an issue having a vital bearing on the overall situation, and the inland areas should take into account the overall situation; when the development in the coastal areas had reached a certain level, more forces should be mobilized from the coastal areas to help the development of the inland areas, which was also an overall situation, the coastal areas should submit to it. In October, 1989, Deng Xiaoping further explained the "two overall situations": "Our development plan is that the coastal areas should be allowed to develop first, and then help the inland areas to develop, so as to achieve common prosperity". The idea of "two overall situations" gives full expression to the relationships between gradient institutional change and gradient economic and technological transfer—the institutional spatial inducement and transfer path should be based on or dependent upon the economic and technological spatial distribution and potential difference. Moreover, the potential institutional difference can reinforce and act on the potential economic and technological difference.

Opening up and regional development are two important aspects of China's Development Path. China's Development Path follows the sequence of regional development and opening up. Therefore, the sequence of the reform-focused regional governance is the sequence of China's regional opening up and development. The point-axis opening up and regional development were selectively initiated in China in the 1980s. Deng Xiaoping believed that the opening up should be accelerated in the coastal areas to make those vast areas with a population of 200 million inhabitants develop quickly first, thus better stimulating the development of the inland areas. Under the guidance of this idea, the *National Land Plan Outline* (*Draft*) followed the theory of the point-axis development strategy and the principle of putting emphasis on efficiency and equity to fully apply and reflect the point-axis development theory into China's economic spatial layout. It also presents the concept of the T-shaped developmental axis which takes the coastal areas and the areas along the Yangtze River as the national first-level developmental axis—the Yangtze

River golden waterway axis and the north-south coastal axis are based upon forming three poles: the north pole—Beijing and Tianjin, the south pole—the Pearl River Delta centering on Hong Kong and Guangzhou, the western pole—Chongqing, center—Shanghai. Based on establishing the four special economic zones, including Shenzhen, Zhuhai, Xiamen and Shantou in 1980, the State Council announced the opening up of 14 coastal cities, including Tianjin, Shanghai, Dalian, Qinhuangdao, Yantai, Qingdao, Lianyungang, Nantong, Ningbo, Wenzhou, Guangzhou, Zhanjiang and Beihai in 1985. The State Council made the strategic decision of developing and opening up the Pudong New Area of Shanghai in 1990. The opening up pattern of the special economic zones (points)—coastal open cities (lines)–basic coastal economic opening-up areas (belts), and the point-axis developmental pattern, including the Pearl River Delta, the Yangtze River Delta and the Southern Fujian Delta took shape. Such patterns are also the regional governance patterns during the early and middle stages of China's reform.

The spatial route of point-axis opening up, development and reform are of great significance for smoothly pushing ahead with China's Development Path, characterized by unbalanced gradual induced development (Table 3.4). China's opening-up has followed the basic trajectory from points to lines, from lines to subareas, from subareas to areas to a combination of subareas and areas, and it is a process of regionally gradual and in-depth advancement. So far, a new all-round opening-up pattern—from the coastal areas to the areas along rivers, from the coastal areas to the areas along the border, from the coastal areas to the areas along the inland railway—has taken shape. Accordingly, China's economy has also been gradually marketized and internationalized within the opening up. The development and opening-up of the newly-launched new areas still follows the trajectory from points to lines, from lines to subareas, from subareas to areas to a combination of subareas and areas, and is based on the spatial governance idea regarding a process of regionally gradual and in-depth advancement. For example, two megacities—Chengdu and Chongqing—as two "points", shape the Chengdu-Chongqing Economic Zone, thus stimulating the formation of the Chengdu-Chongqing Economic Circle among Chengdu, Chongqing and the surrounding cities. The Guanzhong-Tianshui Economic Zone centering on Xi'an is a typical belt area which spreads and extends southward and northward, and then is connected, as a whole, to the Chengdu-Chongqing Economic Belt, constituting the western triangle economic zone with Chengdu, Chongqing and Xi'an as angular points. At present, the "five-point one-line" coastal areas of Liaoning Province, Changchun-Jilin-Tumen, the coastal areas of Jiangsu, the Beibu Gulf of Guangxi and the Western Taiwan Straits Economic Zone are at the initial stage of development with a point-line connection.

Table 3.4 Temporal and spatial sequence of reform-focused regional governance on China's development path

Time	Special zones and ramifications	Functions	Space
1979	Shekou industrial zone	Opening up, experimentation, development	Coastal
1980	Shenzhen, Zhuhai, Shantou, Xiamen pilot special economic zones	Opening up, experimentation, development	Coastal
1984	Coastal open cities	Opening up	Coastal
1984	A decision was made to launch economic and technological development zones	Development	Coastal
1985	The Yangtze River Delta, the Pearl River Delta, the Southern Fujian Delta were designated as the coastal open economic zones	Opening up, development	Coastal
1985	The Shenzhen Science and Technology Industrial Park was established in Shenzhen	Reform, experimentation	Coastal
1988	Hainan became the largest special economic zone in the country	Opening up, development, experimentation	Coastal
1988	The Circum-Bohai-Sea open zone took shape	Opening up	Coastal
1988	The establishment of national high-tech zones was approved	Reform, experimentation	Coastal
1990	The State Council announced the development and opening up of the Pudong New Area	Development, opening up	Coastal
1990	The first bonded zone in China was established	Opening up	Coastal
1992	Five cities, including Wuhu along the banks of the Yangtze River, were opened	Opening up	Along rivers
1992	21 inland provincial capitals, including Hefei were opened	Opening up	Inland
1992	Inland cities along the border, including Heihe were opened	Opening up	Northeastern (along the border)
1994	The establishment of the China-Singapore Suzhou Industrial Park was approved	Opening up, reform	Coastal
1996	The Shenzhen Yantian Bonded Zone, the Zhuhai Bonded Zone were established	Opening up	Coastal

(continued)

Table 3.4 (continued)

Time	Special zones and ramifications	Functions	Space
2000	The establishment of an export processing zone was approved	Opening up	Nationwide
2003	*Closer Economic Partnership Arrangement (CEPA) between the Chinese Mainland and Hong Kong, Macao* was signed	Opening up, development	Nationwide
2004	The integration of bonded zones and ports was carried out	Opening up	Coastal
2005	The Pudong New Area of Shanghai was approved to carry out the pilot comprehensive reform for improving the socialist market economic system	Reform, experimentation	Coastal
2005	The establishment of the Yangshan Bonded Port Area of Shanghai was approved	Opening up	Coastal
2006	The State Council pushed forward the development and opening up of the Binhai New Area	Reform, experimentation	Coastal
2007	The first comprehensive bonded zone was officially completed	Opening up, reform	Coastal
	The agreement concerning the Sino-Singapore Tianjin Eco-city Project was signed	Opening up, reform, experimentation	Coastal
	Chongqing was designated as the national comprehensive reform pilot zone for balanced urban-rural development	Reform, experimentation	Southwestern
	Chengdu was designated as the national comprehensive reform pilot zone for balanced urban-rural development	Reform, experimentation	Southwestern
	The Wuhan City Circle was designated as the national comprehensive reform pilot zone for building an energy-conserving and environmentally-friendly society	Reform, experimentation	Central

(continued)

Table 3.4 (continued)

Time	Special zones and ramifications	Functions	Space
	Changsha-Zhuzhou-Xiangtan was designated as the national comprehensive reform pilot zone for building an energy-conserving and environmentally-friendly society	Reform, experimentation	Central
2008	The Beibu Gulf Economic Zone of Guangxi	Opening up, development	Western
	Guiding Opinions Concerning Further Promoting the Reform, Opening Up, Economic and Social Development in the Yangtze River Delta	Reform, opening up	Coastal
	The Binhai New Area of Tianjin was designated as the comprehensive reform demonstration zone	Reform	Eastern
2009	The Western Taiwan Straits Economic Zone	Opening up, development	Coastal
	Jiangsu coastal areas	Development, reform	Coastal
	The Guanzhong-Tianshui Economic Zone	Development	Northwestern
	The Liaoning Coastal Economic Belt	Development	Northeastern
	The Hengqin New Area	Opening up, development, experimentation	Coastal
	The Changchun-Jilin-Tumen Development and Opening Up Forerunner Zone	Development	Northeastern
	The Reform and Development Plan for the Pearl River Delta Region (2008–2020)	Reform, opening up	Coastal
	The Development Plan for the Yellow River Delta Efficient Ecological Economic Zone	Development, experimentation	Coastal
	The Development Plan for the Poyang Lake Ecological Economic Zone	Development, experimentation	Central
	The Development Plan for the Wanjiang City Belt Demonstration Zone for Undertaking Industrial Transfer	Development, experimentation	Central

(continued)

Table 3.4 (continued)

Time	Special zones and ramifications	Functions	Space
	The Shenzhen Pilot Comprehensive Reform	Reform	Eastern
2010	The Hainan International Tourism Island	Development, experimentation	Island
	The Chongqing Xiyong Comprehensive Bonded Zone	Opening up	Western
	The Liangjiang New Area of Chongqing	Opening up, development	Western
2011	*The Plan for the Central Plains Economic Region*	Development	Central
	The Shandong Peninsula Blue Economic Zone	Development	Eastern
	The Regional Plan for the Chengdu-Chongqing Economic Zone	Development	Western
	The Zhejiang Marine Economic Development Demonstration Zone	Development	Eastern
	The Shenyang Economic Zone was designated as the national comprehensive reform demonstration zone for new-type industrialization	Reform	Northeastern
	Pilot comprehensive reform for international trade in Yiwu City	Reform	Eastern
	The Zhoushan Islands New Area	Development	Eastern
2012	The China Tumen River Regional (Huichun) International Cooperation Demonstration Zone	Development, opening up	Northeastern
	The Wenzhou Financial Comprehensive Reform Pilot Zone	Reform	Eastern
2013	The China (Shanghai) Pilot Free Trade Zone	Opening up	Eastern

3.4.3 Changes in the Spatial Route on China's Development Path

(I) The Areas Along the North-to-South Coastline Starting from the Special Economic Zones

The eastern coastal areas are the forefront of China's opening up, while Hong Kong, Macao and Taiwan are the "bridgehead" for it and the "springboard" for getting access to the world market. In particular, as the international financial center, Hong Kong is an international "market pole" and a "radiation source". Therefore, the breakthrough in China's opening up was first made in the southeastern coastal areas. In August, 1980, the establishment of the four special economic zones, including Shenzhen, Zhuhai and Shantou of Guangdong Province, Xiamen of Fujian was officially approved during the 15th session of the 5th Standing Committee of the National People's Congress. In 30 years, as the connection points or bridges between domestic and international markets, the special economic zones have served as the "second transmitter" in the development of the outward-looking economy. In particular, as the "south pole" for the market economy on the Chinese Mainland, Shenzhen contributed a lot. Based on the significant achievements made in the four special economic zones, in 1988, the State Council decided to designate Hainan as the fifth special economic zone and adopt more flexible policies in it, and to expand the area of the other four special economic zones. As the first step for the opening up, the special economic zones constitute the first level of China's Development Path. From points to lines on this basis, the Chinese Government decided in May, 1984 to open 14 coastal port cities, including Dalian, Qinghuangdao, Tianjin, Yantai, Qingdao, Lianyungang, Nantong, Shanghai, Ningbo, Wenzhou, Fuzhou, Guangzhou, Zhanjiang and Beihai. The areas beyond Shantou, the Zhuhai and Xiamen special economic zones and Wenhai urban areas also enjoyed the same preferential treatment as those cities. Meanwhile, 14 economic and technological development zones were established in those open coastal cities. In 1992, the State Council approved six additional development zones, including Wenzhou, Kunshan, Weihai, Yingkou and Dongshan. As a result, there were 20 national-level coastal development zones called "small special economic zones". Based on establishing the economic and technological development zones in the open coastal cities, in early 1985, the government further decided to designate the Yangtze River Delta, the Pearl River Delta, the Southern Fujian Xiamen-Zhangzhou-Quanzhou Delta as open coastal economic zones. In 1988, the open coastal zones were expanded to Jiaodong Peninsula and Liaodong Peninsula. So far, from lines to subareas, a north-to-south long and wide open belt has taken shape in China's eastern coastal areas. This belt includes 11 coastal provinces, 292 cities and counties by or near the sea, covering an area of 41.7 km^2, accounting for 4.4% of the total national area, with a population of 210 million, accounting for nearly 20% of the total national population. It is the forefront of China's opening up.

(II) The East-to-West Areas Along the Yangtze River

In the 1990s, based on further opening up and development and on the intensification of marketization in the coastal areas, the Central Government attached importance to the opening up and development of the inland areas, and gradually shifted the focus of opening up and market-oriented reform from the Pearl River Delta to the Yangtze River Delta and the Yangtze River Basin. In April, 1990, the Central Government decided to open and develop the Pudong New Area of Shanghai. The Pudong New Area was directly opened to Europe, the USA, Japan and the whole world. The special policies available in the economic and technological development zones, the special economic zones and some special policies necessary for the development of Pudong were adopted in the Pudong New Area. Pudong's opening up and development aimed at re-invigorating Shanghai and rebuilding the international metropolis—turning Shanghai into the flagship of the Yangtze River Basin, one of the international economic, financial and trade centers. With a strong boost from the new development and opening up of Pudong, Shanghai has fully leveraged its advantages in establishing a modern market system. In a few short years, Shanghai built a large market framework based in Shanghai, influencing the whole country and connecting the world. Shanghai has seen the establishment and development of eight major national exchanges covering metal, coal, petroleum, grain and oil, agricultural materials, chemicals, automobiles and building materials, and the establishment of the China Foreign Exchange Trade System, urban-rural equity exchanges and other trading markets. With the formation of these large market patterns, in fact, the focus of China's economic development, reform and opening up has shifted from the southern Pearl River Delta to the Yangtze River Delta centering on Shanghai. Two years after Pudong's opening up and development, the State Council announced the opening up of five cities along the banks of the Yangtze River, including Wuhu, Jiujiang, Wuhan, Yueyang and Chongqing, and the adoption of the open coastal city policy in these cities, and made it clear that, with the approval of the State Council, more development zones could be built in the areas where conditions permitted. In 1992, the Three Gorges Project stimulated the opening up and development of the middle and upper reaches of the Yangtze River. So far, the open coastal city policy has been implemented in more than 10 major cities in the Yangtze River Basin, including Suzhou, Wuxi, Changzhou, Nantong, Nanjing, Zhenjiang, Yangzhou in the lower reaches, and 9 ports have been opened to shape an open belt, with Pudong of Shanghai as the flagship, in the Yangtze River Basin. This policy has vigorously promoted the modernization and marketization of three major regions: the eastern, central and western regions of China.

(III) The Areas from Inland to the Border

Since Deng Xiaoping inspected South China and delivered the famous South Tour Speech in the spring of 1992, China's opening up and marketization have been intensified. In order to strengthen and expand the cooperation with the surrounding countries, the State Council decided to open 13 border cities, counties and towns, including Huichun, Suifenhe, Heihe, Manzhouli, Erenhot, Yining, Tacheng, Bole, Hekou,

Wanding, Ruili, Pingxiang and Dongxing. These open border cities have enjoyed preferential policies that are basically the same as those in the open coastal cities, forming a pattern of opening up along the border. Meanwhile, the Central Government further designated all inland provincial capitals, including Harbin, Changchun, Hohhot, Shijiazhuang, Taiyuan, Hefei, Nanchang, Zhengzhou, Changsha, Chengdu, Guizhou, Xi'an, Lanzhou, Xining and Yinchuan, as open inland cities, and introduced, in these cities, the same preferential policies as those in the open coastal cities. Industrial development zones with high and new technology have been established in most of these cities; furthermore, an economic and technological development zone can also be built in each of these cities where conditions permit. So far, a new pattern of all-round multi-level opening up has basically taken shape in China. With gradual regional opening up, the introduction of foreign capital and foreign trade exports have vigorously carried forward gradual regional reform and opening up.

(IV) All-round Development and Opening up: Development of Western China, Revitalization of Northeastern China and the Rise of Central China

The *Recommendations of the Central Committee of the Communist Party of China for the 10th Five-Year National Plan for Economic and Social Development*, adopted during the 5th Plenary Session of the 15th Central Committee of the Communist Party of China in October, 2000, identified the development of western China and the promotion of coordinated regional development as a strategic task. The development of western China covers 12 provinces, autonomous regions and municipalities directly under the Central Government, including Chongqing, Sichuan, Guizhou, Yunnan, Tibet Autonomous Region, Shaanxi, Gansu, Qinghai, Ningxia Hui Autonomous Region, Xinjiang Uygur Autonomous Region, Inner Mongolia Autonomous Region and Guangxi Zhuang Autonomous Region. On September 10, 2003, the State Council convened an executive meeting to study the implementation of the strategy for revitalizing the old industrial bases, including the region of northeastern China, and outlined the guiding thoughts, principles, tasks and policy measures for revitalizing Northeast China. In October, 2003, the Central Committee of the Communist Party of China and the State Council issued *Several Opinions Concerning Revitalization of Old Industrial Bases Including the Northeast China Region*. In response to the relatively slow development in Shanxi, Anhui, Jiangxi, Henan, Hubei and Hunan in central China, in April, 2006, the State Council issued *Several Opinions Concerning Promoting the Rise of Central China*, which included 36 policy measures and stated efforts to turn central China into a nationally-important base for the production of grain, a base for energy raw materials, modern equipment manufacturing and high-tech industry, as well as a comprehensive transportation hub. A relatively complete set of regional developmental strategies for the upsurge of eastern China, the development of western China, the revitalization of northeastern China and the rise of central China came into being. The implementation of these strategies was an improvement in and a supplement to the unbalanced regional reform and development in China. It corrected and compensated for the imbalance caused by the first-ever implementation of preferential policy in the coastal areas during the preliminary stages of the reform. However, the development of western China, the revitalization of northeastern China and the rise of central China are merely the industry-driven regional developmental modes, rather than efforts towards achieving the regional strategic goals through the growth poles of key development areas on China's Development Path. The development of western China and the rise of central China meant that the Central Government was launching key construction projects in western China and central China to drive local economic development forward. As the Pudong New Area of Shanghai, the Binhai New Area of Tianjin, Chengdu-Chongqing had been upgraded to comprehensive reform pilot zones, and various types of regional development zones had been approved to be incorporated into the strategies for the upsurge of eastern China, the development of western China, the revitalization of northeastern China and the rise of central China in the past 1–2 years, the regional developmental strategies on China's Development Path have begun again. Various ramifications of the special economic zones on China's Development Path in recent years have materialized this overall roadmap; in particular, the national comprehensive reform pilot zones and the economic development zones upgraded to a national strategy have mirrored China's strategic thoughts regarding regional development in the new period.

Since the beginning of the new period, especially the whole 11th Five-Year Plan period and the 12th Five-Year Plan period, the strategies of China's Development Path have been upgraded more quickly. The upgrading of the Pudong New Area of Shanghai, the Binhai New Area of Tianjin and Shenzhen to comprehensive reform pilot zones in the socialist market economy country is the giving of a special economic zone function involving first-ever implementation of pilot programs amidst the improvement of the socialist market economic system during the stage of intensification of the reform. Such upgrading guarantees the regional developmental strategy for the upsurge of eastern China. It reinforces and improves the three existing coastal economic growth poles: the Yangtze River Delta, the Circum-Bohai Sea Region and the Pearl River Delta. The Central Government has unveiled several medium and long-term regional plans, including the *Guiding Opinions Concerning Further Promoting the Reform, Opening Up, Economic and Social Development in the Yangtze River Delta*, the *Reform and Development Plan for the Pearl River Delta Region (2008–2020)* and the *Regional Plan for the Beijing, Tianjin and Hebei Metropolitan Circle*. The Jiangsu coastal areas, the Western Taiwan Straits Economic Zone, the Zhuhai Hengqin New Area, Shenzhen Qianwan are the important parts of the regional governance design for the upsurge of eastern China. The designation of Chengdu and Chongqing as the national comprehensive reform pilot zones for a balanced urban-rural development, the upgrading of the Guanzhong-Tianshui Economic Zone to a national strategy, the designation of Xi'an as a national comprehensive reform pilot zone for the coordination of scientific and technological resources, the opening up and development of the Beibu Gulf of Guangxi regard the regional governance design of China's Development Path for the development of western China in the new period. The inclusion of the Wuhan City Circle and Changsha-Zhuzhou-Xiangtan into the national comprehensive reform pilot zones for building a resource-conserving and an environmentally-friendly society is an important move for the rise of central

China. The recently-approved regional development zones, including the Liaoning Coastal Economic Belt and the Changchun-Jilin-Tumen Development and Opening Up Forerunner Zone, as well as the plan for the revitalization of the old industrial base in northeastern China constitute the strategic intent to revitalize northeastern China. In particular, since the State Council approved, in 2009, eight regional development plans, including the *Reform and Development Plan for the Pearl River Delta Region (2008–2020)*, the *Several Opinions Concerning Supporting Fujian Province to Accelerate the Construction of the Western Taiwan Straits Economic Zone*, the *Development Plan for the Guanzhong-Tianshui Economic Zone*, the *Development Plan for the Jiangsu Coastal Areas*, the *Overall Development Plan for Hengqin*, the *Development Plan for the Liaoning Coastal Economic Belt*, the *Plan Outline for the Cooperative Development of the Tumen River Region, China*, the *Plan for Promoting the Rise of Central China*, China's new regional economic patterns have gradually taken shape, including the Yangtze River Delta, the Pearl River Delta, Beibu Gulf, the Circum-Bohai-Sea, the west coast of the Taiwan Straits, three provinces in northeastern China, central China and western China. Meanwhile, the regional economic plans have been newly introduced in various areas, such as the Huaihai Economic Zone, Tangshan Bay in the Circum-Bohai-Sea region, the western triangle economic circle, the Yellow River Delta Economic Zone, the Poyang Lake Ecological Economic Zone and the Liangjiang New Area of Chongqing. This shows that China has entered the historical stage of all-round construction and improvement of the socialist market economy. This also indicates that China's regional development and opening up pattern has increasingly improved and become clear in the new period, and the spatial route on China's Development Path has ultimately taken shape.

Chapter 4
Theoretical Contributions of the Special Economic Zones to China's Development Path

Brilliant economic achievements have been made in China in more than 30 years of reform and opening up. The GDP has grown rapidly in consecutive years, the people's enthusiasm for production has been continuously aroused, and the levels of living and wealth have dramatically increased. The efficiency of resource allocation in the market has significantly improved. Enterprises have been ceaselessly vitalized in production, creating huge material wealth. The government has gradually identified its own boundary and functions. The macroeconomic regulation and control means have become increasingly diverse, ensuring rapid, orderly and stable economic growth in China. With these economic achievements, China's development path towards modernization with distinctive characteristics is gradually taking shape. As the outcome of special policies, the special economic zones are the experimental fields and forerunners in China's reform and opening up. The special economic zones have explored at a practical level and have become the first to build a path towards modernization that is fit for China's development, and have made important theoretical contributions to gradually forming China's Development Path. These theoretical contributions mainly cover the following three levels: First, the practice in the special economic zones has helped determine the direction of market-oriented reform in China; the socialist market economic theory has been successfully practiced and experimented with in the special economic zones, laying a solid foundation for building, developing and improving that new theory; second, the special economic zones have enriched the property rights theory of the socialist market economy, affirmed that public ownership remains the mainstay and that multiple forms of ownership develop side by side; the flow of production factors has been promoted in the special economic zones to form a labor market, and the distribution theory, that is the work-based distribution and the distribution made according to production factors complement each other, has been developed; third, the special economic zones have become the first to clarify the boundary between the government and the market, shape the modern governmental structure, transform the government from an omnipotent entity into a

© Social Sciences Academic Press and Springer Nature Singapore Pte Ltd. 2018
Y. Tao and Z. Lu, *Special Economic Zones and China's Development Path*,
Research Series on the Chinese Dream and China's Development Path,
https://doi.org/10.1007/978-981-10-3220-2_4

service-oriented one, eliminate the administrative intervention in the microeconomic units on the market, emphasize macroeconomic regulation and control, and clearly pinpoint the government's functions under a socialist market economic system.

4.1 Contributions from the Special Economic Zones to China's Socialist Market Economic Theory

Since the founding of new China, the experimentation regarding China's economic system has covered several different stages: the planned economy was first practiced, followed by the adoption of the planned economy as the mainstay with the market economy as a supplement, equal emphasis on both economic forms, and the planned commodity economy, until the socialist market economic system was ultimately established. Apparently, that was not a smooth process. In that process, China experienced two heated national debates—one focused on whether or not to initiate the reform and opening up; the other one involved the nature of the reform and opening up. In both debates, the special status and roles of the special economic zones could not be overlooked. After comrade Deng Xiaoping, the chief architect of the reform and opening up, inspected the special economic zones twice, with careful consideration and a group discussion by the Party Central Committee for pooling the wisdom, the direction of market-oriented reform was ultimately upheld, and the socialist market economic system was established. In that process, the socialist market economic theory was gradually developed.

4.1.1 The Direction of the Market-Oriented Reform Was Established in the Special Economic Zones

The socialist political economic system was established and the planned economic system was practiced during the initial stage of new China, during which stage the planned economic system was conducive to China's stability and development; however, with the economic and social development in China, the disadvantages of the planned economic system loomed large; with a deeper understanding of the traditional planned economic system, the market elements were gradually introduced into the reform of our economic system, and being market-oriented, it became dominant. Under the compulsive institutional arrangement made by the Central Government, as the outcome of the special policies, the special economic zones emerged and were charged with the important mission of breaking the ideological and practical fetter of the original planned economic system and blazing new trails. The special economic zones met the people's expectations as the market-based regulation mechanism was established at their inception, a relatively well-functioning market system took shape and huge achievements were made in the special economic zones. This also established the overall direction for the reform of China's economic system.

After ten chaotic years and the downfall of the Gang of Four, the Party and the government gradually shifted the focus of their work to economic construction; in particular, the Party and the government launched the national debate on the truth criterion and reestablished the ideological line of emancipating the people's minds and seeking truth from facts. At that time, comrade Deng Xiaoping sharply pointed out that China's fundamental problem consisted in institutions. When the people are subject to great ideological shackles, the emancipation of their minds and the exploration of the institutional change and transitional path is exactly the general background for establishing the special economic zones. The special economic zones emerged and grew along with the reform and opening up. The people's doubts and debates about the reform and opening up inevitably touched upon the establishment and development of those zones. The national debate on the establishment of those zones spurred the whole party and the people across the country to emancipate their minds and clarify the direction of the reform.

Comrade Deng Xiaoping first vowed to fully and accurately understand Mao Zedong's Thought and stressed that seeking truth from facts was the quintessence of Mao Zedong's Thought, so as to ideologically bring order out of chaos. The predecessors of the proletarian revolution also gradually, from different perspectives, made it clear that it was necessary to restore and carry forward the fine style of work of seeking truth from facts and considering practice as the sole criterion for testing truth. In 1978, an extensive debate on the truth criterion was carried out nationwide. That debate broke the ideological fetter of the "two whatevers"—"we will resolutely uphold whatever policy decisions Chairman Mao made, and unswervingly follow whatever instructions Chairman Mao gave", pushed forward ideological emancipation across the country, making important ideological preparations for convening the Third Plenary Session of the 11th Central Committee of the Communist Party of China and providing the ideological guarantee for establishing the special economic zones.

It is widely believed that the first debate on reform occurred in the early 1980s and focused on the relationship between planning and the market. The Third Plenary Session of the 11th Central Committee of the Communist Party of China, convened in 1978, marked the beginning of China's reform. That session opened a new chapter for the reform and opening up. Although the decision about the reform and opening up had already been made, Deng Xiaoping's reform proposition still met with many controversies and difficulties; for example, the target institutions towards which the reform was carried out were vague and the reform path was unclear; breaking the old system called for conquering the barriers created by the people with vested interests; the continuity of economic and social development should be maintained along with the breaking up of the old system.

Faced with difficulties, Deng Xiaoping adopted the move of "crossing the river by feeling the stones" and "taking one step and looking around before taking another". In the meantime, he was also keenly aware that the reform exploration and experimentation were unprecedented, that partial failure and chaos were unavoidable; that was the price which had to be paid in order to go ahead with the reform. Deng Xiaoping envisioned that the reform could not have been finished overnight since development and stability had to be taken as the test criterion and basic goal for the reform. Therefore, a partial reform experimentation was the optimal plan for the reform. The establishment of the special economic zones was the outcome of the interaction among the Central Government, Guangdong Province and Fujian Province. In that process, Deng Xiaoping's advocacy and decisions played an enormously crucial role. Afterwards, with concerted efforts at central and local levels, it took only 20 months to give birth to the special economic zones.

Why were Guangdong Province and Fujian Province chosen to be the settings for the establishment of the special economic zones to make both provinces prosper first? Obviously, the reform certainly encountered various kinds of resistance. Since the Central Government had given the instruction to "allow some regions to become prosperous first", the regions with minimal reform resistance would certainly be chosen by weighing the advantages and disadvantages. What was the resistance? First, resistance of interests: The people with vested interests in the old system might have suffered benefit losses during the reform, thus they were bound to resist the reform. Second, ideological resistance: most of the people were used to the old system and instinctively resisted the reform as a new thing.

As remote coastal areas, the special economic zones represented by Shenzhen were influenced by the advantages of the old system to a very low degree at that time. So, they were prone to accepting new things. Apparently, as the areas least vulnerable to the planned economy, the special economic zones met with less reform resistance. As the number of people with vested interests was small and the level of the people's economic income was low, there was sufficient motivation to withstand the above-mentioned resistance and actively participate in the reform in order to grow into the new interest groups benefiting from the new system. Those special economic zones were part of the areas less exposed to the old system, and were economically underdeveloped and suffered extreme shortage of resources; however, their locations in the coastal areas enabled them to enjoy the excellent conditions for economic development. Moreover, the proximity to Hong Kong and Macao made it convenient for Shenzhen to attract foreign capital and carry out the opening-up policy. There were few indigenous people in the special economic zones, so the policy for encouraging immigration could be adopted. The then political and economic environment helped choose cities such as Shenzhen and Zhuhai as the special economic zones. Those special economic zones energetically shouldered their historical mission and led the direction of the reform.

In July, 1979, the ground was broken for the Shekou Industrial Zone, initiating China's reform and opening up. With the courage of blazing new trails and the spirit of the first mover, the people in the Shenzhen Special Economic Zone fully leveraged the location advantages from proximity to Hong Kong, and broke away from the fetter of the planned economic system to lay the national economic foundation for the special economic zone.

In 1980, the construction of the infrastructures was in full swing in Shenzhen. During the preliminary preparations for establishing the special economic zone, Deng Xiaoping instructed that "the Central Government should give no financial support, you must blaze new trails". However, under the traditional capital construction sys-

Fig. 4.1 A signboard that reads "Time is money, efficiency is life"

tem, it was extremely difficult to make water and electricity available, level the land, and achieve unobstructed transport and telecommunications. The whole process from design and construction to financing and material supply was subject to administrative intervention and allocation. In order to make the impossible possible and overcome mountains of difficulties, Shenzhen became the first to introduce the market mechanism in capital construction, and use bank loans to make investments and deliver returns; so addressing fund shortage during the initial stage of construction in the way of snowballing, which really echoed the instruction that "you must blaze new trails". During the implementation, the competition mechanism was introduced in design and construction, allowing domestic and foreign design personnel and construction teams to participate in competitive biddings. The market of building material was also opened, and the all-round responsibility system for projects was carried out, granting the autonomous right to the contracting units, and fully arousing the enthusiasm and creativity of the constructors. In that period, Shenzhen University was completed and started enrolling students in the same year, and the Shenzhen International Trade Centre Building was erected at an astonishing speed of one storey in three days, creating Shenzhen's Speed. The banner which reads "Time is money, efficiency is life" was even seen on Shenzhen's construction sites, shocking the domestic media (Fig. 4.1).

A great success was achieved in the reform of the capital construction system, carving out the way to fully introducing the market mechanism in Shenzhen. After water, electricity, roads and communication were made available and the land was leveled, Shenzhen moved on to develop an outward-looking economy, to invite investment and to seek economic cooperation with foreign countries. In that process, the people in Shenzhen disrupted the traditional labor employment system, broke the "iron bowl"—a stable, lifelong job, let the market have a say, and developed the contract worker system in line with the trends. Such breakthroughs ensured that enterprises enjoyed a great autonomous right and could recruit workers at their own discretion, specify the pay package to attract talents; there was also a two-way selection between enterprises and workers. That pressed ahead with the reform of the wage system. Afterwards, foreign investors confronted the matter of land when building their factories. Under the planned economic system, they had to go through a strict administrative process and lots of red tape, and have a certain qualification; otherwise, they could not successfully obtain the land use rights. The land use fee was creatively collected in a market-oriented way in Shenzhen. Such a move addressed the transfer of land while keeping the land ownership unchanged, thus offering a new idea and new methods for the reform of the land market. After foreign capital got access to the special economic zone, the matter of foreign exchange surfaced. The Hong Kong dollar was in massive circulation on the market during the initial stage of Shenzhen's construction. Obviously, the traditional administrative prohibition was unfavorable for Shenzhen's development. In 1985, with an innovative spirit, the Shenzhen Municipal Government creatively established the foreign exchange swap center and exercised its management under the principle of "paying attention to both ends and opening the intermediate section"—as long as the source and use were legitimate, the swap price could be determined by both parties. Market orientation once again played a role. The Shenzhen Foreign Exchange Swap Center was the first foreign exchange swap center in China, and it produced a good demonstrative effect on establishing a foreign exchange market in which currencies could be freely converted and the exchange rate could float freely.

A number of measures adopted in Shenzhen enhanced the efficiency of development, emancipated the people's minds and the productive forces, so its economic construction could be rapidly carried out, the GDP grew annually by an average of about 35%, and the social undertakings also developed accordingly. Shenzhen's GDP and per capita GDP were only 196 million yuan and 606 yuan, respectively, in 1979, while Shenzhen's GDP reached 11,566 million yuan in 1989. That achievement produced a great spillover effect, and offered good experience and a demonstration for other special economic zones and cities across the country. From 1980 to 1984, the national economic aggregate grew by 1.5 times, while that figure in Shenzhen, Zhuhai, Xiamen and Shantou was 6, 3, 1.6 and 1.4, respectively (Table 4.1). During the same period, the annual national average economic growth rate was only 10%, while that figure in Shenzhen, Zhuhai, Xiamen and Shantou was 58, 32, 13 and 9%, respectively. Apparently, Shenzhen's development fueled the development of the other special economic zones. These data vigorously prove that the gradual reform path adopted by the Central Government was correct.

In parallel with the bold reform in the special economic zones, a national debate was carried out on whether the planning and the market orientation were adoptable. That debate was, to a great extent, directly related to the special economic zones; for example, the slogan that "Time is money, efficiency is life" greatly upset the people who insisted on the traditional stand; the bold and aggressive market innovation behaviors—the lifting of price controls, the introduction of competition, the establishment of the factor market, etc., —in Shenzhen also annoyed some cautious people in China. Some people said that everything in Shenzhen had become capitalist except that the Five-Starred Red Flag was hung at Kowloon Customs. Some

Table 4.1 GDP in the special economic zones from 1980 to 1984 (*unit* 100 million yuan)

Year	Special zone			
	Shenzhen	Xiamen	Zhuhai	Shantou
1980	2.70	6.40	2.61	10.79
1981	4.96	7.41	3.18	12.62
1982	8.26	8.67	3.53	14.16
1983	13.12	9.44	4.06	13.40
1984	23.42	12.29	6.78	17.40

people compared the special economic zone to the "concession" in the old society. Those people opposed the market economy-oriented reform and strongly advocated a return to the original planned economic system.

The reformist economists represented by Xue Muqiao believed that the socialist economy generally remained a commodity economy and held that the planned commodity economy should be taken as the direction of the reform. The cautious people who took a negative attitude argued that there was a commodity production and exchange in China, but China's economy could not be defined as a commodity economy, and it was essential to stick with the principle that the planned economy was the mainstay while the market regulation served as the supplement. Clearly, those debates focused on whether or not the reform should be carried out and whether or not it should be a market-oriented one.

In the whole process of reform and opening up, the people in the special economic zones responded to the doubts from the objectors by taking practical actions; they quelled that debate through developmental achievements and theoretical innovations, so they were recognized and respected by the Central Government.

Deng Xiaoping always insisted on the wording: market economy. In November, 1979, when meeting with Frank Gibney, Vice-chairman of the Board of Editors at the US Encyclopaedia Britannica, et al., Deng Xiaoping explicitly pointed out: "A market economy is not just available in capitalism", "A market economy was in the bud as early as the period of feudal society, a market economy can also be practiced in socialism", "The view that the market economy is limited to a capitalist society and only a capitalist market economy exists is certainly incorrect", "Why can a market economy not be practiced in socialism?"[1] Those remarks evoked a strong repercussion in the departments in charge of practical affairs and in the theoretical circles. In October, 1985, when meeting with Henry Grunwald, Head of the US Entrepreneurs Delegation, et al., Deng Xiaoping further stated: "There are no fundamental contradictions between socialism and a market economy; the question is in what way can the social productive forces be developed more vigorously", "a combination of a planned economy and a market economy can better emancipate the productive forces and speed up economic development." In the eyes of the Chief Architect, Deng Xiaoping, the special economic zones were always experimental

[1]Deng Xiaoping, The Market Economy Can Also Be Practiced under Socialism (November 26, 1979), *Selected Works of Deng Xiaoping* (Vol. 2), p. 236.

fields. In 1985, when meeting with the delegation of the Algerian National Liberation Front, Deng Xiaoping said: "The Shenzhen Special Economic Zone is experimental, we should make further observations about whether the path is right. It is a new thing in socialism. Success is our aspiration, if it becomes unsuccessful, experience can be gained."[2] According to Deng Xiaoping's remarks about the special economic zones, his goal for China's reform was very clear: to acquire experience from the developed countries and practice a market economy.

In 1986, the production factor market covering technology, labor, land, capital and information had preliminarily taken shape in Shenzhen. The experimentation of the institutional reform in the special economic zone was conducted from a factor market to a product market and from a partial reform to an all-round reform, thus gradually introducing a market economic system. In the Shenzhen Special Economic Zone, the path of market-oriented reform was adopted from the beginning, and the spirit of being bold in making breakthroughs was advocated to fully arouse the enthusiasm of workers to induce production, making tremendous economic achievements, which reflects the superiority of the market economy.

After the establishment of the special economic zones, the debates on its nature never stopped at home or abroad. As the forerunners in the market economy and the experimental fields for the reform and opening up, the special economic zones, including Shenzhen, have been overwhelmed by censure and criticism since their inception. From 1982 to 1983, some leading, nationally-influential newspapers published a large number of criticism-related articles which touched upon the forefront of the reform and opening up—the special economic zones. The objectors generally believed that it was wrong to emphasize the roles of the law of value and market regulation. Comrade Deng Xiaoping always had a consistent attitude toward the opening-up policy. The resolute attitude of comrade Deng Xiaoping came from the chain reaction of the partial reform represented by the practice in the special economic zones, the positive spillover effect coming from them on the national economy and the all-round reform of the national economic system pushed forward in the special economic zones.

As shown by the basic experience gathered from the special economic zones, from the practical perspective, the market economy-oriented reform was carried out and this orientation was upheld in the special economic zones, so that the scarce resources were effectively allocated through the market to achieve an efficient economic growth and rapidly improve the living standard of the people, and make great economic achievements; from the perspective of the driving force at a deep level, the emancipation of the people was respected and expanded in the special economic zones. The reform mobilized the initiative of the players in the market economy, empowered the individuals to participate in the economic activities by giving full play to the subjective initiative and fully emancipating the mind, so as to make the most rational and self-interested judgments and decisions under the law of the market.

[2]Fan Gang, A Study of China's Special Economic Zones-Yesterday and Tomorrow's Theory and Practice, China Economic Publishing House, 2009, p. 46.

Fig. 4.2 Deng Xiaoping writes a dedication for the Shenzhen Special Economic Zone

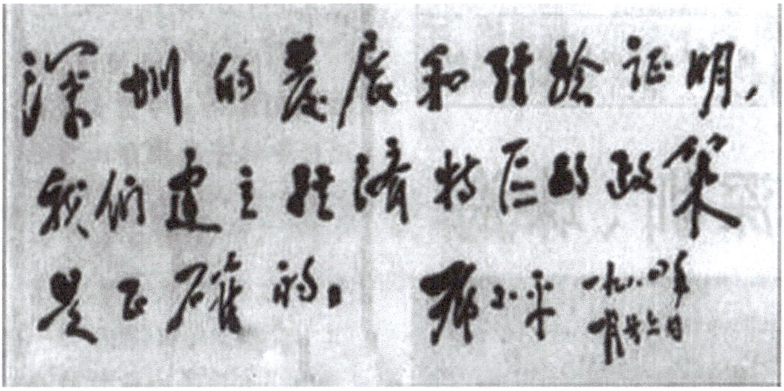

Fig. 4.3 Dedication written by Deng Xiaoping when inspecting the Shenzhen Special Economic Zone

When Guangdong Province vowed to make the market economy dominant in the special economic zones and introduce foreign capital, the views that practicing a market economy amounted to the restoration of capitalism and that the market economy was equivalent to fierce floods and savage beasts prevailed in the rest of the country. In response to this situation, from January 24 to February 15, 1984, Deng Xiaoping inspected three special economic zones, Shenzhen, Zhuhai and Xiamen, and he fully recognized the achievements made in those zones and wrote dedications for them (Figs. 4.2, 4.3, 4.4 and 4.5).

In the conversation entitled "Making the Special Economic Zones Better, Opening More Cities to the Outside World", he said: "As we establish the special economic zones and practice the opening-up policy, the following guiding thought is clear: controls should be relaxed rather than tightened", "the special economic zones serve

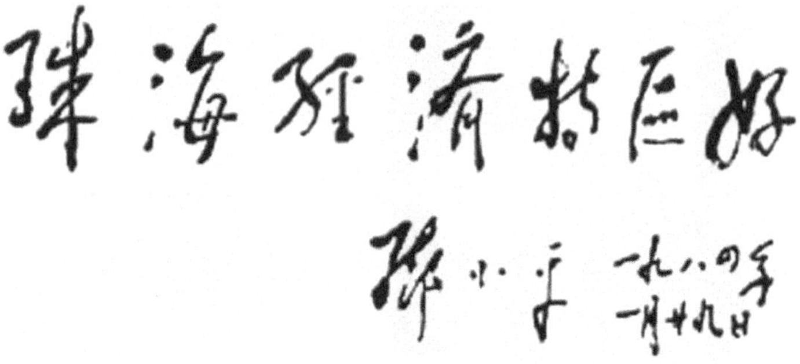

Fig. 4.4 Dedication written by Deng Xiaoping when inspecting the Zhuhai Special Economic Zone

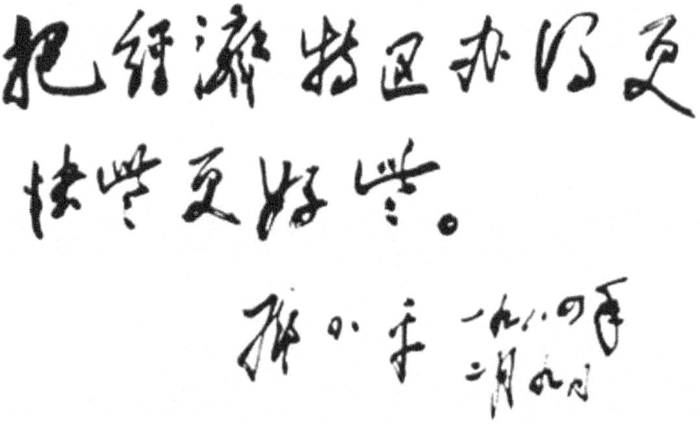

Fig. 4.5 Dedication written by Deng Xiaoping when inspecting the Xiamen Special Economic Zone

as the windows for technology, management, knowledge and external policy; the special economic zones can introduce technologies, acquire knowledge and learn management, while management is also a knowledge. The special economic zones become the bases for opening up, and will benefit us economically and in the cultivation of talents, and will expand China's influence on the outside world."[3] Therefore, the establishment and development of the special economic zones, especially the Shenzhen Special Economic Zone, to a large extent, has proved that the reform and opening up was a correct policy and the only correct policy under the then national conditions. After that inspection, comrade Deng Xiaoping maintained the economic development of the special economic zones, put forward the planned commodity economy, recognized the roles of the market economy, pinpointed the direction for the market-oriented reform, and decided to further carry out the reform and opening up. The people's minds had been emancipated and the reform had been accelerated.

[3]Zhong Jian et al., *Document Literature on China's Special Economic Zones (Vol. 3)*, Social Sciences Academic Press, 2010, p. 5.

4.1.2 The Theory of a Socialist Market Economy Was Practiced and Experimented with in the Special Economic Zones

After the reform and opening up, China gradually developed and enriched the theory of a socialist market economy. As we know, a combination of socialism and a market economy is a big experiment. The establishment of a socialist market economic system with Chinese characteristics is a first-ever event in human history. Combining socialism with a market economy is a great theoretical innovation and a pioneering undertaking in practice. The first-ever successful practice and experimentation of this new theory in the special economic zones, as the experimental fields for the reform, has laid a solid foundation for carrying out a nationwide reform of the socialist market economy, and has played the leading and decisive role in building the whole system of a socialist market economic theory in China.

(I) **A Debate, Triggered by the Special Economic Zones, on Whether the Market Economy Should Be Socialist or Capitalist**

In more than 30 years of reform, the debate between the reformists and the cautious people has never ended. The focus of the debate has varied with the background of the times. Deng Xiaoping said: "There were different opinions on the establishment of the special economic zones from the beginning, there was a worry that capitalism would be practiced."[4] The heated debate on the plan and the market, as mentioned above, resolved many major theoretical differences to realize the establishment of the special economic zones. There was a clearer understanding of the plan and the market. However, the people still had doubts about the reform and opening up as well as the nature of the special economic zones, so a debate on whether the market economy should be socialist or capitalist was once again conducted nationwide.

In fact, the market economy itself has no particular social economic nature, but the market economy must exist in particular social economic institutions, and cannot be free from discussions about whether it should be socialist or capitalist. The market economy initially took shape in the environment of the capitalist economic system, and the capitalist economic system upholds the basic principle that it is based on private ownership and resources are allocated through the market. As early as 1906, Lenin brought forward the concepts of a planned economy and a market economy. In a very long time since then, the economists and the common people have equated the market economy with capitalism, and have believed that the market economy and socialism were two completely contradictory concepts. For a long time, this deep-rooted idea had caused the people to negate the possibility that the market and prices could play the superior role in socialism.

In 1988, very severe inflation occurred in China, followed by political unrest which rocked the whole country in 1989. Some "politicians" and "theorists" who were disgusted with the entire reform attributed the above economic crisis and political

[4]*Selected Works of Deng Xiaoping* (Vol. 3), People's Publishing House, 1993, p. 372.

unrest completely to the reform, and maintained that the cancellation of the planned economy and the adoption of marketization were equivalent to the reform of the socialist system and the adoption of the capitalist system.[5] Therefore, a second great debate on the nature of reform initiated nationwide starting from the reform and opening up.

As the forerunner of the market economy and the experimental field for the reform and opening up, the Shenzhen Special Economic Zone was subject to a lot of criticism and censure while carving out the way for the reform across the country. This is because: First, the line of thought and actions of many cadres of the Party were still affected by rigid ideas at that time; second, the people were prone to approaching a new thing in different ways, which is understandable. A special economic zone was such a new thing. It was very normal that the special economic zones were understood differently in the international community, within and outside the Communist Party of China; last, some of the blame lies with the special economic zones; for example, criminal activities were severe, including rampant smuggling and traffic in smuggled goods, embezzlement and bribe-taking. The special economic zones were not understood, accepted or even criticized due to these faults.

The policy and guideline for rectifying the economic order and comprehensively intensifying the reform were adopted in the Third Plenary Session of the 13th Central Committee of the Communist Party of China, so the reform came to a standstill to some extent. In particular, with the political unrest in 1989, the cautious people seized the opportunity to re-launch the debate on the plan and the market; they believed that the problems in the national economy were, in the final analysis, caused by the wrong direction of the reform. They argued that a market-oriented reform crippled the planned economy; once problems occur, we should return to the planned economic system. Some people even directly linked the debate on the plan and the market to the existence or abolishment of the basic socialist system. Their views mainly included the following: being market-oriented was equivalent to being capitalism-oriented; the market economy meant the cancellation of the public ownership system, adoption of capitalism, negation of the socialist system and the Party's leadership. Therefore, socialism can do nothing but return to the old road of the planned economic system. In that political environment, the views of the cautious people prevailed for a certain period of time, the reform could become retrogressive.

After a period of time, the domestic political environment changed, the reformists bluntly responded to the above views. Famous economists such as Wu Jinglian and Xue Muqiao resolutely upheld the market-oriented reform and stressed that the roadmap of the reform outlined by the Third Plenary Session of the 11th Central Committee of the Communist Party of China should be adopted to firmly safeguard the market orientation. They refuted the view that the planned economy should be combined with market regulation, and clearly stated that we should make a prompt decision and get a clear understanding of the situation to overcome difficulties and achieve prosperity. Overall, the reformists held that our thoughts regarding the reform

[5] Wang Renzhi, Struggle against Bourgeois Liberalization, Speech at the Workshop on the Theory of the Party Building on December 15, 1989, *People's Daily*, February 22, 1990.

and opening up cannot be too rigid; otherwise, we cannot utilize the achievements coming from the reform and opening up to make socialism more attractive and prove the superiority of the socialist system. We must emancipate our minds, be bold in reform, we cannot be bound by prejudice and frightened by the criticism of the cautious people.

Two national debates, during the initial period of the special economic zones, involved major issues of principle. However, in the final analysis, they touched upon whether the special economic zones should be socialist or capitalist. Their essence consisted of the compatibility between the market economy and socialism.

The reform of China's economic system was market-oriented. As the forerunners in the reform, the special economic zones became the first to break the fetter of the planned economic system and introduce the market mechanisms, including the price mechanism, the supply and demand mechanism and the competition mechanism. These measures made breakthroughs in and posed challenges to the traditional socialist road, while many people considered them as variants of capitalism. In the meantime, in order to fully develop the market economy, diverse economic forms emerged and were developed, foreign capital was massively introduced and private enterprises mushroomed in the special economic zones. They were viewed as forms of a capitalist economy at that time. Therefore, they certainly led to domestic debates and panic. In the period during which the "left" line of thought ran wild, many people were greatly bewildered by and resisted the new things, failed to figure out what capitalism and socialism were, they even mistook some policies and guidelines consistent with the socialist system for capitalist ones and thus opposed them.

Apparently, the reform and opening up had to follow the socialist road and could not be separated from the restrictions posed by the Four Fundamental Principles. Therefore, this is particularly important for identifying the boundary between socialism and capitalism. What is socialism? Deng Xiaoping defined it as follows: "The essence of socialism lies in emancipating and developing the productive commodities, eliminating exploitation, removing polarization, and ultimately achieving common prosperity."[6] In order to judge whether the reform is right or wrong and becomes successful or unsuccessful, Deng Xiaoping put forward the famous "Three Favorables" criteria: "When we judge whether the reform and opening up is right or wrong, we must determine whether it is favorable for developing the productive forces in a socialist society, whether it is favorable for enhancing the comprehensive national strength in a socialist country and whether it is favorable for improving the living standard of the people."[7]

The practices in the special economic zones gave the answer to the debate on whether it should be socialist or capitalist—although the market economy was born in a capitalist society, it can also serve socialism. The economic system first developed in the special economic zones is a great combination of socialism and a market economy and is the socialist market economy with Chinese characteristics. The economic system within the special economic zones complies with the fundamental

[6] *Selected Works of Deng Xiaoping* (Vol. 3), People's Daily, 1993, p. 257.

[7] *Selected Works of Deng Xiaoping* (Vol. 3), People's Daily, 1993, p. 295.

socialist principle that public ownership is maintained as the mainstay of the economy and diverse forms of ownership are allowed to develop side by side, and it also tallies with the operations of law and the resource allocation mode which govern the general market economy. However, the practice and tremendous economic achievements in the special economic zones since the reform and opening up have proved that, under the socialist economic system, the means of the market economic regulation can also be used to optimize the allocation of resources in order to release and develop the productive forces, thus making the country prosperous and the people strong, reflecting the superiority of socialism.

In 1992, Deng Xiaoping once again inspected the special economic zones, including Shenzhen, and made the following important remark: "Whether the plan or the market account for a higher proportion is not the essential difference between socialism and capitalism. The planned economy is not equal to socialism since there is also plan in capitalism; the market economy is not equal to capitalism since there is also a market in socialism. Both planning and a market are economic means.[8] This remark essentially removed the traditional thought that the planned economy was socialist and the market economy was capitalist, it laid the foundation for developing the theory of a socialist market economy and indicated the direction for establishing a socialist market economic system. It is generally believed that the South Inspection Speech delivered by Deng Xiaoping in 1992 shocked the whole country, clearly showed the essence of socialism, and ultimately identified the goal for the reform of China's economic system: establish a socialist market economic system. With this as an opportunity, the report to the 14th National Congress of the Communist Party of China explicitly stated, for the first time, that "the goal for the reform of China's economic system is to establish a socialist market economic system".

As shown, the special economic zones became the first to embark on the path towards a market-oriented reform, which remains the socialist road with Chinese characteristics under the guidance of the socialist system. This debate arising out of the special economic zones clarified the nature of a market economy and laid the solid theoretical foundation for the special economic zones to become the first to establish a full-fledged socialist market economy.

(II) Practice and Experimentation of the Theory of a Socialist Market Economy in the Special Economic Zones

The command economy remained dominant in the initial period of the reform and opening up, during which this difference was not very obvious. Meanwhile, those who advocated the European-American mode also believed that, in order to achieve rapid economic development as expected in China, a backward economy, obviously, a powerful government did more good than harm. Therefore, with concerted efforts from the political and academic circles, the reform thoughts of establishing the socialist planned commodity economy took shape in the Third Plenary Session of the 12th Central Committee of the Communist Party of China in 1984. Apparently, this line

[8]*Selected Works of Deng Xiaoping* (Vol. 3), People's Daily, 1993, p. 373.

of thought could be accepted by most of the people. This represented a great step forward in progress compared with the period during which the market economy was considered "a fierce flood and a savage beast" nationwide. The special economic zones represented by Shenzhen made enormous experimentations and innovations in this progress.

"In my opinion, the economic policy should allow some areas, enterprises, workers and farmers to first receive more income and live a better life on the basis of hard work and great performance. Once some people live a better life earlier than others, tremendous demonstration effects would certainly be produced, influencing the neighbors and stimulating the people in other areas and other units to learn from them. Therefore, the whole national economy will continuously develop, and people of all nationalities across the country will quickly get rich."[9]

The practice in the transformation from a planned economic system to a socialist market economic system in China in more than 30 years can be divided into four major stages. During the development of China's gradual economic reform, there was further practice and experimentation of the theory of a socialist market economy in the special economic zones.

1. **The Initial Stage of the Reform (1978–1984)**

The Third Plenary Session of the 11th Central Committee of the Communist Party of China, which convened in December, 1978, marked the beginning of the reform of China's economic system. That stage witnessed deliberations on the institutional reform and evolution of the reform line of thought in China. It is also considered the stage of the initiation of the reform and partial experimentation. The reform in that period was fraught with confused experimentations and hard work.

On the initiative of Deng Xiaoping, China's reform started with the establishment of the Shenzhen Special Economic Zone. Shenzhen was forced to carry out bold institutional innovations in large-scale urban capital construction by opening the construction market and introducing the competition mechanism in capital construction. In 1982, Shenzhen became the first to make a breakthrough in the price reform by putting forward the reform idea of making readjustments dominant, combining a relaxed control with readjustment, and rationalizing the price system step by step. In order to break the constraints laid down by the old system, Shenzhen focused on reforming the capital construction system and lifting controls over prices as a breakthrough, with the first-ever efforts in carrying out a capital construction reform, a price reform, a labor employment and wage reform, and a reform of the management system. Those reforms were only reform experiments at a lower level, but they broke the fetter of the planned economic system, giving play to the role of the market mechanism which had been repelled for a long time.

As a place with an extreme shortage of resources, Shenzhen was subject to the explosion of the population and a shortage of daily necessities after a series of reforms. In order to address the shortage of commodities, Shenzhen resorted to the special policies given by the Central Government to find solutions. At that time, there

[9] *Selected Works of Deng Xiaoping* (Vol. 3), People's Daily, 1993, p. 152.

were state-fixed prices, state-guided prices and free market prices in Shenzhen. In 1984, Shenzhen became the first to fully lift controls over the supply of non-staple food, relax price controls and eliminate all tickets and commodity subsidies. Meanwhile, the new wage system was adopted to directly link the commodity prices to wages, so as to resolve the price reform dilemma that wages were low and subsidies were high. In Shenzhen, the special economic zone policy was utilized to establish an import and export service company, through which purchases were made to address the market supply. As the circulation system with planned purchases and marketing by the State was implemented in China, it was very difficult for the import and export service company to conduct domestic purchasing activities. However, Shenzhen fully leveraged the subjective initiative to creatively use the "foreign exchange" to circumvent the restrictions posed by the domestic planned economy, thus addressing the shortage of commodities. That move broke the three-level circulation system of the planned economy, making a great breakthrough in fully practicing a market economy. After Shenzhen became free from the shortage of commodities, the commodity prices could not be uniformly coordinated by administrative orders, so the law of value in the market economy had to be followed, and the commercial system and the commodity price system had to be reformed.

Shenzhen also became successful in exploring a mechanism in which the socialist market economy could play a role. In Shenzhen, the competition mechanism was introduced in capital construction; the supply and demand mechanism was introduced in the process of improving the commodity market; the first-ever breakthrough was made in the price reform, giving scope to the role of the price mechanism. Of course, with regard to the role of the socialist market mechanism, a coordination between the government and the market was required for more effectively allocating the scarce resources. Meanwhile, it was also necessary to give consideration to the coordination between the economic benefits and social development, so as to ensure that the economic development was not pursued at the expense of the environment. The socialist market system and the socialist market mechanism constitute the socialist market economic system.

The *Decisions of the Central Committee of the Communist Party of China Concerning the Reform of the Economic System*, adopted during the Third Plenary Session of the 12th Central Committee of the Communist Party of China in 1984, established a planned commodity economy based on public ownership.

2. **The Stage of All-Round Reform (1985–1992)**

At that stage, there were major explorations and breakthroughs in China's traditional system, the reform was ambitious and important experimentations were made. The *Decisions of the Central Committee of the Communist Party of China Concerning the Reform of the Planned Economic System* was issued in that period, we made a major breakthrough in understanding the plan and the market, and the reform of the urban economic system was initiated; however, as the reform measures of contracts and leasing operations were implemented, more profits were surrendered to enterprises, so that the central finance bore almost all of the costs of the reform; meanwhile, the transparency of the institutional environment for the reform was destroyed. Moreover, the reform of prices frequently met with setbacks, so the economic reform was interrupted for a period of time after 1989, and even the planned economy came back. The reform was not accelerated until 1992 when Deng Xiaoping made an inspection trip to southern China. In that period, a marked effect was produced in the establishment of the socialist market economic system in the special economic zones, especially in the Shenzhen Special Economic Zone.

In 1985, a foreign exchange swap center was set up in Shenzhen, creating a new method for allocating foreign exchange through the market. In November, 1987, the State Administration of Foreign Exchange recognized and popularized the move made in the Shenzhen Special Economic Zone. In April, 1988, with the approval of the State Council, foreign exchange swap centers were established in the rest of the country. In 1992, the market competition mechanism was introduced in the Shenzhen Special Economic Zone, with the launch of an open market for foreign exchange swaps, so Shenzhen's foreign exchange market became increasingly mature. Institutional innovations in the foreign exchange market are essential for building the order of a market economy. The icebreaking move made by the Shenzhen Special Economic Zone in the field of foreign exchange administration as one of the most unbreakable institutions in China fully reflects the courage and insight of the special economic zone for realizing the new institutions.

On December 1, 1987, Shenzhen saw the first-ever public auction of the right to use the state-owned land. In the late 1980s, the control over 80% of the commodity prices had been lifted and a price system led by market regulation had taken shape in Shenzhen. The first-ever breakthrough in the housing system also occurred in Shenzhen—on July 27, 1989, the Shenzhen Municipal Government released the *Housing Development Plan of the Shenzhen Special Economic Zone*, specifying "two tracks and three categories" in the housing supply and demand, among which two tracks meant government-organized housing construction and housing construction based on investments from the real estate companies, while three categories meant welfare-oriented commodity housing, meager-profit commodity housing and market-oriented commodity housing, or affordable housing at cost price, meager-profit affordable housing and market-oriented commodity housing. On August 10, 1991, the *People's Daily* published a report on the housing reform experience in Shenzhen, which maintained that success was achieved in the conversion of the mechanism involving the housing system through the housing reform, and a housing provident fund was established in Shenzhen.[10]

In Shenzhen, some government departments in charge of economic affairs were transformed into state-owned enterprises, the layout of the state-owned economy was adjusted by invigorating large enterprises while relaxing control over the small ones, and setting up companies involved in electrical and electronic fields; new property rights holders were introduced to some enterprises and a modern enterprise system consistent with a market economy was established. Based on ensuring that public ownership remained the mainstay and multiple forms of ownership developed side

[10]Fan Gang, A Study of China's Special Economic Zones-Yesterday and Tomorrow's Theory and Practice, China Economic Publishing House, January, 2009.

by side, a number of measures for the transformation of the corporate system were introduced in Shenzhen, so that the status of state-owned enterprises as the main market players was established. Furthermore, Shenzhen became the first to practice the all-employee contract system, under which the status of state employees as the main market players was established by enhancing the efficiency and downsizing employees, laying off and redirecting employees. Shenzhen's reform of the state-owned economy gave birth to qualified market players such as the state-owned enterprises and state employees for the socialist market economic system.

Shortly after the establishment of the Shenzhen Special Economic Zone, the reform of the traditional egalitarian distribution system was put on the agenda. A down-top reform was carried out in Shenzhen. Initially, the organization responsible for the construction of the Shekou Port in Shenzhen changed the system of wages for workers and allowed the distribution to be determined by the market in order to arouse the enthusiasm of construction workers and thus improve the efficiency of construction. With Shenzhen's reform of the wage system, enterprises could distribute wages at their own discretion, which was a precedent in China. That reform mirrored the principle of giving priority to efficiency and was of an epoch-making significance for ultimately establishing in China the income distribution system in which work-based distribution is the mainstay and diverse distribution modes coexist. In the market economic environment, only when the reform of the distribution system is intensified can the ideal of common prosperity be ultimately realized.

3. **The Stage of Institutional Innovations in the Reform (1993–2002)**

At that stage, the socialist market economic system preliminarily took shape and was successfully enshrined into the Constitution. In 1993, the *Decisions Concerning Several Issues Involving the Establishment of the Socialist Market Economic System* was adopted during the Third Plenary Session of the 14th Central Committee of the Communist Party of China, which outlined the basic framework of the socialist market economic system. In 1995, the *Recommendations of the Central Committee of the Communist Party of China for Developing the 9th Five-Year National Plan for Economic and Social Development and the Long-term Goals for the Year 2010* was adopted during the Fifth Plenary Session of the 14th Central Committee of the Communist Party of China, which stated that one of the key steps for achieving the goals was the transformation of the economic system from the traditional planned economic system to a socialist market economic system.

Thanks to its proximity to Hong Kong and Macao, Shenzhen enjoys the natural advantage of attracting foreign capital. In fact, this advantage was fully leveraged in Shenzhen, where foreign capital was utilized to reinforce its own construction and the development of the individual economy was encouraged so as to break away from the dominance of the public sector of the economy within a small scope. In 1992, when inspecting southern China, Deng Xiaoping inquired about the proportion of foreign capital in Shenzhen's economic aggregate, and Li Hao, then Shenzhen's Municipal Party Secretary, said that it accounted for about 25%. After listening, Deng Xiaoping was very glad and said: "In Shenzhen, public ownership is the mainstay, foreign capital accounts for only 1/4, furthermore, we can also obtain benefits in tax and labor service from foreign capital! Add more Chinese-foreign joint ventures, Chinese-foreign cooperative enterprises and exclusively foreign-owned enterprises, do not be afraid. As long as we keep a cool head, we have no worry. We have advantages, large and medium-sized state-run enterprises and township enterprises; more importantly, the political power is in our hands."[11] In 2002, private enterprises made up 60% of the total enterprises throughout the city. Meanwhile, the holders of property rights in the state-owned economy became diverse after the strategic reorganization and adjustment of the ownership structure.

On January 14, 1993, a series of supporting measures for transforming the state-owned enterprises and the operational mechanism were released in the Shenzhen Special Economic Zone, further delegating powers to enterprises and putting in place the autonomous right of enterprises in production operations. As from 1994, the reform towards transforming the enterprise operation mechanism was quickened in Shenzhen. In 1995, the *Regulations of the Shenzhen Special Economic Zone for the Management of State-owned Assets* was adopted by the Standing Committee of the Municipal People's Congress. In 2002, the leading municipal group for the liquidation of the non-operating state-owned assets was set up, which was responsible for reappraising the non-operating state-owned assets and standardizing the management. The Shenzhen Special Economic Zone had made the first-ever pilot exploration in the reform of the modern enterprise system.

In Shenzhen, active efforts were made to establish the commodity market and factor markets during the exploration of the socialist market economic system. The commodity market is the foundation for the socialist market system. In the process of exploration, Shenzhen utilized the "foreign exchange" to address the shortage of commodities, so as to build a relatively open and full-fledged commodity market. Apparently, the financial market is the core of the socialist market system. During the exploration of the reform, Shenzhen became the first to establish the foreign exchange market in China, and saw the issuance of the first stock in China, marking the beginning of China's capital factor market. The function of the realization of the resource allocation of a market economy depends upon the flow of the labor force. Shenzhen became the first to reform the labor market in China, giving a boost to the development of China's labor factor market. Science, technology and information are also the important production factors and offer the inexhaustible motivational power for rapid economic development. At the forefront of China's scientific and technological innovation and the birthplace of a number of hi-tech companies, including Huawei and ZTE, Shenzhen has offered successful experiments for the development and improvement of China's factor market for information technology. The real estate market is also an important part of China's socialist market system. Shenzhen witnessed the first-ever public auction of land use rights and reform of China's land system, so that China's real estate market factors could develop. Shenzhen's experience was ultimately applied nationwide, making a beneficial experiment for establishing a uniform national open market system.

---

[11] Liu Jintian et al., *Deng Xiaoping out of Zhongnanhai*, Taihai Publishing House, 2011, p. 361.

Shenzhen became the first to introduce the market competition mechanism, the supply and demand mechanism and the price mechanism, and the first to build a uniform open socialist market economic system, bring about qualified market players, probe the reform of the distribution system, and establish and improve the macro control and regulation system. As the template of the special economic zones, with the spirit of being specially capable of reform, innovation and opening up, Shenzhen has created numerous number ones and has become one of the most prosperous areas in China. Shenzhen has succeeded in developing the market economy under the basic socialist system. Its experience proves that a market economy can serve not only capitalism but also socialism, and socialism can be successfully combined with a market economy. Shenzhen's practice has attracted attention at home and abroad and has been widely recognized. Singaporean Minister Mentor Mr. Lee Kuan Yew highly commended Shenzhen's experimentation. He believed that Shenzhen was unique in China, that China could not do without Shenzhen, and Shenzhen's successful reform proved that Deng Xiaoping's socialist road with Chinese characteristics was feasible; Shenzhen's successful experience was applied across China, pinpointing the direction for establishing the national socialist market economic system.

4. **The Crucial Stage of Reform (2003–Now)**

Since the beginning of the 21st century, the reform of China's economic system has produced all-round effects and has entered a crucial stage. A number of comprehensive reform plans have been implemented in China. The *Decisions of the Central Committee of the Communist Party of China Concerning Several Issues Involving the Improvement of the Socialist Market Economic System,* adopted during the Third Plenary Session of the 16th Central Committee of the Communist Party of China in 2003, specified the main tasks for improving the socialist market economic system. In March, 2005, Premier Wen Jiabao stressed, in two sessions, that the year 2005 would be crucial for the reform.

Since 2003, new fields of reform have been continuously expanded in the Shenzhen Special Economic Zone. In September, 2005, at the 25th anniversary of the establishment of the Shenzhen Special Economic Zone, Premier Wen Jiabao inspected Shenzhen and chaired a symposium regarding the work of the special economic zones. The overall thoughts regarding the reform of the special economic zones gradually became explicit and the comprehensive reform was initiated in a well-targeted manner.

In more than 30 years since the reform and opening up, six administrative management system reforms have been conducted in Shenzhen. The Shenzhen Municipal Government has taken the following concrete actions: enhancing its own public service awareness, strengthening market supervision, reducing administrative intervention in the economic field, encouraging fair market competition and increasing the autonomy of enterprises in their operations, thus offering a good institutional environment and rational institutional arrangements, and ensuring that a free market system can achieve the maximum utility in resource allocation. Meanwhile, in order to support the establishment and improvement of a market system, a number of special economic zone laws and regulations have been made and the basic framework for a complete market economic law and regulation system has been preliminarily developed in Shenzhen. Shenzhen's explorations in transforming the functions of the government have shown to the Central Government that it is important to rationalize the relationships among the market, society and the government, and have helped set the goal for building a service-oriented government and limited government across China. These beneficial experimentations have offered the direction and experience for ultimately establishing and improving a macro control and regulation system in China. This is essential in order for us to establish a socialist market economy.

During this period, the existing market economic system has been improved to some extent in the Shenzhen Special Economic Zone. Further improvements have been made in market reform, factor flow, moderate reform of property rights and the establishment of a credit system. The induced reform has also taken place in social undertakings in the special economic zone. There have been certain reforms and improvements in medical treatment and health, education, culture, rural urbanization, population management, community management, urban planning and construction and in environmental protection. The reform in the Shenzhen Special Economic Zone has been clearly defined as a comprehensive one; this accords with China's reform and developmental trends and the characteristics of Shenzhen's stage of development.

In October, 2007, when delivering his report to the 17th National Congress of the Communist Party of China, comrade Hu Jintao stressed: "We should uphold and improve the basic economic system, in which public ownership remains the mainstay and multiple forms of ownership develop side by side"; the report further stated: "In order to achieve the future economic developmental goals, the key lies in making great progress in accelerating the transformation of the economic developmental mode and improving the socialist market economic system", "it is necessary to deepen the understanding of the law which governs the socialist market economy, institutionally give greater scope to the fundamental role of the market in resource allocation, and shape a macro control and regulation system beneficial to scientific development." On November 9, 2013, the Third Plenary Session of the 18th Central Committee of the Communist Party of China further emphasized the decisive role of the market in resource allocation.

(III) The Practice in the Special Economic Zones Laid a Foundation for Establishing the Socialist Market Economic System

In more than 30 years since the reform and opening up, the people in the special economic zones have been bold in making explorations and innovations, they have broken the fetter of the old system of the planned economy, have vigorously pushed forward the market-oriented reform, and they have made a lot of beneficial experimentations in the capital construction system, labor employment system, land use system and foreign exchange administration. The special economic zones became the first to establish a full-fledged market system, clarify the property rights relations, diversify the market players, identify the positions of the government and the market, and develop a relatively complete set of market rules. The special economic zones became the first to seek out a socialist market economic path fit for China's modernization.

Take the Shenzhen Special Economic Zone as an example; with unremitting efforts for more than 30 years, Shenzhen's economy has grown, annually, by an average of 27.3%, the cumulative GDP has hit 4177.1 billion yuan. Shenzhen has ranked No. 4 in terms of GDP among the large and medium-sized cities across China for several consecutive years; Shenzhen's GDP has exceeded the scale of a moderately developed province. This growth miracle broke Shenzhen's growth ceiling, anticipated by the outside world.

The experiments and development in the special economic zones have stimulated economic growth across China and have resulted in impressive achievements. All of the changes were also concentrated in the GDP. In 1978, when Deng Xiaoping vowed to achieve the ambitious goal of quadrupling the national income by the end of the 20th century, other people, except the famous economist Mr. Sun Zhifang who resolutely supported that view, believed that it was impossible. However, the facts much exceeded people's expectations. China's development was faster than that envisioned by Deng Xiaoping. During the 30–year period since the establishment of the special economic zones, China's GDP doubled in less than a decade, with an annual average growth rate of 9.7%. In 2013, China's GDP reached 9038.66 billion USD and soared from the 13th place in 1978 to the 2nd place in the world, making China the largest economy, only second to the USA. With the rapid growth of the GDP, earth-shaking changes have taken place in China.

The rapid economic growth has laid a solid material foundation for China's socialist construction and has provided the guarantee for the people to become well-to-do after a period of struggling to secure enough food and clothing. The special economic zones have taken advantage of the market to improve efficiency, allocate the scarce resources, arouse the people's enthusiasm, emancipate the productive forces and ultimately achieve economic growth. As the wonderful epitome of the great achievements in socialism with Chinese characteristics, the special economic zones enjoy complete infrastructures, an excellent human environment and developed urban functions; they demonstrate the superiority of the socialist system, national prosperity and the people's mightiness in a new type of socialist country.

The remarkable achievements made in the special economic zones were highly commended and absolutely recognized by Deng Xiaoping. Deng Xiaoping, theoretically, broke the idea that the socialist public ownership was opposite to a market economy, and made way for the ultimate establishment of the socialist market economic system. He keenly pointed out, in 1979, that "the view that a market economy is limited to a capitalist society and only a capitalist market economy exists, is certainly incorrect; why can the market economy not be practiced in socialism? This cannot be considered capitalism. We keep the planned economy as the mainstay while practicing a market economy, but this is a socialist market economy." In 1982, the 12th National Congress of the Communist Party of China officially presented the view that the planned economy served as the mainstay and was supplemented by a market economy. In 1984, the Third Plenary Session of the 12th Central Committee of the Communist Party of China officially stated that the socialist economy was the planned commodity economy based on public ownership. In 1987, the 13th National Congress of the Communist Party of China officially stressed that the system of the socialist planned commodity economy should be a system with internal coordination between the plan and the market.[12]

On June 9, 1992, when delivering a speech at the Party School of the CPC Central Committee, Jiang Zemin upheld, for the first time, the socialist market economic system. On October 12, the report to the 14th National Congress of the Communist Party of China officially stated: "The objective of the reform of China's economic system is to establish a socialist market economic system". In 1993, the Third Plenary Session of the 14th Central Committee of the Communist Party of China made the *Decisions Concerning Several Issues Involving the Establishment of a Socialist Market Economic System*, which designed the basic framework for the socialist market economic system and identified the tasks for the reform of the socialist market economic system on the basis of the understanding of a socialist market economy at that time.[13] Economist Zhang Weiying believed: "Now we should establish a people-oriented system to ensure that people have more enthusiasm, cooperate and help each other, and the market economy is the best system."

The special economic zones have sought out a mode of institutional transformation from a planned economy to a market economy, providing an institutional guarantee for social development. The special economic zones have given birth to a road towards development of general regional cities into international modern central cities, offering the guidance for moving from widespread poverty to common prosperity. The special economic zones have also nurtured an innovative spirit of being bold in making breakthroughs, providing the support of a template for emancipating the people's minds and the productive forces.

As the demonstration of the forerunners in the special economic zones has shown, the adoption of a socialist market economy and a combination of socialist public ownership and a market economy are favorable for developing productive social forces, enhancing the comprehensive national strength and improving the people's living standard; such adoption and combination can also more fully arouse the workers' initiative, enthusiasm and creativity, more effectively achieve an optimal allocation of resources, better coordinate efficiency with equity, thus making it possible to ultimately realize the goals of common prosperity and social equity.

It is generally believed, in the academic circles, that China has carried out the reform and opening up through the establishment of the special economic zones, and the reform and opening up has basically focused on the path of the market economy. With the explorations of the goals of the reform of the economic system from 1984 to 1987 and the twists and turns from 1989 to 1991, more people have become keenly aware that we should take the market economy prevalent in the modern countries as the new goal of our economic system. During this institutional transformation, the plan should be replaced by the market to allocate the economic resources, the microeconomic issues, including the types and quantities of goods made by the

[12]Liu Wenge et al., *Theory and Practice of the Socialist Market Economy*, Peking University Press, 2012, p. 19.

[13]Socialist Market Economy, www.lnd.com.cn, *Liaoshen Evening News*, June 18, 2011.

enterprises, consumer group, and the distribution mode should be determined by the market.

In order to affirm the achievements of the socialist construction made in the special economic zones, comrade Jiang Zemin made the following remarks at the 20th anniversary of the establishment of the special economic zones: "The special economic zones have played an important role of experimental field in the historical process of transformation from the previous planned economy to the socialist market economy, and have served as important windows and bases in the historical process of the reform and opening up; they have played the important roles of demonstration, radiation and simulation in the historical process of achieving common development across China."[14]

In 2012, 20 years after the South Inspection Speech, comrade Xi Jinping, the new generation leader of the Party and State, inspected the Shenzhen Special Economic Zone, he encouraged the special economic zones to explore new institutions by saying "Delegate powers to yourself, be bold in going ahead". As shown, the experimentations from the special economic zones in establishing a socialist market economic system and its institutions were spoken highly of by several generations of leaders. The experimentations and innovations made in the special economic zones have ensured a gradual establishment of China's socialist market economic system, the formation and progressive improvement of the theory of a socialist market economy.

4.2 Contributions from the Special Economic Zones to the Theory of Socialist Property Rights and to the Distribution Theory

The establishment of the social market economic system is a systematic project and entails experimentations, development and improvements in different aspects of the entire economic operations system. At their inception, the special economic zones embarked on the market economy-oriented reform, and became the first to explore and develop the property rights system and the distribution system in the socialist market economic system, thus laying a solid foundation for establishing a socialist market economic system across the country and enriching the theory of property rights and the distribution theory concerning a socialist market economy.

---

[14]Jiang Zemin, Speech at the 20th Anniversary of the Establishment of the Shenzhen Special Economic Zone, *People's Daily*, November 15, 2000.

4.2.1 The Property Rights Reform in the Special Economic Zones Laid the Foundation for Establishing the Socialist Market Economic System

The form of ownership as a relationship of property ownership is legally defined as property rights.[15] The delimitation of property rights is very important in pushing forward China's reform for completing institutional transformation by establishing the special economic zones. According to Coase Theorem II, if the transaction cost is higher than zero, different delimitations of property rights will lead to a different efficiency of resource allocation.[16] Coase believed that the initial delimitation of lawful rights would exert an impact on the efficiency of economic institutional operations. An arrangement of rights would generate more output than other arrangements. However, unless this was an adjustment of the rights established under the legal system, the market costs for creating the same consequence through transfer and merger were so high that the optimal rights allocation and the resulting higher output would never be achieved.[17] As shown, the delimitation of property rights is the basic prerequisite for market transactions. In the process of achieving economic development, clearly delimited property rights have a direct impact on the effective operations of the market and the ultimate result of economic development.

According to the economist Zhou Qiren, China's course of reform is a history of unfinished property rights reform. The property rights reform aims at clarifying the property rights and establishing the status of the market players. Theoretically, it is designed to shape the microeconomic foundation for a socialist market economy. The property rights relations are based on a particular ownership relationship. The Third Plenary Session of the 18th Central Committee of the Communist Party of China pointed out: "Property rights are the core of ownership", "Property rights of both public and private sectors of the economy are inviolable". Therefore, the comprehensive understanding of the ownership issues is of great significance for the institutional change made by establishing the special economic zones as those units that were to break the traditional system and achieve a gradual transformation from a planned economy to a market economy across China.

(I) **The Diversification of the Ownership Structure is the Primary Issue in the Reform of Property Rights**

1. **A Different Understanding of the Ownership Structure**

Ownership is the most basic relationship of production. The institutional precondition for developing the productive forces is the perfect form of ownership. The debates on

---

[15]Su Dongbin, Special Frontier Issues Concerning China's Special Economic Zones, China Economic Publishing House, 2000, p. 196.

[16]Chang Xiuze, et al., *Property Rights Exchange—Theory and Operation*, The Economic Daily Press, 1995, p. 2.

[17]Ronald Harry Coase, *Property Rights and Institutional Change*, Shanghai Joint Publishing Company, 1991, p. 20.

the ownership structure covered the whole process of the reform of China's socialist economic system, while the issues involved in these debates varied in the different stages. During the initial period of the special economic zones, the debate on the ownership theory focused on whether ownership was the means or the objective. One view held that ownership was the means. They believed that developing the productive forces and increasing the aggregate of social wealth was the fundamental objective of all social forms, including socialism. Ownership was an important part of the relationship of production and was subject to the productive forces and it served the development of the productive forces. Another view was that ownership was the objective. Public ownership had the essential connection with the social system and economic system. Socialist public ownership had an inherent and inevitable connection with the essence of socialism. Keeping socialist public ownership as the mainstay was the indispensable basic premise and an important guarantee for embodying and realizing the essence of socialism. The second view led to undue emphasis on large-scale people's commune and a high level of social public ownership with the people's commune with respect to the form of ownership; it severely ignored the institutional design and continuous improvement in the operation of the public property rights; it also hindered a further reform of the ownership structure and inhibited a further healthy development of the non-public sectors of the economy.

As indicated above, both views were inappropriate. The ultimate objective of socialism is neither public ownership nor the development of the productive forces; on the contrary, it is the universal improvement of the material and cultural living standard of all of the people; comrade Deng Xiaoping called it "common prosperity". In the opinion of comrade Deng Xiaoping, the essence of socialism lies in emancipating and developing the productive forces, eliminating exploitation and polarization and ultimately achieving common prosperity. In this essence, the emancipation and development of the productive forces is the means, while the realization of common prosperity is the objective. Public ownership, exploitation-free work-based distribution and a planned economy make sense only when compared with capitalism; this shows that they are the characteristics—but not the essence—of socialism. This is because public ownership and the absence of exploitation occurred as early as the primitive society, and were not exclusive to socialism.

As mentioned by Professor Su Dongbin, the objective of socialism can be summarized as common prosperity, while its means can be summarized as one policy—developing the productive forces; its condition can be summarized as one system—keeping public ownership as the mainstay. In this regard, the objective is eternal, the means are diverse and the conditions are changing.[18]

With the development and improvement of the special economic zones, fewer and fewer scholars advocate single public ownership and complete privatization; the debates on the ownership structure mostly focus on whether public ownership or

---

[18]Su Dongbin, Dialogue Concerning Deepening the State-owned Enterprise Reform—An Interview with Professor Su Dongbin, Economist, Director, Taiwan, Hong Kong and Macao Economic Research Institute, Shenzhen University, *Shenzhen Special Economic Zone Daily*, September 4, 1996.

private ownership should be kept as the mainstay. Those who insist that it should be public ownership maintain that only when public ownership is maintained as the mainstay can the essence of socialism be retained. The essence of socialism consists in keeping public ownership as the mainstay. When the practice has proved that private ownership is more efficient and is more able to promote the development of the productive forces than public ownership in many fields and under many circumstances, keeping public ownership as the mainstay will run counter to the criterion: productive force. In order to persist in such a criterion, the move of keeping public ownership as the mainstay must be abandoned. As a result, keeping public ownership as the mainstay contradicts such a criterion. The people who insist on developing private ownership as the mainstay, the constitution and the laws relating to private property are confronted with a contradiction between the elimination of exploitation and the protection of private property. This is because both sides recognize that there is an inevitable relationship between private ownership and exploitation. So when you curse the act of exploitation, you will certainly vent your anger on private ownership. When you stress that it is necessary to vigorously develop private economy and protect private property, you have to tolerate exploitation.

Although the heated debate over private ownership still exists, people are no longer afraid of talking about it. Private ownership was considered as a "fierce flood and a savage beast" at the beginning; afterwards, it was gradually regarded as the beneficial supplement to public ownership; finally it has become an important part of a socialist market economy and enjoys the protection equivalent to that of public ownership in the constitution. The Third Plenary Session of the 18th Central Committee of the Communist Party of China further made it clear that both public and non-public sectors of the economy are important parts of a socialist market economy, and the important foundation for China's economic and social development.

2. **Important Status and Roles of the Private Economy in the Special Economic Zones**

The private economy enjoys an important status and plays an important role in economic development. After the Second World War, many western European countries, including the UK, France and Austria had a considerable number of state-owned enterprises. However, in 1979, the British Prime Minister Margaret Thatcher initiated a large-scale privatization reform of the state-owned enterprises and introduced the competition mechanism, which lasted for 10–20 years. As state-owned enterprises failed to address inefficiency, the proportion of state-owned enterprises was very small in those countries. In 1980, the output value created by the state-owned enterprises accounted for about 11% of the UK's total GNP, while now this proportion is only 2%. According to the economist Hu Zuliu, the existence of state-owned enterprises is indeed unnecessary in a full-fledged market economy because private enterprises can do better with higher efficiency with regard to the same thing in a profitable competitive enterprise.

The special economic zones were exceptions against the general background of a planned economy in China. The market economy was practiced in the special economic zones from the beginning. Shenzhen has always been serving as the model for the special economic zones. Take Shenzhen as an example, market regulation has become dominant since its inception and a diversified pattern in which the public sector of the economy, the foreign investment economy, the economy under the collective joint-stock system and the private economy jointly developed took shape in Shenzhen in a short period of time. The proportion of the original publicly-owned enterprises in Shenzhen was smaller than that in China's inland areas at the outset of the reform. During the high-speed development of the special economic zone, the foreign investment economy and the private economy rapidly developed, and almost took turns in ups and downs. With active attraction of foreign investments and the development of the individual economy, the long-term dominance by the public sector of the economy in China was broken in Shenzhen.

After Deng Xiaoping inspected southern China in 1992, the private economy developed by leaps and bounds. One impressive achievement was the rapid growth of the FDI, along with economic development in the special economic zones. In 1978, FDI were almost zero across China. However, with the more than 30-year-long reform in the special economic zones, China has become one of the largest destinations of FDI in the world. The growth of FDI in China has been mainly attributable to the development of the special economic zones. In 1985—at the beginning of the implementation of the opening-up policy, 37% of the FDI settled in the special economic zones. In 2005, China became the largest destination of FDI in the world, and 93% of those investments were based in the special economic zones.

With the rapid development of the private economy and the practice of the market-oriented economic reform, people have rediscovered the status and role of the private economy in China's economic development. The well-known economist Tong Dalin, former Deputy Director of the State Commission for Restructuring the Economic System, evaluated the roles of the private economy as follows: "In the process of China's reform and opening up, the private economy has developed and expanded along with the socialist market economy. Both fall within a large scope. Without the private economy, the socialist market economic system is nothing but a mere skeleton. If the private economy is separated from the socialist market economy, the private economy will become half-dead. Both constitute a community with a common destiny in the economic field. In this sense, the private economy is a very important part of the socialist market economy. It can be believed to enjoy a legitimate status rather than the supplement or the beneficial supplement. It is not the inessential supporting actor; on the contrary, it is the leading actor."[19] The constitutional amendment adopted in the Second Session of the 9th National People's Congress in early 1999 established that "public ownership remains the mainstay, and multiple forms of ownership develop side by side" as one basic economic system at the primary stage of socialism, and the non-public sectors of the economy as an important part of China's socialist market economy; they were included into the *Constitution of the People's Republic of China*, revised in that year. That was a far-reaching theoretical breakthrough. It removed the obstacles to diversifying and

[19]Tao Yitao, Lu Zhiguo, *China's Economic Zones: Design, Implementation, and Impact*, Social Sciences Academic Press, 2008, pp. 110–111.

rationalizing China's ownership structure. That also meant that the status and roles of the non-public sectors of the economy, especially the private economy in China's economic structure, had been officially recognized.

The 16th National Congress of the Communist Party of China fully affirmed the status of the private economy, and scientifically positioned the private entrepreneurs as the socialist builders, and stressed that we should judge whether an individual made political progress by focusing on the origin and whereabouts of their properties rather than the existence and quantity of those properties. Those breakthroughs further affirmed the status and roles of the "private".[20] The development of the private economy in Shenzhen has not only given a strong boost to Shenzhen's economic growth, but it has also helped seek out the path towards the adjustment of ownership across China.[21]

3. **The Diversified Structure of Ownership in the Special Economic Zones Has Laid a Micro Foundation for the Socialist Market Economic System**

Professor Su Dongbin stated early on: "We must acknowledge that the operational mechanism which governs the market economy cannot be built on the micro foundation of the planned economy, its ownership structure has to be diversified."[22] At the initial stage of the special economic zones, the Central Government clearly required the special economic zones to go beyond the existing system. For the sake of experimentation, the special economic zones could follow the principle that "special cases are handled with special methods, new things are done in new ways, the stand is unchanged and methods are novel", and fully serve as the experimental fields, so as to explore the path to the reform of China's economic system and acquire experience. In fact, from the beginning, the special economic zones focused on the market-based allocation of resources as the means for regulating the economic activities and made experimentations regarding the establishment of the socialist market economic system, including the practice of diversifying the ownership structure.

According to archival documents, the officials of Guangdong Province first proposed, in 1979, to carry out the work on attracting foreign capital in pilot cities and authorize Shenzhen and Zhuhai to act as pilot cities; they also suggested that after the pilot work had become successful, similar pilot work should be carried out in other cities. One priority of the pilot work was the attraction of foreign capital and development of the export-oriented industries. The *Regulations of Guangdong Province for Special Economic Zones*, promulgated on August 26, 1980, provided that "the special economic zones encourage foreign nationals, overseas Chinese, Hong Kong and Macao compatriots and their companies and enterprises to make investments and set up factories, or cooperate with the Chinese side in the form of joint ventures

[20]Su Dongbin, *Selected Records of China's Contemporary Economic Thinking*, Social Sciences Academic Press, 2009, p. 269.

[21]Su Dongbin, *Brief History of Chinese Special Economic Zones*, Guangdong Economic Press, 2001, p. 316.

[22]Su Dongbin, Three Major Requirements of the Market Economic System for the Ownership Structure, *Economic Research Journal*, 1998 (12).

to establish factories, enterprises and other undertakings, and protect their assets, due profits and other legal incomes according to laws." The establishment of the special economic zones broke the longstanding convention that the players engaged in market activities were only those from the public sector of the economy in China, and shaped a new pattern for the market system in which diverse sectors of the economy—including the economy under the ownership of all of the people, the economy under collective ownership, various types of joint operation economies, private economy and individual economy—coexisted in the special economic zones and various economic situations linked and influenced each other, and jointly developed. In particular, foreign investors were allowed to enter the material production market, which was a major breakthrough, both theoretically and in practice. Afterwards, with respect to the ownership structure, the 14th National Congress of the Communist Party of China explicitly brought forth the policy of long-term joint development of diverse sectors of the economy.

In November 1993, the *Decisions Concerning Several Issues Involving the Establishment of the Socialist Market Economic System* was adopted during the Third Plenary Session of the 14th Central Committee of the Communist Party of China, which stated efforts to further transform the operational mechanism of the state-owned enterprises and establish a modern enterprise system which would adapt to the requirements of the market economy and ensure that the property rights were clearly delimited, rights and responsibilities were well defined, the government functions were separated from enterprise management, and the management was scientific. The Shenzhen Special Economic Zone became the first in China to establish the modern enterprise system on a pilot basis. In the later period, the state-owned enterprises were restructured according to the corporate system in an all-round way, and all state-owned enterprises in the competitive industries were transformed into limited liability companies and incorporated companies. The development of the mixed ownership economy further stimulated the diversification of the holders of the property rights of state-owned enterprises. The practice of diversifying the ownership structure in the special economic zones induced historical breakthroughs in the theory of ownership. The report to the 15th National Congress of the Communist Party of China officially stated: "Keeping public ownership as the mainstay and allowing the economy with diverse forms of ownership to develop side by side is a basic economic system at the primary stage of socialism in China", "Public ownership can and should be realized in various ways", "The state-owned economy controls the lifelines of the national economy and plays the leading role in economic development", "The non-public sectors of the economy are an important part of China's socialist market economy", "The public sector of the economy includes not only the state-owned economy, the collective economy but also the state-owned sector and collective sector of the mixed ownership economy".

After the 16th National Congress of the Communist Party of China, the basic economic system of keeping public ownership as the mainstay and allowing the economy with diverse forms of ownership to develop side by side was further improved and developed. The 16th National Congress of the Communist Party of China vowed to uphold and improve the above basic economic system according to the requirements for emancipating and developing the productive forces. The 16th National Congress insisted on unswervingly consolidating and developing the public sector of the economy, steadfastly encouraging, supporting and guiding the development of its non-public sectors. The 16th National Congress required that keeping public ownership as the mainstay and promoting the development of the non-public sectors of the economy should be coordinated in socialist modernization and must not oppose each other. Proceeding from the new starting point of historical development, based on the above "unswerving" and "steadfast" policies, the 17th National Congress of the Communist Party of China vowed to provide equal protection for the real rights and shape a new pattern in which the economy with diverse forms of ownership competes on an equal footing and mutually promotes itself, so as to deepen the understanding of the basic economic system of socialism. According to the report to the 18th National Congress of the Communist Party of China, measures should be taken to unswervingly encourage, support and guide the development of the non-public sectors of the economy, ensure that the economy with diverse forms of ownership can get equal access to the production factors, equally participate in market competition according to the laws and be equally protected by those laws. As further stated during the Third Plenary Session of the 18th Central Committee of the Communist Party of China, both public and non-public sectors of the economy are important parts of the socialist market economy and the important foundation on which to base China's economic and social development. We must unswervingly consolidate and develop the public sector of the economy, keep public ownership as the mainstay and give play to the leading role of the state-owned economy, continuously enhance the vigor, controlling force and influence of the state-owned economy. We must steadfastly encourage, support and guide the development of the non-public sectors of the economy, and arouse the vigor and creativity of those sectors of the economy.

Regarding China's socialist economy, in the more than 60-year period of China's economic development from the initial period of new China to the period since the 18th National Congress of the Communist Party of China, carrying out the reform and opening up, and establishing the special economic zones to develop a socialist market economy has been the most important practice and has achieved unprecedented achievements. With the development and improvement of the structure of ownership in the special economic zones, China's socialist market economy has witnessed, in continuous practice, the gradual formation and improvement of a new pattern, that is, that public ownership remains the mainstay and multiple forms of ownership develop side by side.

(II) The Shareholding Reform of Enterprises has Enabled the Special Economic Zones to be the First to Build the Foundation for the System of Modern Enterprise

The stockholding system is a form of capital organization of modern enterprises. It is conducive to separating ownership from management power, enhancing the efficiency of the enterprise and of the capital operations. The corporate shareholding reform of publicly-owned enterprises, including the state-owned enterprises in the special economic zones, can ensure that the publicly-owned enterprises adapt to the development of the market economy and are reformed into market players and legal entities responsible for their own management decisions, profits and losses, and they can gradually improve the structure of the corporate governance within the framework of the corporate stockholding system. Therefore, as publicly-owned enterprises, especially the state-owned enterprises, are reformed into modern companies, among which the important enterprises are state-controlled—particular ones are solely state-owned, they can keep pace with the modern companies in countries with a general type of market economy, and they can not only compete equally with the market players with a non-public ownership, such as foreign-funded enterprises and private enterprises, but they can also participate in competition on the international market. As shown, the stockholding system offers a new line of thought for enterprise reform and helps find a way and route to combine China's public ownership, especially state ownership, with a market economy.

1. **A Pilot Shareholding Reform was Carried Out in the Special Economic Zones**

The Shenzhen Special Economic Zone greatly moved ahead in reform: Upon its establishment, it followed the international practice and initiated the shareholding reform of state-owned enterprises by diversifying shareholders and allowing foreign capital and private capital to hold shares, and enterprises to go public. China's stock market kicked off in the Shenzhen Special Economic Zone. On July 8, 1983, the first stock company in new China—Baoan County Joint Investment Co., Ltd.—was issued in Shenzhen. In October, 1986, the Shenzhen Municipal Government officially issued the *Interim Regulations of the Shenzhen Special Economic Zone for a Pilot Shareholding Reform of State-owned Enterprises*, which officially launched the experimentation of the corporate shareholding reform, and specified the stipulations for the internal organization of the incorporated companies and the enterprise system, with immediate implementation. On March 3, 1987, the Shenzhen Municipal Government released the *Interim Measures of the Shenzhen Special Economic Zone for Pilot Registration Concerning the Stockholding System of State-owned Enterprises*, which officially initiated the zone's pilot shareholding reform of enterprises and stock issuance, and further standardized the regulations and the actual operating procedures for the shareholding reform of the state-owned enterprises. The shareholding reform was piloted in six large municipal state-owned enterprises. On December 28, 1987, the Shenzhen Development Bank, the first regional joint-stock commercial bank owned by the State, enterprises and private persons in China, convened the first shareholders meeting and was officially established.

The explorations and experimentations in Shenzhen were recognized and supported by the Central Government and the Guangdong Provincial Government. On February 10, 1988, in the official reply to the application filed by Guangdong Province for intensifying the reform and expanding the opening up to speed up economic development, the State Council approved the following regulations: Enterprises can issue shares to the general public and individuals within the province, the economic central cities can be approved to set up a number of enterprise credit rating agencies and securities companies specializing in issuing as agent, underwriting, purchasing and selling shares and bonds, and the stockholding system can be adopted in large and medium-sized state-owned enterprises. On April 25, 1988, the Shenzhen Municipal Government issued the *Interim Provisions of Shenzhen City for the Work on the Board of Directors at Municipal State-owned Enterprises* and the *Interim Provisions of Shenzhen City for the Work on Managers and Factory Directors of Municipal State-owned Enterprises*, which required the adoption of the general manager responsibility under the leadership of the board of directors of the joint-stock enterprises, and standardized the management of the joint-stock enterprises. In December, 1988, Shenzhen Vanke Enterprise Co., Ltd. issued shares to investors at home and abroad, and became the first enterprise to issue shares according to the international standard in China. In 1988, in the Shenzhen Special Economic Zone, the shareholding reform was attempted in all enterprises, and five enterprises were chosen for pilot share issuance and listing. In 1989, there were 189 joint-stock companies in Shenzhen, among which five were listed companies which officially issued shares. In 1991, there were 11 listed companies and a number of unlisted share companies were reorganized. In 1992, the *Interim Provisions of Shenzhen City for Joint-stock Companies* was issued in Shenzhen, which provided for the issues concerning joint-stock companies from the establishment to termination and liquidation so as to establish the legal status of the joint-stock companies. Since then, the pilot shareholding reform of enterprises has been fully conducted in Shenzhen (Table 4.2).[23]

The shareholding reform of the state-owned enterprises in the Shenzhen Special Economic Zone involved prohibitions on public ownership, so it was subject to a lot of criticism. Critics mostly approached the treatment of private capital under the stockholding system from a negative perspective, and they stressed that the opposite side of the social production materials, such as the old form of personal property, already existed in the shareholding system, and the transformation towards shares was still confined within the boundary of capitalism, so the transformation did not overcome the contradiction between the nature of wealth as social wealth and the nature of wealth as private wealth, so the contradiction developed in a new form. However, after the shareholding reform of the state-owned enterprises, the previous longstanding drawbacks quickly disappeared, the people had to take the state-owned enterprise reform seriously, and reanalyze the shareholding system. They believed that the shareholding system was only an economic form, that it could be adopted in both capitalism and socialism, and that it did not involve the nature of socialism. For what concerns the social nature of joint-stock companies, Karl Marx maintained that, with the establishment of joint-stock companies, the capital which was built through a social production mode and was conditional upon the social concentration of production materials and labor force directly took the form of social capital and became opposed to private capital, while its enterprises appeared to be social enterprises and were in opposition to private enterprises; these assets were no longer the private properties of the mutually-separated producers; on the contrary, they were

[23]Fan Gang, *A Study of China's Special Economic Zones-Yesterday and Tomorrow's Theory and Practice*, China Economic Publishing House, 2009, p. 66.

Table 4.2 Great events of the pilot shareholding reform in the special economic zone

Time	Great events
1983-07-08	The first stock in new China—Baoan County Joint Investment Co., Ltd.—was issued in Shenzhen
1986-10-15	The Shenzhen Municipal Government officially issued the *Interim Regulations of Shenzhen Special Economic Zone for the Pilot Shareholding Reform of State-owned Enterprises*
1987-03-03	The Shenzhen Municipal Government released the *Interim Measures of Shenzhen Special Economic Zone for Pilot Registration Concerning the Stockholding System of State-owned Enterprises*
1987-12-28	The Shenzhen Development Bank convened the first shareholders meeting and was officially established
1988-02-10	The State Council approved, in principle, the *Application Filed by Guangdong Province for Deepening the Reform and Expanding Opening Up to Speed Up Economic Development*, which was filed by Guangdong Province on January 7, 1988
1988-04.25	The Shenzhen Municipal Government issued the *Interim Provisions of Shenzhen City for the Work on the Board of Directors at Municipal State-owned Enterprises* and the *Interim Provisions of Shenzhen City for the Work on Managers and Factory Directors of Municipal State-owned Enterprises*
1988-12	Shenzhen Vanke Enterprise Co., Ltd. issued shares to investors at home and abroad
1992-02-19	The *Interim Provisions of Shenzhen City for Joint-stock Companies* was issued in Shenzhen

the properties of the united producers—social properties.[24] The practice in the Shenzhen Special Economic Zone firmly proves that the shareholding system is the main form of public ownership during the primary stage of socialism. Subsequently, the theoretical perspective that the shareholding system is the form for realizing public ownership has been gradually accepted by the people.

2. **Securities and Property Rights Exchange Markets Were Established in the Shenzhen Special Economic Zone**

In traditional socialist political economics, the explanation of capital given by Karl Marx was adopted: Capital is the value capable of bringing surplus value, capital is the patent of capitalism and the tool for capitalists to exploit workers; it is the element which reflects the essence of capital. Therefore, Karl Marx always denied capital and believed that "capital" should not exist in a socialist system. The mistake in this view is that the specific form of capital is not considered. If the ownership relationship is taken into account, under the condition of socialist public ownership, capital mainly takes the form of public ownership; capital still possesses the right to control labor, the right to claim and control labor surplus, it still vests with capital, but it is ultimately jointly owned by workers, and the surplus value is converted into capital in order

[24] *Selections of Karl Marx and Frederick Engels* (Vol. 2), People's Publishing House, 1995, p. 516.

to expand the productive forces of the whole society, and common prosperity is ultimately achieved. Generally speaking, capital refers to all those factors which can deliver income or profits to its owner. The forms of capital are diverse, including currency, land, goods, technology, information and power.

According to the *Decisions of the Central Committee of the Communist Party of China Concerning Several Issues Involving Improvement of the Socialist Market Economic System,* adopted during the Third Plenary Session of the 16th Central Committee of the Communist Party of China, property rights are the core and main part of ownership, including real rights, creditor's rights, stock rights and intellectual property rights. At present, most of the people in economic circles accept such a view: Property rights involve a scope which includes, but is much more extensive than, ownership; besides ownership, property rights also include the right of possession, the right to control, the right to operate, the right to obtain income and the right of disposal. Property rights are exclusive, mobile and diverse in form. Generally speaking, property rights mean the rights which can deliver income or profits to their owner, thus property rights fall within the scope of capital.

The establishment of the securities market is the inevitable result of the shareholding reform. Li Hao, then Party Secretary and Mayor of Shenzhen City, said that the establishment of joint-stock enterprises called for the emergence of a securities market. The securities market includes a securities issuance market and a securities trading market. The securities issuance market arose along with the corporate shareholding reform in the special economic zone. When the securities issuance market reached a certain scale, the securities trading market developed. In the late 1980s, the shareholding reform was piloted in more and more enterprises. Some enterprises printed and issued shares by themselves for over-the-counter trading, resulting in a disorderly operation. Shenzhen's proximity to Hong Kong caused a craze for shares in Shenzhen. On May 10, 1987, the Shenzhen Development Bank raised, for the first time, a share capital worth 7.90 million yuan from the general public in the form of subscription fees, thus the curtain on Shenzhen's stock issuance market rose. Subsequently, Shenzhen Special Economic Zone Securities Co., Ltd., the Shenzhen Guotou Securities Department and the Bank of China Securities Department were open for business, making preparations for stock trading. In 1988, the Shenzhen Development Bank became part of over-the-counter trading at Shenzhen Special Economic Zone Securities Co., Ltd., making the Shenzhen Development Bank one of the first joint-stock companies involved in over-the-counter trading in Shenzhen. Soon afterwards, Vanke, Gintian, Anda, Yuanye also issued shares and got involved in over-the-counter trading. With the increase in the volume of stock trading, there was an urgent need for larger, more regular and professional trading institutions. On November 26, 1990, the Shanghai Stock Exchange was established with the approval of the People's Bank of China. On December 1, 1990, the Shenzhen Stock Exchange was put into trial operation. The State Council set up the China Securities Regulatory Commission. On April 11, 1991, the Shenzhen Stock Exchange was officially established upon approval. On May 15, 1991, the Shenzhen Municipal Government issued the *Interim Regulations of Shenzhen City for the Management of Stock Issuance and Trading*, which were the first-ever stock market management regulations in China.

On July 3, 1991, with the official reply from the State Council, the Shenzhen Stock Exchange was officially put into operation. In December, Shenzhen saw the issuance of B shares to overseas investors.

After the establishment of the Shanghai Stock Exchange and the Shenzhen Stock Exchange, locally-issued shares—five old stocks in Shenzhen and eight old stocks in Shanghai—were traded (Table 4.3). Afterwards, the corporate shares issued in the rest of China were listed on the Shanghai Stock Exchange and the Shenzhen Stock Exchange. In 1992, when inspecting southern China, Deng Xiaoping affirmed the role of pilot stock issuance, which triggered a round of rises in the securities market. In 1995, the Shenzhen Municipal Government carried out a series of reforms and innovations in the securities market management system, operational system and technical conditions, and transformed the originally independent Shenzhen Securities Registration Co., Ltd. into a clearing house wholly-owned by the Shenzhen Stock Exchange, and established a unified operations management system, thus exercising an integrated type of management covering securities issuance, listing, trading and clearing, reducing the intermediate segments, and providing the institutional guarantee for improving the operating efficiency and service quality, effectively reinforcing the supervision. In 1996, Shenzhen Securities Registration Co., Ltd. was merged into the Shenzhen Stock Exchange, and the original secondary clearing for securities trading was turned into primary clearing under the exchange; in May, 1996, the system for centralized management and clearing of shares was officially implemented. In 2000, the State Council approved, in principle, Shenzhen's plan for establishing a growth enterprise market. In October, the Shenzhen Stock Exchange released the *Consultation Paper Concerning the Rules for a Growth Enterprise Market.* In November, the trading clearing system for the growth enterprise market was put into place. In July, 2001, the Shenzhen Securities Communication Center was formally completed, thus the preparatory work for the growth enterprise market had been completed. After the reform of non-tradable shares was basically completed, China's securities market got on the right track and became the barometer of China's macro economy.

With respect to the property rights trading market, on February 8, 1993, the Shenzhen Assets and Equity Exchange, the first cross-regional property rights trading institution in China, was established and put into operation, so the property rights of enterprises were formally transferred to the market. On October 13, 2000, the Shenzhen International Hi-tech Assets and Equity Exchange was established, which was the first assets and equity exchange to be established under the corporate system, and it was mainly engaged in trading the high and new technology achievements, projects or growth-type property rights in China. On November 16, 2009, the Shenzhen United Assets and Equity Exchange and the Shenzhen Cultural Assets and Equity Exchange were established. The Shenzhen United Assets and Equity Exchange results from a resource integration based on the original municipal assets and equity exchange center and the Shenzhen International Hi-tech Assets and Equity Exchange; it is the uniform comprehensive property rights trading market in Shenzhen. The Shenzhen United Assets and Equity Exchange effectively solves problems concerning market segmentation, small scale, insufficient radiation and the influence of Shenzhen's property rights market; and it further improves the multi-level capital market system.

Table 4.3 Five old stocks in Shenzhen

Issue time	Company name	Abbreviation and code	Overview of issuance
1987-05	Shenzhen Development Bank	Shen Fa Zhan (000001)	A total amount of 7.90 million yuan was raised from the general public through free subscriptions. The price per share was 20 yuan. Only 49.9% of the planned 795,000 shares were completed, 396,500 shares were actually issued. The actual proceeds amounted to 7.93 million yuan
1988-11	Shenzhen Vanke Enterprise Co., Ltd.	Shen Vanke (000002)	28 million shares were issued to domestic and foreign investors. The price per share was 1 yuan
1989-02	Gintian Industry Co., Ltd.	Shen Gintian (000003)	27,400 shares with a face value of 100 yuan were initially issued. 5.22 million shares were issued to the general public in the following year
1989-12	Shenzhen Shekou Anda Transport Co., Ltd.	Shen Anda (000004)	12.50 million shares with a face value of 1 yuan were issued, among which 5 million shares were issued to the general public
1990-03	Sino-foreign joint venture: Shenzhen Yuanye Industry Co., Ltd.	Shen Yuan Ye (000005)	9 million shares with a face value of 10 yuan were issued to the general public

The securities and property rights markets are the property rights trading markets. The continuous development and improvement of the securities market and the property rights market creates favorable conditions for ensuring that the market economic system is compatible with and combined with the basic socialist system. The practices of the special economic zones explore the path and offer experience for the reform towards the establishment of the socialist market economic system across the country.

3. **The Special Economic Zones Became the First to Build the Foundation for the Modern Enterprise System**

The modern enterprise system is associated with socialized mass production and reflects the requirements of a market economic system and it also enables the enterprises to really become legal entities and players in market competition. The modern enterprise system refers to a number of norms and modes relating to a series of acts, including modern enterprise organization, operation and management. It mainly covers the enterprise property rights system, the organization management system, the enterprise bankruptcy and merger system, the personnel system and the social security system.

In a large country with a 30-year history of a planned economy and deep-seated ideology, as the institutional change in breaking the traditional system is made by establishing the special economic zones, the dominance of state-owned enterprises is the inevitable prerequisite for reform during the gradual transformation from a planned economy to a market economy throughout the country. The establishment of the modern enterprise system of the state-owned enterprises is naturally crucial for the reform of China's economic system. The reason is that, although the introduction of the non-public sectors of the economy changes the ownership structure of China's economy, it occurs beyond the basic objects subject to the traditional planned economic system. The mainstream in China's economic life consists of state-owned enterprises, and the state-owned enterprises are the lifeline and fiscal pillar of the national economy. Therefore, Shenzhen's establishment of a modern enterprise system—in particular, the property rights reform—within the basic objects subject to the planned economic system has attracted attention nationwide.

Identifying the establishment of the modern enterprise system as the direction for the reform of state-owned enterprises is neither invented by the theorists in the special economic zones, nor the decision solely made by the governments of the special economic zones; however, the people in the special economic zones represented by Shenzhen have found a new way—the operational system based on three-level authorizations—to achieve ownership by all of the people and they have sought out an effective path for making public ownership compatible with and combined with a market economy, so as to become the first to build the micro foundation for a nationwide market economy. In July, 1987, Shenzhen became the first to set up the first special state-owned assets management body in China—Shenzhen Investment Management Co., Ltd., and continuous experimentations, practice and improvements were made by following the principle developed by the State that "state-owned assets are owned by the State, subject to differential supervision by the government and operated by enterprises at their discretion". The state-owned assets management commission led by the municipal government was established in September, 1992. In April, 1994, the first batch of (43) state-owned enterprises were granted the certificate of authorization. In March, 1995, the first state-owned assets operation company in Shenzhen—the Shenzhen Materials Corporation—was set up, so a new state-owned assets management system with operations based on three-level authorizations gradually took shape in the Shenzhen Special Economic Zone. The basic structure is as follows: The first level, the municipal state-owned assets management commission, exercises the all-round macro supervision and management of the state-owned operating assets, non-operating assets and resource assets across the city; the second level, the municipal state-owned assets operation company authorized by the municipal state-owned assets management commission, is specially engaged in operating the municipal operating state-owned assets and exercises the ownership of state-owned assets on behalf of the municipal government; the third level, the municipal state-owned assets operation company, grants the state-owned enterprises the certificate of authorized occupation of state-owned assets, and authorizes enterprises to exercise the property rights of the legal person and carry out the activities of production operations.[25]

If the modern enterprise system is considered the foundation for a market economy, identifying the owner representative who is to shape the property rights constraint mechanism is the foundation for building a modern enterprise system. The operation based on a three-level authorization in the Shenzhen Special Economic Zone has diversified property rights in state-owned assets, so it has, to a large extent, established the status of state-owned enterprises as the enterprises making their own management decisions, and has forced the state-owned enterprises to be solely responsible for their profits or losses; more importantly, this new system identifies the representative in the ownership of the state-owned assets and addresses the previous absence of an owner—previously, nobody was responsible for the state-owned assets, but now there is someone responsible for them, so that a crucial step has been taken in the property rights reform. This innovation has reformed the management system of the government as the superstructure; more importantly, it has fundamentally shaped micro players in the market economy, providing the basic condition and prerequisite for a sound operation of the market economy. The adoption of the system of operations based on three-level authorization in the Shenzhen Special Economic Zone has marked the emergence of a new form of property rights in the principal-agent system within the modern enterprise system. Apparently, in this process, the people in Shenzhen have advanced step by step and come across a solid stone, and they have boldly removed it instead of bypassing it. Shenzhen has contributed to the system of operations based on three-level authorization. This is the brilliant practice of and an enrichment of the Deng Xiaoping Theory.[26]

4.2.2 The People in the Special Economic Zones Have Explored and Developed a Distribution System Which Is Suitable for a Socialist Market Economy

In a sense, the reform of the economic system is a process of adjusting the relations of interest among different economic players and is reflected in the reform and adjustment of the system of income distribution. According to Karl Marx, any distribution of consumable materials is nothing but the result of the distribution of the production conditions, and the distribution of the production conditions mirrors the nature of the production mode. Under market economic conditions, whosoever possesses the production conditions can participate in the income distribution in the

[25]Luo Qinghe, *Introduction to the Economics of the Special Economic Zones*, Central Compilation & Translation Press, 2001, pp. 409–410.

[26]Su Dongbin, *Special Frontier Issues Concerning China's Special Economic Zones*, China Economic Publishing House, 2000, p. 155.

capacity of the owner of the production conditions. During the primary stage of China's socialism, the distribution of production conditions among the members of the society involves the distribution of the public and non-public production conditions. The multi-ownership structure dominated by public ownership requires that multiple distribution modes adapt to it.

(I) The Reform of the Wage Distribution System in the Special Economic Zones

1. The Special Economic Zones Became the First to Establish Various Types of Basic Wage Systems and Wage Distribution Modes, and the First to Reform the Highly Concentrated Enterprise Wage Distribution System

The reform of the wage distribution system in the Shenzhen Special Economic Zone started by granting the enterprises the autonomous right to distribute, and ensured that enterprises could choose, at their own discretion, the internal wage system, determine the total wages, the wage standard and distribution mode in light of their own production operation characteristics and economic benefits. In 1982, the reform of the wage system—a new wage system of basic wage + wage attached to posts + floating wage—was piloted in the Sino-Hong Kong joint venture Bamboo Garden Hotel and Youyi Restaurant in the Shenzhen Special Economic Zone. In 1983, the pilot reform was extended to nine state-owned enterprises and several collective enterprises by mainly giving a certain wage management authority to enterprises and linking wages to the economic benefits, as well as focusing on removing the drawback from egalitarianism—wages were not linked to work under the traditional wage system. With the reform practices, the eight-level wage system was broken, flexible enterprise wage systems and wage modes were adopted, including more than ten basic enterprise wage systems covering the structural wage system, the floating wage system, the system of wages attached to posts, the technical grade-based wage system, the post wage system, the wage system based on seniority and the wage system based on post technical grade. In April, 1984, the municipal government released the *Wage Reform Plan of Shenzhen City for Industries and Factories*, which stated that enterprises can choose the wage distribution mode at their own discretion. The *Trial Plan of the Shenzhen Special Economic Zone for Comprehensive Reform of the Internal Management System*, released in August, 1984, provided that the structural wage system dominated by floating wages was generally carried out in state-owned enterprises in the special economic zone. The innovation in the structural wage system was conducted on two levels: First, the individual work performance determined most of the wage income so that "the big rice bowl" in which there was equality without considering the work performance was abandoned; second, the total wages were based on the production operations at the enterprises, and enterprises fixed their employees' wage level according to individual work performance. This reform shattered China's traditional wage system and made, for the first time, state-owned enterprises determine the distribution at their own discretion; this reform was of epoch-marking significance for the reform of the enterprise distribution system across the country.

The first-ever reform of the distribution system of the enterprises in the Shenzhen Special Economic Zone had the characteristics of arising from the instincts of the grass-roots level; it had no premise of legality, so a reverse transmission of pressure was made to promote interaction between the high and low levels so that the reform could be realistically carried out beyond the existing system, and it became successful.[27]

2. **A New Wage Determination System was Established in the Special Economic Zone, Breaking the Two "Big Rice Bowls" in the Wage Distribution Within Enterprises**

In the Shenzhen Special Economic Zone, with the separation of government functions from enterprise management, the government pushed enterprises to the market; as a result, the state-owned enterprises lost the condition for enjoying "the big rice bowl" given by the State. The power to determine wage distribution shifted from the government to enterprises, and the mechanism of wage determination became market-oriented. Meanwhile, the reform of the labor employment system and the system of internal distribution to the enterprises eliminated "the big rice bowl" for the employees. As early as 1980, the Shenzhen Special Economic Zone became the first to pilot the system of labor contract for Sino-foreign joint ventures, and effectively stimulated foreign-funded enterprises to choose the employment mode and the system of wage distribution at their own discretion. In 1981, the People's Congress of Guangdong Province promulgated the *Interim Provisions for Labor Wage Management of Enterprises in the Special Economic Zones*. In 1982, this system was extended to state-owned enterprises and public institutions. In 1983, the system of labor contracts was identified as the direction for labor employment in the special economic zones, and new provisions concerning recruitment, use, wages and insurance were made. In 1984, part of the regular workers were included in the contract system, and the boundary between the enterprise cadres and workers was broken, and the labor contract management or labor service contract management was performed among temporary workers and labor service workers. Afterwards, Shenzhen's labor employment was fully shifted to the labor contract system.

In 1984, a new wage system was practiced in Shenzhen. Wages tended to become market-oriented, and the level of the wage of employees was basically determined by the equilibrium wage rate formed on the labor market. The wage levels for different types of work forces at different levels became available on the market. The labor remuneration for employees became dependent on their contributions and the relationship of market supply and demand. The labor remuneration for employees at state-owned enterprises also became market-oriented to varying degrees. It took fewer than five years for Shenzhen to complete the reform of the labor employment system by replacing the old system with a new flexible one, which was one of the most successful institutional reforms in the special economic zones.

[27] Fan Gang, *A Study of China's Special Economic Zones-Yesterday and Tomorrow's Theory and Practice*, China Economic Publishing House, 2009, p. 57–59.

3. **The Wage Guarantee System Mainly Characterized by Socialization was Established and the Single Wage Guarantee System was Disrupted in the Special Economic Zone**

With the development of the economy with diverse forms of ownership in the market economic system, the wage guarantee system needed to be shifted from the government to society, and the Shenzhen Special Economic Zone became the first to do relevant experimentation (Table 4.4). First, the minimum wage guarantee system was set up. In 1992, Shenzhen saw the release of the minimum wage standard. In November, 1994, the *Regulations of the Shenzhen Special Economic Zone for Minimum Wages* was adopted during the municipal people's congress, which required that the minimum wage guarantee system should be established according to international practice. Second, the wage arrearage system was established. Shenzhen drew on international and Hong Kong's practice and experience in the wage protection system to develop a wage protection system in light of Shenzhen's reality. In October, 1996, the *Regulations of the Shenzhen Special Economic Zone for Wage Protection* was promulgated by the people's congress, which mainly required that the government should adopt the mode of mutual social aid to raise funds for advancing the wage arrears incurred to employees due to enterprise bankruptcy, safeguarding the basic rights and interests of workers and stabilizing the social order.

(II) **The Special Economic Zones Became the First to Establish the System Under Which Diverse Production Factors Were Allowed to Participate in Distribution**

According to the traditional theory, labor, capital and land constitute the production factors. The composition of production factors is not always unchanged; as the productive forces develop and science and technology, management and information play increasing roles in production, they are also to be considered as production factors, but these factors are the attached productive forces since they play a role through the improvement in the substance of substantive factors or a combination of substantive factors. With the intensification of the reform in the special economic zones and the development of the economy with diverse forms of ownership, in fact, the distribution mode has also greatly changed. In the non-public sectors of the economy, including private enterprises, Chinese-foreign joint ventures, Chinese-foreign cooperative enterprises and exclusively foreign-owned enterprises, the production factors, including capital and technology were incorporated into the income distribution as from the establishment of these enterprises. With the development of the joint-stock system, besides wage income, employees can also participate in profits on the basis of shares by purchasing company shares. Therefore, the incorporation of the production factors, including capital and technology into the income distribution is the inevitable result of the objective practice and development, and is the objective embodiment of reform practice and a theoretical improvement.

Table 4.4 Great events in the reform of the wage distribution system in the special economic zone

Time	Great events
1980	The labor contract system was piloted for Sino-foreign joint ventures
1981	The People's Congress of Guangdong Province promulgated the *Interim Provisions for Labor Wage Management of Enterprises in the Special Economic Zones*
1982	A new wage system of basic wage + wage attached to posts + floating wage was piloted in Bamboo Garden Hotel and Youyi Restaurant
1983	The labor contract system was identified as the direction for labor employment in the special economic zones, and new provisions concerning recruitment, use, wages and insurance were made
1984	Part of the regular workers were included in the contract system, and the boundary between enterprise cadres and workers was broken, and the labor contract management or labor service contract management was performed among temporary workers and labor service workers
1984-04	The municipal government released the *Wage Reform Plan of Shenzhen City for Industries and Factories*, which stated that enterprises could choose the wage distribution mode at their own discretion
1984-08	The *Trial Plan of the Shenzhen Special Economic Zone for Comprehensive Reform of the Internal Management System* provided that the structural wage system dominated by floating wages was generally carried out in state-owned enterprises in the special economic zone
1992	Shenzhen Municipal City released the minimum wage standard
1994-11	The *Regulations of the Shenzhen Special Economic Zone for Minimum Wages* was adopted during the municipal people's congress, which required that the minimum wage guarantee system and the wage protection system should be established according to international practice
1996-10	The *Regulations of the Shenzhen Special Economic Zone for Wage Protection* was promulgated by the people's congress

1. **Inclusion of Capital in Distribution**

Capital is the blood vital for the operation of an economic entity. The inclusion of capital in distribution is very common. With respect to the investments in enterprise legal persons, distribution is based on the amount of the contribution. In the special economic zones with Shenzhen as the template, capital is included in distribution, mainly in two ways: First, the joint stock system is practiced, under which dividends and bonuses are obtained on the basis of the number of shares held, so as to incorporate capital into distribution. The first-ever pilot reform of the joint-stock system in China was launched in the Shenzhen Special Economic Zone. This joint stock system is available principally in the following forms: (1) listed companies: the people purchase company shares to participate in the operations of the capital market and obtain investment returns from the capital; (2) within the issuing companies: employees are not only workers but also shareholders of companies; besides the wages distributed according to work, workers also enjoy dividends based on shares; (3) employee stock ownership within companies; (4) joint-stock cooperative companies established by transforming the rural collective economy: villagers become shareholders and obtain income according to shares. Second, private individuals make investments to establish economic entities and obtain returns from capital investments. With the rapid development of the special economic zones, and the increase in the level of personal income and accumulated capital, people obtain returns from capital investments through multiple investment channels, including joint investment in establishing economic entities.

2. **Inclusion of Land in Distribution**

Land is incorporated into distribution in two ways: First, the land use rights is contributed to become a shareholder so as to obtain dividends and bonus; second, the land use rights are leased to collect site use fees.

In 1979, in Shenzhen, the site use right was contributed to establish Sino-foreign joint ventures or site use fees were collected from Sino-foreign joint ventures. The land use rights can serve as the investment from the Chinese side in joint ventures.[28] In 1980, the concept of land as a commodity occurred in the national working conferences on city planning. In the same year, the State Council approved the policy of collecting land use fees from foreign-funded enterprises. Afterwards, the land use system was reformed, and the land ownership was separated from the land use rights; the previous unpaid and perpetual use of the land use rights was changed into paid and time-bound use. In 1981, the *Interim Provisions of the Shenzhen Special Economic Zone for Land Management* was adopted during the 13th Session of the Standing Committee of the 5th People's Congress of Guangdong Province, which approved the adoption of the following land policy in the special economic zone: administrative allocation, development of divided areas, decentralized operation and collection of use fees. On May 21, 1987, the *Land Management Reform Plan of the Shenzhen Special Economic Zone* was unveiled in Shenzhen, which stated that land was put into commercialized operation, the real estate market was opened, and paid use of land was carried out in an all-round way; however, the primary land market was monopolized by the government, the land use rights were transferred to investors by public auction, bidding and agreement; land was permitted to be circulated, transferred, traded and mortgaged; the competitive mechanism was introduced to ensure that land would become available as a commodity on the market. The *Regulations of the Shenzhen Special Economic Zone for Land Management* was adopted during the 13th Session of the Standing Committee of the 6th People's Congress of Guangdong Province, which provided that "the municipal government can transfer the land use rights through agreement, bidding and public auction". On April 12, 1988, the *Amendment to the Constitution of the People's Republic of China* was adopted during the 1st Session of the 7th National Congress of the People's Republic of China, which provided that "the State carries out the system of paid use of state-owned land according to laws, the land use rights can be transferred, leased and mortgaged according to laws". In the same year, real estate exchanges were established in cities across China and specialized banks set up a real estate credit department.

[28]Fan Gang, *A Study of China's Special Economic Zones-Yesterday and Tomorrow's Theory and Practice*, China Economic Publishing House, 2009, pp. 63–64.

In 2000, the first-ever local regulations concerning land trading in China—the *Regulations of Shenzhen City for Land Trading Market Management*—were issued, which provided that "the secondary and tertiary land use rights are permitted to be traded on the tangible market, but all trading of the operating land must be conducted at the real estate trading centers, and the system for the operating land shall be changed from the multi-track system to the single track system." In 2005, the bidding, listing and auction of industrial land was piloted, which was hailed as another major breakthrough in China's land use system and the construction of a factor market after the first auction took place in Shenzhen in 1987.

3. **Inclusion of Technology in Distribution**

Technology is incorporated, as an independent factor, in distribution in two ways: First, the patented or non-patented technologies introduced by groups or individuals outside the enterprises are directly converted into company shares, so that these groups or individuals enjoy profits; second, the technological achievements made within the enterprises are distributed to key technical personnel according to their contributions.

The Shenzhen Special Economic Zone developed relevant regulations and policies to encourage the inclusion of technology in distribution. In 1987, the *Interim Provisions of the Shenzhen Municipal People's Government for Encouraging Scientific and Technical Personnel to Establish Private Technology Enterprises* were promulgated, which stated that the "scientific and technical personnel can contribute their patented, proprietary technologies and trademark rights as well as other industrial property rights owned by them as investments which are then converted into shares". Afterwards, the *Regulations of the Shenzhen Special Economic Zone for the Protection of Technical Secrets* and the *Interim Measures of the Shenzhen Special Economic Zone for the Management of the Appraisal of Intangible Assets* as well as other regulations were made. In September, 1998, the Shenzhen Municipal Government issued the *Administrative Measures of the Shenzhen Special Economic Zone for the Conversion of Technological Achievements into Shares*, which further encouraged the inclusion of technology in distribution and standardized conversion of technology into shares.

The technological market was established and improved to promote the inclusion of technology in distribution. As from 1993, the scientific and technological achievements trading center, the technology market promotion center, the technology brokerage house, the patent service center, the intangible assets appraisal firm, the technical contract arbitration commission and the intellectual property rights tribunal were established in Shenzhen, boosting the establishment and improvement of the technological market system, promoting the commercialization of patented technologies and their conversion into productive forces. In 1988, the *Administrative Measures of the Shenzhen Special Economic Zone for the Conversion of Technological Achievements into Shares* was introduced, which provided that "the owner of technological achievements can contribute their technological achievements as capital to become a company shareholder". Since 1999, the annual China Hi-Tech Fair has been held, which has played a very important role in promoting the combination of technology and production. In 2000, the Shenzhen International Hi-tech Assets and Equity Exchange was set up, which is the first assets and equity exchange to have been established under the corporate system, and it is mainly engaged in trading the high and new technological achievements, projects or growth type property rights in China; this exchange has further propelled the combination of technology and production and the inclusion of technology in distribution.

The non-state-owned enterprises can contribute technology in order to become shareholders by agreements: the foreign side contributes technology, management and market exploitation to become a shareholder; or the Chinese side contributes technology, while the foreign side participates with capital; or Shenzhen's local enterprises contribute capital, while the enterprises from the inland areas contribute technology to become shareholders. For example, Shenzhen Kaifa Technology Co, Ltd. is a Sino-foreign joint venture, in which the foreign side contributes technology to become a shareholder, and technology is included as an independent factor in distribution. Huawei, ZTE and other private enterprises contribute key technical personnel and important technologies to become shareholders. This distribution mode fully arouses the enthusiasm of scientific and technical personnel so as to ensure a good development of the enterprises.[29]

4. **Inclusion of Management in Distribution**

Management is also a production factor. As the work of managerial personnel is special, the management labor of managers plays a special, irreplaceable role in the activities of production operations of the enterprises and their survival and development. As management work is a special kind of production work, the managerial personnel should obtain a relatively high income.

In the non-state owned enterprises, management can be embodied as complex work with high wages and bonuses. In some foreign-funded enterprises and private enterprises, besides higher wages and bonuses, the senior managerial personnel are also given bonus shares, in which case, management is included as a special production factor in distribution. For most of the operators at state-owned enterprises, management is incorporated into distribution by means of wages and bonuses. As from 1994, in Shenzhen, a new way for "management to be included in distribution" was investigated, and the *Interim Measures of Shenzhen City for Pilot Annual Salary System Involving Operators of State-owned Enterprises* was developed for the pilot implementation of an annual salary system concerning operators at state-owned enterprises. In 1997, the Shenzhen Municipal Government issued the *Interim Provisions of Shenzhen City for a Pilot Annual Salary System Involving Operators of State-owned Enterprises*. According to the provisions of the new annual salary system, the operators can be amply rewarded with cash, shares and convertible bonds, and the reward funds can be deducted from after-tax profits.

[29]Wu Xianduo, An Attempt at Keeping Work-based Distribution as the Mainstay and Coexistence of Multiple Distribution Modes—A Review of the Distribution System Reform in Shenzhen Special Economic Zone, *Practice and Theory of SEZS*, 2000 (9).

The Shenzhen Special Economic Zone became the first to explore and practice the inclusion of multiple factors in distribution, and combine the work-based distribution with the distribution made according to the production factors to ensure that the system of income distribution is adapted to the development of a market economy. This offers valuable experience and a vivid sample for the reform of the distribution system across the country.

(III) The Reform of the Distribution System in the Special Economic Zones has Enriched the Significance of the Socialist Distribution Theory

The previous theory of socialist distribution only focused on work-based distribution without other distribution principles and other distribution modes. In the new period of the reform and opening up, with the development of the market economy in the special economic zones, the single mode of work-based distribution has been broken and other production factors have been gradually included in distribution. In the practice of the special economic zones, with the adoption of the joint-stock system, the share-based bonus has become a distribution mode which cannot be ignored; interest is no longer a symbolic encouragement but a real distribution mode; land rent has actually existed as a result of paid use of land; the capital profit shared in an association has become the rational income of capital owners, including the State, the collective and individuals; technology can be converted into shares; the emergence and development of different distribution modes different from the work-based distribution, including contract income, rents and commissions, show that their existence is necessary and rational. As indicated, the product distribution is governed not merely by the law of work-based distribution but by a law of overarching and extensive distribution. This is the law according to which the products are distributed according to production factors.

The report to the 13th National Congress of the Communist Party of China affirms the fact that distribution is carried out according to production factors, and states that the distribution mode cannot be a single one during the primary stage of socialism, that we must follow the principle that the work-based distribution becomes dominant and is supplemented by other distribution modes. The report to the 14th National Congress of the Communist Party of China continues the statement in the report to the 13th National Congress of the Communist Party of China: "With respect to the system of distribution, work-based distribution becomes dominant and is supplemented by other distribution modes, considerations are given to both efficiency and equity". According to the report to the 15th National Congress of the Communist Party of China, we should adopt the system in which work-based distribution becomes dominant and multiple distribution modes coexist; we should combine work-based distribution with the distribution according to production factors. The report to the 16th National Congress of the Communist Party of China further states that we should establish the principle of including production factors such as labor, capital, technology and management in distribution, and improve the system in which work-based distribution becomes dominant and multiple distribution modes coexist. This shows that we deepen the distribution theory of the primary stage of socialism and there is a new breakthrough in the distribution theory and distribution policy during the current stage in China. The report to the 17th National Congress of the Communist Party of China further makes it clear that we should uphold and improve the system of distribution in which work-based distribution becomes dominant and multiple distribution modes coexist, and we should make the system perfect in which production factors, including labor, capital, technology and management, are included in the distribution according to contributions. The report to the 18th National Congress of the Communist Party of China stresses that the basic system of a socialist economy and system of distribution should be upheld.

The improvement and supplementation in the new distribution theory in the Party's and national reports have continuously affirmed the experiments and practice of the new system of distribution under the socialist market economic system in the special economic zones. This is also a theoretical contribution from the special economic zones to China's development path towards modernization.

4.3 Contributions from the Special Economic Zones to the Theory of the Government's Functions Under a Socialist Market Economic System

During the establishment of China's socialist market economic system, the market system has been gradually improved, market players have gradually become full-fledged and the mechanism of market operations has become increasingly well-functioning. Meanwhile, as an important player in the market economy, the government has also gradually clarified the boundary between it and the market and has transformed its functions to gradually change from an omnipotent government to a service-oriented government. The transformation of the government's functions under the socialist market economic system is mainly conducted in the following ways: The government gradually delegates powers to the market, and withdraws its intervention in the micro market players to become a limited, effective and service-oriented government; the government functions are gradually concentrated in exercising macro control and regulations, improving the market mechanism, and addressing the market failure to ensure the stable operation of the socialist market economy. Being market-oriented, China's special economic zones are charged with heavy responsibilities for seeking out the path for China's economic system and exploring the relationships between the government and the market and the new position of the government's functions under the new system. First, the special economic zones have fully leveraged their policy advantages to probe the relationships between the government and the market under the socialist market economic system, and define the boundary of government functions; second, the governments of the special economic zones have actively searched for a path towards building a limited, effective and service-oriented government and have offered the original sample for determining the boundary of government functions under the market economic system. Furthermore, the experiments and practice in the special economic zones have also enriched and developed the theory and means of governmental macroeconomic regulation and control under the socialist market economic system, providing valuable experience for the placing of the government's functions under China's socialist market economic system.

4.3.1 The Special Economic Zones Became the First to Clarify the Relationships Between the Government and the Market and Preliminarily Explore the Boundary Between the Government and the Market Under the Market Economic System

From the perspective of the historical development of the theory of a market economy, the relationships between the government and the market involve the issue concerning the origin of the market economy. The market economy is the economic system or economic form in which the market mechanism plays the fundamental role in resource allocation, but the market mechanism fails to address the short supply of public goods, the market monopoly, externalities and macroeconomic disequilibrium in the market economy. Market failure calls for active intervention from the government. On the other hand, both excessive and insufficient intervention from the government reduces the efficiency of economic operations. This gives rise to the issue concerning the relationships between the government and the market in the development of the market economy. Hungarian economist Janos Kornai compared the relationships between the government and the market to a marriage which cannot be broken up, and he believed that there was a complementary relationship between the two. In fact, the debate on the relationships between the government and the market has never ended since the emergence of the market economy in China.

The quintessence of the market economy is that the government should be a limited government that can properly deal with the relationships between the government and the market, while the key lies in rationally identifying the boundary of governmental functions. That boundary neither depends on the government itself, nor is it simply defined by "big government" and "small government"; that boundary is determined by the market environment and the objects which interact with government activities, and it varies with the changing environment and objects. Comrade Deng Xiaoping said that our leading organizations at various levels ran many affairs which should not have been handled, that cannot be properly dealt with by them or that were beyond their capacity; as long as these affairs were transferred to the lower levels, enterprises, public institutions and social organizations for being handled under the system of democratic centralism according to certain regulations and rules, they could be handled well; however, once they were centralized with the Party and the government's leading organizations, the departments and commissions under the central leadership, it was very difficult to handle them properly because none of these organizations was adept at dealing with the burdensome matters unfamiliar to them.[30] The government's functions and powers should be confined within the government's capacity, and it is also important to clarify what the government should, can, should not and cannot do.

For the boundary of the government's functions, the government under the socialist market economic system is a limited government. There is no universally applicable criterion for determining the proportions of market regulations and economic regulations which should be conducted by the government. The rational proportions vary with different fields. In today's society, the economy is no longer purely a choice made by the market and the government; it is often a choice based on different combinations of both. Generally, in the cases where self-regulation and self-management are possible on the market and in the society, the government should not act beyond its functions and powers. Where there is no permission according to laws, the access for the government is denied. Where there are no prohibitions from laws, the market is provided with access.

The socialist market economic system is a great combination of socialism and a market economy and a successful experiment. In this experiment, the governments of the special economic zones shoulder the heavy responsibility for exploring the boundary of the government's functions under the new system while developing the market economy. Based on the above analysis concerning the theory of the boundary of the government's functions, we believe that the governments of the special economic zones were the first to make the following beneficial experiments.

(I) **Investigations Regarding the Market Coverage and Scope**

Shenzhen is one of the first-established special economic zones in China. The Central Government established the special economic zones by giving policies without financial support. This required the special economic zones to seek production factors and sell products through both domestic and international markets, and take the path towards a market economy. In the Shenzhen Special Economic Zone, the spirit of being bold in making breakthroughs was carried forward, and the whole administrative system was reformed and reconstructed several times in a market-oriented way in light of the actual conditions. Based on giving full play to the role of the market mechanism, the breadth and intensity of the market-oriented reform was expanded by carrying out a series of breakthrough reform experiments in reforming the enterprise system, cultivating the market system, establishing the macroeconomic regulation system and improving the distribution and social security system. With efforts from the government of the Shenzhen Special Economic Zone, that special economic zone became the first to establish ten large systems involving the market economy, which are the classic cases concerning the explorations of a path towards a market economy. During its reform and development, the Shenzhen Special Economic Zone has always followed the overall direction of being market-oriented. In 1994, according to the decisions made during the 14th National Congress of the

[30] *Selected Works of Deng Xiaoping* (Vol. 2), People's Publishing House, 1993, p. 328.

Communist Party of China and the Third Plenary Session of the 14th Central Committee of the Communist Party of China, the *Overall Plan for Building a Socialist Market Economic System* was developed in the Shenzhen Special Economic Zone and that special economic zone became the first to put forward the goal of building the socialist market economic system. In 1997, the basic framework, mainly made up of ten large systems, for the socialist market economy preliminarily took shape.[31]

On May 21, 1997, the Xinhua News Agency released the news: The State Institutional Reform Commission conducted a special research survey and believed that Shenzhen's socialist market economic system has been preliminarily formed.[32] With 10–20 years of reform, ten large systems involving the socialist market economy have been shaped in the Shenzhen Special Economic Zone. These systems include: (1) the ownership system in which public ownership is kept as the mainstay and diverse sectors of the economy compete on an equal footing and develop side by side; (2) the market system based on the commodity market and supported by factor markets; (3) the market system dominated by indirect means and supported by factor markets; (4) the market-based price system; (5) the state-owned assets supervision, management and operation system with capital as the bond; (6) the system of distribution in which work-based distribution is dominant and multiple distribution modes coexist; (7) the social security system which combines mutual social aid with personal security; (8) the system of social service supervision dominated by intermediary organizations; (9) the national economic accounting and enterprise financial accounting system which caters to the needs of the market economy; (10) the law and regulation system which adapts to the needs of the socialist market economic system. The ten large systems involving the socialist market economy in the Shenzhen Special Economic Zone constitute the main part of the basic framework for the socialist market economic system and serve as an important reference and basis for establishing China's socialist market economic system.

(II) Explorations Regarding the Reform of the State-Owned Enterprise Management System

In more than 30 years, the reform of state-owned enterprises has been continuously intensified in the Shenzhen Special Economic Zone, while the successful experience in the reform of state-owned enterprises in the special economic zone has produced the demonstration effect on and set an example for the reform of state-owned enterprises across the country. The reform of the autonomous right for enterprises was expanded and the reform of the state-owned enterprise property rights system was preliminarily investigated in the Shenzhen Special Economic Zone at the beginning of its establishment. In July, 1983, the first large state-owned joint-stock company—Baoan County Joint Investment Co., Ltd.—was set up in Shenzhen. Fruitful

[31] *Circular Concerning Printing and Distribution of Shenzhen's Plan for Comprehensively Establishing the Relatively Perfect Socialist Market Economic System*, (1997) No. 24 Document of CPC Shenzhen Municipal Committee and Municipal Government, December 31, 1997.

[32] Su Dongbin, Zhong Ruoyu, A Study of China's Special Economic Zones, The Commercial Press, 2010, pp. 274 and 275.

reform explorations regarding state-owned enterprises were made by establishing the modern enterprise system in the Shenzhen Special Economic Zone as from 1992 after the reform involving the contracted managerial responsibility system and the joint-stock system. These experimentations mainly include diversification of property rights, reform of the state-owned assets management system and of the internal management system of enterprises, the strategic adjustment and transformation of state-owned enterprises. With the intensification of the reform of the property rights system, the system of distribution, the management system and of the supervision and restriction mechanism, as well as the gradual introduction of more reform measures, the Shenzhen Special Economic Zone became the first to establish the modern enterprise system in China.

The reform of state-owned enterprises started early and has been vigorously pushed forward in the Shenzhen Special Economic Zone. An experiment was made in transforming the state-owned enterprise system in the Shenzhen Special Economic Zone as early as its initial stage; the Shenzhen Special Economic Zone became the first to reform the labor employment system, the enterprise operational mode and system, and promulgate the shareholding reform regulations in China. The enterprises under the corporate system were regulated. In the Shenzhen Special Economic Zone, the industrial structure of the state-owned economy and state-owned enterprises was strategically reorganized—under the guideline that "there is both withdrawal and entry, actions are taken in some areas while there are no actions in other areas", measures were taken to invigorate large enterprises while relaxing control over small ones to make some state-owned enterprises leave the competitive fields, so as to enhance the quality of state-owned assets, optimize the economic structure and generally enliven the state-owned enterprise economy. Thanks to the advantage of their location due to their proximity to Hong Kong, Shenzhen's state-owned enterprises have enjoyed more opportunities for participating in international competition, and they have been able to get access to more information early and they quickly drew on the advanced management philosophy and management experience from enterprises in the developed countries; moreover, they have been able to swiftly adapt to the changes in domestic and foreign markets. The enterprise operation mechanism has also become relatively flexible. In the special economic zones at the forefront of the reform and opening up, since their establishment, government institutions have embarked on continuous reforms and innovations as well as more thorough separation of government functions from enterprise management than their counterparts in the inland areas.

(III) **Analyses of the Reform of the State-Owned Asset Management System**

In order to further realize the separation of the government's functions from enterprise management, and define the status and responsibilities of the contributor of the state-owned capital, the people in the Shenzhen Special Economic Zone followed the requirements of the modern enterprise system to make reform investigations of the state-owned capital operation and supervision system and establish it. It consists of three levels: the municipal state-owned assets management commission—a state-owned assets management company—enterprises (see the figure below). As a

Fig. 4.6 Shenzhen's three-level system of state-owned capital operations and supervision

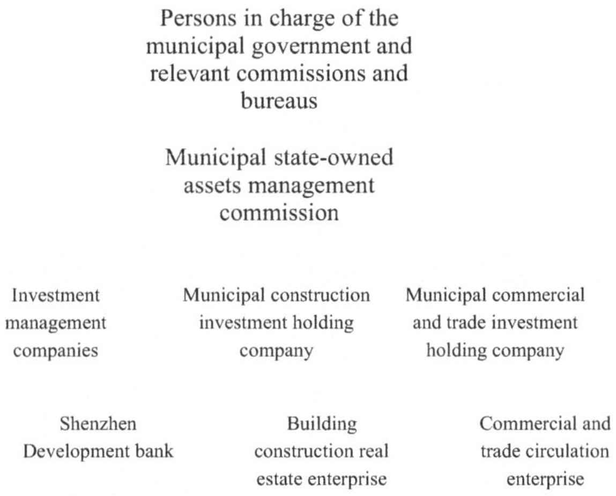

new way to achieve ownership by all of the people, it effectively combined public ownership with the market economy, so that the Shenzhen Special Economic Zone became the first to build the micro foundation of a market economy across the country (Fig. 4.6).

Under the three-level system of state-owned capital operations and supervision, the separation of the government's functions from capital and enterprise management is achieved at the first and second levels, and the separation of the State's ultimate ownership from the ownership of the enterprise legal person is achieved at the third level. With multi-level authorization and establishment of the responsibility system, the administrative subordination relationship between the government and enterprises under the planned economic system has been changed into a capital bond relationship between the principal and agent in the market economy, and a state-owned assets operation company has been shaped as the property rights holder and responsible party so as to better address the absence of the party responsible for state-owned assets, and offering the precondition for state-owned enterprises to enjoy the status of a legal person and become the independent entities capable of making their own management decisions. During the investigations of the state-owned assets management system, the three-level system of state-owned assets management was a great innovation in the Shenzhen Special Economic Zone. However, with the intensification of the reform of state-owned enterprises, the new system of operations based on a three-level authorization and a two-level management structure, etc. has basically failed to solve the problems concerning the state-owned enterprises and the state ownership, which should be further explored.

(IV) First-Ever Pilot Implementation of the Quasi-public Goods Supply Mechanism

In 2006, the Shenzhen Special Economic Zone saw the all-round reform of the organizational system and the separation of the government's functions from public institutions: The public institutions without the functions of public welfare were surrendered to the market, while the public welfare-oriented public institutions were supported by the financing of the government. As from the second half of 2002, urban public utilities including water, gas and public transportation were open to international bidding and available for the introduction of strategic investors. Shenzhen became the first to issue the *Administrative Measures for the Franchised Operation of Municipal Public Utilities* in China, which was later revised as the *Regulations for the Franchised Operation of Municipal Public Utilities*. Subsequently, there has been a legal basis for managing the franchised enterprises. As from 2006, Shenzhen further improved the supervisory system of public utilities, and established the special fiscal subsidy mechanism for urban pipeline gas and public transportation to effectively achieve the alignment between social public welfare and enterprise-oriented operations. In 2007, the system of purchase of services from social organizations by the government was established in Shenzhen, giving full play to the roles of citizens and social organizations in the management of public social affairs. In 2008, nearly 3/4 of Shenzhen's general budget expenditure was arranged for public services and the people's livelihood, showing that the fiscal expenditure had favored people's livelihood. In 2011, the 12th Five-Year Plan period began, the 26th Summer World University Games were held in Shenzhen, the expenditures of the Shenzhen Municipal Government for general public services and the development of undertakings concerning the people's livelihood accounted for more than 80% of the general budget expenditures.[33] In 2013, first priority was given to guaranteeing the expenditures for people's livelihood, and equal access to the basic public services was accelerated in the Shenzhen Special Economic Zone. The full-year municipal fiscal expenditure in five programs concerning people's livelihood, including education, medical treatment and health, social security, employment and housing security amounted to 51.8 billion yuan, up 14%, up 4.5 percentage points compared with the municipal public fiscal revenue in the same year.[34]

Thanks to its special social structure, policies and geographical advantages, the Shenzhen Special Economic Zone has provided the complete sample and base for experimentation and demonstration in improving the quasi-public goods supply mechanism. Being adjacent to Hong Kong and Macao, Shenzhen is an outward-looking port city with the largest quantities of both ports and inbound and outbound personnel in China, and is closely connected to the international community and it is able to quickly get access to a great deal of information. As the successful model in the reform and opening up, the Shenzhen Municipal Government can exert a far-reaching international influence through its actions. It should continue to better serve as the window and produce the demonstration effect in investigating and improving the socialist market economic system with Chinese characteristics and fully showcasing the institutional charm of socialism with Chinese characteristics.

---

[33]Qiao Jiahua, Report on the 2011 Budget Implementation and the 2012 Drafted Budget of Shenzhen City, *Shenzhen Special Economic Zone Daily*, February 10, 2012.

[34]Qiao Jiahua, Report on the 2012 Budget Implementation and the 2013 Drafted Budget of Shenzhen City, *Shenzhen Special Economic Zone Daily*, February 9, 2013.

In the construction of the quasi-public goods supply mechanism, the delimitation of the boundary among the government, enterprises and society should ensure high efficiency, intensified supervision, greater transparency and reflect equity and justice. In order to avoid widespread turmoil in the society, Shenzhen's first-ever implementation of pilot programs is of special political and historical significance.

The Shenzhen Special Economic Zone became the first to clarify the relations between the government and the market in China. In the special economic zone, the boundary of the government's functions under the market economic system has been preliminarily analyzed to further extend the reform to the field of public services. Breakthroughs have been made in defining the government's service functions, cultivating the market system, simplifying administrative examination and approval procedures, standardizing the government procurement system and establishing the social security system. Its institutional achievements take the lead nationwide and institutional information has spilled over to various domestic reform fields through demonstration effects.

4.3.2 Beneficial Attempts Have Been Made to Build a Limited, Effective and Service-Oriented Government in the Special Economic Zones

The establishment of the new political system with a "small government, big society" in the Hainan Special Economic Zone is one of the experimentations and practices in building a limited, effective and service-oriented government. Upon becoming a province, Hainan followed the requirements of the reform of the political system to separate the functions of the Party from those of the government, separate the government's functions from enterprise management, streamline the governmental organs and establish more economic entities. In Hainan, the setting up of government institutions has dispensed with the existing institutional mode in other provinces and autonomous regions, with an emphasis on high capability and efficiency to realize a "small government, big society". Hainan's reform of the political system has a particular definition: The state administrative organs should be small, while the overall system for the people's survival, life and development should be large. A "small government" is a limited and effective government and means that a large number of economic functions are surrendered to society; the governmental institutions are simplified; the government's functions and work style are transformed; the efficiency of the work is improved. A "big society" means that a service-oriented government is built; the economic autonomous right of individuals and enterprises is recognized and guaranteed; enterprises forge an alliance to form enterprise groups at their own discretion; the independence of public institutions is affirmed and guaranteed. All matters which the government should not handle are dealt with by enterprises; the law of economics is followed and the extensive democratic autonomy is gradually practiced.[35] During the initial stage of the Hainan Special Economic Zone, the issue regarding where the government's functions lay was preliminarily addressed while developing the socialist market economy. The government of the special economic zone was bold in delegating its own powers, reducing its powers in the examination and approval indicators, and strengthening the services for investors and the general public. Meanwhile, full scope has been given to the roles of social intermediary organizations in the market economy. The experimentations and reforms in building a limited and effective government in the special economic zone are of demonstrative and referential significance.

The pilot comprehensive reform in Pudong has also resulted in many experimentations in building a limited, effective and service-oriented government. The public service function of the local government has been strengthened in Pudong. As the government's functions in public services and social management became relatively weak after China's reform of the tax system, the government of Pudong reinforced the financial guarantee for sub-districts, and stripped its investment attraction function so as to shift its focus towards public services. In Pudong, the market lever was used to achieve political purposes. In Pudong, the market forces were leveraged to set up a number of funds, including the scientific and technological development fund under commercialized operations, the venture capital investment guidance fund, with a shift from financial aid without payment towards paid use, which produced a good effect and carved out the path towards exploring how to improve the efficiency of governmental funds under the condition of a market economy. The government guides but does not intervene in the market. In Pudong, the governmental funds guide the social funds, while social funds are used to promote the optimization and reorganization of the enterprises and independent innovations. The government does not directly intervene in enterprise behaviors and acts in full compliance with the law of the market. This effectively ensures that governmental funds deliver massive returns when used on a small scale and are put into business operations. This gives a vigorous boost to the transformation of the developmental mode. With a typical significance, these experimentations have shown the clear direction for the government to carry out the macro policies and plans under the condition of a market economy.

The experiments in the special economic zones accord with the transformation of the government's functions and the requirements of the construction of the public finance; the experiments are correct in their direction, of great significance and have a far-reaching influence. They can be practically applied in the eastern developed coastal areas. With further development and improvement of China's socialist market economic system, they also serve as a strong reference for and have a good demonstration effect on the grass-roots government in western China in terms of transformation of the government's functions.

Being market-oriented, China's special economic zones are charged with the heavy responsibility for probing the path for the national economic system. During the reform in establishing the socialist market economic system, the building of a

[35]Chen Xiaoxing, *China's Largest Special Economic Zone—Hainan*, Shaanxi Tourism Press, 1988, p. 33.

limited and effective government actually represents the dialectical unity in breaking and making governmental functions. The establishment of the socialist market economic system means that the traditional planned economic system is abandoned; full play is given to the decisive role of the market in resource allocation; the economic activities follow the law of value; the price lever and the competition mechanism are leveraged to make the economy vibrant. However, an emphasis on the role of the market neither denies the function of planning nor fully rules out the role of the government. The adoption of the market economic system in the special economic zones is a reply to the objective requirement of the outward-looking economic development in the special economic zones. The requirement for building a limited and effective government in China's special economic zones reflects the general law of the modern market economy and the characteristics of the market economic development in those zones.

In the modern market economic system, the economy cannot do without the government and the market. The market is the foundation for economic operations and resource allocation. Maintaining the effective operation of the market economy is the focus of the government's intervention in economy. The combination of the government and the market is a logical unity of the mechanism of governmental intervention—the visible hand—and the market mechanism—the invisible hand. Therefore, under no circumstances does the intervention of the government weaken and replace the role of the market; on the contrary, the intervention of the government aims at creating a good internal and external order for an effective operation of the market. With the experimentations and practices in building a limited, effective and service-oriented government, we should thoroughly correct the creed, in the traditional market economic system, that the government with less intervention is the best government, and now we should uphold the idea that the government with the most appropriate intervention is the best government.

4.3.3 The Experimentations and Practices in the Special Economic Zones Have Enriched the Theory and Means of Governmental Macro Regulations and Control Under the Socialist Market Economic System

(I) **The Experimentations in the Special Economic Zones Have Shown the Necessity for Governmental Macroeconomic Regulation and Control**

A sound macroeconomic regulation and control system is essential for the socialist market economic system. With effective management, regulation and control, the government can ensure a balanced development and stable operation of the whole economy at the macro level, offset the imperfections in the market economy and guarantee social equity. Macroeconomic regulation and control is mainly exercised by the central government; however, the economic operation of a region may be accompanied by a variety of contradictions and problems, thus it is necessary for local governments to carry out macro management, regulation and control in order to ensure the sustained and healthy development of the national economy. Therefore, it is absolutely necessary to build a society-wide system for economic management regulation and control in a region. The experimentations in conducting a market-oriented reform and building a socialist market economic system in the special economic zones are accompanied by the establishment and improvement of the government's macroeconomic regulation and control system. The combination of both hands—the government's and the market's—is the internal requirement for economic development in the special economic zones.

First, the economic foundation was weak and there was acute shortage of resources in the special economic zones at their inception. If only the spontaneous effort of the market had been relied upon to accumulate the capital for building the infrastructures necessary for supporting a sustained, rapid economic development, it would have been impossible to make the special economic zones rapidly grow and take the lead nationwide; planned and step-by-step implementation was necessary. Therefore, on the one hand, the microeconomic operation should be regulated by the invisible hand and conditions should be created to leverage the role of the market, and all the fields where the market can play a role, should be regulated by the market. On the other hand, the macroeconomic operations should be regulated by the visible hand. The issues which cannot be addressed merely by the market can be dealt with by the government. Only when both hands are combined can the rational allocation of resources and the best interests be effectively realized to fulfill the government's purpose for the allocation of the productive forces and boost a sustained, rapid and healthy economic development in the special economic zones.

Second, as the experimental fields for national reform and the windows for opening up, the special economic zones cannot smoothly engage with international capital and further explore the socialist market economic system unless the macroeconomic regulation and control is strengthened and the costs for the reform are reduced. The special economic zones made the first move to reform the traditional system and build a new market economic system. The formation of the market price mechanism, the cultivation of the market system and the establishment of the modern enterprise system had a vital bearing on the overall situation, and they involve complicated interest relations, thus they would certainly meet with resistance from those with vested interests. The transformation from a planned economic system to a market economic system is a great historical transformation with far-reaching significance, and a great transformation is inevitably accompanied by risks. Where macroeconomic regulation and control is reinforced and various conflicts of interest are properly handled, the reform risks and the reform friction costs can be reduced to ensure that such a transformation can be safely and steadily carried out as far as possible. Meanwhile, the basic line of thought of China's opening up is the participation in the international division of work and entry into the world market. We should boldly draw on all civilization achievements created in human labor, all advanced operational models and management methods which reflect the modern socialized mass production from various countries in today's world, including the developed capitalist countries,[36] in order to develop socialism. In this regard, there were choices between the introduction of and resistance to something from foreign countries during the first-ever implementation of pilot programs in the special economic zones, and these choices were made by the authority and power of the government.

Third, China's special economic zones are areas with a multi-level ownership structure and diverse stakeholders. Priority is given to efficiency but equity is also taken seriously. The government's macroeconomic regulation and control is indispensable for preventing the market from increasing income inequality and special economic zones from veering off the socialist path.

The necessity for macroeconomic regulation and control in the special economic zones also mirrors that for national macroeconomic regulation and control. According to economist William Arthur Lewis, governmental intervention is little in a stable society, but the government should treat nothing lightly in a rapidly-changing society.[37] This remark, made by William Arthur Lewis half a century ago, remains of great significance for China's transformation from the traditional planned economic system to a socialist market economic system. A good macroeconomic regulation and control is crucial for performing the government's economic function and is the core of this function. Strengthening macroeconomic regulation and control is the inevitable requirement for developing a socialist market economy. In China, as a socialist country, the establishment of the new type of a macroeconomic regulation and control system is the reform of the original traditional planned economic system and an institutional innovation in discarding the functions and modes of traditional governmental management. The Third Plenary Session of the 18th Central Committee of the Communist Party of China stressed a better leverage of the government's role while carrying forward the decisive role of the market in resource allocation. Better giving play to the government's role in macroeconomic regulation and control is the inevitable requirement for developing the economy and establishing a socialist market economic system.

(II) The Experiences of the Special Economic Zones Offer the Rest of the Country Valuable Lessons on Macroeconomic Regulation and Functional Transformation of the Government's Functions

The qualified parties responsible for regulation and control determine the efficiency of the government's macroeconomic regulation and control. In the special economic zones, under the principle of separating the government's functions from enterprise management and public institutions, keeping a good macroeconomic regulation and control and relaxing the control over the micro aspects, the roles of the government, as the social administrator, the state-owned assets owner and the macroeconomic regulator and controller are explicitly defined. As the social administrator, the government should make various necessary regulations, cultivate the factor markets and promote their operation, shape relatively excellent market rules and order to ensure a level playing field for enterprises and individuals.

---

[36] *Selected Works of Deng Xiaoping* (Vol. 2), People's Publishing House, 1993, p. 373.

[37] William Arthur Lewis, *The Theory of Economic Growth*, The Commercial Press, 1983, p. 465.

As the owner of state-owned assets, the government should let professional management organizations engage in the management of these assets, and replace direct micro-management with indirect management. As the macroeconomic regulator and controller, the government should better carry out the economic development forecast, the overall balance regulation, the layout planning of the productive forces in major structural domains, and rationally identify the strategic goals, develop and apply the corresponding economic policies, guide and adjust a coordinated development of the national economy.

1. **Separate the Government's Functions from Enterprise Management, Transform the Functions of the Government as the Regulator**

The market economy requires the government to relinquish control over production operations. The government should refrain from interfering in the economic behavior of enterprises, and limit its involvement to keeping market order and pursuing fairness and equity. As the market players, enterprises enjoy the legal status of commodity producers and operators which engage in independent operations, they are solely responsible for profits and losses, they pursue self-development and exercise self-regulation. The market economy is governed by its own rules of the game. Milton Friedman pointed out, the government is needed to establish and to implement rules of competition.[38] If the market economy is compared to a sports competition, the government is comparable to the referee.

The transformation of the functions of the government as the administrator aims at defining enterprises as the market players. For this purpose, in the special economic zones, the principle of separating the government's functions from enterprise management has been followed to reduce the authority and functions of relevant government departments in enterprise management, and grant the autonomous right to enterprises, making way for establishing modern enterprises. For example, in Shenzhen, as from 1985, the organization structuring department phased down the organization structuring management of the enterprises; in 1988, the authority for managing the organization structuring of the enterprises was basically removed. The autonomous right to production operations has been fully granted to enterprises, so that the enterprises have really become the commodity producers and operators which engage in independent operations, and are solely responsible for profits and losses, pursue self-development, exercise self-discipline, and they become the enterprise legal persons which independently enjoy the civil rights and undertake civil obligations. The administrative subordination relationships between enterprises and the government have been eliminated; the longstanding practice in which state-owned enterprises were granted administrative ranks has been changed; the internationally accepted indicator system has been adopted to divide the state-owned enterprises into nine classes, under three categories on the basis of scale and economic benefits, and the enterprise-related benefits have been directly linked to the class and category of the enterprises. The function of examination and approval of relevant

[38]Wang Shenzhi, *Western Economic Think Bank* (Vol. 3), Economic Science Press, 1991, p. 1661.

government departments has been weakened. All newly-established enterprises consistent with the industry's policies and relevant regulations of the special economic zones are not subject to examination and can directly obtain approval from and register with the industry and commerce department. A reform has been carried out to free enterprises from the competent administrative department; the main tasks of the government's comprehensive economic department are as follows: quicken the establishment and improvement of the national macroeconomic regulation and control system, strengthen the survey of, research on and formulation of the strategies and policies for national economic, social, scientific and technological development, reinforce the function of the social management of the government, and conduct comprehensive coordination. Other administrative departments of the government adopt the industry-wide unified management and working standard for the economic entities with different types of ownership in different organizational forms, providing a level playing field for all enterprises.

2. **Separate the Government's Functions from Assets, Transform the Functions of the Government as the Owner**

The government in a market economy has two functions. On the one hand, as the holder of political power, the government performs the functions of social administration; on the other hand, as the owner of state-owned assets, the government carries out those functions that come with such ownership. Under a traditional planned economic system, the government is both the owner and the manager of state-owned assets. The government allocated state-owned assets according to the plan and assumed the unlimited responsibilities for assets profits and losses. As the assets operators, enterprises actually occupied and used assets, but shouldered no responsibilities for profits and losses. As a result, the operation of state-owned assets was inefficient or there was a massive erosion of the state's assets.

In order to change the above situation, the special economic zones have followed the principle of separating ownership from management rights to transform the functions of the government as the owner. With a focus on rationalizing the property rights relationships, the management of the state-owned assets has been profoundly reformed to establish a new structure characterized by a state-owned assets management commission—the state-owned assets operation company—and state-owned enterprises, thus shaping a new pattern in which the property rights operators become diverse, and they compete and promote each other. The relationships between the government and enterprises, between large enterprises and subordinate enterprises have been changed from the previous administrative relationships between upper and lower levels to property rights relationships with capital as the bond. This really reflects the reform requirements: Under the conditions of a market economy, the government properly administrates the ownership, relaxes the control over the management rights, and exercises the power of macroeconomic regulation and control. This has pushed forward the establishment of the mechanism in which enterprises independently carry out operations and are solely responsible for profits and losses. Under the conditions that the property rights are explicit and the responsibilities are well defined, the enterprises can fully utilize their resources and production factors to develop and grow to guarantee the safety and appreciation of the state-owned assets.

3. **Establish a Pragmatic, Incorrupt and Efficient Governmental System**

The performance of the government's functions is based on the rational setting up of government institutions. Under the traditional planned economic system, the institutions were set up according to personnel, causing overstaffing. The government departments were enthusiastic about micro management and were used to adopting administrative examination means and "strengthening" the management of the economic activities with "restless hands". This led to red tape in examination and affairs handling, administrative inefficiency, an increase in work randomness and bureaucracy.

Take the Shenzhen Special Economic Zone as an example: Bold and resolute institutional reforms were carried out during the earliest stages of the special economic zone—five reforms were conducted in 12 years from 1981 to 1992, with one reform in about every two years, on average.[39] Upon its establishment, the special economic zone focused on the transformation of functions, by the fixing of the institutions, their functions and staffing level. According to the principle of downsizing, unity and efficiency and the requirement of coordination among decision-making, execution and supervision as specified in the report to the 16th National Congress of the Communist Party of China, the governmental administrative reform continued to be driven forward. The plan for the administrative separation of power was put forward in Shenzhen in January, 2003. According to the plan, the decision-making departments only have decision-making power without executive power; the executive departments only have executive power without decision-making power; the supervisory bureau and audit bureau are supervisory departments directly under the mayor. In 2009, the gigantic departmental reform in Shenzhen further intensified the integration of the institutions with similar functions to carry out a comprehensive set-up. Fifteen government departments were removed, accounting for 1/3 of the total number; nearly 1/3 of the administrative examination items were cancelled and adjusted. The decision-making was preliminarily separated from execution so as to further rationalize the governmental organizational structure. The Chief of the Scientific Research Section of Guangdong Academy of Social Sciences said that the gigantic departmental reform was the largest institutional reform since the reform and opening up; once it becomes successful, it may be carried out in the Pearl River Delta. Downsizing and cost reduction are only secondary goals, while the most important goal is to improve administrative efficiency and reduce the excessive intervention in micro entities—enterprises– by means of reform.

[39]Zhang Huiping, A Law-based Government: Advance amid Self-revolution—Report on Shenzhen's Reform of the Administrative Approval System, Legislative Affairs Office of the Shenzhen Municipal People's Government, February 5, 2010.

(III) The Special Economic Zones Have Enriched the Government's Macroeconomic Regulation and Control Means Under the Socialist Market Economic System

Under the conditions of a market economy, the government's macroeconomic regulation and control function is generally dominated by indirect regulation and control. Since their inception, the special economic zones have always been market-oriented; as the breadth and depth of reform are different from those in the inland areas, the special economic zones differ from the inland areas in terms of their economic system and economic structure. Under the conditions of a socialist market economy, the government's macroeconomic regulation and control is based on the market mechanism and is conditional upon not hindering market operations and giving full play to the market forces. The macroeconomic regulation and control means in the special economic zones feature a combination of economic lever and other regulation and control means.

1. Planning Means

A market economy does not exclude planning. As two basic means for allocating the scarce social resources, both planning and market have advantages and disadvantages. The coordination function of planning is fully leveraged, the advantages of the beforehand plan—scientific, forward-looking and overarching—are utilized to develop the guidance plan covering the special economic zones, and the beforehand plan is practiced for continuous development and improvement. The plan is programmed, but it is not a rigid restriction. At the beginning of the special economic zones, the Central Government only gave policies without financial support; the planning means adopted in the special economic zones were dominated by guidance plans, mainly covering the economic development strategy, the medium and long-term economic plan, industrial, investment, fiscal and monetary policies. These plans and policies did not directly restrict the behavior of the market players in the special economic zones, but they could provide authoritative information to them and serve as their reference for making correct choices in the production operations. More than 30 years of practice prove that the overall developmental strategy, the staged development plan and industrial policy developed in the special economic zones are basically correct, and the coordinating function of planning has played an important role in macroeconomic regulation and control in the special economic zones.

2. Economic Means

The economic means show that the government, based on consciously following and using the law of value, draws on the regulation and control role of the economic lever to exercise macroeconomic regulation and control of the national economy. The economic lever associated with interests is the regulator of the economic interests; it prompts enterprises to respond to the economic information and market developments, so as to make decisions about the direction for and the scale of their production operations. Various economic means with a regulatory role are comprehensively used to basically align the production operation activities with the macroeconomic goals. The development of the special economic zones in more than 30 years has been a process in which efforts have been made to explore and summarize how to adopt various economic levers to regulate and guide the economic behavior of the market players, and change the dominant role from a direct one to an indirect one so as to achieve the government's macroeconomic regulation and control.

Price is an important economic lever for macroeconomic regulation and control. The price reform was initiated during the initial stage of the special economic zones. In 1984, the mandatory prices were basically removed, and a price operation system with a dominance of market prices and a combination of market prices, floating prices and planned prices preliminarily took shape in the Shenzhen Special Economic Zone. With the establishment and operation of this system, the government could regulate and control production, exchange, distribution, consumption and reproduction links. In 1995, the Shenzhen Municipal Government issued the *Shenzhen Special Economic Zone's Regulation of Price Management*, putting Shenzhen's price management under the legal system. As from 1997, the national treatment of prices has been made in the Shenzhen Special Economic Zone—a unified treatment has been provided for partial domestic and foreign capital, domestic and foreign residents with respect to electricity prices, medical charges, property management fees and other charges and prices. In 1999, various charging acts were standardized and steps were taken to further improve the mechanism of price formation and operation for public utilities including water, power supply, telecommunications and public transportation; regulations concerning price self-discipline, price hearing and anti-profiteering were made to curb price dumping, price monopoly, price fraud and price discrimination.[40] In order to protect the environment and encourage citizens to save electric power, the multistep electricity price plan has been implemented in the Shenzhen Special Economic Zone since 2012.

3. **Administrative Means**

Administrative means were adopted to intervene in the economic imbalance to maintain a basic balance of the economic aggregate and dynamic optimization of the economic structure in the special economic zones. When it comes to the administrative means for regulating and controlling the economy, the administrative bodies made mandatory orders, instructions, stipulations, and specified mandatory tasks or some restrictions in exercising macroeconomic regulation and control. Primarily, there were different degrees of intervention in, regulation and control of investment demand and consumer demand prone to becoming overheated in the special economic zones.

For example, the construction of the scale of capital was reduced and the investment structure was adjusted in the special economic zones. Take Shenzhen as an example: In 1986, the special economic zone followed the decisions made during the national working conference on the special economic zones to greatly cut down

[40] *Several Recommendations of the Shenzhen Municipal Price Bureau for Adopting a Price Lever to Promote Shenzhen's Economic Development*, November 6, 1999.

the scale of the construction of capital, make administrative orders to remove 51 high-rise building projects, and slash the capital construction investments by more than 2 billion yuan, with a focus on reducing the construction of hotels and restaurants. From late 1988 to late 1989, in order to resolutely carry out the instructions of the Central Government for improvement and rectification, 280 projects with a building area of 302 m^2 were suspended and the capital construction investments were decreased by 2.6 billion yuan in the Shenzhen Special Economic Zone.[41] Afterwards, with the aim of controlling the capital construction investments in a more effective way, the permit system for investment project construction was implemented in Shenzhen to ensure the construction of infrastructures, including industry, transportation, energy and ports. The overheating in investment demand was brought under control and the investment structure was optimized.

4. **Legal Means**

A market economy is an economy under the rule of law. Strictly speaking, laws serve as the guarantee for exercising macroeconomic regulation and control and for maintaining market order; however, as shown by the role of some legal provisions in regulating the economic activities, laws can also be considered as macroeconomic regulation and a means of control. Legal means are adopted to ensure that the market competition in the special economic zones is fair, orderly and effective. Since the establishment of the special economic zones, the people have been strongly encouraged to adopt the legal means to regulate the economy on the basis of law-based governance of the market and law-based administration, so that the economy in the special economic zones has been operated under the game rules which govern a market economy.

At the beginning of the special economic zones, in response to the need for introducing foreign capital and engaging in external economic and technical cooperation, a number of single laws and regulations were made, covering the management of inbound and outbound personnel, the introduction of technology, enterprise registration, economic contracts involving foreign interests, labor wages, land management and commodity housing management, incorporating the economic activities in the special economic zones into law-based management as much as possible. The special economic zones, including Shenzhen, Hainan and Xiamen, have fully leveraged the advantages from the legislative power granted by the Standing Committee of the National People's Congress to make various necessary economic laws and regulations and administrative regulations in light of their actual conditions, to regulate the basic rules for enterprise behavior and the norms for acts of government, adjust the economic relations among various parties, and ensure the implement of the economic policies, measures and economic contracts, thus guaranteeing orderly social production and circulation. Meanwhile, the government can apply these laws, regulations and rules to regulate the procedure of economic operations in the special economic zones and restrict the economic behavior of the market players; it can adopt the judicial means involving the economic affairs, to hear the economic cases and settle

[41] Shao Hanqing, *Explorer's Way*, Haitian Press, 1995, p. 157.

the economic disputes, check and correct the passive phenomena in the economic development, combat the economic criminal activities and punish criminals in order to effectively promote a rapid, coordinated and healthy development of the economy in the special economic zones.

The special economic zones have followed the mode of dominance by market regulation to carry out the reform of the economic system. This has given birth to the unique features of the special economic zones, and it also represents a successful experiment in building the national socialist market economic system, nationwide. The macroeconomic regulation and control means in the special economic zones give full play to the roles of the plan and the market in resource allocation, and are also combined with the economic levers and other regulation and control means to further enrich the government's macroeconomic regulation and control means under the socialist market economic system; they also serve as the reference for establishing and improving the macroeconomic regulation and control system across the country. Given the new situation in which the degree of economic marketization has significantly increased, the market players have become diverse and the relations of interest are complicated in China, the Central Government has repeatedly stressed that emphasis should be placed on the actual effects, the economic, legal and necessary administrative means should be comprehensively utilized, and importance should be attached to the role of the market mechanism; moreover, the behavior of the market players should be correctly guided so as to achieve the goal of macroeconomic regulation and control. For example, in 2004, the Central Committee of the Communist Party of China and the State Council further strengthened and improved the decision-making regarding the macroeconomic regulation and control, comprehensively applied the economic, legal and necessary administrative means to curb the excessively rapid growth of the fixed assets investments, shore up the weaknesses in economic development, and reinforce the economic operations regulations in order to produce marked effects in the macroeconomic regulation and control.

On November 9, 2013, the much-anticipated Third Plenary Session of the 18th National Congress of the Communist Party of China was convened, which vowed to make the market play a decisive role in resource allocation. Meanwhile, the decision concerning the establishment of the leading group for comprehensively intensifying the reform also became the focus of attention at home and abroad. From a planned economy to a market economy, from the special economic zones to the extension of China's Development Path, China experienced bitter investigations and painful lessons, but made tremendous achievements. The practice in the special economic zones has helped identify the direction of the market-oriented reform in China. The special economic zones have successfully practiced and experimented with the theory of the socialist market economy; they have enriched the property rights theory of the socialist market economy in which "public ownership is kept as the mainstay and diverse forms of ownership coexist"; they have developed the distribution theory that work-based distribution and distribution based on production factors complement each other. Meanwhile, the special economic zones have become the first to clarify the boundary between the government and the market, shape the modern government's structure, transform the government from an omnipotent one to a service-oriented one, leave the administrative intervention in the micro economic entities in the market, and emphasize macroeconomic regulation and control. The more than 30-year reform of the economic system has turned China into the second largest economy in the world; what will China look like in the next 30 years? That depends on a new round of reform. With regard to how to develop China's development path towards modernization, the special economic zones are still experimenting and China is still forging ahead, the story of reform continues and the developmental path is long and arduous.

Chapter 5
Institutional Contributions from the Special Economic Zones to China's Development Path

From the perspective of institutional economics, the practice in China's special economic zones is a top-down compulsory institutional change. From the bringing forth of the concept to the formulation of policies and practical guidance, the special economic zones have been under the leadership of the Central Government. Meanwhile, the practice in China's special economic zones is also a gradual institutional change. At the beginning of the special economic zones, Deng Xiaoping put forward the strategy of "crossing the river by feeling the stones", showing a step-by-step, experimental and gradual process.

The primary institutional contribution to the success in the special economic zones is that the special economic zones have offered a market economic system to China and thus have presented China's Development Path—the special economic zones were established to complete the institutional transformation and achieve economic development in China (Tao Yitao 2010). Institutional transformation is a transformation from the traditional planned economic system to a market economic system. Another important institutional contribution from the special economic zones is that they prove that mixed ownership is feasible in a market economy.

The special economic zones have not only sought out the path towards a market economy, but they have also driven forward China's political reform. The practice of separation of the administrative power, voting system and direct elections in the special economic zones has vigorously promoted the reform of China's political system. Deng Xiaoping pointed out that if there were only a reform of the economic system without a reform of the political system, the reform of the economic system would not be successful.[1] This is because the government under a planned economic system is an authoritative and investment-oriented government, while a market economy requires the government to be a service-oriented and politically democratic government which mainly provides public services. The transformation of the economic system entails the transformation of the political system; thus, after the development of the market economy has proven that the transformation of the

---

[1] *Selected Works of Deng Xiaoping* (Vol. 3), People's Publishing House, 1993, p.164.

© Social Sciences Academic Press and Springer Nature Singapore Pte Ltd. 2018

Y. Tao and Z. Lu, *Special Economic Zones and China's Development Path*,
Research Series on the Chinese Dream and China's Development Path,
https://doi.org/10.1007/978-981-10-3220-2_5

economic system has been basically successful, it will be necessary to reform the political system accordingly. The great foresight of Deng Xiaoping has guided us to make continued efforts to reform the political system.

The rapid economic development in China since the reform and opening up has borne a resemblance to the economic prosperity in East Asia during the 1960s–1970s. As the boundary between the government and the market was not properly defined, the East Asian Model showed many drawbacks, including the wasting of resources, a structural imbalance, a lack of public goods, social injustice and corruption. Now the East Asian countries have broken away from that model, and their governments have been transformed from authoritative ones to democratic and service-oriented ones, so as to achieve all-round modernization, economically and politically.

In China, the institutional contributions from the special economic zones to China's modernization involve both economic and political levels, so the special economic zones have become the windows for showcasing the institutional self-confidence of socialism with Chinese characteristics. Regarding the special economic zones as the windows, experimental fields and forerunners of China's reform and opening-up, their successful experience has become a model applied nationwide and has produced the effect of institutional spillover. Therefore, with economic success and experimentations in political reform, the special economic zones have made important institutional contributions to China's modernization.

5.1 The Special Economic Zones Are the Windows for Showcasing the Institutional Self-Confidence of Socialism with Chinese Characteristics

The successful practice in the special economic zones makes them capable of and eligible for becoming the windows for demonstrating the institutional self-confidence of socialism with Chinese characteristics. The original task for the special economic zones to experiment with the reform of the market economic system in China has been completed and thus the special economic zones are no longer special; however, as the special economic zones are charged with the task of and have been given the function for comprehensively intensifying the reforms, including the public institutional reform and the reform of the political system under the new situation, they will continue to be special. The special features of the special economic zones and their resulting success are the reasons why they serve as the windows for showcasing the institutional self-confidence of socialism with Chinese characteristics.

5.1.1 The Special Economic Zones Are the Integral Part of Socialism with Chinese Characteristics and Cover the Whole Process of the Socialist Cause with Chinese Characteristics

The establishment of the special economic zones in China's coastal areas was a major decision made by the Central Government and the State Council, on the initiative of comrade Deng Xiaoping, in response to domestic and international situations under the new historical conditions, with the aim of quickening the reform and opening-up and the drive towards socialist modernization. The original purpose of establishing the special economic zones was to reinvigorate the economy, increase foreign trade to earn foreign exchange, accelerate economic development, seek out the path and gather the experience for China's modernization—blaze new trails as stressed by comrade Deng Xiaoping. At the time when the special economic zones were established, they were granted the autonomous right to introduce projects and assume full fiscal responsibility, so that the commodity economy could be reinvigorated within the special economic zones. At their inception, the special economic zones went beyond the traditional planned economic system: Diverse sectors of the economy coexisted within the special economic zones, the capital mainly came from foreign investments, and the whole economy was an outward-looking one; government regulation and control was dominated by indirect regulation and control. The special economic zones embarked on the path of a market economy from the beginning, serving as the experimental fields for pushing ahead with the socialist cause with Chinese characteristics.

The goal of "blazing new trails"—establishing the socialist market economy with Chinese characteristics—as stressed by comrade Deng Xiaoping has been basically achieved through the leading role of the special economic zones. With the gradual expansion of the national opening-up, the original preferential policies peculiar to the special economic zones have been applied in the coastal and inland areas, fully indicating the role of the special economic zones as the frontrunners in the socialist cause with Chinese characteristics; moreover, the special economic zones have always been at the forefront, nationwide, in institutional innovations, industrial upgrading and expansion of the opening-up, and they have always taken the lead, producing demonstration and radiation effects across the country.

There is no experience to be drawn on in the socialist cause with Chinese characteristics; the establishment of the special economic zones is a new thing in a socialist country. As the levels of economic and social development are different among the areas of China, the reform and opening-up modes inevitably vary with the areas. The practice in the special economic zones proves that: (1) The socialist theory with Chinese characteristics is feasible, and the practice sheds light on what socialism with Chinese characteristics is; (2) The establishment of the special economic zones has proven to be a great pioneering undertaking which combines the universal principles of Marxism with the actual conditions in China, and is a great achievement of socialism with Chinese characteristics; (3) It has been proven through practice that socialism can create a higher economic developmental speed than capitalism; (4) What has been done successfully in the special economic zones has proven that the emancipation of people's minds is the important magic weapon for developing socialism with Chinese characteristics.

5.1.2 The Special Economic Zones Have Played the Role of Vanguard in the Reform and Opening-up in the Great Socialist Cause with Chinese Characteristics

Essentially, the socialist theory with Chinese characteristics is a theory concerning the emancipation and development of the productive forces. It is the theoretical foundation for the special economic zones. The reasons for choosing the coastal areas as special economic zones for first-ever implementation of pilot programs in the reform and opening-up are as follows: On the one hand, they enjoy geographical advantages; on the other hand, they were less subject to the traditional planned economic system and were the areas where the proportion of a state-owned economy was very low, the reform and opening-up met with less resistance, there were many favorable conditions and extensive room for developing the non-public sectors of the economy. During the initial stage of the reform and opening-up, the outward-looking economy was most suitable for cultivating a market economy.

The development of the special economic zones features a trajectory of continuous reform and opening-up. The special economic zones have gained valuable experience in establishing and improving the socialist market economy, including: (1) reforming the rigid and highly centralized planned economic system, introducing a market economy, strengthening the shareholding reform and establishing the modern enterprise system; (2) setting up Chinese-foreign joint ventures, Chinese-foreign cooperative enterprises and exclusively foreign-owned enterprises, thus creating fiscal revenue for the country, learning advanced foreign technologies and management experience, cultivating the enterprise operation management talents for China and more quickly integrating China's economy into the world economy; (3) carrying out a series of reforms in the systems, involving employment, insurance, housing, registered permanent residence and land, acquiring the experience for a national reform.

Overall, the basic experience from the special economic zones through the reform and opening-up includes the following: being bold in making breakthroughs, unswervingly driving forward the reform in a market-oriented way, audaciously drawing on the market economic experience from the developed countries; keeping the correct guidance of public opinion across the country to create a good environment for the reform; correctly dealing with the relationships among reform, development and stability; making full use of the legislative power and legal means to consolidate the achievements of the reform; properly conducting the overall planning to press ahead with the reform in a coordinated and integrated way. What Shenzhen has done proves that the adoption of mixed ownership is possible in a market economy, which is logically consistent with the statement, made in the Third Plenary Session of the 18th National Congress of the Communist Party of China, that both public ownership and other systems of ownership are important parts of a socialist market economy. Besides innovations in the economic system, the special economic zones are at the forefront of the whole country regarding the innovations in the political and cultural systems. It took almost 20 years for the Shenzhen Special Economic Zone to finish the path towards modernization. That was accomplished by the Western countries in a period of 100–200 years. As the bridges for economic contacts among Hong Kong, Macao and Chinese Mainland, the Shenzhen and Zhuhai Special Economic Zones have played important roles in Hong Kong's and Macao's return to the motherland and the implementation of the "one country, two systems" policy.

The success of the Shenzhen Special Economic Zone in the reform and opening-up is first attributable to the granting of the right by the Central Government to the special economic zone for first-ever implementation of pilot programs and the Central Government's trust in the special economic zone. Deng Xiaoping said that the establishment of the special economic zones had been decided by the Central Government on his initiative (Leng Rong and Wang Zuoling, 2004). In 1982, Shenzhen's development became stagnant due to the debate on whether it was to be socialist or capitalist. In this regard, Deng Xiaoping said, before the leading body of Guangdong Province: "If you believe that it is good, you should keep on it". This greatly inspired the people in the special economic zone to continue the reform and opening-up. In 1992, when delivering his South Inspection Speech, Deng Xiaoping pointed out that whosoever opposed the reform and opening-up would be beaten by the people (Tian Bingxin 2004). The success of the Shenzhen Special Economic Zone is also attributable to the advantage of its location—proximity to Hong Kong – making it convenient for attracting foreign capital. Its success also results from a crop of doers with the spirit of reform, including Ren Zhongyi, Wu Nansheng, Liang Xiang and Yuan Geng. They creatively used the special policies given by the Central Government and converted the policies and environmental advantages into practical productive forces.

The practice in Shenzhen and other special economic zones in China has helped seek out China's Development Path—a path of market-oriented reform with compulsory gradual institutional change, which is different from the Soviet Model, dispenses with egalitarianism and is built on the special economic zones as breakthroughs. What the special economic zones have successfully done fully proves that the reform and opening-up is the inevitable way to emancipate and further social productive forces.

5.1.3 The Practice in the Special Economic Zones Embodies the Scientific Outlook on Development

The practice in the Shenzhen Special Economic Zone fully proves that development is the absolute principle and scientific development is the fundamental way of building a well-off society in an all-around way and achieving modernization. The growth and development of the Shenzhen Special Economic Zone has been a process of constantly adjusting the developmental strategy amid lessons and setbacks, optimizing the industrial structure, transforming the developmental mode and experimenting with a gradual transition from an economic growth-focused society to a welfare-oriented society with all-round development (Tao Yitao 2010).

The Shenzhen Special Economic Zone started mainly from processing the materials supplied by foreign clients, processing according to the buyer's samples, assembling the parts supplied by foreign clients and engaging in compensation trade, and by earning foreign exchanges through exports. This was determined by the national condition where the labor resources were abundant and the State needed to earn foreign exchanges at that time. During industrial transformation and upgrading, Shenzhen opportunely shifted its focus to high and new technological industries and chose the path of sustainable development. During that transformation and development, the government established the diversion of funds and offered preferential policies to fill the fund gap resulting from high input during the initial period and to mitigate the risks for enterprises with investments in high and new technological industries; as a result, numerous well-known new high-tech enterprises were attracted to Shenzhen and a large number of well-known domestic and foreign institutions of higher learning and scientific research institutions set up educational and research institutions in Shenzhen.

In the Shenzhen Special Economic Zone, initially, there was a focus on processing the materials supplied by foreign clients, processing according to the buyer's samples, assembling the parts supplied by foreign clients and engaging in compensation trade in a labor-intensive way to earn foreign exchanges; afterwards, the capital and technology-intensive high and new technology industries were developed and independent innovations were encouraged; now, the economic growth mode is transforming into the economic field to achieve economic and social development; the above process represents the innovations in the developmental philosophy and changes in the developmental mode; these innovations and changes have first boosted the rapid and coordinated development of the special economic zones and have shown a bright prospect for scientific development. The philosophy of scientific development has extended the developmental outlook from the transformation of the growth mode to social development, from the economic field to various fields of social life. In more than 30 years since their establishment, the special economic zones have always given first priority to scientific development, and Shenzhen's GDP has annually grown by an average of 30%. Shenzhen's rise from its previous status as a small border county into a large modern city bears the most convincing testimony to the vitality of the special economic zones, making Shenzhen, as the representative of the special economic zones, the window for demonstrating the institutional self-confidence of socialism with Chinese characteristics.

5.2 The Special Economic Zones Have Stimulated the Chinese Government to Experiment with Reforms and Innovations in Public Institutional Arrangements

During economic development, the special economic zones have been fettered by the original traditional administrative system to varying degrees and have shown some drawbacks to the original administrative system, thus there is an urgent need for them to quicken the reform of the administrative system, transform the government's functions and enhance the efficiency of the government. The Shenzhen Special Economic Zone has always been the first to carry out pilot programs in the reform of the administrative system, which has produced remarkable effects. In May, 2009, the State Council approved the *Shenzhen City's Overall Plan for Comprehensive Reform*, under which Shenzhen should follow the national strategic arrangements for reform and development to start the first-ever implementation of pilot programs regarding the following four aspects: First, major national measures for intensifying the reform and expanding the opening up; second, an institutional design consistent with the international practice and the widely accepted rules as well as China's future developmental direction; third, institutional innovations which exert important impacts on Shenzhen's economic and social development and can produce great demonstrations and driving effects across the country; fourth, major matters concerning nationally intensified cooperation between the Chinese Mainland and Hong Kong. With continued experimentations and innovations in the reform of the administrative system, the special economic zones have been the first in China to establish the system and mechanism for scientific development, gaining fresh experience for developing socialism with Chinese characteristics.

5.2.1 Improve the Efficiency of the Government and Build a Service-Oriented Government

With a slew of reform measures, the Shenzhen Special Economic Zone is committed to defining the boundary between the government and the market well and to building a service-oriented government. Its reform measures have come out in front in China and have yielded significant effects. The policy of reducing the items of the administrative examination has been adopted nationwide. The differential reform of public institutions, the cultivation of social organizations, reforms of the commercial registration system and the cultural system remain at the forefront of the country, and have delivered tremendous social and economic benefits. The reforms in the civil servant system and government performance management have become remarkably successful. The service-oriented government has basically taken shape.

(I) **Reform of the Administrative Examination System**

The reform of the administrative examination system is the most important reform for transforming the government's functions and improving the efficiency of the government. In July, 2012, the *Work Plan Concerning the Reform for Accelerating the Transformation of the Government's Functions and Intensifying the Reform of the Administrative Examination System* was released in Shenzhen. The reform of the administrative examination system in Shenzhen has brought about the following four significant achievements.

1. **Clear up the examination items and improve the mechanism for the management of examination and approval**

According to the *Catalogue of the Shenzhen Municipal People's Government for the Items Concerning the Reform of the Administrative Examination System in 2012* as released in December, 2012, Shenzhen undertook 180 items, delegated and entrusted by the governments at higher levels, removed, transferred and changed 90 items which were no longer subject to administrative examination, delegated and entrusted 23 items to the departments of the district governments, and cleared up more than 30% of the items. The examination items have been put under the catalogue-based management. In 2012, Shenzhen carried out the *Administrative Measures of Shenzhen City for the Catalogue of Administrative Examination Items*, specifying the conditions and procedures for various departments to increase or decrease the administrative license and non-administrative license examination and registration items, and stipulating that the administrative license examination items and non-administrative license examination items should not be set up or set up in a disguised form if no laws and regulations serve as the basis. The regulations and normative documents of the municipal governments have been comprehensively reorganized to the extent that the inappropriate documents have been repealed and revised.

The government's powers cannot be exercised if there is no authorization by laws. The cancellation of unnecessary examination items and the reform of the examination management mechanism can remove the unnecessary restrictions on enterprises, thus reducing the transaction costs and improving the efficiency of the overall economic operation. At the economic level, this is beneficial for achieving economic transformation and upgrading; at the political level, this is helpful for transforming the government from an authoritative one to a service-oriented one.

2. **Transform the government's functions, cultivate social organizations**

In October, 2012, the *Work Plan for Clearing up the Functional Items of Government Departments* was released in Shenzhen City. According to this plan, the functions must be cancelled, transferred and delegated to the lower levels, and services must be purchased; the transfer of the government's functions and the purchase of services must be intensified by transferring the services which can be undertaken by social organizations from the government to social organizations; the field of social organizations must be reformed more quickly; the scope of directly registered social organizations must be expanded to eight categories of social organizations covering industry, commerce and economy, public benefit and charity, social welfare; a dual system of registration and filing of community social organizations should be adopted to promote the development of community social organizations; experimentation should be carried out to establish the differential access system for social organizations; social organizations should be actively guided to apply for social service projects in which the central finance supports the social organizations to participate, and for the special fund of Guangdong Province for cultivating and developing social organizations; the behavior of social organizations msut be regulated and supervised; the legal person liability of the social organizations must be strengthened and an industrial self-disciplining mechanism should be established; the legislative work on social organizations must be pushed forward; the fiscal support for social organizations must be increased.

Social organizations can handle many affairs which should not be dealt with by the government, so the boundary between the government and the market can be better defined. Social organizations have close connections with and extensive participation from the ordinary people, thus this helps enhance the people's satisfaction and sense of ownership as well as efficiency. The government can really transform from excessive management to focus more on the supply of public goods.

3. **Innovate in the examination and approval mode, optimize the examination and approval functioning system**

Various departments have set up service offices to handle the administrative examination affairs in a relatively centralized way; joint examination and approval have been conducted and granted; the examination and approval process has been reengineered; multiple examination and approval procedures and evidentiary materials have been simplified and optimized; the classification standard of the handling time has been developed; coordination and information sharing have been strengthened; the administrative examination and approval system has been continuously improved. On September 24, 2012, the coordinated handling platform under the administrative examination and approval system was put into operation among 16 departments, thus enabling full offline forward handling and sharing of results. This marked an all-round routine operation within the reform involving inter-departmental coordinated handling of investment projects at the level of the Shenzhen Municipal Government. Meanwhile, the municipal service system, the municipal administrative examination and approval system and the Shenzhen Branch of the Provincial Online Service Hall have been planned and improved to fully integrate the existing relevant resources of the information system. The reform involving the inter-departmental coordinated handling of investment projects has been expanded. The online service hall has been continuously improved. Shenzhen Government Online ranked No.1 among the sub-provincial cities nationwide in terms of the assessment of the performance of the government's website for the third consecutive year in 2013. The standardization of administrative examination and approval has been steadily promoted.

4. **Improve the mechanism of supervision, strictly ascertain where the responsibility lies**

Actions have been taken to expand electronic supervision over administrative examination and approval, intensify the management of administrative examination and approval performance and strictly ascertain where the responsibility of the examination and approval lies. This applies modern science and technology in work management and can effectively improve the efficiency of supervision, guarantee the results of supervision and promote the transformation of the government into a modern one.

(II) Reform of the Commercial Registration System

Major breakthroughs have been made through the reform of the commercial registration system in Shenzhen—a new commercial registration management system has taken shape, in which the qualification of the commercial subject is separated from the business qualification, examination and approval are combined with supervision, and the subscription system is adopted for registered capital. The reform of the commercial registration system gives more autonomy to enterprises, enhances social self-discipline and gives further scope to the fundamental role of the market; the reform caters to the need to exercise administration according to laws, transform the government's functions and build a service-oriented government. In April, 2010, the reform of the commercial registration system was launched in Shenzhen. On October 30, 2012, the *Several Regulations of the Shenzhen Special Economic Zone for Commercial Registration* was passed by the Shenzhen Municipal People's Congress. Six major breakthroughs have been made through the reform of the commercial registration system in Shenzhen, including:

First, the commercial registration system which centers on business licensing has been reformed to separate the commercial subject qualification from the business qualification, rationalize the interrelations between the registration of the commercial subject and the business qualification license, and establish the registration system with the highest combination of examination, approval and supervision. The registration of the commercial subject qualification and the licensing of the business qualification can be independently conducted. The business qualification license is no longer the precondition for the commercial subject registration. The new business license has been adopted and does not specify the business scope of the commercial subject; the business license becomes merely the certificate of the qualification of the commercial subject, while the business scope is specified in the articles of the association, agreement or application form and made public. The general business items are not subject to examination for a license. Examination and approval are combined with supervision; the responsibility for the examination items and the routine industrial supervision remain with the relevant examining department and the competent industrial department. This policy removes the procedure of the registration of the scope of business, which imposes restrictions on the commercial subject, and is conducive to creating a good business environment and helps the operators reduce site costs.

Second, the paid-in registered capital registration system for limited liability companies has been changed into the registered capital subscription registration system, and the structure of the internal governance of companies has been improved. This policy reduces the capital cost for establishing companies, enhances the efficiency of capital utilization, arouses enthusiasm for starting a business, removes the "registered capital credit" bubble and helps build a real and reliable social transaction security and credit system.

Third, the commercial subject supervision mode has been reformed; the directory system for operational anomalies has been adopted; innovations have been made in the credit supervision mode. This policy helps guide commercial subjects to attach importance to credit and regulate their credit, and to improve the overall degree of integrity in society.

Fourth, the annual checking system for enterprise registration has been reformed by adopting the annual report filing system for the commercial subjects and building an information foundation for effectively collecting and searching for information about the actual operating conditions of the commercial subjects.

Fifth, the public notification system for commercial registration has been reformed by establishing a unified platform for public notification of the registration authorization of the commercial subject and credit information and really sharing the information resources. This move is conducive to building a credit-based society.

Sixth, the traditional registration mode has been reformed by carrying out online registration in an all-round way, establishing the electronic business license system, achieving electronic and networked commercial registration and adopting the registration system for integrating the business license, the organization code certificate, and the taxation registration certificate into one document. This policy makes it convenient for the general public to file an application; it helps reduce the social costs, improve the efficiency of registration for the commercial subjects and cuts down the administrative costs.

The reform policy for the commercial registration system in the Shenzhen Special Economic Zone was fully implemented as from March 1, 2013, so Shenzhen has seized the developmental opportunity and has seen an increasing number of local people starting a business, as more and more people have flocked to Shenzhen to establish their businesses. The application costs for enterprises have declined and the business environment has been further optimized. There is a great possibility that enterprise registration materials will be accepted and processed, thus effectively improving registration efficiency. The number of intermediary bodies which act as agents has decreased and the market is no longer available for intermediary bodies in large quantities, effectively mitigating the risks of corruption. The Shenzhen Special Economic Zone comes first nationwide in terms of this reform, and it is bound to exert an impact on China's commercial registration system across the board, generally enhancing the efficiency of commercial registration in China.

(III) Reform of the Civil Servant Management System, Reform of Public Institutions, Gigantic Reform of the Departmental System and Management of Government Performance

In Shenzhen, actions have been taken to actively and steadily push forward reforms involving the differential management of civil servants and the contractual employment system for civil servants; the *Opinions Concerning Further Deepening of the Reform Regarding the Classified Management of Civil Servants* was adopted in 2012, which spells out the measures to adopt in order to further improve the civil servant placement system, civil servant management system (based on the contractual employment system and more quickly solve the problems left over by the reform. In 2012, the civil servants in the local taxation bureau and the social security bureau were transformed into posts of the type which correspond to administrative law enforcement posts established to separate the promotion and benefits of civil servants from administrative ranks, and other departments studied steps to carry out the same kind of transformation. The reform involving the contractual employment system for civil servants in the Party-masses system was launched, and the courts in Futian District and Yantian District were indicated to conduct the pilot reform concerning the differential management of court personnel and the professionalization of judges.

In July, 2006, the differential reform of public institutions was fully initiated in Shenzhen. In Shenzhen, the existing public institutions were reformed in a differential way, to the extent that these public institutions were divided by function into three major categories, including supervision and administration, public services and operational services, and then were included in the differential reform by being incorporated into an administrative management series, being retained (integrated) or revoked, and being transformed into enterprises, respectively. The organizations not committed to performing public services were separated from public institutions; the administrative ranks of public institutions were abolished, so that the public institutions became non-administrative ones; the pilot reform of statutory bodies was energetically experimented. In 2010, the differential reform of public institutions was basically completed, thus the days when the government agencies and public institutions ran enterprises had ended. In the next step, institutional and mechanism innovations would be carried out in public institutions in Shenzhen.

The *Overall Plan of Shenzhen City for Comprehensive Reform*, approved by the State Council in May, 2009, required Shenzhen to initiate first-ever implementation of pilot programs in four aspects. In July, 2009, the State Commission Office of Public Sectors Reform approved the *Institutional Reform Plan of the Shenzhen Municipal People's Government*; according to the plan, 15 departments of the Shenzhen Municipal People's Government would be removed, accounting for 1/3 of the departments. The gigantic reform of the departmental system could effectively reduce the departmental communication costs and fiscal expenditure as well as improve the efficiency of collaboration. Shenzhen had actively explored the administrative operational mechanism in which decision-making, execution and supervision restrict and coordinate each other, and had moved towards market, efficiency and service to carry out a new round of the reform of government institutions. The functionally coordinated huge system of departments preliminarily took shape in 2010.

The management of governmental performance has been fully performed in Shenzhen. In November, 2004, the first electronic supervision system for administrative examination and approval in China was established in Shenzhen; since then, electronic supervision has been rapidly practiced with an increasing amount of contents; four large systems—an electronic supervision system for administrative examination and approval, an electronic supervision system for the examination and approval of major investment projects, an electronic supervision system for administrative information resource sharing and a system for the assessment of governmental performance—have been built. The administrative system of electronic supervision enables real-time supervision over main administrative items and three-level networked supervision over the streets in urban areas. Since the beginning of the operation of the electronic supervision system for administrative examination and approval, the proportion of the examination and approval items which have been successfully handled in Shenzhen has soared from the less than 3% to an average 87.5% in 2007, while the examination and approval items which were successfully handled by municipal departments in advance, accounted for 99.7% in 2012.

(IV) **Reform of the Cultural System**

With the spirit of the special economic zone as first mover, Shenzhen was the first to put forward and implement the strategy of building the city through culture, with innovations made in the whole process of cultural reform and development, to seize the opportunities and pursue development by leaps and bounds. The breakthroughs in Shenzhen's cultural reform and innovations are mainly reflected in the following five areas. First, innovations in basic philosophyidea: new ideas are adopted to promote the practice of culture. Shenzhen has brought forth a number of cultural philosophies—winning and losing are judged by culture; the levels are determined by politeness; success depends upon spirit; the winner is measured by culture and ideas; refining and carrying forward are stressed; cultural reform and development are boosted by the strong cultural self-consciousness and high cultural self-confidence. Second, management innovations: the function of the government's cultural management has practically been transformed. On the one hand, something has been added: the *Plan for Revitalization and Development of the Creative Culture Industry* and its supporting policies have been introduced; the functions of policy regulation, market supervision, social management and public services have been strengthened; on the other hand, something has been removed: the number of municipal cultural administrative examination and approval items has been reduced from 102 to 11. Third, institutional innovations: cultural development has been vigorously vitalized. The state-owned cultural organizations have generally established a vibrant and efficient mechanism of operational management. Steps have been taken to make state-owned cultural groups large and strong and build performance-oriented groups. The social forces have been guided to implement the cultural programs and branded cultural activities, including the Reading Month and Citizens' Cultural Lecture have been carried out. Fourth, service innovations: the cultural rights and interests of citizens are guaranteed; the cultural enjoyment service system, the cultural participation service system and the cultural creation service system have been established and improved. Fifth, business type innovations: the integrative development of culture, science and technology is being actively promoted. Shenzhen has witnessed experimentations of new modes for industrial development, including "culture + technology", "culture + creativity", "culture + finance", "culture + tourism". The China (Shenzhen) International Cultural Expo, co-hosted by the Ministry of the People's Republic of China, the State Administration of Radio, Film and Television, the General Administration of Press and Publication of the People's Republic of China, the Guangdong Provincial People's Government and the Shenzhen Municipal People's Government, has been held in Shenzhen each year since 2004. It has become the No. 1 Cultural Expo in China—the only national-level comprehensive Cultural Expo in China. It centers on exposition and trading. It stimulates the development of China's cultural industry and has played an important role in introducing Chinese cultural products to the world.

5.2.2 Reforms and Investigations of the Land Use and Housing Systems in the Shenzhen Special Economic Zone

Since the beginning of the 20th century, many changes have taken place in China's land use system; in particular, in the past 20 years or more, China has embarked on a distinctive path of adopting the paid land use and transfer system under socialist public ownership. The Shenzhen Special Economic Zone enjoys a special and important status in China's reform and opening up. The urban land reform policy was initiated in Shenzhen, while most of its experiences and achievements have been applied nationwide. Shenzhen is a typical case. The research on Shenzhen's land use system is highly representative, overarching and forward-looking.

(I) **Reform of the land use system in the Shenzhen Special Economic Zone**

When new China was founded, socialist public land ownership was established. The constitution clearly stipulates that no organization or individual shall appropriate, sell, lease land or illegally transfer land in other forms. China's urban state-owned land was subject to the single administrative allocation system—the State supplies the land use rights to users on an unpaid basis with an indefinite duration; the land use rights could not be transferred among land users—until the reform and opening-up.

1. **The initial reform**

The Shenzhen Municipal Government drew on Hong Kong's experience to cooperate, regarding land, with Hong Kong to build houses, around 1980. This method addressed the issue of funds for the government in building houses and started the era of commodity housing on the Chinese Mainland. In November, 1981, the *Interim Provisions of the Shenzhen Special Economic Zone for Land Management* was adopted during the Standing Committee of the 5th People's Congress of Guangdong Province, which specified land expropriation, planning, ownership, operation, fee standards and the duration of the use in the special economic zone, so the period of paid land use arrived. Different use fees based on the quality of the urban land were collected in light of actual conditions in Shenzhen as from 1982. This system fundamentally recognized that land could be leased. During this period, the land use right was supplied with and without payment in Shenzhen, but the transfer of the land use right was permitted only between the Shenzhen Municipal Government and land users and occurred only by means of allocation. From 1979 to 1985, the capital construction investments in Shenzhen totaled 6.36 billion yuan, while the investments in urban infrastructure construction and real estate development accounted for 31.5% of the total capital construction investments—if the real estate investments in industry, commerce, transport, agriculture, forestry and water conservancy were included, these investments made up more than 60% of the total investments (Zheng Jingsheng 1987).

In April, 1987, the State Council announced that land use rights could be transferred on a paid basis; Shenzhen became the first to transfer land use rights—the right to use the land lot covering an area of more than 5,000 m^2 with a duration of 50 years was transferred. On December 1, 1987, Shenzhen saw the first auction involving paid transfer of state-owned land use rights in China. This landmark auction marked the beginning of the reform of the land use system in China. Afterwards, paid transfer of land use rights was rapidly applied nationwide. Shenzhen took a step forward in the reform of the land use system—initially, fees were collected from foreign investors in the form of cooperative land development in Shenzhen, and then land use fees were collected; subsequently, the right to use state-owned land was publicly transferred on a paid basis. In January, 1988, the Standing Committee of the People's Congress of Guangdong Province became the first in China to issue and implement the *Management Regulations of the Shenzhen Special Economic Zone*. According to the regulations, the land use rights in the special economic zone were monopolized and transferred by the municipal government on a paid basis by means of agreement, bidding and public auction. Since then, Shenzhen's land market has preliminarily taken shape.

In 1988, the First Session of the 7th National People's Congress revised the provision, in the *Constitution of the People's Republic of China* adopted in 1982, that land transfer was not permitted; according to the revised provision, land use rights could be transferred according to the laws, and the system for paid use of state-owned land was adopted. In 1990, the State Council promulgated the *Interim Regulations of the People's Republic of China for the Transfer of Urban State-owned Land Use Rights*. According to the regulations, land use rights could be used, transferred, leased, mortgaged or used in other economic activities according to the laws and the allocated land consistent with the requirements could be transferred after payment of the land price. During this period, users could obtain land use rights through unpaid allocation and paid transfer by means of an agreement-based transfer, public bidding, auction, sales, exchange and grant. As from 1994, the plan of administrative allocation of land was cancelled, all land transfer had to be based on signing a land transfer contract and administrative allocation of land was changed to an agreement-based transfer in Shenzhen.

2. **Order No. 100**

In 2001, an agreement-based land price was officially abolished and it was stipulated that all land transferred through agreement had to be based on market land prices in Shenzhen. In 2002, the Shenzhen Municipal Land and Resources Bureau issued the *Regulation for the Use of State-owned Land Transferred through Bidding, Auction and Listing*, adding a new way to transfer land in Shenzhen—listing.

In March, 2001, the *Administrative Regulations of Shenzhen City for the Land Transaction Market* (Order No. 100 of the Shenzhen Municipal Government) was made public and became effective. These were the first local regulations for land transactions in China. Shenzhen's land transaction market was officially put into operation at the same time. The regulations mainly stipulated that the secondary and tertiary land use rights could be traded on the tangible market; all operating land had to be listed and traded in the land and real estate trading center; the original multi-track system for the supply of the operational land was changed to the single-track system.

3. **The Third Revolution**

Land nationalization was completed in Shenzhen as early as 1992; however, as the development was too fast, no land was available in Shenzhen for a long time. In 2004, with full coverage through urban planning, Shenzhen achieved the urbanization goal of becoming the first city in China without rural areas by turning 270,000 farmers into urban residents; as all the land covering an area of 260 km^2. Outside the special economic zone became state-owned, Shenzhen became the first city in China without a rural organizational system. In December, 2005, the first industrial land lot was publicly transferred on Shenzhen's tangible market for land transactions. This marked the expansion of the scope of market-oriented land resource allocation in Shenzhen from the original single operational land to industrial land. This was the third revolution in the land use system in Shenzhen after the first auction in 1987 and Order No.100 in 2001.

4. **"Deep water area" reform**

As a highly urbanized city in China, Shenzhen has always come out in front in the reform of the land system. However, with the 30 years of rapid development, there is a certain degree of misalignment between land management and urban development transformation in China, such as, between the manner of land use and the new requirements for urban transformational development, between the land resource allocation mode and the new requirements for intensifying the reform of the market economic system, between the land interest allocation mode and the new requirements for building a harmonious society, between the mechanism of the land management system and the new requirements for transforming the government's functions.

In May, 2012, the Ministry of Land and Resources and the Guangdong Provincial Government jointly approved the *Overall Plan of Shenzhen City for the Reform of the Land Management System* as the degree of urbanization was high, all land became state-owned, the incremental space was extremely limited and the contradiction between land supply and demand was very acute. The plan centered on ensuring efficient utilization of construction land during industrialization and urbanization, establishing a new land management mechanism for promoting urban scientific development, achieving scientific and rational land use, and comprehensive, coordinated and sustainable economic and social development. The plan covered eight reform priorities, including innovation of the mechanism for secondary land development utilization, improvement of the state-owned land property rights system and reinforcement of land legislation. The plan focused on paid land use, market-oriented land allocation, unified expropriation and transfer for guaranteeing the supply of new construction land, investigation into the use of land reserves for promoting the transformation of the economic developmental mode. This secondary land renewal use model further clarified the complex property rights of the existing land and houses, turning the illegal gains into legal gains and converting potential interests into realizable interests, ultimately maximizing the benefits and increasing the value.

It is worth noting that the nationalization of land has been completed in Shenzhen, but the leftover problems concerning land ownership in urbanization are very complicated; the land of the original village collectives has been expropriated and has become state-owned land according to the planning, the formalities for making compensation concerning much of the land have not yet been completed, so this land is, in essence, still owned by the village collectives and joint-stock companies; meanwhile, the original village collectives have not yet gone through the formalities, thus the collective cannot use this land; there are even illegal buildings, leaving the land resources unused or causing inefficient utilization of them; as a result, both the government and the original village collectives have suffered losses.

Shenzhen's urbanization is accompanied by some problems left over from history: The rights and interests in part of the land are controversial, so the government cannot recover this land and the collectives cannot use it; some organizations which have received land from the original village collective economic organizations in Shenzhen use the land to build low-end factories and lease the land at low prices. In order to liquidize the land resources and further make room for Shenzhen's transformation and upgrading, in January, 2013, "1 + 6" documents concerning the promotion of Shenzhen's industrial transformation and upgrading were released. According to one of these documents—the *Measures of Shenzhen City for Improving the Industrial Land Supply Mechanism and Expanding the Industrial Land Space (Trial)*, the organizations which had received land from the original village collective economic organizations were given the possibility to apply to let legal industrial land enter the market. This document was a major breakthrough in the reform of the domestic land management system considered as a restricted zone. It is the policy-derived result and innovation from the land reform plan of Shenzhen City approved by the Ministry of Land and Resources and Guangdong Provincial Government. It is conducive to increasing the land use value and boosting the industrial transformation and upgrading of village joint-stock companies. This reform of the land management system in Shenzhen is deemed to start adopting the double-track system for land supply and investigate the path towards the reform of the land system in future urbanization. It also marks the entry of land reform into the deep-water area (Table 5.1).

(II) Exploration of the Housing System in the Shenzhen Special Economic Zone

1. Reform Plan of the Shenzhen Special Economic Zone for the Housing System

During the initial stage of the Shenzhen Special Economic Zone, the population growth was not fast, and the ratio of the registered population to the permanent resident population was about 1:1 in 1988. In order to address the shortage of houses,

Table 5.1 Adjustments of the land use system in Shenzhen since 1981

Year	Content
1981	The *Interim Provisions of the Shenzhen Special Economic Zone for Land Management* was adopted during the Standing Committee of the 5th People's Congress of Guangdong Province
1988	The *Administrative Regulations of the Shenzhen Special Economic Zone for Land Management* was promulgated during the Standing Committee of the People's Congress of Guangdong Province
1990	*Measures of the Shenzhen Special Economic Zone for the Collection of Land Use Fees*, the State Council issued the *Interim Regulations of the People's Republic of China for the Transfer of Urban State-owned Land Use Rights*
2001	*Administrative Provisions of Shenzhen City for the Land Transaction Market*
2002	The Ministry of Land and Resources issued the *Provisions for Bidding, Auction and Listing for the Transfer of State-owned Land Use Rights*
2006	*Opinions of the Shenzhen Municipal People's Government Concerning Further Strengthening Land Management and Promoting Economical and Intensive Use of Land, Administrative Measures of Shenzhen City for Land Reserve Management*
2012	*Overall Plan of Shenzhen City for the Reform of the Land Management System*
2013	*Measures of Shenzhen City for Improving the Industrial Land Supply Mechanism and Expanding the Industrial Land Space (Trial)*

the housing investment channels became diverse in the special economic zone, mainly including: The government invested in building houses for the working personnel from government institutions and public institutions; organizations built houses by themselves to mainly provide houses for their employees; the real estate development companies invested in developing houses mainly for personnel from foreign-funded enterprises, some enterprises and public institutions, individual workers and residents in sub-districts; individuals built houses by themselves. During this period, urban housing developed rapidly at a rate apparently higher than that of the growth of the urban population, achieving coordinated development of housing, urban economy and society. From 1980 to 1998, the per capita living area within the special economic zone increased from 6.60 to 15.3 m^2. In 1992, the Shenzhen Municipal Housing Bureau was granted the UN-Habitat Scroll of Honour Award by the United Nations Human Settlements Programme (Ma Chunhui 2010).

However, since the 1990s, the permanent resident population has grown rapidly and exceeded the registered population. The ratio of the permanent resident population to the registered population was about 3:1. The growth of the urban population was obviously faster than that of urban housing, so addressing the urban housing problem was an important issue during the initial stages of the special economic zone. In October, 1988, the *Reform Plan of the Shenzhen Special Economic Zone for the Housing System* was released and became effective; Shenzhen became the first in China to stop physical housing distribution and monetize housing distribution; the concept of commodity housing appeared in the eyes of the people and was spread nationwide for the first time. The year 1988 was symbolic for Shenzhen's housing reform. In that year, the government and relevant departments intensively introduced a number of normative documents concerning the housing reform, such as *Nine Detailed Rules for the Reform Plan of the Shenzhen Special Economic Zone for the Housing System, Provisions for New Housing Standards.*

In 1989, the Shenzhen Municipal Government released the *Housing Development Plan of the Shenzhen Special Economic Zone*, specifying the overall goal for addressing the housing issue in the special economic zone: address the housing issue for the employees of the Party and government organs as well as public institutions within 3–5 years; mitigate the housing shortage in the special economic zone within 5–8 years; basically ensure that all eligible citizens would have an apartment house and the housing supply and demand would be basically balanced in the special economic zone by 2000 or in a longer period of time. In the same year, the government also released the *Circular Concerning Relevant Issues in the Implementation of Shenzhen's Housing Reform Plan*, the *Circular Concerning Approval and Distribution of the Work Report of the Municipal Housing Management Bureau and the Supervision Bureau on Strengthening Housing Reform Supervision and Law Enforcement*, the *Opinions Concerning the Handling of Several Issues Involving the Housing Reform at the Party and Government Organs and Public Institutions*. In 1990, the Shenzhen Municipal Government issued a number of housing reform documents including the *Circular Concerning the Printing and Circulation of the "Guiding Thoughts and Measures for the Housing Reform at State-owned Enterprises in the Shenzhen Special Economic Zone" Developed by the Housing System Reform Office*, the *Circular Concerning the Issues Involving the Original Houses of Employees in the Shenzhen Special Economic Zone After Job Transfers*, the *Circular Concerning Several Issues Involving the Enterprise Housing Reform* and *Provisions for the Handling of Several Issues in the Housing Reform*. The overall guiding thought lies in applying the public housing policy and achieving housing socialization.

According to the *Reform Plan of the Shenzhen Special Economic Zone for the Housing System*, the houses newly built after the housing reform should be small, rational, practical and available in various types, and the same housing construction funds can meet the housing needs of more families. Along with the implementation of the small house policy, the system for area price differences was also adopted with the economic means for controlling the need for large-area houses in Shenzhen in 1992. The specific measure under the system for area price differences is as follows: with 70 m^2 as the benchmark, the total housing price increases by 1% if the housing area rises by 1 m^2. In late 1988, the Shenzhen Branch of the China Construction Bank established the real estate credit department in order to coordinate the implementation of the housing reform plan. This credit department mainly aimed at extending mortgage loans at preferential interest rates to citizens who had the desire to purchase affordable houses, offering working capital loans to the government for building affordable houses and establishing special accounts for managing enterprise housing provident funds. In 1994, the Shenzhen Branch of the Industrial and Commercial Bank of China set up a special body for extending mortgage loans at preferential interest rates to citizens who planned to purchase affordable houses at meager-profit prices.

With economic development and the shortage of urban land, subject to giving play to the roles of the State, collectives, enterprises and individuals, the housing supply in the Shenzhen Special Economic Zone featured the "double-track three-category" mode: the government's housing management bureau organized efforts to build welfare-oriented housing and meager-profit houses; the real estate development companies invested in building commodity houses. From 1988 to 1999, more than 400,000 citizens owned houses through the housing reform, and about 155,500 affordable houses were sold in the Shenzhen Special Economic Zone; the Shenzhen Municipal Housing Management Bureau cumulatively sold about 45,000 units of affordable housing (Wen Zhe, 2000).

In October, 1999, the *Several Provisions of Shenzhen City for the Reform of the Housing System of State Organs and Public Institutions* was issued and became effective. 职工只要将所购安居房补交全成本微利差价和缴纳有关税费后, 即可拥有住房的全部产权, 而且住房可以进入市场交易. 这标志着深圳市住房商品化, 社会化由此迈入全新的发展阶段, 从1999年至2001年, 全国住房制度改革也取得重大突破, 深圳进一步探索和推进深圳市国家机关和事业单位的住房制度改革, 解除安居房的产权约束, 使业主拥有了真正意义上的房屋产. According to the provisions, as of January 1, 2000, once a unit of affordable housing, typically priced just above cost, has been paid for in full, including all necessary fees and taxes, its occupants becomes its legal owner with full property rights over it, including the right to put in on the market. This marked the beginning of a new developmental stage of housing commercialization and socialization in Shenzhen. From 1999 to 2001, major breakthroughs were also made in the reform of the housing system across the country, and in Shenzhen, the reform of the housing system at state organs and public institutions was further explored and promoted, the property rights restrictions on the comfortable houses were removed so that the owners owned the real house property rights.

2. **Interim Administrative Provisions of Shenzhen City for the Housing Provident Fund**

In 1992, the *Interim Provisions of Shenzhen City for Social Insurance* was adopted in Shenzhen, specifying relevant pilot provisions for the housing provident fund. Its core contents are as follows: enterprises voluntarily file an application, the government participates in pilot work after examination and approval, the government bodies and public institutions do not participate in it; there are no mandatory obligations for enterprises; the participating individuals are limited to the employees with registered permanent residence; their own housing provident fund accounts are only available for payment and withdrawal. Only some enterprises practiced the housing provident fund system. The institutional coverage was small. Housing loans could not be offered through the housing provident fund. The housing provident fund paid by these enterprises and employees was managed by the municipal social security bureau. As of the end of 2008, 104,000 employees from various types of organizations were covered by the housing provident fund, the cumulative housing provident fund was about 4.69 billion yuan and the balance was 2.49 billion yuan in Shenzhen.[2]

On April 3, 1999, the State Council issued the *Administrative Regulations for the Housing Provident Fund*. The regulations represented the innovations in the financial system for individual houses during the evolution of China's housing system from a planned one to a market-oriented one. The regulations marked the beginning of a new period for the law-based and standardized development of the system for China's housing provident fund. In 2002, the State Council revised the regulations on the basis of the experience from various areas by considering the development of the national system for the housing provident fund.

For a considerably long time, among large and medium-sized cities across the country, Shenzhen was the only city where the system for the standardized housing provident fund was not established according to the *Administrative Regulations for the Housing Provident Fund* issued by the State Council (effective as of 1999). The housing provident fund system was not officially initiated until the opening of the Shenzhen Housing Provident Fund Management Center in October, 2010. In Shenzhen, Shenzhen branches of the China Construction Bank, the Bank of China and the China Merchants Bank became the first to provide services relating to housing provident fund collection.

3. **Outline Plan of Shenzhen City for the Reform of and Innovation in the Housing Security System**

The affordable housing supply system, focusing on low- and medium-income households and providing social security, and the commodity housing supply system for high-income households were established early in Shenzhen. By the 1990s, industrialization and urbanization had attracted a huge external population to Shenzhen, so the housing demand grew rapidly there. In order to more quickly address the housing issue concerning low- and medium-income households, intensify the development and construction of the economically affordable housing and accelerate the renovation of urban villages, the affordable housing project was carried out in Shenzhen, through which houses were sold to low- and medium-income households at cost prices. Meanwhile, In Shenzhen, the traditional welfare-oriented low-rent public housing policy was abandoned, "houses are built—houses are sold—houses are built again—houses are sold again" greatly quickened the construction of public housing in Shenzhen.

In January, 2013, the *Outline Plan of Shenzhen City for Housing Security System Reform and Innovation* was released. This outline plan expanded the scope of housing security and extended housing security from low-income households with registered permanent residence to homeless households with registered permanent residence, and from households with both housing difficulties and registered permanent residence in households with housing difficulties but without registered permanent residence (Table 5.2). This outline plan stressed efforts to turn Shenzhen

[2]*Shenzhen Special Economic Zone Daily*, December 1, 2010.

Table 5.2 Government Documents on housing system adjustment in Shenzhen since 1985

Year	Content
1985	*Tentative Measures of the Shenzhen Special Economic Zone for Commercialization of Housing for Cadres and Employees of Administrative Public Institutions*
1988	*Reform Plan of the Shenzhen Special Economic Zone for the Housing System*
1989	*Outline Plan of the Shenzhen Special Economic Zone for Housing Development*
1992	*Opinions of the Housing System Reform Office of the Shenzhen Municipal People's Government Concerning Delimitation of Property Rights in Welfare-oriented Housing in the Housing Reform*
2000	*Several Provisions of Shenzhen City for the Housing System Reform of State Organs and Public Institutions*
2002	*Opinions of Shenzhen City Concerning Delimitation of Property Rights in Welfare-oriented Housing in the Housing Reform*
2002	*2001 Measures for the Distribution of Affordable Housing for Employees from the Municipal Party, Government Organs and Public Institutions*
2006	Circular issued by the Shenzhen Municipal People's Government Concerning the Implementation of the *Shenzhen Housing Construction Plan (2006-2010)*
2007	*Circular issued by the Shenzhen Municipal People's Government Concerning Printing and Distribution of the Shenzhen Housing Security Development Plan*
2008	*Administrative Measures of Shenzhen City for Low-rent Housing Security, Interim Administrative Measures of Shenzhen City for Economically Affordable Housing, Interim Administrative Measures of Shenzhen City for Public Rental Housing, Measures of Shenzhen City for Addressing the Housing Issue for High-level Professional Talents (Trial)*
2010	*Regulations of Shenzhen City for Security Housing*
2010	*Interim Administrative Measures of Shenzhen City for the Housing Provident Fund*
2011	*Interim Measures of Shenzhen City for Affordable Housing for Talents, Interim Measures of Shenzhen City for the Construction and Management of Affordable Commodity Housing*
2013	*Outline Plan of Shenzhen City for the Housing Security System Reform and Innovation*

into a model city regarding housing within the reform of the national housing security system. According to this outline plan, the affordable housing queuing system was developed, and all the households with housing difficulties which were eligible for applying for the affordable commodity housing and public rental housing were included in the queuing bank. The queuing sequence was determined according to the time for obtaining Shenzhen's registered permanent residence, and paying the social insurance or filing an application; priority was given to the households with housing difficulties, with disabled members of the household, entitled groups and talents. This also meant that Shenzhen residents without Shenzhen household registration could live in affordable housing. This was in accordance with Shenzhen's situation in which the population with Shenzhen's registered permanent residence was smaller than that without Shenzhen's registered permanent residence. This was also the means for promoting equal access to public services. Shenzhen was at the forefront of the country in this regard.

(III) Contributions from the Shenzhen Special Economic Zone to the reform of the Land Use and Housing System

As one of the areas which was one of the first to embark on the reform and opening up in China, the Shenzhen Special Economic Zone is forward-looking and a typical example nationwide regarding the reform of the urban land system. In 1978, the first land auction in China occurred and the land use mode under which land expropriation was separated from the conversion of land for other uses was experimented with in Shenzhen; in 2004, all collective land was converted into state-owned land in Shenzhen; in 2012, the third land reform was launched to make a breakthrough in industrial land and allow for part of the land whose property rights were actually owned by the original village collectives to enter the market in Shenzhen; relevant systems adopted in Shenzhen were innovative. The land was tapped, while Shenzhen City and the original rural collective economic organizations enjoyed the benefits. The entry of collective construction land into the market has also broken the mode under which industrialization and urbanization was driven merely by government land; the emergence of multiple rights holders is more conducive to healthy urbanization.

In more than 30 years, the Shenzhen Special Economic Zone has accomplished remarkable achievements in the reforms and innovations involving the land use system and the housing policy, laying a solid foundation for creating Shenzhen's economic miracle and carrying out effective experiments in China's land use and housing reform. For example, the first-ever pilot work on the paid use of land across the country has directly resulted in the revision of the constitution, relevant laws and regulations, and in this way initiated the reform of the land use system in China. Shenzhen became the first to carry out a land auction, bidding, listing and transfer, thus driving forward the market-oriented allocation of land resources nationwide. The *Reform Plan of the Shenzhen Special Economic Zone for the Housing System* introduced the concept of commodity housing for the first time and spread it across the country. The experimentation of "three-old transformation" in Shenzhen helped bypass the traditional difficult way of land expropriation, demolition and compensation, and it produced a multi-win outcome to local governments, the farmers whose land was expropriated and whose houses were demolished and the floating population during urban expansion and conversion of rural collective land into state-owned land, so Shenzhen has been hailed as the vanguard in experimenting with "three-old transformation" in China. On December 20, 2013, the first industrial land owned by the original village collective was traded and circulated on the open land transaction market in the history of Shenzhen; this was another historical breakthrough in the land system reform in Shenzhen after the first-ever auction of state-owned land in 1987; this offered a new sample for further breaking land financing, and continued collective ownership of rural land can also maintain social stability and harmony, and help reduce the land transaction costs. This undoubtedly has had an impact and a certain demonstration effect on national economic and social development.

5.2.3 Promote Social Equity, Build a Harmonious Society—Reform the Medical and Higher Education Systems

Rapid economic growth has also been accompanied by the problems similar to those which occurred in the early industrialization of developed countries and some disorders in modern Western society, such as a widening gap between the rich and the poor, corruption, conflicts between the people and between the people and nature. Therefore, some scholars suggested that China should seek out a "modern solution" as early as possible (Qin Xiao 2009). These problems involve a very important theme in economics—efficiency and equity. Achieving efficiency and equity is difficult to do in a market economy. Giving play to the function of the "invisible hand" in resource allocation can deliver efficiency. Equity is mainly achieved by the rational provision of public goods by the government especially in the management of medical and educational programs.

In the process of building a socialist market economy with Chinese characteristics, we should always properly deal with the relationships between efficiency and equity, and give due consideration to equity on the basis of putting efficiency first. In institutional construction, a series of reforms have been carried out in the medical system and the higher education system and equity has been considered while giving first priority to efficiency in order to build a harmonious society in Shenzhen.

(I) **Reform of the Medical System**

In 2011, Shenzhen cooperated with the University of Hong Kong in building Binhai Hospital where the modern hospital corporate governance structure—in which decision-making, execution and supervision power restrict and coordinate each other—and a modern service mode were adopted.

In 2012, the Health and Family Planning Commission of Shenzhen Municipality carried out three tasks in the reform of the medical system involving "innovations in the public hospital management system and experimentations regarding the separation of the clinic from the pharmacy" and "innovations in the system and mechanism for Shenzhen-Hong Kong cooperation in running hospitals and investigations into a new way to international cooperation concerning public interest organizations." These tasks included: First, innovations were made in the public hospital management system—according to the operational mode of statutory bodies, the Public Hospital Administration of Shenzhen Municipality was established to perform the duty of running public hospitals on behalf of the Shenzhen Municipal Government and to accept industrial supervision from the Health and Family Planning Commission of Shenzhen Municipality according to laws; the council of the Public Hospital Administration of Shenzhen Municipality was set up as the decision-making supervisory body. The social capital was guided to run tertiary hospitals; the pattern in which the public medical institutions and non-public medical institutions mutually promote and jointly develop preliminarily took shape. The reform was carried out in specific affairs concerning hospital operations. With respect to the medical pricing system, the funds were allocated according to the quantity of public services supplied, and the medical charges and prices were based on the full cost of medical services to stimulate public hospitals to improve management performance and services. The University of Hong Kong-Shenzhen Hospital adopts the system that all personnel are employed and thus is not included in the management of public institutions, and the hospital determines posts and remuneration at its own discretion. Second, the reform of separating the clinic from the pharmacy was promoted. In 2012, the *Implementation Plan for the Reform of Clinic-Pharmacy Separation at Public Hospitals* was adopted in Shenzhen. Drug price addition was cancelled and changed to treatment and examination fees at public hospitals; the mechanism of competition between drug distribution enterprises and hospital pharmacies was established. Third, innovations were carried out in the system of Shenzhen-Hong Kong cooperation in running hospitals.

The medical system is one of the most important social welfare systems in every country. With cooperation between Shenzhen and the University of Hong Kong, the advantage of location is fully utilized and the social management experience from the advanced economy is drawn on and conveyed nationwide. This was one of the institutional contributions from the special economic zone to China's modernization.

(II) **Reform of the Higher Education Management System**

In Shenzhen, actions have been taken to encourage higher education institutions to combine the offering of specialties with regional economic development, and closely serve the pillar industries, such as high and new technology, finance, logistics and culture and the strategic emerging industries, including new energy, the Internet and biology, adjust the specialties unfit for the industrial and market needs, and add new specialties according to the industrial needs and development forecast, thus, to the greatest extent, protecting the connection with regional industrial upgrading. With specialty adjustments, preponderant disciplines were combined, the setup of colleges and departments was adjusted and the allocation of educational resources within schools was optimized to enhance the overall competitive strength of the schools.

Shenzhen University has become the experimental school for carrying out comprehensive reform involving the self-running of schools and establishing a modern university system. Centering on personnel reform, Shenzhen University has pressed ahead with a number of reforms in an all-round way: two professor committees on personnel and financial accounting have been set up and they are responsible for introducing talents, distributing financial and economic resources, practicing governance of academic and teaching affairs by professors and democratic management, and ensuring academics-led allocation of core resources at higher educational institutions. Intensive teaching is conducted during the whole process. Exquisite classroom teaching is pursued. A new mode of teaching students in accordance with their aptitude is sought. Evaluation is performed according to quality. The management of scientific research is based on the idea of establishing large teams, building large platforms, undertaking large projects and delivering great results. Shenzhen

University has done beneficial experiments in developing the academics-led modern university system in which professors govern the academic and teaching affairs and there is separation of school management, school running and evaluation. The Chinese University of Hong Kong (Shenzhen) jointly run by Shenzhen University and the Chinese University of Hong Kong operates by adopting the school running philosophy and mode of the Chinese University of Hong Kong, offering the fresh experience for the cooperative running of schools.

As the experimental school for national comprehensive reform of higher education, the Southern University of Science and Technology is run by drawing on the successful experience from the world-class universities and innovating the management system and operational mechanism, building an internal governance structure suitable for the development of first-class universities, and attempting to set up the council governance mechanism as well as establishing the academics-led operational model. With regard to the personnel system, the all-personnel employment system has been adopted, the tenure system for professors and the teacher promotion and exit mechanism was established. A comprehensive evaluation and enrollment mode based on college entrance examinations was developed, in which the performance on aptitude tests organized by schools accounts for 30% of the comprehensive enrollment mark. The specialties are not designated for undergraduate students in the first two years of university to reinforce the basic education, while specialized education has been optimized and emphasis is placed on developing an innovative ability and personality in the last two years.

In Shenzhen, great attention is paid to building characteristic colleges, which is considered an important move for pushing forward innovative development, creating "Shenzhen Quality" and accelerating the building of a national innovative city and a modern international advanced city in the new period of the Shenzhen Special Economic Zone. As of 2014, the construction of projects for six characteristic colleges had been initiated in Shenzhen, including BGI College, the Shenzhen College of Advanced Technology, Shenzhen University Kuang-Chi New Materials Characteristic College, the Clinical Medical College of Guangzhou University of Chinese Medicine and the China Capital Market Institute, where there were 1,146 full-time students including 285 undergraduate students and 861 master's degree and doctoral candidates. A number of domestic higher education institutions, scientific research institutions and relevant districts of Shenzhen have offered to build characteristic colleges.

The reform of the educational system at both Shenzhen University and the Southern University of Science and Technology has produced a marked effect. The new mode of teaching students in accordance with their aptitude as adopted at Shenzhen University has become a mature mode of running schools, resulting in effective allocation of teaching and learning resources. The Southern University of Science and Technology has made successful attempts at adopting the international practices concerning student enrollment and education, which will further push forward innovations in the domestic educational system.

5.3 Contributions from the Special Economic Zones to the Reforms of China's Social and Political System

The *Overall Plan of Shenzhen City for Comprehensive Reform* approved by the State Council in May, 2009 stated that Shenzhen should embark on the first-ever implementation of pilot programs regarding four aspects, among which two aspects cover the reform of the political system: an institutional design consistent with the international practices and universal rules, China's future developmental direction, and institutional innovation with an important impact on Shenzhen's economic and social development and the great demonstration effect across the country. The Shenzhen Special Economic Zone has carried out many beneficial experiments regarding reform of the political system; they cannot be considered completely successful, but they are indeed helpful attempts.

5.3.1 Experimentations Regarding Separation of the Three Administrative Powers

In 2003, Shenzhen began the pilot reform in the separation of three administrative powers, acquiring experience for the national reform of governmental institutions.

The separation of three administrative powers was conducted by mainly learning from the administrative reform carried out by the British Government for addressing irrational setting up of institutions, administrative inefficiency and high costs. The enterprise operation philosophy was introduced into the government, and the concepts of cost and benefit were stressed. Three administrative powers were separated in the following way: the government's decision-making was separated from execution and supervision; the important decision-making items were transferred to the core departments of the government; a large number of execution and service duties were separated out and assigned to the specialized independent execution bodies. The result of the administrative reform in the UK was that the execution of specialized and differential management has enabled the government to improve efficiency and lower administrative costs. The UK has separated decision-making from execution, producing a very good effect. Hong Kong has also adopted a similar administrative system, and has become the main source of learning and reference for the Chinese Mainland. The Government of Hong Kong has a three-tier architecture: the Chief Executive, 3 departments and 11 decision-making bureaus are the high-level decision-making departments, under which there are more than 60 executive bodies; the decision-making departments are separated from the executive departments, they perform their own duties respectively, and these duties are well defined.

The reform attempt in separating the three administrative powers in 2003 was suspended for a few reasons. The reform involving such separation was not restarted until the *Overall Plan of Shenzhen City for Comprehensive Reform* was introduced in 2009. This plan explicitly stated that the functionally coordinated huge department system should first be piloted in the setting up of government institutions, according to the requirement that the decision-making power, the executive power and the supervisory power mutually restrict and coordinate. Such mutual restriction and coordination of the decision-making power, the executive power and the supervisory power means separation of three administrative powers and is the core of the huge department system operation.

5.3.2 The Mechanism of Open Recruitment and Voting in Cadre Selection

Open recruitment of the leading cadres from the society is an important measure taken in Shenzhen for reforming the cadre selection and appointment system and introducing the competition mechanism to reinforce the building of the group of leaders. At the beginning of the Shenzhen Special Economic Zone, the demand for high-caliber talents was huge and talents were recruited and transferred from the rest of the country to Shenzhen. In 1983, the Organizational Department of the Central Committee of the Communist Party of China issued a document, permitting Shenzhen to recruit cadres from Shanghai, Beijing and Tianjin. As from 1986, the bureau-level leading cadres were openly recruited through examination at the Shenzhen Municipal Standard and Meteorological Bureau and Audit Office. In October, 1986, the leading bureau-level cadres for eight departments, including the labor bureau, the judicial bureau and the industrial and commercial bureau were openly recruited through examination across the city. The praiseworthy aspect of open recruitments conducted in Shenzhen in more than 30 years is the introduction of the mechanism of competition, through which talents are screened on the basis of merit through examination and evaluation in various forms, from different perspectives and by multiple means. As an attempt at reform, open recruitment of the leading cadres has proven to be successful over many years of practice in various areas and has been widely applied nationwide.

At present, the voting system has been universally adopted by the Party and government organs across the country in making important decisions. It was initially implemented in Longgang District of Shenzhen. In 1997, the 15th National Congress of the Communist Party of China vowed to quicken the reform of the cadre system and expand democracy. In order to carry out the decision made at the 15th National Congress of the Communist Party of China, in response to the situation in which the top leaders in the leading groups and contingent of cadres had the final say, the Committee of Longgang District of Shenzhen developed the overall reform idea of internal coordination which included ten major measures, one of which was the adoption of the voting system for appointing the cadres of the Party committee leadership. In August, 1998, the *Voting System for Appointing the Cadres of the Leadership of the Party Committee (Leading Party Group)* was developed in Longgang District, and the Party Committee of Buji Town and the Buji District Court were chosen for pilot implementation, and the Party Committee of Pingshan Town also actively participated in pilot work. The voting system is carried out basically in the following way: (1) determine the scope of voting, incorporate the cadre appointments on which the Party Committee and the leading Party group have the right to decide and the cadre appointments subject to decision made by the personnel departments of the Party Committees or organizations at higher levels into the scope of voting; (2) determine the voting form, explicitly state that all members involved in the voting by the Party Committee and the leading Party group are subject to a vote by more than 2/3 of the required attendees, and the voting result should be announced on site; they are not adopted unless more than 1/2 of the required attendees cast affirmative votes; (3) standardize the voting procedure—the candidates are reviewed by the personnel department of the organization, public opinions are solicited and the review opinions are expressed before voting; and the review is introduced by the personnel department, deliberation and discussions are conducted, secret voting is carried out in the voting meeting, the formalities for taking office are completed according to relevant regulations after voting. In 1999, the voting system was applied across the Longgang District. The first-ever pilot implementation of the voting system in Longgang District was successful and attracted wide attention. It was specially reported by the *People's Daily*. The voting system introduced a breakthrough in cadre appointment. It converted the appointment power of the top leader into that of all members of the Party Committee and the leading Party group, and changed the decisive vote of the top leader into an ordinary vote like that of the other members. It changed the situation in which the top leader had the final say over cadre appointment and built a new paradigm of democratic participation. The voting system increases the democratic and scientific levels of decision-making regarding cadre appointment. The voting system promotes and maintains the solidarity of the group as well as boosting the correct use of the personnel. The Shenzhen Municipal Party Committee decided to make reference to Longgang's practice—the candidates to be appointed and the recommended candidates for the chief of the Party Committee and the government's leading group during the change of office term of the leading group at the district level are nominated by the standing committee of the Party Committee at the next level, deliberated by all committee members and are subject to secret voting. In April, 2002, the Guangdong Provincial Party Committee adopted the system of voting by all committee members in promoting and appointing three Party and government chiefs at the prefecture level, and announced that, subsequently, the candidates to be appointed and the recommended candidates for the Party and government chiefs at the prefecture level were subject to voting conducted according to the *Trial Measures for Voting on Candidates for New Party and Government Chiefs at the Prefecture Level*. In May, 2002, the General Office of the Guangdong Provincial Party Committee issued the *Trial Measures for Voting on Candidates for New Party and Government Chiefs at the Municipal, County and District Levels*, extending the voting system to the county level. The voting system originated in Shenzhen and then was adopted in Guangdong Province, and now it has been applied nationwide.

5.3.3 Democratic Election Experiment in Direct Election

As the vanguard in the reform and opening-up, Shenzhen has carried out many beneficial experiments in direct elections. In the Shekou Industrial Zone, a democratic experiment was carried out from 1983 to 1986, in which all employees were evaluated and elected through voting, even the leading group was directly elected through the contest. In early 1999, a reform experiment of electing the town chief through the competitive "three-round two-vote" system was made in Dapeng Town, Longgang District, Shenzhen. In 2000, a provincial and municipal joint research group led by Zhang Gaoli, then Secretary of the Shenzhen Municipal Party Committee, conducted *A Study of the Historical Mission for Cross-century Development—Turning Shenzhen into A Model City which is Based on Socialism with Chinese Characteristics and Becomes the First to Basically Achieve Modernization*. According to this study, it was planned that Shenzhen would become the first to directly elect a town chief, even a district chief might be directly elected in particular districts of Shenzhen in the next ten years. In 2008, the *Several Opinions of the Shenzhen Municipal Committee of the Chinese Communist Party of China and the Shenzhen Municipal People's Government Concerning the Building of the Socialist Model City (Exposure Draft)* and the *Outline Plan for Recent Reforms in Shenzhen (Exposure Draft)* were released on the Internet, specifying the overall line of thought regarding the designing of the reform of the structural system involving State power, including: put the building of democracy and the legal system before other reforms; in the next three years, innovate the working system and mechanism of the people's congress, explore the pilot adoption of the system for direct election of deputies to the people's congress at the district level through a contest, introduce the mechanism of competition to the inner-party elections, gradually expand the scope of the direct election of the leading group at the grass-roots Party organizations, improve the system of competitive election of the Party Committee at the municipal and district levels, strive to become the first in China to implement the property declaration system involving the Party and leading government cadres at the municipal and district levels. The direct election practice in Shenzhen has played the role of active guide and vanguard in reforming the socialist political system with Chinese characteristics.

The election based on the "two-vote system" in the Longgang District of Shenzhen is the first-ever attempt at direct elections. The "two-vote system" has brought about top-down democratic elections from conscious pilot implementation to mechanism guidance, all-round promotion and institutionalization. The "two-vote system" changes the previous practice that the Party Committee at the higher level determined the candidates and the election was carried out by Party members. Under the "two-vote system", with recommendations made by the masses, members of the rural grass-roots Party organizations are elected by Party members. Its procedure is as follows: Candidates are first recommended by the representatives of villagers and Party members, and Party members recommend themselves, they are nominated by the current Party branch, and a qualification examination is conducted, election speeches are delivered and opinion polls are conducted; the candidates for the Party branch members are determined under the principle that the candidates are at least 20% more than the positions, and then they are elected in the meeting of Party members. The first vote in the "two-vote system" is a recommendation vote, a public opinion vote, designed to examine the degree of recognition of the recommended people by the masses and this provides the basis for determining the official candidates. The second vote is the one cast by the officially electing Party members and is the inner-party election vote. With the recommendation and the election, the "two-vote system" closely combines the public opinion foundation with the election. In October, 1998, one administrative village was chosen from each of the ten towns in Longgang District to carry out pilot elections under the "two-vote system". In May, 1999, as an election system innovation, the "two-vote system" was widely adopted during elections upon the expiration of the office term of the Party branch in the rural areas throughout Shenzhen. The "two-vote system" is legitimate in the operating procedure, extensive in democratic participation and impartial in the determination of candidates. The "two-vote system" expands the channels for making use of personnel, helps establish the effective incentive mechanism and guarantees the quality of the election. During the election upon the expiration of the office term of the rural Party organizations in 2001, the "two-vote system" was changed to "two recommendations, one election"; the difference is that the preliminary candidates are subject to the approval by the examining group of the town Party committee and the weight given to the examining group of the town Party committee increases. Its election process is basically the same as that under the "two-vote system".

Later, the "two-vote system" developed into "public recommendation and direct election". Both the "two-vote system" and "two recommendations, one election" share this similarity: the nomination and approval by the department at the higher level comes first. "Public recommendation and direct election" open a new chapter for democratic elections. In January, 2007, when the first Party committee at a private enterprise in Guangdong Province was established in the Tongtiandi Mobile Communication Market in Futian District, the competitive election based on public recommendation and direct election was conducted. The whole election process was open; the Party organization at the highest level neither recommended candidates, nor designated the candidates for the Party secretary; all Party members directly cast votes for the election according to their own will. The candidates were determined through joint recommendation by the Party members and the masses and self-recommendation. Immediately after the recommended candidates were determined, they were released by public announcement and their qualifications were examined, they were reviewed by the organization and democratic appraisal was conducted. The votes involving democratic appraisal were counted and released on site, and the result was publicly announced. The "public recommendation and direct election" in the communities of Futian District aroused a great repercussion in Shenzhen. This election mode is conducive to enhancing the prestige of the leading groups of the grass-roots Party organizations and substantively improves the credibility and transparency of grass-roots elections. In 2008, the working committees at Shenzhen's municipal organs carried out a pilot "public recommendation and direct election" for the Party committees of the organs. In late July, the Party committees of the Shenzhen

Municipal Supervision Bureau, the Shenzhen Municipal Land and House Property Management Bureau, the Shenzhen Municipal Statistical Bureau and the general Party branch of the Shenzhen Municipal Work Safety Bureau underwent elections upon the expiration of the office term through "public recommendation and direct election". In the "public recommendation and direct election" of Shenzhen's municipal organs, the candidates for members of the Party committees are recommended by the Party organizations, including the Party organizations at the same and higher levels, and they are jointly recommended by more than three Party members and they recommend themselves.

Among the measures in the reform of Shenzhen's political system, open recruitment has become a common way of cadre selection and has been conducted nationwide to a large extent. The voting system and direct elections have also been put into practice to a great degree. This represents a step forward in the democratic politics with the extensive participation and a correct check and balance. It is a beneficial institutional attempt at transformation from an authoritative government to a democratic service-oriented government. This process has not yet been finished and is still on-going. It is believed that the reform measures concerning the political system in the special economic zones represented by Shenzhen will continue to help move China's Development Path forward smoothly and completely.

Chapter 6
Economic Contributions from the Special Economic Zones to China's Development Path

In recent years, the special economic zones have played a very important role in continued economic and social innovations and further development in China—the strategy of economic gradient development, which is pole-driven development, the point-to-line and line-to-area development, from the coastal areas to the inland areas, along the rivers and the border.

Against such a background, the method which combines quantitative analysis with qualitative analysis is attempted to comprehensively and objectively review the roles of the special economic zones in the modernization of China: On the one hand, such a driving and radiation role can be measured to enhance the attainment of the expected result in policy implementation; on the other hand, the leading industrial and demonstration effect from the special economic zones can be evaluated to identify the entry point in the industrial planning so as to achieve more with less effort.

6.1 Basic Background for the Development of the Special Economic Zones

At present, China has entered a crucial period of reform and development—the institutional dividend has slowly faded away; there are bottlenecks and constraints in various aspects of social and economic development, including political and legal factors, economic factors, technical factors, social factors, cultural factors and ecological resources. The original developmental mode is no longer sustainable and China needs new engines for economic growth. The special economic zones have continuously innovated, developed and played the leading role in the above aspects, so they undoubtedly provide China with a developmental path full of opportunities and challenges.

Against the new background at home and abroad at the present stage, China's economy is advancing from the "old normal" to the "new normal". This calls for

© Social Sciences Academic Press and Springer Nature Singapore Pte Ltd. 2018
Y. Tao and Z. Lu, *Special Economic Zones and China's Development Path*,
Research Series on the Chinese Dream and China's Development Path,
https://doi.org/10.1007/978-981-10-3220-2_6

renewing systems and institutions and for achieving fresh economic development, carrying out benign interaction to promote the optimization and upgrading of the industrial structure, driving forward institutional innovations and those regarding the mechanism and going global, so as to boost economic, institutional and cultural integration and development between the special economic zones and the areas other than the special economic zones in different regions, at various levels and on different developmental paths during the future development and opening-up. Therefore, in our view, the successful convening of the Third Plenary Session of the 18th Central Committee of the Communist Party of China in 2013 marked a new great milestone in initiating a new round of China's reform and opening up. The China (Shanghai) Pilot Free Trade Zone is a comprehensive experimental site for all-round reforms, from the economic system to the supervisory system to the administrative system; with regard to the significance of further improving the structure of China's economic system, it can be compared to the Shenzhen Special Economic Zone established in the first round of reform through opening-up. It will offer valuable experience for innovations to China's institutions and mechanism and to international development in the future.

6.2 Current Growth of the Special Economic Zones: Scale and Speed

In recent years, various types of special economic zones have adapted to the new situation, made new progress and realized new leaps in promoting scientific development and building the Chinese Dream.

Specifically, tremendous development and progress have been achieved in five major special economic zones—Shenzhen, Shantou, Zhuhai, Xiamen and Hainan—and six national-level new areas—the Lanzhou New Area in Gansu Province, the Liangjiang New District in Chongqing, the Zhoushan Archipelago New Area in Zhejiang Province, the Nansha New District in Guangzhou, the Pudong New Area, and the Tianjin Binhai New Area. Furthermore, as the efforts for expanding the development, the experimental zones for reform and opening-up—demonstration zones and cooperation zones—have been established and regional planning has been developed. The national bonded zones, bonded logistics parks, national hi-tech zones, national bonded port areas, bonded logistics centers, export processing zones, border economic cooperation zones, special economic development zones, comprehensive bonded zones and key experimental zones for development and opening-up as well as other types of special economic zones have seen further improvements in their developmental potential. With a review of the latest economic development in the special economic zones, a good and solid theoretical and practical foundation is provided for further reforms in the special economic zones, and a new direction is defined for further social and economic development—at the economic and industrial levels, the levels of political and social factors, cultural factors and ecological resources—in China.

6.2.1 The Scale and Speed of Economic and Industrial Development in the Special Economic Zones

(I) Analysis of the Developmental Trends in Shenzhen

Table 6.1 shows the data concerning the GDP, fixed asset investments, total working population, the output value of the transportation, warehousing and postal industries in Shenzhen from 1990 to 2012. Comparisons can reveal the trends in economic development in the Shenzhen Special Economic Zone.

Table 6.1 Data concerning the GDP, fixed asset investments, working population, and the output value from the warehousing and postal industries in Shenzhen from 1990 to 2012

Year t	GDP Y_t (10,000 yuan)	Fixed asset investments K_t (10,000 yuan)	Total working population L_t (10,000 people)	Transport, warehousing and postal industries W_t (10,000 yuan)
1990	1,716,665	623,380	109.22	61,162
1991	2,366,630	912,324	149.32	93,946
1992	3,173,194	1,782,322	175.97	154,369
1993	4,531,445	2,477,875	220.81	187,473
1994	6,346,711	2,819,413	273	299,651
1995	8,424,833	2,758,243	298.51	249,416
1996	10,484,421	3,275,270	322.12	294,605
1997	12,974,208	3,930,657	353.53	398,958
1998	15,347,272	4,803,901	390.33	417,028
1999	18,040,176	5,695,878	426.89	282,095
2000	21,874,515	6,196,993	474.97	367,972
2001	24,824,874	6,863,749	491.3	308,935
2002	29,695,184	7,881,459	509.74	261,890
2003	35,857,235	9,491,016	535.89	823,019
2004	42,821,428	10,925,571	562.17	734,274
2005	49,509,078	11,810,542	576.26	1,265,170
2006	58,135,624	12,736,693	609.76	1,674,594
2007	68,015,706	13,450,037	647.11	2,477,602
2008	77,867,920	14,676,043	682.35	2,819,570
2009	82,013,176	17,091,514	723.61	3,936,762
2010	95,815,101	19,447,008	758.14	3,650,747
2011	115,055,298	20,609,180	764.54	3,362,286
2012	127,956,227	24,044,311	#	4,719,911

Source Shenzhen Statistical Yearbook (1991–2013) [M]. Statistics Press. ("#" means no published statistical data)

Table 6.2 Comparisons of economic levels between Shenzhen and Hong Kong, Singapore (unit: 100 million USD, USD)

Year	Shenzhen		Singapore		Hong Kong	
	GDP	Per capita GDP	GDP	Per capita GDP	GDP	Per capita GDP
1990	36	1824	388	12,745	769	13,480
1991	44	2254	452	14,412	888	15,444
1992	58	2326	520	16,099	1040	17,930
1993	79	2604	605	18,250	1200	20,328
1994	74	1967	732	21,421	1355	22,458
1995	101	2341	871	24,702	1442	23,428
1996	126	2706	952	25,929	1590	24,702
1997	157	3097	993	26,158	1763	27,170
1998	185	3346	850	21,647	1669	25,508
1999	218	3593	849	21,442	1633	24,714
2000	264	3962	943	23,414	1691	25,375
2001	300	4207	877	21,194	1666	24,811
2002	359	4877	906	21,705	1638	24,285
2003	433	5682	960	23,319	1586	23,558
2004	517	6553	1127	27,046	1659	24,454
2005	604	7422	1254	29,400	1778	26,093
2006	729	8585	1457	33,114	1899	27,698
2007	894	10,031	1776	38,700	2071	29,943
2008	1121	12,013	1900	39,255	2154	30,952
2009	1201	12,318	1856	37,220	2093	30,017
2010	1415	13,930	2274	44,790	2242	31,914
2011	1781	17,096	2598	50,123	2437	34,457
2012	2080	19,799	2765	52,051	2655	36,660

Source Annual Statistical Yearbooks of Shenzhen, Hong Kong and Singapore [M]. Statistics Press

As shown above, the momentum of economic development was good, the growth was relatively rapid, and the modern industries were directly proportional to the urban economic development in Shenzhen. The added value of relevant industries constantly grew in Shenzhen, which coordinated well with the economic development in the whole city. According to the above analysis, Shenzhen has an important role and status in China's economy and society and has made significant contributions to the development of China's modern economy.

In addition, according to comparisons regarding per capita GDP between Shenzhen and the advanced international cities (as shown in Table 6.2), Shenzhen's per capita GDP was 19,799 USD in 2012, Shenzhen had the leading position in this regard nationwide; however, it was only equivalent to the levels of Hong Kong and

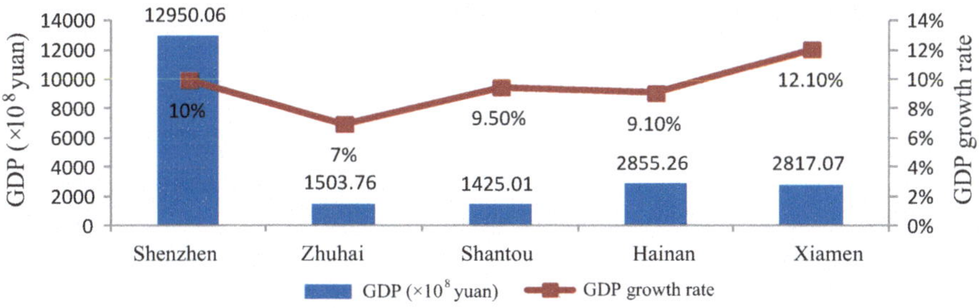

Fig. 6.1 Trends of change in the GDP of the three main industries and growth rates in the five major special economic zones in 2012

Singapore in 1992 and 1993, showing a developmental gap of nearly 20 years. Given the developmental trends of the service industry in the advanced international cities, there is still a relatively large amount of room for development in Shenzhen, which is at the level of a moderately developed city.

(II) Analysis of the Current Development in Five Major Special Economic Zones, Including Shenzhen, Zhuhai, Shantou, Xiamen and Hainan

The GDP in the five major special economic zones, Shenzhen, Zhuhai, Shantou, Xiamen and Hainan (shown in Fig. 6.1), increased from 1,924,817 million yuan in 2011 to 2,155,116 million yuan in 2012, with their GDP growth rates higher than the national growth rate—Shenzhen and Xiamen enjoyed a double-digit growth. Per capita GDP in Shenzhen, Zhuhai and Xiamen was higher than 10,000 USD, while that in Shantou and Hainan was still lower than 5000 USD. Shenzhen, Hainan and Shantou witnessed double-digit growth of per capita GDP.

At the present stage, it is more urgent to transform the economic developmental mode in China amidst international economic downturn and stagnant external demand. The industrial output value steadily increased, but its growth rate apparently declined compared with the same period of the previous year in the special economic zones with a relatively high degree of dependence upon foreign trade—Zhuhai, Xiamen and Shenzhen experienced relatively large decreases in growth rate, with these decreases being 8.4, 6.3 and 5.3% points, respectively. The industrial added value in Shantou and Xiamen grew by 12.4 and 12.8%, respectively, higher than the national level. The industrial added value in Shenzhen, Zhuhai and Hainan grew by only 7.3, 6.4 and 8.8% respectively, lower than the national level (Table 6.3).

In the five major special economic zones, the economic growth is structurally slowing down, the traditional industries are being steadily transformed and upgraded, and the industrial structure is being optimized. In such special economic zones as Shenzhen, Shantou, Zhuhai, Xiamen and Hainan, the traditional industries have been continuously extended, step by step, from the low end of the value chain to its high

Table 6.3 Industrial output value and its growth rates in five major special economic zones

Economic indicators	Shenzhen[a]	Zhuhai	Shantou	Xiamen	Hainan
Industrial added value (100 million yuan)	5091.4	740.2	667.8	1164.0	521.2
Industrial added value growth rate (%)	7.3	6.4	12.4	12.8	8.8
Growth compared with the previous year (%)	−5.3	−8.4	−1.7	−6.3	−4.6
Added value growth rate at state-owned enterprises (%)	1	8.7[a]	4.9[ab]	–	25.4
Growth compared with the previous year (%)	−9.2	−8.8	12.7[ab]	–	11.2
Added value growth rate at joint-stock enterprises (%)	15.7	21.3	16.3[ab]	–	15.4
Growth compared with the previous year (%)	−12	1	−4.1[ab]	–	−3.7
Added value growth rate at foreign-funded, Hong Kong, Macao and Taiwan-funded enterprises (%)	0.1	−1.8[a]	5.1[ab]	18.2[ab]	−0.6
Growth compared with the previous year (%)	−3.2	−15.2	−7.6[ab]	–	−10.2
Added value growth rate in the light industry (%)	10	6.5	–	5[ab]	14.5
Growth compared with the previous year (%)	7.4	−18.6	–	−6.8[ab]	4
Added value growth rate in the heavy industry (%)	6.6	6.0	−2.6[ab]	16.9[ab]	7.5
Growth compared with the previous year (%)	−8.7	−2.8	−0.8[ab]	−4.7[ab]	−7.7

Source Statistical Communiqués on the 2011 and 2012 National Economic and Social Development in the Five Major Special Economic Zones
Note [a]Industries above the designated size, [b]total industrial output value

end, and the adjustment and upgrading of the industrial structure has been accelerated. In recent years, Shenzhen has become the first to introduce a plan for revitalization and development of the strategic emerging industries and the supporting policies, focusing on developing six major strategic emerging industries, including biology, the Internet, new energy, new materials, new-generation information technology and the creative cultural industry. In 2012, the scale of the strategic emerging industries in Shenzhen totaled 1248 billion yuan, accounting for 27% of Shenzhen's GDP, up 25.5%, higher than the double of the economic growth rate. Currently, Shantou has been home to the strategic emerging industries including new materials, high-end electronic information, biological medicine, semiconductor lighting, animation, solar photovoltaic, environmental protection and software. In Shantou, there has been a certain foundation for the development of such industries as zirconium, Beidou Navigation Satellite Systems and satellite remote sensing, big data and new environmentally-friendly materials. Under the principle of "developing some areas while refraining from other areas" and "carrying out major projects to take the lead and foster the development of industrial agglomerations", Shenzhen has been active in building the developmental pattern of "3 + 4" strategic emerging industries, making breakthroughs in new-type high-end electronic information, biological medicine, new energy and new energy automobiles, and developing new materials, aviation, ocean engineering, energy conservation and environmental protection industries. Under the principle of combining high agglomeration with relative concentration, subject to the requirements of integration within and outside the island, high starting points, high standards and high levels, Xiamen has relied on the Xiamen Scientific & Technological Innovation Park, the Torch Industrial Zone, the Haicang Biological Medicine Port, and characteristic parks for software and machinery to actively promote the development of agglomeration of the strategic emerging industries. Hainan has attached great importance to cultivating and developing the strategic emerging industries, and has been vigorous in establishing the special funds dedicated to developing the strategic emerging industries to guide the flow of capital to the above industries. Hainan has encouraged and given priority to the development of such strategic emerging industries as new energy, new materials, software, electronic information and biological medicine. With the construction of a number of large projects including Hainan Yingli, the Haikou Pharmaceutical Valley, the Hainan Resort Software Community and the Sanya Creative Industry Park, the strategic emerging industries represented by biological medicine, high-end equipment manufacturing, information, new energy and new materials have gradually taken shape in Hainan.

Shenzhen's GDP was 1,295,006 million yuan, up 10.0% compared with the previous year (the same below), higher than the average national and provincial levels. Shenzhen continued to rank No. 4 among the cities on the Chinese Mainland in terms of GDP. Shenzhen's per capita GDP was 123,247 yuan, up 11.62% (Fig. 6.2). In the evaluation of the technological industrialization capability of the cities at and above the sub-provincial level across the country in 2012, Shenzhen ranked No. 1, showing a high endogenous power for industrial development.

Zhuhai's GDP was 150,376 million yuan, up 7.0% compared with the previous year. Zhuhai's per capita GDP was 89,794 yuan, up 6.32%. Shantou was relatively backward among the five major special economic zones. In 2012, Shantou's GDP totaled 141,501 million yuan, up 9.5% compared with the previous year. Shantou's per capita GDP was 23,596 yuan, up 11.17%. Xiamen's GDP was 281,707 million yuan, up 12.1% compared with the previous year at a comparable price. Xiamen's per capita GDP was 70,832 yuan, up 9.27%. Hainan's GDP was 285,526 million yuan, up 9.1% compared with the previous year at the comparable price. Hainan's per capita GDP was 32,374 yuan, up 12.03%.

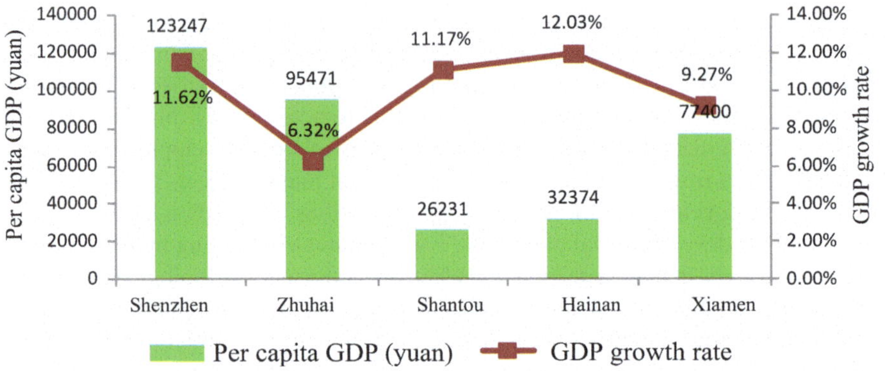

Fig. 6.2 The trends of change in per capita GDP and growth rates in the five major special economic zones in 2012

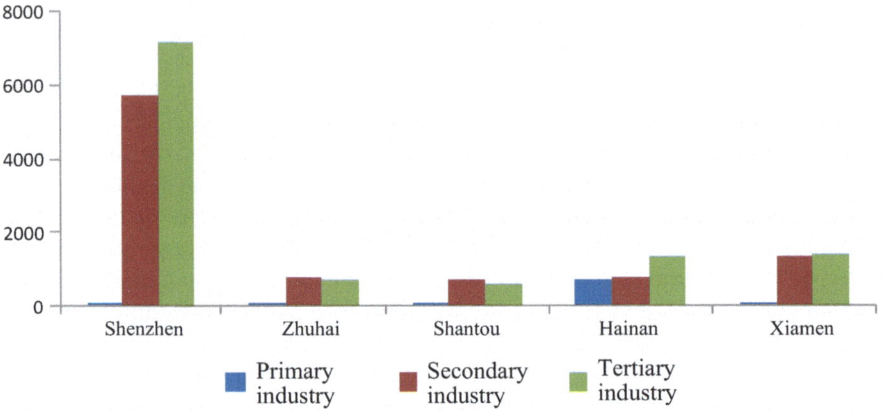

Fig. 6.3 Added value from the three industries in the five major special economic zones in 2012 (100 million yuan)

6.2.2 *Levels of Industrial Structural Transformation in the Special Economic Zones*

The added value from the primary, secondary and tertiary industries was 630 million yuan, 573,764 million yuan and 720,612 million yuan in Shenzhen in 2012, up 0.1, 7.3 and 12.3%, respectively (Fig. 6.3).

The added value from the primary, secondary and tertiary industries was 3902 million yuan, 77,636 million yuan and 66,870 million yuan in Zhuhai, up 4.9, 3.1 and 8.0, respectively. The added value from the primary, secondary and tertiary industries was 8044 million yuan, 74,020 million yuan and 60,437 million yuan in Shantou, up 4.2, 11.9 and 7.3%, respectively. The added value from the primary, secondary and tertiary industries was 2521 million yuan, 137,401 million yuan and 141,785 mil-

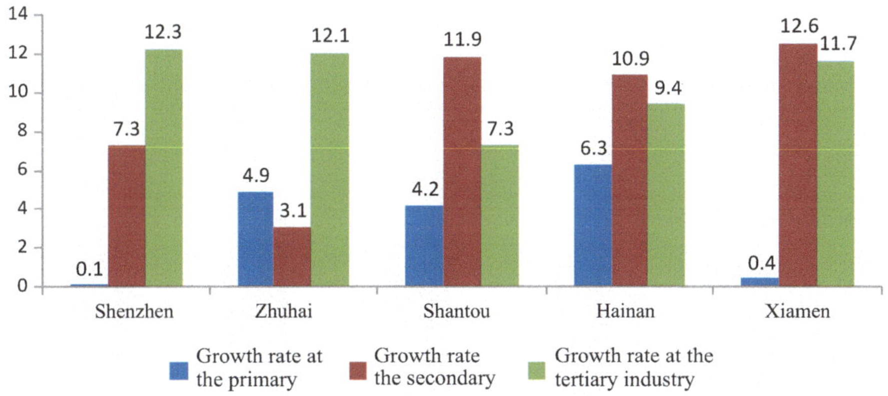

Fig. 6.4 Growth rates of the three industries in the five major special economic zones in 2012

lion yuan in Xiamen, up 0.4, 12.6 and 11.7%, respectively. The added value from the primary, secondary and tertiary industries was 71,147 million yuan, 80,367 million yuan and 134,012 million yuan in Hainan, up 6.3, 10.9 and 9.4%, respectively (Fig. 6.4).

The structure of the three industries in Shenzhen was adjusted from 0.0:46.5:53.5 in 2011 to 0.0:44.3:55.7 in 2012, with further optimization of the industrial structure. The structure of the three industries in Zhuhai was adjusted from 2.6:54.4:43.0 in 2011 to 2.6:52.9:44.5 in 2012. The structure of the three industries in Shantou was adjusted from 5.8:50.9:43.3 in 2011 to 5.8:51.5:42.7 in 2012. The structure of the three industries in Xiamen was adjusted from 1.0:51.4:47.6 in 2011 to 0.9:48.8:50.3 in 2012, while that in Hainan was adjusted from 26.1:28.3:45.6 to 24.92:28.15:46.94 (see Fig. 6.5).

The proportion of the primary industry in the GDP in Shenzhen, Zhuhai and Shantou was similar to that in the previous year. The proportion of the secondary industry in the GDP in four special economic zones, except Shantou, declined compared with the previous year. The proportion of the tertiary industry in the GDP in four special economic zones, except Zhuhai, rose compared with the previous year.

In Shenzhen and Xiamen, the tertiary industry made up the largest proportion among the three industries, followed by the secondary industry and then the primary industry, and the proportion of the tertiary industry exceeded 50%, showing that the industrial structure was evolving towards a relatively advanced stage. In Zhuhai and Shantou, the secondary industry made up the largest proportion, followed by the tertiary industry and then the primary industry, and the proportion of the secondary industry exceeded 50%, indicating that industrialization was expanding. In Hainan, the tertiary industry made up the largest proportion, followed by the primary industry and the secondary industry, suggesting the path of evolution in different directions with the impact of special factor endowment, location and other factors.

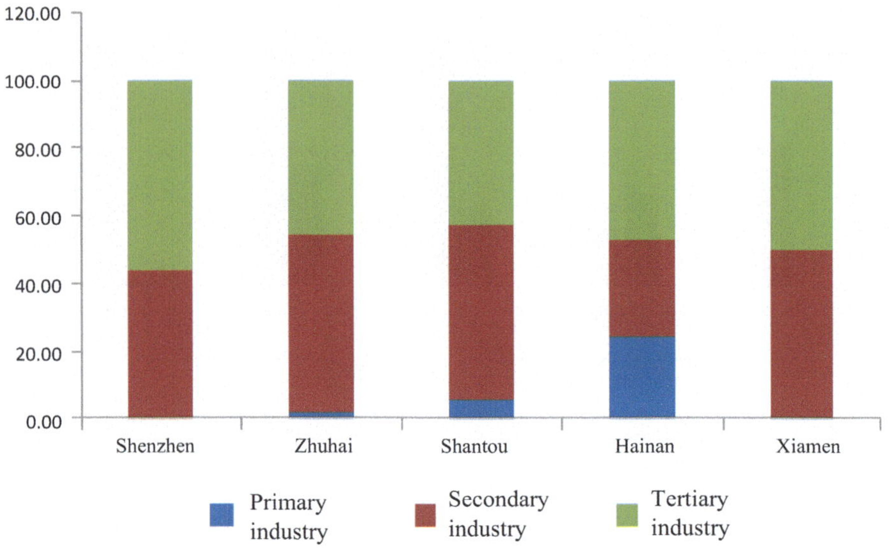

Fig. 6.5 Composition of the three industries in the five major special economic zones in 2012

In order to better illustrate the overall changes in the structure of the three industries in the special economic zones, the change value C_{ij} of the industrial structure in the special economic zones can be calculated. It is assumed that $C_{ij} = \sum \left| Q_{ij1} - Q_{ij0} \right|$, where, Q_{ij} is the proportion of the *j*th industry in the whole industrial structure in the *i*th special economic zone, the subscripts 0 and 1 represent 2011 and 2012, respectively. The higher the C_{ij} value is, the larger the change is in the industrial structure in the special economic zone; the lower such a value is, the smaller the change is.

According to the results of the calculation, the change values of the industrial structure in Shenzhen, Zhuhai, Shantou, Hainan and Xiamen compared with the previous year were 4.39, 5.55, 6.09, 2.67 and 5.46%, respectively (see Fig. 6.6). As shown, among the five major special economic zones, Shantou saw the highest change value of the industrial structure, followed by that in Zhuhai, Hainan and Shenzhen, while Xiamen showed the lowest change value.

Besides the overall changes in the industrial structure in the special economic zones, in order to know the direction and intensity of changes in the three industries in the special economic zones, the trend value in industrial change, B_{ij} should also be calculated. It is assumed that $B_{ij} = \frac{Q_{ij1}}{Q_{ij0}}$, when B_{ij} is larger than 1, the proportion of the *j*th industry in the *i*th special economic zone increases—the *j*th industry expands; when B_{ij} is equal to 1, the proportion of the *j*th industry remains unchanged; when B_{ij} is smaller than 1, the proportion of the *j*th industry decreases—the *j*th industry contracts. The larger the distance is between B_{ij} value and 1, the higher is the intensity

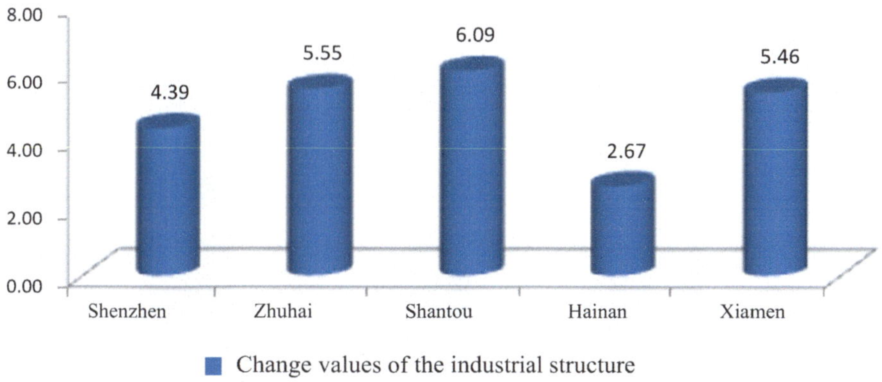

Fig. 6.6 Change values of the industrial structure in the five major special economic zones

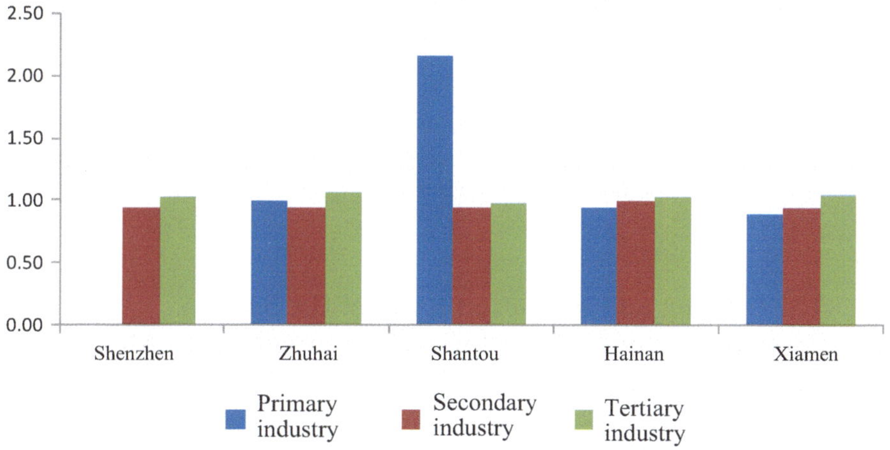

Fig. 6.7 The trends of change of the three industries in the five major special economic zones

of the expansion or contraction of the *j*th industry. The smaller the distance is, the lower the intensity is.

According to the results of the calculation, as shown by the average values of the trends of change of the three industries, the proportion of the primary industry was generally unchanged in the five major special economic zones, while the secondary industry tended to contract and the tertiary industry was set to expand (Fig. 6.7).

The five major special economic zones showed different characteristics. According to the values of the trend of change of the primary industry in the five major special economic zones, the primary industry contracted in Shenzhen, Hainan and Xiamen, while it expanded in Shantou and Zhuhai. According to the values of the trend of change of the secondary industry in the five major special economic zones, these zones displayed exactly the same trend—the proportion of the secondary indus-

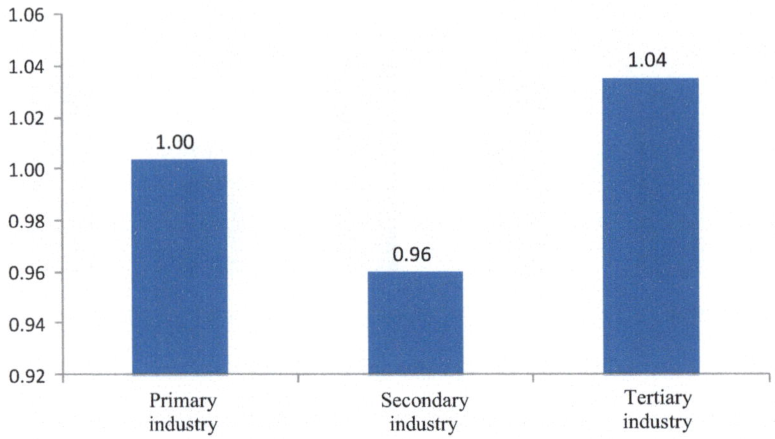

Fig. 6.8 Average values of the trends of change of the three industries in the five major special economic zones

try declined. According to the values of the trend of change of the tertiary industry in the five major special economic zones, the tertiary industry expanded in four special economic zones, except Shantou (Fig. 6.8).

6.3 The Driving and Radiation Roles of the Special Economic Zones in the Macro Economy: From a Macro Perspective

The economic development of the special economic zones is increasingly aligned with the national economic development; it exerts an impact through the factors determining the regional economic development to stimulate the economic growth of the whole region. In order to more explicitly display such a role, this section will build up a time series model and adopt the metrological method to analyze the contributions from the special economic zones to economic growth.

6.3.1 Indicator Selection and Data Source

(I) **Indicator Selection (Output Value of the Advanced Technology-Based Manufacturing Industry and the Modern Service Industry)**

In this research project, the indicator (ZZL)—the level of development of the output value of the advanced technology-based manufacturing industry and the modern service industry is adopted to approximately describe and measure the development of the special economic zones: On the one hand, this is because the level of development of the output value of the advanced technology-based manufacturing industry and the modern service industry is the main part of the economy in the special economic zones; on the other hand, this is because its statistics have become mature after many years of development, and data are available and reliable. Meanwhile, the level of development of the advanced technology-based manufacturing industry and the modern service industry is a physical indicator, so the level of development of the advanced technology-based manufacturing industry and the modern service industry is used in this research to reflect the economic development of the special economic zones.

The economic growth of the special economic zones can mean "quantitative" epitome—continued increase in total national output; this is the center of economic growth. If the "qualitative" improvement is considered, economic growth becomes economic development, which includes not only the economic growth rate, the degree of growth steadiness and the result of growth, but also the average quality of life of the people in a country or territory such as the educational level and the health standard, the overall progress in the whole economic structure and social structure. With respect to economic growth, this research project measures the economic development only from the "quantitative" perspective; given the availability and validity of the data, the Gross Regional Product (GRP) of the special economic zones is chosen as the indicator for measuring the economic growth rate.

(II). **Data Source and Processing**

In this paper, relevant data concerning the special economic zones from 1990 to 2012 were chosen for analysis, while the data came from the *Statistical Yearbooks of the Special Economic Zones (1991–2013)*; however, the Gross Regional Product (GRP) was based on the current year's prices while inflation was not considered. In order to make data comparable and prevent system errors in analysis, in this research, data were processed and the Gross Regional Product of the special economic zones was converted into the constant price in 1990, thus removing the impact of the price factor on the Gross Regional Product.

6.3.2 Test Results and Descriptions

In order to eliminate the impact of heteroscedasticity on the model and reduce data fluctuation, the original indicators were converted into logarithmic indicators before the building of the model: $\ln grp$ is the logarithmic value of GRP, while $\ln zzl$ is the logarithmic value of the level of development of the advanced technology-based manufacturing industry and the modern service industry.

(I). **Unit Root Test of Variables**

In practice, most of the economic and financial data are nonstationary time series. For nonstationary time series, the numerical characteristics of time series vary with

Table 6.4 ADF test of variables

Variable	Test type	ADF test value	Critical values at significance levels			Test results
			1%	5%	10%	
ln*grp*	(C, 0, 0)	0.283074	−3.689194	−2.971853	−2.625121	Nonstationary
*D*ln*grp*	(C, 0, 0)	−0.568588**	−3.699871	−2.976263	−2.627420	Stationary
ln*zzl*	(C, 0, 0)	−0.780027	−3.689194	−2.971893	−2.625121	Nonstationary
*D*ln*zzl*	(C, 0, 0)	−4.479087*	−3.699871	−2.976263	−2.627420	Stationary

Note 1. *D* is the first difference; *means that the test value at the significance level of 1% is significant; **means that test value at the significance level of 5% is significant; the absence of any mark means that the test value is not significant

time—the stochastic law of nonstationary time series is different at various time points, it is difficult to figure out the stochastic nature of time series through the known information of the series.

The rapid economic growth in the special economic zones and the continuous development of the level of development of the advanced technology-based manufacturing industry and the modern service industry render time series data nonstationary. Therefore, in order to test the time series characteristics of data, Augment Dickey Fuller (ADF) was adopted for conducting the tests. The test results are shown in Table 6.4.

According to the above table, the ADF test statistics of both ln*grp* and ln*zzl* are larger than the critical value at the significance level, so the null hypothesis cannot be rejected, the series ln*grp* and ln*zzl* have a unit root and are nonstationary values, but the ADF test statistics of the first difference of both ln*grp* and ln*zzl* is smaller than the critical value at the significance level of 5% (the ADF test statistics of Dlnzzl is smaller than the critical value at the significance level of 1%), so the null hypothesis is rejected, the first difference of series lngrp and ln*zzl* has no unit root, and the time series is generally stationary—ln*grp*-*I*(1) and ln*zzl*-*I*(1) test values are significant.

(II). **Co-Integration Test of Variables**

In order for a co-integration analysis, the VAR model of ln*grp* and ln*zzl* was built, and the AIC information criterion and the SC criterion were used to determine that lag order was 1; the Johansen test was adopted to examine the co-integration among variables. The results are shown in Table 6.5.

According to the Johansen co-integration test results, at the significance level of 5%, there is a co-integration relationship between the special economic zones' GRP and the level of development of the advanced technology-based manufacturing industry and the modern service industry—there is a long-term stable relationship between the level of development of the advanced technology-based manufacturing industry and the modern service industry and economic growth.

Table 6.5 Johansen co-integration test results

Number of assumed co-integration equations	Characteristic root Eigenvalue	Maximum characteristic root statistics Max-Eigen Statistic	5% critical value at the maximum characteristic root statistics	*P* value
None*	0.389261	20.90098	20.26184	0.0408
At most 1	0.244990	7.587663	9.164546	0.0987

Note *Means that the null hypothesis is rejected at the significance level of 5%, the maximum characteristic root test shows that there is a co-integration equation

Table 6.6 Granger test results

Null hypothesis (Hypothesis)	F-statistic	*P* value (Probability)
ln*zzl* is not Granger cause for ln*grp*	4.06851	0.04406
ln*grp* is not Granger cause for ln*zzl*	4.61484	0.03262

(III). **The Granger Causality Test**

Some economic variables are significantly correlated, but they are not necessarily meaningful; judging whether a change is the cause for another change is a common issue with an economic model; this requires a Granger causality test to judge the causal relationship among variables (Table 6.6).

The *P* value in the above table means the probability of accepting the null hypothesis—the smaller the numerical value is, the higher the capability of the variable is for predicting the dependent variable. According to the above table, there is a two-way causal relationship between economic growth and the level of development of the advanced technology-based manufacturing industry and the modern service industry—economic growth can promote the development of the advanced technology-based manufacturing industry and the modern service industry. The development of the advanced technology-based manufacturing industry and the modern service industry is a Granger cause for economic growth and can also fuel economic growth.

(IV). **Building of the VAR Model and Estimation**

The AIC and SC minimum criterion is adopted to determine that the lag order P is the first order, and the VAR model is used to make an estimation. The results are shown below:

In*grp*(−1)	0.885706	0.026414
	(0.04082)	(0.03519)
	[21.6979]	[0.75057]
In*zzl*(−I)	0.434131	0.884575
	(0.14650)	(0.12631)
[2.96327]		[7.00343]
C	−1.806224	0.576556
	(0.65047)	(0.56079)
	[−2.77678]	[1.02811]
R-squared	0.997637	0.976625
Adj. R-squared	0.997448	0.974755
Sum sq. resids	0.091154	0.067753
S.E. equation	0.060384	0.052059
F-statistic	5277.109	522.2570
Log likelihood	40.45339	44.60706
Akaike AIC	−2.675242	−2.971933
Schwarz SC	−2.532506	−2.8291966
Mean dependent	6.273359	6.118530
S.D. dependent	1.195264	0.327646
Determinant resid	covariance (. adj.)	9.49E−06
Determinant resid	covariance	7.57E−06
Log likelihood		85.62027
Akaike information criterion		−5.687162
Schwarz criterion		−5.401690

Note *Means that the null hypothesis is rejected at the significance level of 5%, the maximum characteristic root test shows that there is a co-integration equation

According to the above table, we can list the following two equations:

$$
\begin{aligned}
\ln grp_t &= 0.885707 \ln grp_{t-1} + 0.434132 \ln zzl_{t-1} - 1.802565 \\
&\qquad (21.6737) \qquad (-2.67534) \qquad (-2.77653) \\
R^2 &= 0.99763 \qquad AIC = -2.67523 \qquad SC = -2.53252
\end{aligned} \tag{6.1}
$$

$$
\begin{aligned}
\ln zzl_t &= 0.026722 \ln grp_{t-1} + 0.884578 \ln zzl_{t-1} + 0.5802565 \\
&\qquad (0.7505) \qquad (7.03534) \qquad (1.0276) \\
R^2 &= 0.9766 \qquad AIC = -2.97523 \qquad SC = -2.8252
\end{aligned} \tag{6.2}
$$

As shown in the above equations, most of the estimated parameters are statistically significant, and only particular ones are not significant, but these coefficients are generally significant.

In Eq. (6.1), the first order lag of $\ln grp_t$ has a relatively large positive impact on it. The first order lag of $\ln grp_t$ and $\ln zzl_t$ also has a relatively strong positive relationship, showing that the development of the advanced technology-based manufacturing industry and the modern service industry can positively boost economic growth.

In Eq. (6.2), $\ln zzl_t$ has a relatively strong association with its first order lag value and this is a positive relationship; the first order lag values of $\ln zzl_t$ and $\ln grp_t$ also have a positive relationship.

Overall, the economic growth in the special economic zones can greatly promote the development of the advanced technology-based manufacturing industry and the modern service industry, while the development of the advanced technology-based manufacturing industry and the modern service industry can positively stimulate economic growth. Thus, efforts should be made to further reinforce the development of the advanced technology-based manufacturing industry and the modern service industry, so that the development of the advanced technology-based manufacturing industry and the modern service industry can further fuel economic growth. Measures should be taken to make it become the new growth point in future economic development.

6.4 The Demonstrative Effect of the Special Economic Zones and Their Effect as Industry Leaders

An evaluation of the special economic zones in China's economic development should focus on not only their direct contributions to urban GDP, but also their guarantee and support for the development of the society, economy and other industries, and their maintenance of coordination in the industrial chain. Therefore, there is an urgent need for expanding and enhancing the industrial linkage of the pillar industries and the strategic emerging industries in the special economic zones, for closely following the pace of their transformation and upgrading, for promoting the standardized, information development, networking, intensive and fine construction, and for keeping a high degree of alignment with the development of other industries. This section will adopt the measuring software SPSS15.0 to evaluate the demonstrative effect of the special economic zones and their effect as industry leaders.

6.4.1 Design of the Evaluation Indicator System for Industrial Transformation in the Special Economic Zones

(I). **Design Principles for the Evaluation Indicator System**

The evaluation system for industrial transformation in the special economic zones is designed to more objectively reflect the process of the development of industrial transformation in the special economic zones and thus identify, through comparisons, the key and difficult points as well as problems in the industrial transformation in the five major special economic zones. The design of the evaluation system for industrial transformation in the special economic zones should follow the general principles concerning the building of the indicator system and give prominence to the typical theme in this research.

1. Systematic

The evaluation system for industrial transformation in the special economic zones is a large, complete system. We must reveal the essence of industrial transformation through the design of the indicators as far as possible. An indicator system should be built on the basis of the internal logic of the development of industrial transformation and should include industrial development and growth, structural upgrading, scale expansion, etc.

2. Operable

The design of the indicators should take into account the data foundation of the five major special economic zones. The contents of the indicators should be explicit, specific, available for measurement and easy to use. The quantitative indicators should facilitate the acquisition or calculation.

3. Representative and dynamic

In the design of the indicators, it is necessary to choose and set the indicators which are, as far as possible, directly related to the evaluation objectives for the development of industrial transformation in the special economic zones; the differences of different indicators in significance should be identified in light of the characteristics of the development of transformation in the special economic zones and the main needs for industrial transformation; the key and most representative indicators should be chosen while abandoning the general indicators.

4. Guidance

The evaluation system for industrial transformation in the special economic zones aims at evaluating the development of industrial transformation in the five major special economic zones and thus accelerating the industrial transformation in the special economic zones.

(II). **Determination of the Evaluation Indicator System**

The above four major principles for designing the evaluation system for industrial transformation in the special economic zones are followed, and reference is made to domestic and foreign literature concerning the evaluation of industrial transformation to determine the evaluation indicator system, as shown in Table 6.7.

Relevant quantitative data in the evaluation indicator system mainly come from the *Guangdong Statistical Yearbook*, the *Shenzhen Statistical Yearbook*, the *Xiamen*

Table 6.7 Evaluation system for industrial transformation in the special economic zones

Evaluation objectives	Primary indicators	Secondary indicators
Evaluation system for industrial transformation in the special economic zones	Industrial growth level	Industrial added value growth rate
		Added value growth rate in the hi-tech manufacturing industry
		Growth rate in the modern service industry
	Structural transformation level	Proportion of added value from the advanced manufacturing industry in the industries above the designated size
		Proportion of added value from the hi-tech manufacturing industry in the industries above the designated size
	Scale level	Output value of new products
		Output value of the modern service industry
	Benefit level	Per capita output
		Output per area of land
	Relevant supporting conditions (market and technical innovations)	Internal expenditure of R&D funds
		New product exportation proceeds
		Number of patent applications

Statistical Yearbook, the *Hainan Statistical Yearbook,* the *Shantou Statistical Yearbook,* the *Zhuhai Statistical Yearbook* and other statistical yearbooks and annual reports released by relevant provincial and municipal governments.

6.4.2 Quantitative Evaluation Process and Results

The evaluation of the development of industrial transformation in the special economic zones is mainly based on principal component analysis (Tables 6.8, 6.9 and 6.10). The principal component analysis is a statistical method which proceeds from the interrelation among multiple numerical variables and draws on the correlation among the original variables and the idea of dimensionality reduction as well as interpreting the original polytomy variables by a few original linear combinations. It is a common method of analysis for simplifying the data structure. Its advantage is that it can eliminate the impact which indicators exert as a result of different dimensions and overcome information overlapping caused by the correlation among indicators and the problems from the artificial determination of indicator weight coefficients, so it has very good application prospects in comprehensive evaluation.

Specific steps for principal component analysis:

1. Standardize the original data;
   Test the significance of factor analysis. According to the results of the Bartlett test, the Bartlett value is 281.39, the degree of freedom is 45, the significance probability P in the test is lower than 0.0001, showing that the relevant matrix is

Table 6.8 Summary of total variance interpretation degree

Component	Original characteristic value			Extraction square and loading			Rotation square and loading		
	Total	Variance %	Cumulative %	Total	Variance %	Cumulative %	Total	Variance %	Cumulative %
1	8.213	68.441	68.441	8.213	68.441	68.441	5.134	42.783	42.783
2	2.171	18.088	86.529	2.171	18.088	86.529	4.440	37.000	79.783
3	1.081	9.008	95.537	1.081	9.008	95.537	1.890	15.754	95.537
4	0.536	4.463	100.000						
5	3.482E−16	2.902E−15	100.000						
6	2.998E−16	2.499E−15	100.000						
7	1.140E−16	9.501E−16	100.000						
8	7.284E−17	6.070E−16	100.000						
9	−2.021E−17	−1.684E−16	100.000						
10	−8.254E−17	−6.878E−16	100.000						
11	−3.361E−16	−2.801E−15	100.000						
12	−3.815E−16	−3.179E−15	100.000						

Extraction method: principal component analysis

Table 6.9 Rotated common factor loading matrix

	Component		
	1	2	3
Zscore (x1)	−0.221	0.017	−0.893
Zscore (x2)	−0.063	−0.967	−0.116
Zscore (x3)	0.286	0.624	0.595
Zscore (x4)	0.564	0.785	0.202
Zscore (x5)	0.714	0.647	0.216
Zscore (x6)	0.943	0.262	0.196
Zscore (x7)	0.978	0.085	0.186
Zscore (x8)	0.563	0.636	0.527
Zscore (x9)	0.396	0.824	0.405
Zscore (x10)	0.960	0.200	0.179
Zscore (x11)	0.961	0.204	0.175
Zscore (x12)	−0.080	−0.917	0.247

Extraction method: principal component analysis; Rotation method: orthogonal rotation with Kaiser standardization
[a]Rotation converges after four iterations

Table 6.10 Common factor score coefficient matrix

	Component		
	1	2	3
Zscore (x1)	0.127	0.139	−0.691
Zscore (x2)	0.132	−0.305	0.031
Zscore (x3)	−0.121	0.104	0.355
Zscore (x4)	0.043	0.168	−0.053
Zscore (x5)	0.109	0.100	−0.060
Zscore (x6)	0.243	−0.058	−0.084
Zscore (x7)	0.280	−0.122	−0.080
Zscore (x8)	−0.012	0.079	0.234
Zscore (x9)	−0.066	0.179	0.149
Zscore (x10)	0.261	−0.080	−0.095
Zscore (x11)	0.261	−0.078	−0.099
Zscore (x12)	0.037	−0.328	0.330

Extraction method: principal component analysis, Rotation method: orthogonal rotation with Kaiser standardization

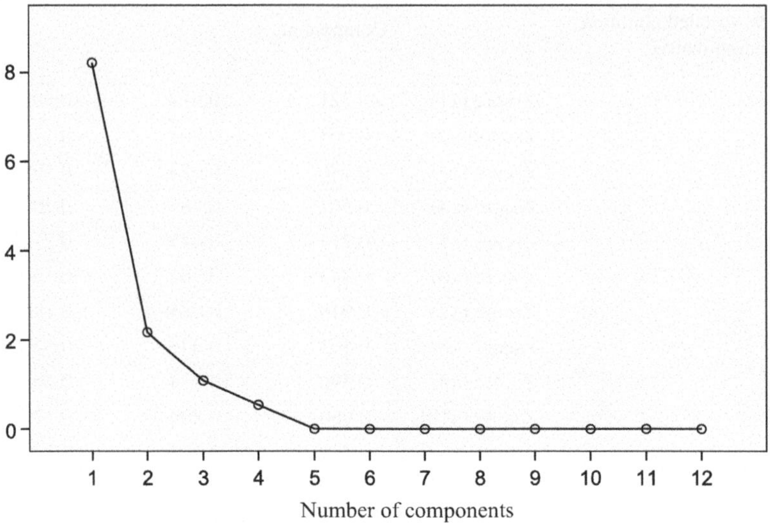

Fig. 6.9 Characteristic values of common factors

not a unit matrix and it is fit for factor analysis. As shown by the results of the analysis, KMO is 0.621, higher than 0.5, indicating that observational variables are acceptable for factor analysis.

3. Extract the common factors. According to an analysis of Fig. 6.9, the characteristic values of the first three common factors are larger than those of the subsequent ones and all of these characteristic values are larger than 1; the characteristic values of the 4th common factor and its subsequent ones are smaller than 1 and steadily change; Table 6.9 shows that the cumulative contribution rate of the first three common factors is 95.537%, so it is relatively appropriate to extract the first three common factors.

   The statistical significance of the data in this table refers to the correlation coefficient between each common factor and the original indicator contained in it—load. According to Table 3, five factors—proportion of added value from the hi-tech manufacturing industry in the industries above the designated size ($X5$), the output value of new products ($X6$), the output value from the modern service industry ($X7$), internal expenditure of R&D funds ($X10$) and new product exportation ($X11$)—have relatively high loads in the first common factor, which can be considered the transformation effect factor with the greatest contribution (42.783%). The added value growth rate in the hi-tech manufacturing industry ($X2$), the growth rate in the modern service industry ($X3$), the proportion of added value from the advanced manufacturing industry in the industries above the designated size ($X4$), per capita output ($X8$), output per area of land ($X9$), the number of patent applications ($X12$) have more loads in the second common factor, which can be considered as a transformation process factor with a con-

Table 6.11 Ranking of the comprehensive scores of industrial transformation in the five major special economic zones

	F_1	F_2	F_3	Comprehensive score	Ranking
Shenzhen	0.73569	0.078178	0.270903	1.084771	1
Xiamen	−0.08555	0.312339	−0.09874	0.128048	2
Zhuhai	−0.38215	0.275668	0.193368	0.086883	3
Shantou	−0.16092	−0.06322	−0.21258	−0.43672	4
Hainan	−0.10707	−0.60297	0.066166	−0.64387	5

tribution of 37%. The industrial added value growth rate ($X1$) has more load in the first common factor, which can be regarded as the transformation foundation factor with a contribution of 15.754%.

4. Calculate the scores of common factors. The regression method is used to calculate the scores of common factors; According to the common factor score coefficient matrix (Table 6.11), the equations for the scores of common factors can be obtained:

$$
\begin{aligned}
F_1 &= 0.127X1 + 0.132X2 - 0.121X3 + 0.043X4 + 0.109X5 + 0.243X6 + 0.28X7 \\
&\quad - 0.12X8 - 0.66X9 + 0.261X10 + 0.261X11 + 0.037X12 \\
F_2 &= 0.139X1 - 0.305X2 + 0.104X3 + 0.168X4 + 0.100X5 - 0.058X6 - 0.122X7 \\
&\quad + 0.079X8 + 0.179X9 - 0.080X10 - 0.078X11 - 0.328X12 \\
F_3 &= -0.691X1 + 0.031X2 + 0.355X3 - 0.053X4 - 0.60X5 - 0.084X6 - 0.080X7 \\
&\quad + 0.234X8 + 0.149X9 - 0.095X10 - 0.099X11 + 0.330X12
\end{aligned}
$$

The indicator values of the five major special economic zones are introduced into the above equations to work out the scores of factors. The degrees of contributions from variances of nine common factors in the total variance interpretation table are used to build the comprehensive evaluation model:

$$F = 0.42783F_1 + 0.37F_2 + 0.15754F_3$$

Factor scores are introduced into the above equation to obtain the comprehensive scores of industrial transformation in the five major special economic zones (Table 6.11).

6.4.3 Evaluation Analysis

In terms of comprehensive scores concerning industrial transformation, Shenzhen ranked No. 1 among the five major special economic zones, followed by Xiamen,

Zhuhai, Shantou and Hainan. For three major factors which constitute the comprehensive score, Shenzhen enjoys the leading position in the transformation effect among the five major special economic zones thanks to its apparent advantages in proportion of added value from the hi-tech manufacturing industry in the industries above the designated size ($X5$), the output value of new products ($X6$), the output value from the modern service industry ($X7$), internal expenditure of R&D funds ($X10$) and new product exportations ($X11$) and its increasingly mature transformation mode. For the transformation process, Xiamen and Zhuhai have witnessed rapid improvements in added value growth rate in the hi-tech manufacturing industry ($X2$), growth rate in the modern service industry ($X3$) and proportion of added value from the advanced manufacturing industry in the industries above the designated size ($X4$), thus they are frontrunners among the five major special economic zones in terms of industrial transformation. A solid industrial foundation is the necessary condition for quickening the development of industrial transformation. In this regard, Shenzhen, Zhuhai and Hainan enjoy excellent advantageous conditions and have a solid foundation for industrial transformation.

6.5 Future Development of Industrial Transformation in the Special Economic Zones

(I) The special economic zones have played the evident roles of the stimulator and model in China's economy and will enjoy a large amount of room for development in the future; they are expected to become the important indicators for measuring China's future modernization. Therefore, along with coordinating the development in the central and western regions, undoubtedly, it is also necessary to increase the policy support and resource allocation for the special economic zones, and spare no efforts in guaranteeing the future development of the special economic zones; the policy support for encouraging the development of the modern industries in the special economic zones cannot be decreased and should be strengthened to quicken the economic transformation and upgrading in the special economic zones, including Shenzhen, and enhance the efficiency of resource allocation.

(II) The evaluation of the special economic zones in China's economic development should focus on not only their direct contributions to urban GDP, but also their guarantee and support for the development of the society, the economy and other industries, their maintenance of coordination in the industrial chain. Therefore, there is an urgent need for intensifying and enhancing the industrial linkage of the pillar industries and the strategic emerging industries in the special economic zones, for closely following the pace of their transformation and upgrading, and for promoting the standardized, information development, networking, intensive and fine construction, and keeping a high degree of alignment with the development of other industries.

(III) The special economic zones are at a crucial period of development. In the long term, the overall and fundamental obstacles to the institutional innovations in the special economic zones are looming increasingly large; the advantages of institutional innovation that the special economic zones enjoy in development are on the decrease relative to the inland provinces and municipalities; the growth vitality and space induced by institutional innovations are declining. In the short term, economic development in the special economic zones is increasingly aligned with the national economic development. In recent years, the economic growth rate in the special economic zones has fallen though it has remained higher than the national level. Amidst the international economic downturn and increasingly stagnant external demand, the industrial development in the special economic zones with a relatively high degree of dependence upon foreign trade has been exposed to more external risks and uncertainties. In 2013, during the 18th National Congress of the Communist Party of China, the Central Committee of the Communist Party of China vowed to quicken the pace of implementing the strategy of innovation-driven development and take it as a priority for accelerating the improvement of the socialist market economic system and transformation of the economic developmental mode; it stressed efforts to adapt to new changes in the domestic and foreign economic situation, speed up the formation of a new economic developmental mode and drive forward the development by shifting the focus to quality and improvement of performance. Against such a background, the industrial transformation in the special economic zones should be carried out by proceeding from the overall situation of strategic transformation in the special economic zones; given such current striking problems as an inadequate capacity of science and technology input and output and a low level of scientific and technological innovation in most of the special economic zones, it is necessary to actively tap the endogenous growth impetus induced by technological innovations to accelerate profound industrial transformation in the special economic zones.

(IV) Except in Shenzhen, where a strong scale, performance, scientific and technological support foundation has been built over many years of industrial development, the other four special economic zones are still subject to a number of prominent problems, including a lack of long-term impetus for industrial transformation, a relatively low level of industrial structural transformation and a small scale of high-tech industries. For example, with respect to the developmental scale of hi-tech products, the new product output value in Zhuhai, Shantou and Xiamen was 72,791 million yuan, 13,994 million yuan and 12,378 million yuan, respectively, in 2012. Such an output value in Shenzhen was 8, 44 and 5 times that in Zhuhai, Shantou and Xiamen, respectively. The imbalance in the speed and performance of the new industrial development among the special economic zones is extremely salient. According to the quantitative evaluation of the capability for development of industrial transformation of the special economic zones, Shenzhen has taken the lead in the proportion of added value from the hi-tech manufacturing industry in the industries above the designated size and the output value from the modern service industry, but Shenzhen has seen a slowdown in the growth of added value from the hi-tech manufacturing industry and the growth of the modern service industry after many years of development; Zhuhai has an overall productivity similar to that of Shenzhen, but Zhuhai lags far behind Shenzhen in industrial scale, R&D input and other indicators; compared with the other four major special economic zones, Hainan is still at a relatively low level of industrial structure, and Hainan has a great gap with respect to the other special economic zones in the effect and supporting conditions of industrial transformation; Shantou is a special economic zone with a relatively small economic aggregate, which, to a certain extent, restricts effective industrial agglomeration radiation and weakens the innovative resource aggregation and derivation effect, and it puts Shantou in a disadvantageous position amid high-end competition; Xiamen enjoys an excellent foundation for the development of industrial transformation, but Xiamen is greatly inferior to Shenzhen in its capacity for science and technology input and output and the level of its scientific research, thus imposing tremendous constraints on the endogenous growth impetus for industrial transformation in Xiamen. In the general environment with the increasingly acute environmental constraints from resource factors, only when the five major special economic zones advance in continuously enhancing their capability for industrial transformation in response to the weaknesses in the development of industrial transformation can they seize the new historical opportunities in the new period of the reform and opening-up and put their industrial development in place so as to stimulate the national industrial development.

Chapter 7
Cultural Contributions from the Special Economic Zones to China's Development Path

Remarkable achievements have been made since the special economic zones were established in China; in particular, the Shenzhen Special Economic Zone has been highly commended by the leaders of the Central Committee—Hu Jintao said: "Shenzhen has created the miracles in the world history of industrialization, modernization and urbanization"; Xi Jinping said: "Shenzhen's development is a representative work of China's reform, China's miracle and also the world's miracle". However, as the special economic zones originally aimed at and focused on promoting economic development, in a considerably long time, domestic and foreign attention was mainly paid to the achievements of economic development and to the reform of the economic system in the special economic zones, while there was less attention to and research on the cultural situation and innovations in the special economic zones and their cultural contributions to China's modernization. In fact, the rapid development in the special economic zones is largely attributable to the cultural spiritual impetus; the economy and culture have flourished side by side and supplemented each other in the special economic zones. The special economic zones have given birth to not only great economic achievements, but also tremendous cultural achievements which cannot be ignored, showing a function of impressive cultural innovation and of making some widely-recognized important contributions to the drive of China's modernization.

When it comes to cultural innovation and development, the Shenzhen Special Economic Zone is the most typical and representative. In this regard, a feature article entitled the *Power of Culture Continues New Legends in Shenzhen* written by the editorial group of the *People's Daily* (Overseas Edition) makes the most accurate and vivid descriptions: "In more than 30 years of reform and opening up, Shenzhen has created both economic and cultural miracles and has evolved from a barren border town to a model global city for the promotion of nationwide reading and a city of design. If the special economic zones are considered the models of the material

© Social Sciences Academic Press and Springer Nature Singapore Pte Ltd. 2018
Y. Tao and Z. Lu, *Special Economic Zones and China's Development Path*,
Research Series on the Chinese Dream and China's Development Path,
https://doi.org/10.1007/978-981-10-3220-2_7

civilization in China, cultural Shenzhen is undoubtedly the model of the spiritual civilization in China."[1] Given this, discussions, in this chapter, about the cultural contributions from the special economic zones to China's modernization focus on the Shenzhen Special Economic Zone as an example to showcase the cultural image of and cultural contributions from the special economic zones.

7.1 Functional Expansion, Generation and Development of the Function of Cultural Innovation in the Special Economic Zones

The cultural innovations in the special economic zones are closely related to the functional orientation of the special economic zones. In more than 30 years of the reform and opening up, with the development of the situation and the requirements of the times, great changes have occurred in China's developmental path and developmental mode, and the overall pattern of socialist modernization with coordinated economic, political, cultural, social and ecological development has gradually taken shape. In this historical process, the functional orientation, status and roles of the special economic zones have changed accordingly. Culturally, if the special economic zones are only considered as the experimenters of cultural renewal under the condition of the opening up at the early stage after their establishment, they have changed into the vanguards and front-runners in cultural innovations along with the generation and development of their function of cultural innovation.

7.1.1 Functional Expansion and Extension of the Special Economic Zones Under the New Situation

At their inception, the special economic zones were basically positioned as the zones designed to explore the new path for economic development and reform of the economic system under the condition of opening up and offer successful experiences for developing a socialist market economy. However, with China's socialist modernization, the reform and opening up has generally developed from the first-ever implementation of pilot programs in the special economic zones in the early years to widespread reform and opening up across the country. Accordingly, significance the roles and status of the special economic zones have become more complex: in addition to being the forerunners, windows and experimental fields in the reform and opening up, they also serve as demonstration zones for pursuing scientific development and comprehensive deepening of reform. For example, the National Development and Reform Commission has newly positioned the Shenzhen Special Economic Zone as

[1] *Culture Shenzhen*, 2014 (7), p. 9.

the national pilot zone for comprehensive reform, the national central city for economics, the national innovation-oriented city, the international city and the model city based on socialism with Chinese characteristics. As the status and roles of the special economic zones are redefined and there are new requirements for such status and roles, the basic functions of the special economic zones will certainly expand and extend, and it will be necessary to probe new lines of thinking and measures for cultural innovations and development to gradually generate and give prominence to the function of cultural innovation while quickening economic development.[2] Only when we realize this can we gain a full understanding of the status and roles of the special economic zones in China's modernization and know their cultural contributions, and can we clearly understand the new historical mission of the special economic zones under the new situation of comprehensively intensifying the reform.

7.1.2 Generation and Development of the Function of Cultural Innovation in the Special Economic Zones

The prerequisites for cultural contributions are cultural innovations, cultural achievements and cultural influence. The cultural innovations are the key since cultural achievements and cultural influence cannot exist without cultural innovations. The special economic zones have experienced a process of natural generation and development from spontaneous cultural innovations to gradual formation of the function of cultural innovation, while there are many causes for cultural innovations.

(I) **The Functions and Mission of the Special Economic Zones Have Spurred Their Cultural Innovations**

The special economic zones are the outcome of the reform and opening-up. They have basically functioned as the practical explorers, providers of successful experience, models and stimulators, the reform and opening-up front-runners, windows and experimental fields for the socialist economic construction with Chinese characteristics and China's reform of the economic system. Cultural innovations were not the original purpose of establishing the special economic zones, nor did the then policy-makers and special economic zone builders pay attention to cultural innovations. However, cultural development follows its own law, and cultural innovations are inevitable in the special economic zones with rapid economic development. In a sense, this is an inexorable trend independent of man's will.

1. **The Establishment and Construction of the Special Economic Zones Has Objectively Driven the Emancipation of the Mind and the Renewal of Ideaideas As Well As Cultural Innovations**

In early 1992, when inspecting south China, comrade Deng Xiaoping very profoundly pointed out: "The main experience from Shenzhen is the courage to blaze new trails."

[2] *Culture Shenzhen*, 2014 (7), p. 9.

In essence, the enterprising spirit of Shenzhen's people came out of pressure to a certain extent. At the beginning of the Shenzhen Special Economic Zone, the Central Government gave no financial support though it offered preferential policies, and Shenzhen's people took actions to make breakthroughs by themselves. Originally, Shenzhen was a border town with a population of only about 20,000; in order to serve as the front-runner, window and experimental field in the reform and opening up, it was necessary for Shenzhen to create the material conditions, build the basic facilities, introduce talents and develop a novel idea of the reform and opening up. These necessities cannot be addressed by adopting the old way of thinking; on the contrary, the mind must be emancipated and the ideaideas must be renewed to proactively break away from the fetters of the longstanding old line of thinking and ideaideas under the planned economic system to break new ground and build a new world. Therefore, there were extraordinary slogans such as "time is money, efficiency is life", the reform measure that "land is used on a paid basis" and the Shenzhen Speed of building one storey in three days, the bold attempt in opening up the labor market and relaxing controls on prices, the personnel management system and the reforms of the system of distribution ...a series of reform measures reverberated throughout the country and also stimulated the rapid development of the Shenzhen Special Economic Zone. These reform measures and the modern line of thought and ideaideas adopted in them have naturally evolved into ideological and cultural ideaideas and cultural phenomena, which have spread across the country through media, while Shenzhen has moved forward in cultural innovations.

2. **It Is Essential for the Special Economic Zone to Drive Cultural Innovations Forward in the Process of Persisting in Reform and Innovations and Assuming its Historical Mission**

In the early period of the Shenzhen Special Economic Zone, the task of economic development became evident and urgent due to a lack of historical and cultural deposits, so cultural construction lagged behind economic development. Furthermore, some people in China had doubts about and did not recognize the establishment of the special economic zone, thus the cultural underdevelopment in Shenzhen was often intentionally exaggerated—they described Shenzhen as a cultural desert and a city with deformed development, which damaged the image of the special economic zone to a certain degree. The necessity and urgency for quickening the cultural construction and improving the cultural image became obvious. At that time, Shenzhen's economic strength was not high; there was even a relative shortage of fiscal funds, but the Shenzhen Municipal Party Committee and the Municipal Government allocated special funds to build the basic cultural facilities including television stations and libraries, and vowed to run Shenzhen University better by tightening the belt; this fully shows the foresight and spectacular vision which the early leaders of the Shenzhen Special Economic Zone had for cultural construction.

After the necessary cultural hardware facilities were preliminarily available in Shenzhen, a number of scholars and far-sighted personages from other places moved to Shenzhen. They had rational reflections and anticipated forecasts about the cultural situation and developmental trends in Shenzhen, and became the first ones to put forward the concept of a special economic zone culture, which was recognized and supported by the Ministry of Culture. The cultural elites in Shenzhen and from the rest of the country published articles in the special column "Cultural Square" in the *Shenzhen Economic Daily* to express views on Shenzhen's culture—Mr. Yang Dongping claimed, "There is a northern expedition of Guangdong's culture amid the reform and opening up"; Mr. Yu Qiuyu stressed, "Shenzhen should play the role of creating a new culture"; Mr. Liu Mengxi said, "Shenzhen has a multiculture and is full of cultural innovation vitality"; Shenzhen's scholars said, "Shenzhen should build up its cultural self-confidence", "Shenzhen is not a cultural desert; on the contrary, it shows a new cultural form", "Shenzhen's cultural construction should go beyond the reference and incorporate the innovative elements". These views exerted an extensive influence in the domestic, and even in the overseas cultural community. People have started reexamining and evaluating Shenzhen's culture, and have gradually recognized the new ideas, characteristics and forms of Shenzhen's culture, and their influence on the new cultural construction within the new situation. Culturally, Shenzhen has taken on a new look, with its influence from Guangdong to the rest of the country, so Shenzhen has acted as a cultural innovator.

3. **Cultural Innovations are Requisites for the Special Economic Zones to Accomplish the New Mission Entrusted by the Central Government**

After the beginning of the 21st century, the Central Committee of the Communist Party of China put forward a range of new philosophies and strategies for governing the country, including the Scientific Outlook on Development, the building of a harmonious socialist society, an innovation-oriented country and a culturally powerful country. The implementation of these philosophies and strategies is certainly a process of active exploration and accumulation of experience. As the forefront of the reform and opening up and the vanguards which have made great contributions to the socialist economic and cultural construction with Chinese characteristics and have offered a lot of successful experience, the special economic zones are duty-bound, under the new historical conditions, to undertake the new mission of making continuous experimentations for carrying out these new philosophies and strategies. In order to accomplish the new mission entrusted by the Central Government, there are no other ways except reforms and innovations, including cultural innovations. Therefore, the Shenzhen Special Economic Zone has decided to implement the strategy of building the city through culture and plan the building of an innovation-oriented city and a culturally advanced city; the strategic conception of building "three cities" has come out; a new platform for developing the cultural industry—China (Shenzhen) International Cultural Expo—has been created; the cultural system reform has been accelerated; a number of major reform measures have been adopted and implemented at the institutional level. These measures for reform and innovation have elevated Shenzhen's cultural innovations to a new level, so Shenzhen has entered a new stage of development.

(II) Cultural Innovations in the Special Economic Zones

As the forefront of the reform and opening up, the special economic zones are greatly influenced by outside cultures. Facing Taiwan that is across the Taiwan Strait, the Xiamen Special Economic Zone has long been influenced by Taiwan's culture. Being close to Macao, the Zhuhai Special Economic Zone is inevitably exposed to cultural influence from Macao. Adjacent to Hong Kong, as an emerging city growing out of a small border town, the Shenzhen Special Economic Zone is under the influence of Hong Kong's culture and regional cultures introduced by immigrants from various regions, and is bound to develop diverse immigrant cultures. The fusion of diverse cultures has, to some extent, catalyzed cultural innovations, while the influence of external cultures is the fundamental catalytic factor. In this regard, the Shenzhen Special Economic Zone is a typical example.

1. **Neighboring Hong Kong, Shenzhen is Exposed to External Cultural Influence Through Many Channels**

When the Shenzhen Special Economic Zone was established and became the first to be open to the outside world from the late 1970s to the early 1980s, the reform and opening up in China's inland areas had not yet been carried out in an all-round way. As Shenzhen took the first opportunity from the reform and opening up, Shenzhen was unrivalled by the inland areas in the intensity of the reform and the breadth of opening up at that time. Thanks to first-ever opening up, an open cultural atmosphere was fostered in Shenzhen and Shenzhen became the soil prone to accept the external cultural ideas. A variety of external cultural ideas quickly took root in Shenzhen and became an integral part of Shenzhen's culture, and they further evolved into new cultural ideas and awareness. For example, the self-awareness of displaying personality, the tolerant awareness of not intervening in others' private lives, the awareness of acting according to laws and regulations, cherishing time and stressing efficiency were first recognized and carried forward in Shenzhen with the influence of external cultures.

After the establishment of the Shenzhen Special Economic Zone, under the general atmosphere of opening up, the economic cooperation and cultural exchange activities between Shenzhen and Hong Kong were very frequent. Moreover, the people in Shenzhen could be free to watch television and listen to the radio from Hong Kong at that time; numerous books and magazines published in Hong Kong flocked to Shenzhen in various ways; many people from Hong Kong made investments and bought properties in Shenzhen; a large number of people from Hong Kong travelled between Shenzhen and Hong Kong to visit their relatives or engage in exchanges. All of these became the channels for Hong Kong's culture, even the Western culture, to influence Shenzhen. With smooth channels and an open mind, cultural exchanges and cultural influence became inevitable. Some people have said, "The scene in Shenzhen is like that in Hong Kong".

2. **The Fusion of Chinese and Foreign Cultures Brings about Cultural Innovations and New Cultural Forms**

As the frontier of the reform and opening up and an immigrant city, Shenzhen is a melting pot of external cultures, immigrant cultures from various regions and Guangdong's local culture, which is accompanied by a process of shock, fusion and formation of new cultural forms. The inherent spirit of excellent national cultures, the progressive modern cultural ideas and the cultural spirits advocated by the Communist Party of China and the government have blended together, resulting in a new cultural system of the special economic zone, which integrates ancient and modern, Chinese and foreign cultures; they are widely spread and deeply rooted among the people, acceptable to and adopted by the people of the special economic zone. A new modern cultural form has come into being. This cultural form brings together Chinese, foreign, immigrant cultures and Guangdong's local culture; it has these cultural characteristics: rich, diverse, modern and innovative; it cultivates and influences the mindsets and behaviors of all of Shenzhen's people; it produces an effect of cultural radiation on the outside world. An important factor contributing to the creation of this cultural form is the influence and penetration of external cultural ideas.

(III) **Rapid Economic Development has Stimulated Cultural Innovations in the Special Economic Zones**

Rapid economic development in the special economic zones has improved the people's living standards and has changed the people's lifestyle, providing the necessary material foundation for renewing the mindsets of citizens in the special economic zones and enhancing their cultural quality, and also arousing their awareness of and impetus for innovation, to a great extent driving cultural innovations forward. The Shenzhen Special Economic Zone exceptionally stands out in this regard.

1. **The Improvement in the Material Standard of Living has Uplifted the Spiritual Cultural Needs**

With the rapid economic development in Shenzhen and its increasing contributions to the country, the level of Shenzhen's urban modernization is rising and the living environment and the basic living conditions, including clothing, food, housing for its residents and transportation, have greatly improved. Shenzhen, as a whole, has become the first to enter the well-off society; the life of some citizens in Shenzhen has surpassed the well-off level and has reached the level of the moderately developed countries. It is often said that human subsistence first relies on daily necessities, followed by lyre-playing, chess, calligraphy and painting, and then flowers, birds, fishes. This suggests that the improvement in the material standard of living will certainly result in an increase in the spiritual cultural needs and attention to the spiritual life and living quality. After Shenzhen has become the first to enter the well-off society, citizens focus on how to renew their lifestyle, improve their living quality and pursue artistic goals rather than solve the problem of food and clothing and address other basic living needs. This presents Shenzhen's policy makers, cultural and artistic workers with the real task for expediting cultural development, boosting cultural innovations in order to meet the growing spiritual cultural needs of its residents. Therefore, a number of modern cultural facilities, including central libraries, music halls and youth palaces, have sprung up. Famous songs originating from Shenzhen, including *The Story of Springtime, Entering the New Era, Marching towards the Revival*, have been sung in Shenzhen, even throughout the country. TV play series originally produced in Shenzhen, including *How the Steel is Tempered, The Empty Mirror, Family Tradition, Destiny*, have appeared on screen and have been well-received. Shenzhen is also home to a galaxy of piano art talents, including Li Yundi and Chen Sa. Many excellent original literary and artistic works from Shenzhen have been given awards at home and abroad. Cultural innovations have built a culturally and artistically thriving Shenzhen and have made widely recognized outstanding contributions to satisfying the spiritual cultural needs of its residents.

2. **High-end Cultural Facilities Promote the Innovative Development of Culture**

The high-end cultural facilities built in Shenzhen since the beginning of the new century have covered the shortage of cultural facilities and have changed the layout of urban cultural facilities. These cultural facilities broaden the cultural horizon of its residents, attract citizens to the palaces of culture and art, upgrade their cultural quality and taste and arouse their cultural innovation awareness.

Cultural innovations cannot merely rely on spontaneous actions of citizens, but must be guided and promoted by the government. In Shenzhen, cultural lectures are available to guide citizens to experience culture and art, increase their level of appreciation and develop a high cultural taste; the Reading Month activity is carried out to encourage all of the people to fundamentally make ideological and cultural improvements. A series of cultural forms of innovations, including cultural lectures for citizens and the Reading Month are, to a certain degree, closely related to Shenzhen's economic foundation. From the perspective of the "biological chain" for development, such a process is clear: strong economic foundation → high-grade cultural facilities → citizens' willingness to utilize and enjoy high-grade cultural facilities → cultural innovation activities for fulfilling citizens' willingness. This process vividly demonstrates the role of economic development in stimulating and promoting cultural innovations.

3. **Transformation of the Economic Development Model and Industrial Restructuring Facilitate Growth of the Cultural Industry**

As early as the end of the 20th century, the contradiction between rapid development and a shortage of resources and energy loomed large in Shenzhen. The Shenzhen Municipal Party Committee and the Municipal Government vowed to transform a speed-focused Shenzhen into an efficiency-oriented Shenzhen, and build a harmonious and efficiency-oriented Shenzhen. The Shenzhen Municipal Party Committee and the Municipal Government stressed that importance should be attached to the cultural industry such as the high and new technology industries, and the low-cost and low-consumption cultural industry should be taken as one of four pillar industries in Shenzhen; moreover, city-wide efforts should be made to accelerate its development. Therefore, the *Decisions of the Shenzhen Municipal Party Committee and the Municipal Government Concerning Vigorously Developing the Cultural Industry*, which is full of innovation awareness and innovation measures, was released in Shenzhen; the new platform for trading cultural products—the China (Shenzhen) International Cultural Expo—was created; a number of ingenious cultural industry bases and cultural industry parks came forth. These actions of cultural innovation cater precisely to Shenzhen's needs for changing the economic developmental mode. The relationship between economic development and cultural innovations is evident.

(IV) Sense of Cultural Self-reliance as a Source of Innovation in the Special Economic Zones

The special economic zones are the front-runners, windows and experimental fields for the reform and opening up. Given these roles, the special economic zones are required to develop the awareness of building a good image by themselves and achieving cultural self-reliance, and they should strive to create the conditions for accomplishing their historical missions with a relatively perfect cultural image and a high cultural taste. However, the cultural foundations of several major special economic zones are different. As an emerging city with a short history, Shenzhen lacks cultural deposits. This further reinforces its awareness of cultural self-reliance. This awareness naturally evolves into the internal impetus for cultural innovations and ignites its cultural innovations.

1. Urban Competition and Development Pressure Have Fueled Cultural Innovation and Development in Shenzhen

Since the 1990s, China's socialist modernization has shown an interesting phenomenon: the economic aggregate and cultural image of large and medium-sized cities across the country have become the important indicators for experts and scholars to evaluate the regional economic development and the building of a harmonious society. A series of activities launched and advocated by the media, including the ranking of city comprehensive competitiveness, appraisal and selection of the most attractive cities and the most livable cities, have helped shape the pattern of city competitions. In this pattern of competition, the highest pressure on Shenzhen is a lack of cultural deposits and cultural charm. The only way for Shenzhen to stand out in this pattern of competition lies in translating pressure into impetus and adopting a new line of thought beyond the reference to push cultural innovations forward. The Shenzhen Municipal Party Committee and the Municipal Government have identified the developmental goal of building a high-grade international city to arouse and mobilize its residents' spirit of cultural innovation, and have made great decisions regarding the intensification of the reform of the cultural system and quickening the development of the cultural industry. The public cultural institutions and large and medium-sized cultural enterprises have been exploring new ways towards cultural innovations in the reform of the cultural system. As a result, the Publicity Department of the Shenzhen Municipal Party Committee and cultural enterprises have jointly produced TV play series such as *How the Steel is Tempered*; Shenzhen artists have created theme songs like *Entering the New Era*; the first new urban literature has been advocated; the large-scale Statue of Deng Xiaoping with a great social and historical significance has emerged in Shenzhen; various artistic activities including Joy Together, Square Concert, Grand Theatre Art Festival and Artistic Classic Performance Season have been unveiled in Shenzhen; romantic cultural dreams such as "the building of a famous modern cultural city" and "calling Shenzhen's school of thought" have gone wild in Shenzhen. Shenzhen bears witness to a poet's saying: The sun is new every day!

2. **Urban Development Strategy Boosts Cultural Self-reliance and Drives Innovations**

In order to achieve the developmental goal of building a high-grade international city, promoting a balanced economic and cultural development and building a harmonious and efficiency-oriented Shenzhen, the Shenzhen Municipal Party Committee and the Municipal Government have made the strategic decision to build the city through culture, with the determination to consolidate and develop Shenzhen's characteristics and status by means of culture and build the image of a more attractive city. This great decision has upgraded the people's awareness of cultural innovation with efforts to achieve the urban developmental goals and carry out the urban developmental strategy, providing a stronger spiritual impetus and fostering a good atmosphere for stressing and discussing culture in the whole society. High-level cultural forums, including the Think-tank Forum, the Taiwan-Hong Kong-Shanghai-Shenzhen Cultural Seminar, and the China Cultural Industry Forum have been held in Shenzhen, broadening the cultural horizon of Shenzhen's people. The national foreign trade culture research base, the cultural industry development demonstration base and other important cultural research and cultural construction bases have been built in Shenzhen. The Shenzhen Special Economic Zone has served as the cultural model and has advanced from the first mover in economic reform to the cultural model.

7.1.3 Augmented Cultural Innovation Prowess Leads to Changes in the Cultural Identity

In more than 30 years of the reform and opening up, great achievements have been made in China's modernization, and profound changes have taken place in the economic, political, cultural, social life and ecological civilization. Domestic social and cultural changes and international globalization have presented a very realistic issue: Which culture should be chosen in contemporary China, how should the proper direction for cultural construction and development be pinpointed? In response to this issue, the Central Committee of the Communist Party of China stated the direction of keeping the advanced culture and the great historical task for developing the national scientific popular socialist culture geared towards modernization, the world and the future. In order to complete this task, it is necessary to proceed from the practice of the reform, opening up and modernization, focus on the frontier of the world's cultural development, carry forward the fine tradition of the national cultures, draw on the strong points of nations around the world and actively innovate in substance and form to continuously enhance the attraction and appeal of the socialist culture with Chinese characteristics. In this sense, the function of cultural innovation of the special economic zones has given rise to a change in the cultural role of the special economic zones, so that they become the vanguards and leaders in building an advanced culture in contemporary China.

First, the cultural innovations in the special economic zones should follow the trends and should produce the guidance and demonstration effects on the cultural choice and comprehensive cultural innovations in contemporary China, with the adoption of a new path for integrating diverse cultures and displaying unique features with a combination of cultural choices and cultural synthesis.

Second, the cultural innovations in the special economic zones should cater to the needs for building a harmonious society, give expression to a high degree of cultural self-consciousness, and give full scope to the role of vanguard and leader. For example, the philosophies of cultural development first developed in the Shenzhen Special Economic Zone, including the realization of citizens' cultural rights and the building of the public cultural service system, show, at the new ideological and theoretical level, the new thinking of putting the people first in the cultural construction and of promoting social harmony through cultural construction.

7.2 Cultural Innovations and Cultural Development

Cultural innovations should be either aroused by external forces or supported by the internal thought foundation. The thought foundation for cultural innovations in the special economic zones is a high degree of cultural self-consciousness, while cultural self-consciousness gives birth to cultural self-reliance and cultural self-reliance stimulates cultural innovations.

7.2.1 Cultural Self-consciousness and Cultural Innovations

Cultural self-consciousness means the self-knowledge of the people living in a particular culture regarding their culture, its origin, process of formation, unique characteristics and developmental trends.[3] Specifically, cultural self-consciousness mainly refers to the cultural consciousness and awakening of a nation or a party, including the profound understanding of the status and roles of culture in its historical progress,

---

[3]Fei Xiaotong, *Fei Xiaotong's Views on Culture and Cultural Self-consciousness*, Qunyan Press, 2007, p. 235.

the correct understanding of the cultural development law and active assumption of the historical responsibility for cultural development. Cultural self-consciousness is an inherent spiritual power, the burning desire to make and the persistent pursuit of the progress of civilization; it is the ideological basis and the precondition for promoting cultural prosperity and development.[4] Overall, cultural self-consciousness is the awakening and the elevated consciousness of cultural builders and the important foundation for thoughts for cultural prosperity and development.

The cultural self-consciousness in the special economic zones is reflected in the top-level design of strategic thinking and the philosophy of cultural development—the current cultural situation and development at different stages of the special economic zones are considered to scientifically develop the strategy for cultural development, constantly renew the philosophy of cultural development, identify the direction and path of cultural development to fundamentally drive cultural innovations forward. In this regard, the Shenzhen Special Economic Zone is the widely recognized, typical and representative case.

In more than 30 years since the establishment of the Shenzhen Special Economic Zone, remarkable achievements have been made regarding various aspects; full play has been given to the role of the special economic zone as the window, front-runner and experimental field in the reform and opening up, and successful experience has been gathered for seeking out the socialist developmental path with Chinese characteristics; an impressive city development has been achieved, thus the Shenzhen Special Economic Zone has become the most attractive avant-garde city with the strongest sense of modern culture and the greatest number of developmental opportunities among large and medium-sized cities in China. Shenzhen has been granted honorary titles such as the City of Design and the Global Model City for the Promotion of Nationwide Reading by the United Nations Educational, Scientific and Cultural Organization. Shenzhen has been awarded the title of the Outstanding Developing Knowledge City at the Knowledge Cities World Summit. Shenzhen ranks No. 1 among large and medium-sized cities across China in terms of urban cultural competitiveness. In this sense, Shenzhen is hailed as the model of cultural self-consciousness and cultural innovations and the indisputable representative among several major special economic zones in China. An analysis of Shenzhen gives the general picture of the cultural self-consciousness and cultural innovations in the special economic zones.

The period from the 1980s to the early 1990s was the initial phase of start-up and urban development of the Shenzhen Special Economic Zone. In that period, cultural self-consciousness appeared out of pressure. It was mainly embodied in strengthening the construction of the cultural infrastructure, promoting the renewal of cultural ideas, with the purpose of refuting the untrue remarks made by some people to belittle and deny the Shenzhen Special Economic Zone and throwing away the label of cultural desert imposed on Shenzhen, safeguarding the political image of the special economic zone and building a good cultural image of an emerging

[4] Yun Shan, Cultural Self-consciousness, Cultural Self-confidence, Cultural Self-reliance, *Red Flag Manuscript*, 2010 (15).

city. This resulted in preliminarily changing the urban cultural image of Shenzhen and laying a solid foundation for the subsequent cultural construction and cultural development in Shenzhen.

From the early 1990s to the beginning of this century, Shenzhen entered a new stage, creating new advantages and enhancing competitiveness in urban development. In that period, Shenzhen saw an apparent improvement in its cultural self-consciousness. It was mainly reflected in promoting the cultural developmental plan, specifying the developmental goals for the urban cultural construction, attempting to carry out the reform of the cultural system to boost the urban cultural competitiveness through multiple channels in an all-round way, with the aim of building a famous modern cultural city. This brought about an evident improvement in Shenzhen's cultural image and cultural status and the removal of the label of cultural desert that had been imposed on Shenzhen.

Since the beginning of the 21st century, Shenzhen has assumed the heavy historical responsibility of being the first to build a scientific developmental demonstration zone and taken on the role of "providing the cultural conditions for promoting scientific development" in urban cultural construction and cultural development. In this period, Shenzhen's cultural self-consciousness has reached a new level thanks to efforts in constantly renewing the philosophies of cultural development, conscientiously developing the strategy for cultural development, vigorously driving the development of the cultural industry forward, intensifying the reform of the cultural system, building a public cultural service system, realizing the cultural rights of citizens and actively fostering cultural brands and excellent literary and artistic works, so as to improve the urban cultural soft power, provide a new spiritual impetus and industrial support for urban development and offer good cultural conditions for promoting scientific development. As a result, there was a historical evolution from the so-called cultural desert to a cultural oasis, the cultural influence and cultural radiation power was continuously enhanced, and the urban cultural image was widely recognized and praised by the people at home and abroad, creating important preconditions for building a culturally powerful city.

Overall, Shenzhen's cultural self-consciousness shows a clear self-knowledge of its own cultural situation, a correct understanding of the status and roles of culture in urban development and the law of cultural development, and an active assumption of the historical responsibility of building an advanced socialist culture. This is the self-consciousness of an emerging special economic zone in expanding the functions of the special economic zone and energetically pushing forward cultural innovations. This is also the cultural self-consciousness of a pioneering city in making self-improvements and leading the trend on the threshold of new times. Shenzhen is a breathtaking landscape of cultural creation in the great practice of socialism with Chinese characteristics. It is also an outstanding model in the process of China's modernization. A journalist from the Xinhua News Agency acclaimed, "The Shenzhen Special Economic Zone has ascended to the first echelon of national cultural development in an all-round way, and the Shenzhen Model of cultural development mirrors the path towards growth of the special economic zones in more than 30 years".

7.2.2 *Rapid Development and Continuous Cultural Innovations in the Special Economic Zones*

With unceasing development and changes in the historical process of China's socialist modernization, the function of the cultural innovation of the special economic zones has varied with different stages. Shenzhen is either a special economic zone or an emerging city growing from a small town. Shenzhen needs to not only perform the function of reform exploration of the special economic zones, but also to accelerate the urban cultural development and uplift the cultural image. With such a dual identity and dual function, Shenzhen is considered the unquestionable representative among the special economic zones in cultural innovations.

Shenzhen was officially designated as a city in 1979 and became a special economic zone in 1980. Its urban development and its development as a special economic zone occurred basically at the same time. From the perspective of either the development as a special economic zone or of urban development, development can be roughly divided into three different stages; the cultural innovations at each stage were based on new developmental philosophies, constantly renewed and enhanced.

(I) **Cultural Innovations at the Initial Stage of the Shenzhen Special Economic Zone and Its Urban Development**

The period from the establishment of the Shenzhen Special Economic Zone to the early 1990s coincided with the initial stage of the Shenzhen Special Economic Zone and its development. At that stage, Shenzhen's cultural innovations were the objective embodiment of the forced strive-to-be-strong consciousness in the cultural field. As a special economic zone, Shenzhen was required to be the first to break the fetters of the traditional planned economic system and take the lead in practicing the reform of the market-oriented economic system and quicken economic development, blaze new trails for the national reform and opening up. Meanwhile, it was necessary to change the situation of the cultural underdevelopment in the initial period of the special economic zone as soon as possible—no good cultural facilities, no local mainstream media and no cultural celebrities—and build an urban cultural image commensurate with the status of the special economic zone, and refute, with facts, the remarks made by some people to debase and deny the special economic zone's image, cast off the label of cultural desert imposed on Shenzhen and achieve cultural revitalization.

1. **Consciously Renew the Ideological and Cultural Ideas**

In the early 1980s, the people in the Shekou Industrial Zone of Shenzhen renewed the ideological ideas and put forward the famous slogan that "time is money and efficiency is life" to sum up some spiritual things about the reform and opening up. This slogan fully reflects the new ideological and cultural idea of cherishing time and stressing efficiency; it is reputed as the first spring thunder in breaking the ideological shackles; as this slogan had a great impact on the mindsets and behavioral mode under the traditional planned economic system, it quickly caused a sensation across the country and was recognized and commended by comrade Deng Xiaoping.

2. **Vigorously Strengthen the Construction of Cultural Infrastructures**

In 1983, subject to a lack of fiscal funds, the Shenzhen Municipal Party Committee and the Municipal Government took bold actions and tightened their belt to build eight major basic cultural facilities, including a science museum, a museum, a library, a grand theatre, a TV station, Shenzhen University, a stadium and a news center, which were put into operation in the mid- and late 1980s or the early 1990s, and local mainstream media, including *Shenzhen Special Economic Zone Daily*, Shenzhen TV, *Party's Life in the Special Economic Zone, Special Economic Zone Literature*. With a modern design and attractive appearance, they help project a new image of Shenzhen's urban culture. The local mainstream media have not only helped free Shenzhen residents from excess dependence on Hong Kong's radio and television programs, and newspapers and magazines, but also increased recognition of Shenzhen's own culture among both local residents and Shenzhen's residents visitors.

3. **Fully Understand and Take a Correct Attitude Towards the Influence of External Cultures**

Being adjacent to Hong Kong and at the forefront of the reform and opening up, Shenzhen was greatly exposed to a complex mixture of both good and bad external cultures, including advanced cultural ideas and decadent cultural consciousness. Therefore, with an open mind peculiar to the special economic zones, the Shenzhen Municipal Party Committee and the Municipal Government sized up the situation and gained a correct understanding to put forward the guidelines that "we introduce the good ones while resisting the bad ones", "we oppose the dirt rather than foreign things", carefully learn, draw on and assimilate all of the advanced science, technology, managerial experience and excellent achievements of human civilization from foreign countries such as Hong Kong, Macao and Taiwan, thus effectively promoting the optimization of Shenzhen's cultural structure, driving Shenzhen's cultural innovations forward and showing the openness and magnanimousness of the special economic zone city.

4. **Actively Advocate Theoretical Research on the Special Economic Zone Culture**

Shenzhen's culture from the 1980s to the early 1990s was in a disadvantageous position among the large and medium-sized cities across China, but it exhibited new cultural characteristics and cultural significance. As the longstanding settlers in Shenzhen, with the cultural sensitivity and theoretical self-consciousness of the special economic zone people, some farsighted intellectuals in Shenzhen's cultural circles creatively developed the concept of the special economic zone culture, called for "special things" in the special economic zone culture and advocated theoretical research on the special economic zone culture. This cultural sensitivity and theoretical self-consciousness were recognized and praised by the leaders of the Ministry of Culture, so the National Working Conference on the Special Economic Zone Culture was held; the Ministry of Culture and Shenzhen jointly set up the Cultural Research Center of the Shenzhen Special Economic Zone, the new cultural bright spot had been formed in the Shenzhen Special Economic Zone.

(II) Cultural Innovations at the Stage of Fostering New Advantages and Strengthening the City's Competitiveness in the Special Economic Zone

The period from the 1990s to the beginning of this century saw the emergence and growth of new comparative advantages and competitiveness in Shenzhen. During this time, the Shenzhen Special Economic Zone and its urban development were subject to new tests and requirements from the changing domestic and international condition. Internationally, upheavals occurred in Eastern Europe and the Soviet Union collapsed, evoking deep reflections on the traditional socialist model and the failure of the Soviet Union's reforms; domestically, the ultra-left trend of thought surged and triggered the debate on whether the special economic zones were socialist or capitalist, and attempted to deny the reform and opening up as well as the special economic zones. At this critical juncture, comrade Deng Xiaoping vigorously turned the tide—in early 1992, at the age of 88, he inspected south China, including Shenzhen, and delivered the famous South Inspection Speech. He explicitly pointed out, "development is a top priority", "Shenzhen's important experience is the courage to blaze new trails", "Shenzhen's construction achievements give a definite answer to the anxiety-ridden people, and the special economic zones are socialist rather than capitalist". His South Inspection Speech repelled the left-leaning countercurrent of denying the reform, opening up and the special economic zones and set off the second round of mind emancipation in China. In June, 1994, Jiang Zemin, then General Secretary of the Communist Party of China, inspected Shenzhen and encouraged Shenzhen to develop new advantages and move to a higher level, foster the advantages of a spiritual civilization, the ideological political advantages and the all-round advantages of social progress while adding more economic and material civilization advantages. The full affirmation from comrade Deng Xiaoping and the warm encouragement from comrade Jiang Zemin brought new impetus for the Shenzhen Special Economic Zone and its urban development. The Shenzhen Municipal Party Committee and the Municipal Government developed the strategic line of thinking of starting a business for the second time and set up the goals for building a modern international city.

In this period, Shenzhen's cultural innovations also reached a new level. The decision-makers equated cultural development with economic and social development, and a pattern of striving to be strong through competition took shape. When it comes to this completion, first, efforts were made to win honor for the Shenzhen Special Economic Zone, promote Shenzhen's urban development through cultural development, develop the new advantages of the special economic zone, build a new urban cultural image, refute, with facts, the untrue remarks which denied the special economic zone, and live up to the expectations of comrade Deng Xiaoping and the Central Committee of the Communist Party of China about Shenzhen; second, the opportunities for urban development were sought. Under the new pattern in which the level of urban development was judged by management and standards in the world, Shenzhen's urban cultural construction was quickened to inject the cultural impetus for Shenzhen's urban development; third, actions were taken to elevate urban development to the highest level. Given the actual situation where Shenzhen was distinctive in modern culture but weak in historical culture, the goal of building a famous modern cultural city was put forward to present a new height and new image commensurate with a famous historical cultural city.

1. **Formulate the Long and Medium-Term Plan for Cultural Development, Identify the Overall Goal of Cultural Development**

In March, 1995, the Shenzhen Municipal Party Committee and the Municipal Government held a special meeting on Shenzhen's cultural work to discuss the *1995–2010 Plan for the Cultural Development of Shenzhen (Discussion Draft)*. That plan specified for the first time the strategic goal of building a famous modern cultural city. In March, 1998, the Shenzhen Municipal Party Committee and the Municipal Government officially printed, issued and implemented the *1998–2000 Three-Year Plan and 2010 Long-term Goal for Shenzhen's Cultural Development* based on the 1995 plan. That plan further defined the overall goal of Shenzhen's cultural development: "Shenzhen will be turned into a famous modern socialist cultural city by fitting in with the needs for building a modern international city".

If the proposal for building a famous modern cultural city is considered the salient hallmark of Shenzhen's cultural self-consciousness and cultural innovations at this stage, its significance lies in not only the image positioning in the overall goal of cultural development, but also the poetic pursuit of cultural development; the latter is more charming and more deeply rooted among the people. When Beijing, Nanjing, Xi'an and other ancient cities were awarded the title of famous historical cultural cities, Shenzhen, with a short history of fewer than 20 years and full of cultural confidence and cultural romance, brought forward a resounding concept: building a famous modern cultural city, and dividing the significance of a famous modern cultural city into a window for Sino-foreign cultural exchanges, a cultural goods trading market, a modern cultural product manufacturing base and an excellent cultural products and fine cultures center. In particular, for Shenzhen's people, gratifyingly, 13 years later, Shenzhen was awarded the title of the City of Design by the United Nations Educational, Scientific and Cultural Organization, so the concept of a famous modern cultural city had become reality.

2. **Building More High-end Cultural Facilities for the Development of a Culturally Global City**

In 1995, the Shenzhen Municipal Party Committee and the Municipal Government followed the overall goal of building an international city to incorporate the construction of public cultural facilities into the overall plan for urban development, and decided to build, in stages, a number of future-oriented iconic cultural facilities with high technological and cultural content and foster the cultural image of an international city in the 9th Five-Year Plan period and the first ten years of the following century. Afterwards, according to the construction plan, the Guan Shanyue Art Museum, Shenzhen Book City, the Shenzhen Special Economic Zone Press Tower, the Shenzhen Economic Daily Building, the Shenzhen Fine Arts Institute, Shenzhen Cable Television, the Huaxia Art Center and the He Xiangning Art Museum were built. In the late 1990s, six major new cultural facilities, including the Shenzhen Library (New Library), the Central Book City, the concert hall, the youth palace, the radio and television center and the new museum were built. In 10–20 years, a number of modern high-grade cultural facilities mushroomed in the center of Shenzhen, presenting a new cultural image of a modern international city.

3. **Introducing More Progrms to Encourage Reading and Learning**

In November, 2000, in order to foster a scholarly urban atmosphere, build a new cultural tradition in Shenzhen, an emerging special economic zone city, and turn Shenzhen into a city respected thanks to reading, Shenzhen became the first city in China to initiate the Reading Month activity. Subsequently, the Reading Month activity has been carried out once a year, and each activity has a distinctive theme for displaying the cultural function of the Reading Month. For example, the theme of the 10th Reading Month was that reading is advocated by and changes cities, which vividly depicts the relationship between the Reading Month and urban development. The Reading Month guides citizens to seek a perfect cultural self-consciousness and make cultural innovations for elevating their urban cultural taste. The Reading Month creates the basis for a new annual cultural festival, providing good conditions for acquiring cultural knowledge, enriching one's spiritual elements and exerting an extensive impact nationwide. So far, it has become a cultural brand of Shenzhen and sets an example for nationwide reading programs.

4. **Becoming a Leader in Cultural System Reform, Exploring Ways to Build an Overarching Cultural Management Framework**

In the early 1990s, the people in Shenzhen were keenly aware of the new situation that "urban development hinges on management" and decided to initiate a pilot reform of the cultural system to improve the management of urban culture. The reform started from promoting all-round cultural management and comprehensive law enforcement to integrate the cultural, radio and television, press and publication and the cultural relics managerial functions of the municipal government, and incorporate the press and publication bureau, the radio and television bureau and the cultural relics bureau into the bureau of culture, so that the first four-in-one big system of cultural management in China took shape in Shenzhen. In the meantime, according to the requirements of the "two-level government, three-level management, four-level network" and the "delegation of powers to those levels and to local management", the first comprehensive cultural law enforcement agency in China—the cultural inspection brigade at both municipal and district levels—was set up and a management mechanism for comprehensive law enforcement gradually took shape.

(III) Cultural Innovations Against the Backdrop of Scientifically-Sound Development and Expansion of Shenzhen's Urban Functions

Since the beginning of the 21st century, Shenzhen has become the first to assume the heavy historical responsibility of building a scientific development demonstration zone, and its cultural construction and cultural development have the function of "providing the cultural conditions for promoting scientific development". Meanwhile, Shenzhen's urban functions have been newly expanded and enhanced, with an increase in the significance of building a culturally powerful city and an international culturally-creative fashion center. In that period, Shenzhen's cultural innovations reached a new height.

In 2003, comrade Hu Jintao, then General Secretary of the Communist Party of China, developed the major strategic idea of the Scientific Outlook on Development, so China entered a new historical stage of the reform, opening up and modernization. In the general pattern of competition for comprehensive national power amidst globalization, the 16th National Congress and the 17th National Congress of the Communist Party of China explicitly stated that it was necessary to quicken cultural construction and cultural development, improve the national cultural soft power and comprehensive competitiveness, and promote an extensive socialist cultural development and prosperity during the implementation of the Scientific Outlook on Development. In the new situation, the Central Government set new and higher requirements for the development of the Shenzhen Special Economic Zone, and required Shenzhen to accelerate its development, take the lead in development and seek a coordinated pattern of development, offering more beneficial experience for exploring the scientific developmental mode.

With the development of the situation, the Central Government had increasingly explicit requirements for Shenzhen and positioned Shenzhen more clearly. In 2006, the National Development and Reform Commission designated Shenzhen as the only national pilot innovation-oriented city in China. The *Reform and Development Plan for the Pearl River Delta Region*, issued by the National Development and Reform Commission in 2008, defined Shenzhen as the national pilot zone for comprehensive reform, the national central city for economics, the national innovation-oriented city, the model city based on socialism with Chinese characteristics and an international city. That marked the unequivocal positioning, at the national level, of Shenzhen—a special economic zone and an emerging city—within the new situation and with a clear definition of functions, roles and development goals for reform.

In that period, Shenzhen's cultural innovations were based on the new philosophy of development and developmental thinking of the cultural construction led by the Scientific Outlook on Development reaching a high degree of self-consciousness. Shenzhen showed the basic situation of advancing with heavy responsibilities in the new pattern of city competition where the winner was judged by culture; Shenzhen actively shouldered the heavy historical responsibility for exploring the scientific developmental mode and for building its contemporary new culture; moreover, Shenzhen strove to become the demonstration zone for scientific development and the demonstration zone for advanced socialist cultural construction. During that period,

Shenzhen's cultural innovations featured the conscious establishment of a cultural development strategy, the conscious renewal of the philosophy of cultural development, and conscious innovations in the cultural construction and cultural developmental mode. Its core significance and main hallmark was innovation. Innovation can be considered as the prominent bright spot in Shenzhen's cultural construction and development in that period.

1. **Making Culture the City' Soul and Source of Pride**

In January, 2003, the Sixth Plenary Session of the Third Shenzhen Municipal Party Committee specified five strategic goals for turning Shenzhen into an international city—one of these goals was the building of a high-grade cultural and ecological city—and the strategy of building the city through culture. In March, 2004, a working meeting on implementing the strategy of building the city through culture was held in Shenzhen, which stated efforts to vigorously carry out the strategy of building the city through culture and turn Shenzhen into a culturally advanced city. This shows that the Shenzhen Municipal Party Committee and the Municipal Government have a deeper understanding of the status and roles of culture in urban development than the previous two stages, that they have reached a new level, and have realized that, in the pattern of global competition, Shenzhen must shift its previous emphasis on economy and management to culture, it must win the new urban commanding height with cultural taste and a cultural image, and link its strategy for cultural development to that of urban development.

The strategy of building the city through culture is Shenzhen's comprehensive strategy for promoting urban development within the new situation—a priority is given to developing culture by taking it as the leading and basic factor for building an international city; culture is incorporated into the economic, political, social, scientific, educational and environmental fields and into other fields to drive rapid urban development and all-round social progress forward in Shenzhen, as well as to comprehensively improve the cultural significance and cultural taste of the whole city and turn Shenzhen into a high-grade international city. Building the city through culture is, in a certain sense, the development of the people through culture—culture and the enhancement of the value of people are elevated to the center of economic and social development. Therefore, building the city through culture is a great innovation in transforming Shenzhen's economic developmental mode and building a harmonious city, and it is also a significant measure for creatively carrying out the Scientific Outlook on Development and reflecting the idea of putting the people first.

2. **Libraries, Pianos and Design: The Three Pillars of Shenzhen's Distinct Cultural Strength**

A city is an abstract concept, and prominent cultural characteristics are required for making its image distinctive. In order to implement the strategy of building the city through culture, a strong supporting point is needed and real things which are visible and clear are necessary. For this purpose, while implementing the strategy of building the city through culture, Shenzhen's people have built "three cities"—turning

Shenzhen into the city of the library, the city of the piano and the city of design. This indicates that Shenzhen's cultural innovations are made not only by emancipating the mind, adopting the explicit philosophies, but also proceeding from the actual conditions, finding out the feasible solutions and perfectly combining the avant-garde line of thought with pragmatic actions.

The building of "three cities" is a strategic choice with local characteristics for Shenzhen's future cultural development, a choice made by Shenzhen according to the existing advantages and basic conditions for cultural development; it is also the specific way to implement the strategy of building the city through culture and building a culturally advanced city. It presents a sensible and visible developmental goal and the physical objects available for evaluation in terms of the strategy of building the city through culture. This combines the creation of Shenzhen's cultural advantages with Shenzhen's cultural characteristics, and quickens the formation of Shenzhen's symbol for a cultural brand and image. In another sense, the building of "three cities" is also the concept and design with Shenzhen's characteristics for its urban cultural development, and brings about three large bright spots on Shenzhen's cultural map; it reflects a high degree of cultural self-consciousness and awareness, rich cultural imagination and practical cultural style of its policy-makers.

3. **Better Protection of Cultural Rights and Improved Public Cultural Service System**

Citizens' cultural rights is a realistic issue which has, for a long time, attracted international attention. However, the extensive public opinion about it has not yet formed and it has not yet become the basic philosophy and guiding thought of the government for cultural administration in China for various reasons. Based on the cultural spirit which should be available in a pioneering city, with a high level of cultural self-consciousness and awareness, Shenzhen became the first, at the beginning of this century, to vow to realize the cultural rights of citizens and consider the realization of those rights as an important step for successful urban cultural development, as well as to consider the realization of the cultural rights of citizens as the basic theme of urban cultural competition and development, and the important content of Shenzhen's cultural developmental strategy and future urban developmental strategy; the government organs have been required to follow the goal of realizing the cultural rights of its residents in order to establish a new cultural administrative philosophy, adjust the cultural administrative means so that citizens can really obtain the right to enjoy cultural achievements, participate in cultural activities, carry out cultural creation and protect the spiritual and material interests in cultural creation.

Striving to realize the cultural rights of citizens is a loud voice first coming from Shenzhen during China's building of the advanced socialist culture. This shows that Shenzhen's cultural innovations have reached a higher level and it embodies the foresight and profound thought of the policy-makers—paying attention to the cultural construction and the building of a cultural image, the improvement of the cultural spirit and the maintenance of cultural rights; adding splendor to the building of a harmonious Shenzhen, combining the building of the city through culture with putting the people first, reflects a high realm of and a high taste in cultural innovations, becoming another innovative measure taken by Shenzhen for carrying out the Scientific Outlook on Development. Making efforts to promote the realization of the cultural rights of citizens is taken as one of the basic philosophies for cultural development and has really changed the longstanding ideology of emphasizing publicity in cultural construction but paying less attention to the cultural rights of citizens. This is a revolutionary change. Its significance and impact cannot be evaluated too much.

In order to safeguard and practically realize the cultural rights of citizens, Shenzhen has also become the first to put forward the idea of building a public cultural service system, and take it as the necessary social condition for realizing the cultural rights of citizens, so it has become the important part of Shenzhen's philosophical system for cultural development. In recent years, in Shenzhen, a lot of work has been done in order to accelerate the construction of public cultural facilities, innovate the forms of public cultural activities, enrich the contents of public cultural services and improve the mechanism of guarantee of public cultural services; a number of high-grade cultural facilities have been added; three major activities, including the Weekend Culture, Flowing Culture and High Art have been unveiled; various cultural brands such as the Reading Month, the Social Sciences Culture Popularization Week, the Shenzhen Culture Forum, Creative December and the Shenzhen Golden Autumn Art Festival have been developed; a public cultural service system for boosting the realization of the cultural rights of citizens and meeting citizens' spiritual cultural needs has preliminarily taken shape and will gradually be improved.

4. **Speeding up the Development of the Cultural Industry and Making it the Fourth Pillar Industry**

A vigorous development of the cultural industry is the necessary way to enhance the national cultural soft power and the comprehensive competitiveness of the nation. The historical mission of building a scientific development demonstration zone and a model city based on socialism with Chinese characteristics requires Shenzhen to expedite the development of its cultural industry, offer successful experiences in the coordinated development of non-profit cultural undertakings and an operating cultural industry, and explore the new line of thought and mode concerning the development of the cultural industry. In this regard, Shenzhen always has complete rational knowledge and a high degree of cultural self-consciousness. Since the strategy of building the city through culture was established in 2003, accelerating the development of the cultural industry and enhancing cultural self-consciousness and awareness regarding cultural competitiveness have become clearer and have been regarded as the lever for optimizing the urban industrial structure and sharpening the urban cultural competitive edge. The Fourth Party Representative Congress of Shenzhen, held in May, 2005, stated actions to develop the cultural industry as the fourth pillar industry in Shenzhen following high and new technologies, financial and logistics industries. The working meeting on Shenzhen's cultural industry, held in Shenzhen in November, decided to make city-wide efforts to promote the development of the cultural industry. Afterwards, a number of regulatory and policy documents, including the *Decisions of the Shenzhen Municipal Party Committee and the Municipal People's Government Concerning the Vigorous Development of the Cultural Industry* and the *Developmental Plan of Shenzhen for the Cultural Industry (2007–2020)* were released, and the development of the cultural industry was incorporated into the *11th Five-Year Plan of Shenzhen for Economic and Social Development*. In 2008, the Shenzhen Municipal Party Committee and the Municipal Government set the clear goals for developing a cultural industry: by 2010, the total value of Shenzhen's cultural industry will account for more than 10% of the GDP; by 2020, Shenzhen will become the domestic first-class, Asia-leading and world-famous culturally avant-garde city, and the added value of the cultural industry will make up about 11% of the local GDP.

The accelerated development of the urban cultural industry is one of Shenzhen's urban cultural developmental philosophies. Its cultural self-consciousness and innovative measures in the planning and implementation are reflected in the following four levels:

First, the China (Shenzhen) International Cultural Expo has been held, serving as an international cultural product display platform, cultural project trading platform and cultural information exchange platform for developing the cultural industry; second, the Shenzhen Culture Assets and Equity Exchange was established, providing a never-ending Cultural Expo and a new path for developing the cultural industry which combines culture with finance; third, the technological content has been increased in developing the cultural industry and a mode for the development of the cultural industry which integrates culture and technology was created; fourth, a priority has been given to developing the creative design industry, and the national-level creative industry park has been planned and built from a high starting point at a high level, the cultural industry has gradually been elevated to a creative cultural industry, and a new cultural industrial development mode which combines culture with creative elements has come into being.

The creative development and practice in Shenzhen's cultural industry show that Shenzhen has consciously advanced in realizing and safeguarding the cultural rights of its residents, meeting the citizens' diverse cultural needs and promoting rapid urban development; and the operations of the cultural industry have been earnestly developed while making progress in non-profit cultural undertakings and have been taken as an important means for boosting urban development and enhancing cultural competitiveness and the competitiveness of the city.

5. Promoting Residents' Cultural Caliber and Boosting the City's Soft Power

A humanistic spirit is the fundamental spirit reflected by human culture and the inner soul in the whole human cultural life. It centers on pursuing a lofty value ideal, including the true, the good and the beautiful. Its ultimate goal is the freedom and all-round development of the people. An urban humanistic spirit is the core value of a city, a high-level embodiment of the urban cultural significance and cultural taste as well as the fundamental part of the urban cultural soft power. Shenzhen's intensified efforts at building an urban humanistic spirit have a special significance and significance. On the one hand, Shenzhen has become the first to break the fetter of the planned economic system to carry out a number of first-ever market-oriented reforms; in Shenzhen, new thoughts and new ideas have emerged one after another, the cultural ideas are diverse; it is urgently necessary to strengthen the building of a host culture; it is essential to build the socialist core value system and adopt socialist core values to guide the healthy development of diverse cultures; on the other hand, it is necessary to opportunely summarize the new thoughts and cultural ideas with a sense of modern culture and consistent with the developmental needs of the times naturally formed in Shenzhen during the reform and opening up, and they should be accepted so as to epitomize the modern urban humanistic spirit and become an important part of the contemporary new culture and the spiritual significance of socialist core values. Therefore, the reinforced building of an urban humanistic spirit is a concentrated reflection of Shenzhen's cultural self-consciousness and also a major move made by Shenzhen in building the socialist core value system.

The Fifth Plenary Session of the Fourth Shenzhen Municipal Party Committee, held in December, 2006, vowed to strengthen the building of an urban humanistic spirit. As shown in the report to this session, nowadays, city competition and regional competition are reflected not only in the production of material wealth, but also in the humanistic and spiritual level; in the final analysis, the winner is judged by culture, the level is determined by civilization and success is defined by the spirit. Within the new situation in which the significance of the completion of the city is changing, Shenzhen has more conditions and necessities for building a humanistic urban spirit and pursuing the all-round development of the people, putting the people first and constantly fostering, creating, enriching and elevating the humanistic urban spirit. This is the greatest soft power of the city.

In Shenzhen, the building of a humanistic urban spirit is combined with the establishment of the socialist core value system; the significance of the humanistic spirit of the times has been interpreted, so the humanistic spirit becomes the important embodiment of socialist core values, socialist core values are rooted in production and living practices, and the humanistic spirit is converted into a group social consciousness and group behavior, and internalized as the humanistic gene of mainstream urban culture. In Shenzhen, the humanistic urban spirit is summarized as follows: putting the people first, stressing care and mutual help, respecting dignity; upholding self-reliance, competition, tolerance, harmony, friendly affection, benevolence and righteousness; advocating openness and inclusiveness, assimilation of good points, vitality, innovation and creation; emphasizing rules of etiquette, the rule of law, sincerity, goodness, self-examination, self-discipline, honesty and absence of deception; seeking civility and truth, being scientific, rational, rigorous and pragmatic. This indicates that Shenzhen's cultural self-consciousness has ascended from the general consciousness of the cultural subject to the conscious action of implementing the Scientific Outlook on Development and building the socialist core value system, and it has become the new philosophy and new measure for Shenzhen to be the first to achieve scientific and harmonious development.

The innovation in Shenzhen's building of a humanistic urban spirit is that such building is taken as an important measure for developing intangible urban resources and is extended to urban economic, political, cultural and social construction, so that such building really epitomizes the urban soft power and becomes the solid foundation and inexhaustible source for urban core competitiveness. In Shenzhen, a clear and feasible strategic idea of building the cultural soft power has been developed to build a well-enhanced public cultural service system, enhance the overall quality of its residents, forge an urban cultural brand, improve Shenzhen's urban cultural image, expand its urban cultural influence and cultural radiation force, strengthen the construction of cultural human resources and the protection of its historical and cultural heritage. Efforts are being made to move towards the following goals for cultural soft power construction and development: make the cultural innovation vitality commensurate with the status of the special economic zone, foster a first-class cultural power commensurate with Shenzhen's first-rate economic strength, gather excellent cultural capital which matches the strategy of building the city through culture, cultivate international influences consistent with the goal of building an international city and build an international cultural creative center commensurate with the statuses of Shenzhen and Hong Kong as metropolises.

6. **Strengthen Cultural Innovative Capacity and Nurturing the Development of New Culture**

Shenzhen is a special economic zone as the window and experimental field in China's reform and opening up and also an emerging sub-provincial city in China's administrative division. When it comes to cultural self-consciousness and cultural innovations, Shenzhen's people naturally combine both statuses and consciously broaden their cultural horizon, closely follow the basic situation of cultural conflicts and cultural fusion amidst globalization, correctly understand the developmental requirements of the national cultural developmental strategy for the construction of the regional culture, as well as rationally identifying the self-positioning according to Guangdong's cultural developmental layout. On the one hand, full scope is given to the function of the reform experimentation of the special economic zone; on the other hand, the function of cultural innovation of the emerging city is strengthened and the cultural innovations are turned into the bright spot of the special economic zone's image and the impetus for urban development; within the new situation, where scientific development is driven forward in an all-round way in China, Shenzhen is active in assuming the heavy historical responsibility of building the contemporary new culture and growing into a scientific developmental demonstration.

China's advanced socialist culture is modern, world-oriented and forward-looking. The building of the contemporary new culture must be based on correctly handling the relationships between Chinese culture and external cultures, between traditional culture and modern culture, between mainstream culture and branch cultures, and on promoting fusion during the development and driving forward development amidst fusion to form a new cultural value system. Shenzhen is highly exposed to external cultures, the foundation of the traditional culture is not strong and diverse cultural ideas exist in Shenzhen. This presents both opportunities and challenges for Shenzhen's cultural innovations. Shenzhen's people have consciously seized the opportunities and actively addressed the challenges. With the Scientific Outlook on Development, Shenzhen's people have made all-round innovations in cultural ideas, cultural developmental philosophy, a mode for the development of the cultural industry, a cultural system and mechanism and they "are good at learning and drawing on all outstanding achievements of human civilization, inheriting and carrying forward all excellent thoughts, virtues and cultural traditions of the Chinese nation, they have effectively withstood the corrosion of various negative and decadent ideologies and cultures and have always kept the socialist spirit and style" (Jiang Zemin's remarks), so the special economic zone has gradually developed Chinese characteristics and styles at the cultural level, exploring the new path for building a contemporary new culture.

The basic goal of Shenzhen's efforts in strengthening the function of cultural innovation and comprehensively carrying out cultural innovations is to improve the urban cultural taste and boost rapid urban development; its ultimate goal is to build a contemporary new culture which represents the direction for an advanced socialist culture. With more than 30 years of development, in particular all-around cultural innovations since the beginning of the new century, Shenzhen's culture has possessed marked features—innovative, smart and powerful—and has shown the embryonic form of the contemporary new culture.

It is innovative because the innovative spirit of the reform is continuously carried forward, cultural ideas and cultural philosophies are constantly renewed, and a trove of creative cultural achievements has been achieved. It is smart because knowledge and rationality have become the fundamental embodiment of the urban cultural spirit, while the humanistic spirit and humanistic sense are the main hallmarks of the cultural urban atmosphere. It is powerful because it is the everlasting source of development, makes and reinforces the appeal, cohesive force, competitiveness, radiation power and the influence of urban culture.

At present, Shenzhen's culture which is innovative, smart and power-oriented is only in its embryonic form, but it has exhibited the sense of modern culture and the cultural charm of a pioneering city; it represents the developmental trend of a modern urban city; it will certainly develop into a new culture which represents the direction for China's advanced socialist culture.

7. **Building a Strong Cultural Identity, Becoming an Innovation Hub for Fashion, Leading the Country in the Development of the Cultural Industry**

Shenzhen's cultural self-consciousness and cultural innovations have advanced with the times and have been continuously improved. The *12th Five-Year Developmental Plan of Shenzhen*, unveiled in 2010, specifies the goal of turning Shenzhen into a culturally powerful city by 2020. This marks the elevation of Shenzhen's cultural self-consciousness and cultural innovations to a new level. If the strategy of building the city through culture is the strategic thought of cultural development which was, is and will be adopted for a considerably long time in Shenzhen, a culturally powerful city is Shenzhen's new developmental goal of carrying out the Scientific Outlook on Development and quickening the building of a modern international city; this means that major quantitative and qualitative breakthroughs will certainly be made in Shenzhen's future cultural development.

Shenzhen's goal of building a culturally powerful city is identified under a particular cultural background. Internationally, in global urbanization, culture has increasingly become the important soft power in city competition and urban development, and overall urban competitiveness will decline unless the urban cultural soft power is constantly enhanced. There is no exception for Shenzhen as an international city. Domestically, China's cultural construction is confronted with many favorable conditions and severe challenges. Seizing the opportunities to accelerate cultural development and enhance China's cultural soft power and international competitiveness is necessary for achieving scientific development. In Shenzhen, more achievements and contributions should be made in this regard. In Guangdong, the Seventh Plenary Session of the Tenth Guangdong Provincial Party Committee, convened in July, 2010, clearly stated the strategic positioning of building Guangdong into a culturally powerful province. The *Plan of Guangdong Province for Building a Culturally Powerful Province* was adopted during that session, specifying new and higher requirements for Shenzhen's cultural construction. Shenzhen is facing a series of realistic issues concerning the accelerated development: transformation of the economic developmental mode calls for increasing the spiritual impetus of culture; high and new technological industries and emerging industries need to be developed to break the bottleneck coming from a shortage of economic developmental resources; the integration of the special economic zone requires a balanced and coordinated development in cultural facilities, cultural environment and cultural services; the spirits of the leading cadres are not high, citizens have some reservations about culture; it is necessary to continue carrying forward the cultural spirit of the times by emancipating the mind, carrying out the reform and opening up, further arousing the vitality of innovation, and better safeguarding the cultural rights of the citizens. The Shenzhen Municipal Party Committee and the Municipal Government have carefully considered the situation and have lost no time in deciding to enhance Shenzhen's Quality and build a quality-focused city; moreover, they have consciously set the developmental goal of building a culturally powerful city, raising the bar for Shenzhen's urban development.

Shenzhen's building of a culturally powerful city is rich in significance, clear in goal and thinking. The guiding thought and goal lie in making the cultural undertaking and industry stronger, enhancing the cultural radiation power and influence as well as the cultural image. Its significance includes: building a socialist core value system with the characteristics of the times and Shenzhen's characteristics, seeking out a new urban civilization mode; improving and optimizing the public cultural service system, better safeguarding the realization of the cultural rights of the citizens; establishing a modern system of cultural industries, building an international creative center for fashion and a cultural flagship city, further consolidating the city of design and the global model city for the promotion of nationwide reading; further improving the cultural market system and the modern system for cultural transmission, becoming the important base for making Chinese culture international.

7.3 Outstanding Contributions from the Special Economic Zones to the Prosperity and Development of Advanced Socialist Culture with Chinese Characteristics

The developmental philosophy and choice of goals of the Shenzhen Special Economic Zone in cultural development fully embody Shenzhen's sense of mission and responsibility for urban practices in building a culturally powerful country, and its frontier experimentation in cultural choices, as well as its practical urban path for continuously implementing the strategy of making the country strong through culture. Every decision is based on Shenzhen's actual cultural conditions and the general situation of national cultural development, making due contributions to the prosperity and development of the advanced socialist culture with Chinese characteristics.

7.3.1 Development of a Dynamic "Theory of Cultural Flow"

As Shenzhen was officially designated as a city in 1979, its history of urban development is only 30–40 years old. However, a miracle of rapid cultural development has been created in Shenzhen, making Shenzhen the "cultural sample" for China's modernization. Understanding and interpreting this "sample" cannot rely on superficial perceptions, but it should proceed on a convincing theoretical basis. The *Cultures Are Flowing*, a new book on cultural theory written by Shenzhen's scholar, Mr. Wang Jingsheng, is designed to describe Shenzhen's culture and lay a theoretical foundation for Shenzhen's cultural self-consciousness and cultural self-confidence; it provides a scientific theoretical system and a vibrant Cultural Flow Theory; its theoretical innovations and practical guidance go beyond Shenzhen and influence the whole country. This shows that Shenzhen has given birth not only to cultural brands, but also to cultural thoughts and theories.

According to the Cultural Flow Theory, cultures are flowing in history and space, and such flow is a process of promoting cultural innovations. The Cultural Accumulation Theory restricts cultural development, social innovations and ideological progress. If it is not denied and criticized, there is a failure to adapt to the changes in today's society and explain the reasons why Shenzhen, an emerging city with a lack of cultural accumulation, can develop rapidly in the cultural field. Cultural development and progress are achieved by continuously challenging the traditional boundary rather than keeping to tradition and adoring the accumulation. If there is excessive dependence on the stock from cultural accumulation while ignoring the increment from cultural flow, cultural accumulation will be turned into a heavy historical burden, so all lively cultural and economic behaviors will be stifled and we will fail to explain the reasons why many cities or areas without cultural accumulation can catch up from behind.[5] Therefore, it is necessary to fundamentally change

[5] Wang Jingsheng, *Cultures Are Flowing*, People's Publishing House, 2013, p. 33.

the theoretical basis for evaluating and judging the cultural generation and cultural development, and expand the theoretical space for cultural innovations, foster a new cultural outlook on innovative development of culture in flow, and understand the original significance and development law of and the real impetus for culture.

Given the new thoughts and views from the Cultural Flow Theory, when evaluating the current cultural situation and predicting the trend in cultural development, we should take into account not only the cultural accumulation and cultural heritage in the country with an ancient five-thousand-year-old civilization, but also the general trend of cultural flow and cultural innovations in today's world; not only fully utilize the original cultural stock, but also be good at innovating and increase the cultural increment; value not only the spiritual guidance role of culture in spiritual values and lifestyles, but also the roles of culture in guiding economic value and boosting development. An emerging city lacks historical cultural accumulation, but it is free from historical burden, so it shows more awareness, impetus and means for cultural innovations and sees more apparent effects; it is completely possible that it can catch up as a latecomer.

7.3.2 *Emergence of New Cultural System of Ideas*

In more than 30 years, Shenzhen's cultural self-consciousness and awareness have promoted the renewal of Shenzhen's cultural ideas and the innovations in its philosophies of cultural development; moreover, an urban spiritual system with reforms and innovations as the spiritual core and the value system with openness and inclusiveness as the main significance have been built. Both major systems can be considered the special economic zone spirit and Shenzhen's idea. A combination of the special economic zone spirit and Shenzhen's idea gives rise to a ideaal cultural system consistent with socialist core values; this injects a strong spiritual impetus into Shenzhen's development, and leads Shenzhen's diverse cultures to developing healthily in a correct direction, and offers a lively "cultural sample" for building China's socialist core values.

(I) **Shenzhen as a Powerful Showcase for What a Country Can Achieve Through Idea Reform and Opening Up**

Some scholars believe that cutting-edge ideaideas are more important than the growth of the GDP. The core of modern urban cultural influence is nothing but ideas which reflect the spirit of the times. In the history of the reform and opening up, the precious values and spiritual wealth created by Shenzhen are the greatest contributions from Shenzhen.[6] This remark reveals precisely what is fundamental in Shenzhen's cultural contributions.

---

[6]Wang Jingsheng, *Top 10 Concepts of Shenzhen*, Publishing House of Shenzhen Press Group, 2011, p. 9.

In 2011, Shenzhen's residents and experts chose ten ideas that most accurately captured the city's character from, many that had become quite popular for quite some time:

Time is money, efficiency is life;

Empty talk does the country no good, hard work is what makes the country powerful;

Never afraid to be the first;

Reform is Shenzhen's root, innovation its soul;

Make the city worthy of respect by turning its residents into book lovers;

Encourage innovations, tolerate failure;

Realize the cultural rights of residents;

If you give a rose to others, fragrance will linger on your hands;

No distance between Shenzhen and the world;

When you come to Shenzhen, you are one of us.

Once the selection result for the ten ideas that best encapsulate Shenzhen's character came out, the *People's Daily* published it immediately, lauding it as a vivid representation of the spirit of the time and process of reform. The *People's Daily* (Overseas Edition) also published an article which attributed the broad recognition and acceptance of these ideas to the fact that not only did they capture what makes Shenzhen but also what makes the time we live in historically distinctive. They are a distillation of the Chinese people's collective memory and experience of reform, and their shared aspiration for a better future.[7]

(II) Form of Expression and Cultural Significance of Shenzhen's Ideas are the "Vivid Samples" for Building Socialist Core Values

The ten ideas that encapsulate Shenzhen's city character constitute a new ideaal cultural system. With respect to the cultural spirit and cultural significance, the top ten ideas epitomize a number of new ideas in Shenzhen; they are the outstanding achievements in Shenzhen's spiritual cultural construction and development; they reflect the special economic zone's spirit and core values with the style of the times and Shenzhen's characteristics; they fully embody the enterprising spirit of stressing efficiency and cherishing time, the unity of knowledge and practice, the realistic approach of opposing empty talk, the exploring spirit of boldly making breakthroughs, the innovative spirit of upholding success and tolerating failure, the caring spirit of openness, inclusiveness, solidarity and mutual help, the human-centered spirit of putting the people first, the global awareness and spirit of integrating into the world. These new ideas and new spirits give full expression to Shenzhen's passion for innovations, its innovative spirit and style; they are the mainstream culture in Shenzhen's multicultural structure and are in the leading position in Shenzhen's urban cultural development; they not only mitigate the negative impact from non-mainstream cultures such as the consumer culture, but also build the spiritual height of Shenzhen's culture; they are the shining spots in Shenzhen's cultural development.

---

[7]Editorial Group of *Culture Shenzhen Weekly* (People's Daily Overseas Edition), Cultural Force Continues New Legends in Shenzhen, *People's Daily* (Overseas Edition), June 11, 2014 (7).

The ideaal cultural system represented by the ten ideas that encapsulate Shenzhen's character has these striking features: oriented towards the times, advanced, inclusive and practical; it is the epitome of the spirit of the times and a vivid expression of the reform and opening up; it is a vivid display of socialist core values in Shenzhen; it belongs to Shenzhen and the whole country; it demonstrates the spiritual facet and ideaal impetus of Shenzhen's development; it sheds light on the great contributions that Shenzhen has brought to China's reform and opening up at the levels of cultural ideas and spiritual values; it provides the strong spiritual impetus for China's reform, opening up and modernization; it treasures the common memories of Chinese people and the spiritual wealth for us to march towards the future.

The form of expression and cultural significance of the ten ideas that encapsulate Shenzhen's character enable them to serve as the "cultural samples" for building socialist core values; these ideas vividly reflect the construction and transmission of culture through a combination of the most basic cultural genes of the Chinese nation and contemporary culture in a popular and extensively participatory way.[8] They make socialist core values lively and easy to accept and operate. In this sense, they demonstrate the important contributions from Shenzhen to the building of China's contemporary culture.

7.3.3 Showcasing to the World China's Distinct Values Cultural Sovereignty by Building World-Renowned Cultural Brands

Cultural brands are the image and symbol of a country, a region or a city; they are also important for augmenting the clout and impact of a culture. Committed to realizing the cultural rights of its residents and providing them with excellent cultural products, the Shenzhen Special Economic Zone has attached great importance to the development of cultural brands, and it has been home to a host of them, including the Shenzhen Culture Forum, the Reading Month, the China (Shenzhen) International Cultural Expo, the Social Sciences Culture Popularization Week, the Chinese and Overseas Excellent Artwork Performance Season, the Grand Theatre Art Festival, the Shenzhen Golden Autumn Community Cultural Art Festival and the Symphony Ode to Humanity. Some of these brands have produced extraordinary cultural effects in China and around the world. These brands have broken a new path for carrying China's cultural sovereignty forward and demonstrating China's value.

(I) **The Shenzhen Culture Forum Serves as a New Platform for Spreading Socialist Core Values**

Established in 2005, the Shenzhen Culture Forum is a special non-profit lecture for residents led by the Party Committee and the government, one of the first of its kind in

[8] Xi Jinping, *Excerpts of Xi Jinping's Expositions on Comprehensively Intensifying the Reform*, Central Party Literature Press, 2014, p. 87.

China. It has been active for ten years, during which more than 800 lectures have been offered, attracting a total audience of about 120,000 people, an annual increase of about 9%; it has 15,000 followers. More than ten million people attend in the lectures by watching them on TV, on the Internet or other media. It was given the Cultural Innovation Award by the Ministry of Culture in 2009; it has been awarded one of the National Top Ten Cultural Innovation Projects, the Learning Party Organization Building Demonstration Contact Point of Guangdong Province and the Shenzhen Demonstration Project for Nationwide Reading.

With the aim of cultivating residents' ability to appreciate high culture, the Shenzhen Culture Forum promotes the humanistic spirit, developing public culture, enriching the citizens' lives and enhancing the taste of the city. More than 700 scholars, including Mo Yan, Tang Yijie, Yi Zhongtian, Yu Dan and Xu Peidong, have been invited to speak at the Shenzhen Culture Forum. Under the mechanism of freedom, equality and easiness, the Shenzhen Culture Forum focuses on literature, art, science, knowledge and a wonderful life, and continuously increases the spiritual, academic, scientific and knowledge content of the city, develops the citizens' pursuit of truth and values, guides citizens to seek the truth, goodness and beauty; it helps discover a new form of the government's provision of public cultural services for its residents; it serves as a new platform for spreading socialist core values and a new carrier for cultivating a healthy cultural life for its residents; it opens a new way for high-quality culture to enter the society and the lives of the citizens and it offers a new mode under which culture can be shared by all of the people.[9]

The Shenzhen Culture Forum has been well received by and sees the passionate participation of citizens. Many citizens have gotten used to attending the Shenzhen Culture Forum at the weekends. Some citizens have humorously said, "We are not doctoral candidates, but we enjoy the treatment of doctoral candidates when listening to the lectures given by scholars and teachers at this forum." Some citizens put the monthly lecture schedule in their study room and attend every lecture. As mentioned by the theme song of the Shenzhen Culture Forum, the curriculum schedule is available in the study room, curiosity goes back to the chest, we return to our school days and jubilantly enter this forum…

(II) The Reading Month as a New Way to Promote Reading and the Exercising of People's Cultural Rights

The annual Shenzhen Reading Month began in 2000 and has lasted for 15 years, during which more than 3500 cultural reading activities have been conducted, and more than 100 well-known experts and scholars have been invited to the reading forum to deliver special speeches, and the number of participating citizens soared from 1.70 million person-times at the first forum to more than 10 million. The Reading Month has created several firsts in China: the first cultural forum focusing on reading, the first middle-school student literary federation, the first special children's library, the first reading association, a number of famous cultural brand activities, including the Shenzhen Reading Forum, Recommended Books for Collection and Reading,

[9] Wang Jingsheng, Cultural Taste Builds Urban Future, *Culture Shenzhen*, 2014 (7).

the Annual Top Ten Excellent Books, Poem World, the Primary and Secondary School Students Composition Contest, Scholarly Family, Scholarly Enterprise, the Book Donation with a Loving Heart, Young Worker Sunshine Reading, Classical Poetic Prose Reading, the Shenzhen Reading Month Debate Contest, the Shenzhen Fairy Tale Festival and the Ocean Culture Forum. Citizens warmly welcome and enthusiastically participate in these activities. With great achievements, the Reading Month has produced good cultural effects in China and has become esteemed around the world. Representatives from more than 20 provinces, autonomous regions and municipalities across the country have come to Shenzhen to learn about the experience of the Reading Month. Shenzhen was awarded the title of the Outstanding Developing Knowledge City during the Knowledge Cities World Summit, and the Global Model City for the Promotion of Nationwide Reading by the United Nations Educational, Scientific and Cultural Organization.

The basic philosophy of the Reading Month in Shenzhen is "making the city respectable because of reading!" The goal is to enhance the urban cultural significance through advocating reading in the city and thus change the quality of the urban spirit.[10] The Reading Month reflects Shenzhen's cultural self-consciousness. It originates from Shenzhen's characteristics and the understanding of the strategy of future urban development. In Shenzhen, as a young immigrant city, citizens generally have the needs for enriching their knowledge, making self-improvement and alleviating the pressure of competition. The Reading Month creates the conditions and provides the conveniences for meeting such needs, especially the needs of migrant worker groups. In the general pattern of completing a culture-based city in the world, it is necessary for Shenzhen, as an emerging city, to increase its cultural depository and improve its cultural tastes; otherwise, a strong cultural competitive power cannot be developed. The Reading Month is Shenzhen's pursuit of the overall high quality and cultural taste of urban culture and also the embodiment of the awareness of a strategy for urban development. Practice proves that the reading enthusiasm that all people have, which is driven forward by the Reading Month, makes Shenzhen praised and commended by the United Nations Educational, Scientific and Cultural Organization.

The fundamental significance of Shenzhen's Reading Month consists in realizing the cultural rights of the citizens by encouraging all people to read. Shenzhen is one of the Chinese cities where attention was paid to cultural rights early on. The Shenzhen Municipal Party Committee and the Municipal Government have taken the realization of its residents' cultural right to reading and seeking knowledge as the cultural responsibility of the Party Committee and the government, and have realized that "reading is the most common and most lasting cultural need in the cultural life of citizens, and the right to read is one of the most basic and most important cultural rights." The Reading Month is a way, carrier and mode for effectively realizing the cultural rights of citizens.[11] Therefore, the Shenzhen Municipal Party Committee and the Municipal Government have actively allocated public resources and organized

[10]Wang Jingsheng, Reading Creates an Advanced Urban Civilization, *Culture Shenzhen*, 2013 (12).

[11]Wang Jingsheng, Reading Creates an Advanced Urban Civilization, *Culture Shenzhen*, 2013 (12).

non-governmental forces to participate in the Reading Month activities, providing the necessary material foundation and realistic conditions for smoothly conducting the Reading Month activities and extensively realizing the cultural rights of citizens, thus making a new mode for encouraging all people to read and realize the cultural rights of citizens.

After Shenzhen's Reading Month exerted a cultural influence in China and became esteemed throughout the world, a new move for encouraging all people to read was made in Shenzhen. In April, 2014, the *Regulations of the Shenzhen Special Economic Zone to Encourage All People to Read (Exposure Draft)* was officially issued. Shenzhen became the first city in China to legislate the encouragement for all people to read by making reference to the international practice. The Regulations specify ten systems for promoting reading among all the people, including: establishing a reading committee to promote reading among all the people, encouraging social forces to participate in building mobile and self-service libraries, newly collecting 0.1 book and electronic literature/people every year, designating November as the Reading Month, implementing the reading promoter system, making 30% of selected works in libraries accessible to minors, setting up a reading fund to promote reading for all people and a welfare lottery with public welfare funds to support reading and establishing a reading assessment research mechanism. The issuance of the Regulations shows that Shenzhen has officially become the first city in China with legislation for guaranteeing the promotion of reading among all people. The Regulations are very concrete and highly operable in citizens' reading rights, resources and facilities for reading activities promoting reading among all the people. With such reading legislation, Shenzhen's Reading Month will permanently exist, regardless of the changes in leaders or other changes, this kind of reading activity will be continued, and Shenzhen will be home to a long-lasting, effective and constant urban reading culture. This will undoubtedly have a guiding role and demonstration effects in promoting reading nationwide.

(III) **The China (Shenzhen) International Cultural Expo is an Important Platform for Making Chinese Culture Go Global**

In November, 2004, the first China (Shenzhen) International Cultural Expo was held in Shenzhen. So far, it has lasted for a decade, during which it has continuously developed and grown. It has become a comprehensive platform which integrates the exposition of cultural products, factor trading of the cultural industry and the information exchange of the cultural industry. It is the only comprehensive Cultural Expo certified by the Union of international Fairs in China. It is hailed, by the journalists of the Xinhua News Agency, as the No. 1 Cultural Expo in China. It has vigorously stimulated the development of China's cultural industry and has more rapidly promoted Chinese cultural products in the international community. Liu Qibao, Minister of the Publicity Department of the Central Committee of the Communist Party of China, acclaimed this fair as an important platform for spreading Chinese culture to the outside world.

With a decade-long growth, the number of exhibitors has increased from 700 in the first fair to 2118 in the ninth fair; visitors, exhibitors and purchasers came from more than 10 countries and territories in the first fair, while that figure rose to 93 in the ninth fair; there was only one sub-fair in the first fair, while that figure and this number increased to 43 in the ninth fair. Since the sixth fair, exhibitors have come from all corners of China, including 31 provinces, autonomous regions and municipalities, Hong Kong, Macao and Taiwan, and it has been difficult to find a vacant booth in some exhibition halls.

During the ten years of this fair, it has been funded by the government for more than 100 million yuan, and it has created a miracle of cultural industrial development and cultural prosperity: transactions worth more than 810 billion yuan have been concluded and cultural exports have exceeded 80 billion yuan. In a sense, this fair has become the barometer of China's cultural industrial development. In this fair, a great number of industry factors, including information, technologies and talents gather and interact with each other, arousing an extensive amount of creativity, boosting the development of China's cultural industry and promoting Chinese cultural products around the world.

This fair has opened a window for observing the developmental trends of the global cultural industry while showcasing the quintessence of Chinese culture, which is conducive to learning about the latest information regarding the development of the international cultural industry. At the tenth fair, there was a strategic cooperation relationship with 16 overseas professional bodies, and a number of overseas bodies, including Russia's art exhibition group and the exhibition groups from Chile and Southeast Asian countries. The overseas exhibition areas accounted for more than 15% of the total area. This shows that this fair has become increasingly international, has played more and more roles in promoting Chinese culture around the world and has made irreplaceable special contributions.

(IV) "Ode to Humanity" as a Symphonic Instrument for Disseminating China's Value

With 8 years of elaborate improvements since 2006, when planning and creation began, the large-scale choral symphony Ode to Humanity, originated in Shenzhen, has developed into a cultural brand which enjoys great prestige throughout the world and serves as the special cultural envoy for spreading China's value and promoting Chinese culture in the world. At the invitation of the United Nations Educational, Scientific and Cultural Organization (UNESCO), the symphony performed at UNESCO's headquarters in Paris, France, on September 21, 2013—the International Day of Peace; it was well received and has become the symphony specially recommended to the world by UNESCO.

The Ode to Humanity is a new attempt to interpret and express the core elements of Chinese Confucian culture with the Western symphony. Five movements focusing on humanity, justice, propriety, wisdom and honesty, the ending song and the epilogue constitute a complete musical work. Notes, movements and the human voice are used to depict a harmonious and elegant landscape of Chinese culture, spreading the value and splendor of Chinese culture, and expressing the life philosophy and attitudes of the Chinese nation.

The symphony—the Ode to Humanity—originated in Shenzhen, and is designed to carry forward the excellent Chinese traditional culture in the context of globalization, an attempt to combine the Western musical form with Chinese traditional values, interpret the Chinese understanding of the true, the good and the beautiful, and adopt the Chinese discourse system to promote and spread the widely recognized values around the world.

After the performance of the Ode to Humanity, the social response and cultural effect went beyond the expectations. After learning about it, the American side warmly invited the symphony orchestra of the Ode to Humanity to jointly perform this magnificent eastern humanistic symphony in the USA in September, 2014. In order to enhance the artistic effect of the performance in the USA, during its visit to Shenzhen in May, 2014, the U.S. Philadelphia Orchestra and Shenzhen Symphony Orchestra rehearsed the Ode to Humanity. The artists from both countries conducted rehearsals for the first time, and their good teamwork brought about a smooth rehearsal and a wonderful performance of the Ode to Humanity. After the rehearsal, Nicholas Platt, senior advisor to the U.S. Philadelphia Orchestra, said that he liked the Ode to Humanity very much and suggested that the song's lyrics, which captured the quintessence of Chinese traditional culture, should be fully revealed during the performance in the USA so that people could get an idea of the beauty of Chinese traditional culture while appreciating the symphony. Allison B. Vulgamore, President of the Philadelphia Orchestra, hailed the Ode to Humanity as a magnificent work, and said, "with the cooperative rehearsal among artists from both countries, we are jointly making history."[12]

The cultures across the Taiwan Strait share the same root, and the Chinese traditional culture is the common spiritual home for the compatriots across the Taiwan Strait. In August, 2014, the Ode to Humanity debuted in Taiwan; it was performed at Taipei's Sun Yat-sen Memorial Hall on August 8, Taichung's Huisun Hall on August 12 and Kaohsiung's Zhide Hall on August 15; as a result, it was well received by Taiwan's audience. The first performance in Taipei on August 8 was highly praised by the audience. After the performance, Taipei's citizen Jia Huixiu said, "After appreciating the Ode to Humanity, I am more proud of the cardinal virtues: humanity, justice, propriety, wisdom and honesty, and the Chinese traditional culture. The people across the Taiwan Strait need such culture and exchanges."[13] After the concert, Kong Chuichang, the 79th generation eldest grandson of Confucius, President of the Chinese Association of Confucius, said, " We can expect that, when the melody of the Ode to Humanity is heard around the world, the universal values, including humanity, justice, propriety, wisdom and honesty, will be understood and accepted by the people from different cultural backgrounds, a world of universal harmony is not far away.[14]

---

[12]Weng Huijuan, We Are Making History Together, *Shenzhen Special Economic Zone Daily*, May 30, 2014, Page A6.

[13]Weng Huijuan, Chen Li, People across the Taiwan Strait Jointly Sang the Ode to Humanity, Resonance Swept throughout China, *Shenzhen Evening News*, August 9, 2014, Page 03.

[14]Weng Huijuan, Chen Li, People across the Taiwan Strait Jointly Sang the Ode to Humanity, Resonance Swept throughout China, *Shenzhen Evening News*, August 9, 2014, Page 03.

7.3.4 Leading the Country's Effort to Develop the Cultural Industry by Discovering a New Rapid Growth Model

The 18th National Congress of the Communist Party of China vowed, from a national strategic perspective, to drive forward the rapid development of the cultural industry, the fusion of culture and technology, to develop new cultural business forms, and increase the scale of, the intensive and professional levels of the cultural industry. Vigorously developing the cultural industry is a necessary way to optimize the industrial structure and improve the national cultural soft power.

With cultural self-consciousness, awareness and the philosophy of cultural innovation, outstanding achievements have been made in Shenzhen's cultural industry; the industrial scale has rapidly expanded, the agglomeration effect is very apparent, continuous innovations have been carried out in the developmental mode and path. The leaders of the Central Government have encouraged Shenzhen to become the front-runner in the development of China's cultural industry.

In recent years, Shenzhen's cultural industry has rapidly expanded against the global financial crisis. Shenzhen has seen a rapid development in cultural sectors such as cultural tourism, modern printing, creative design, newspapers, book distribution, network and computer services, animation and games, performance and entertainment, film, television and audiovisual products manufacturing and high-end arts and crafts. In the past ten years, Shenzhen's creative cultural sector has grown annually by an average of nearly 25%; its added value in 2012 was 115 billion yuan, its proportion in the GDP increased from nearly 3% in 2003 to 9%, and it has become the urban pillar industry, the strategic emerging industry and the important engine for driving the rapid and healthy development of the economy.

The innovative measures and successful experience in the rapid development of Shenzhen's cultural industry have produced a guiding and demonstrative effect with respect to the following three aspects:

(I) Understanding the Significance of a Strong Cultural Industry for National and Regional Development, Making It a Key Policy Objective

In Shenzhen, as a pioneering city under the influence of modern cultural ideas, people always maintain the philosophy of advanced cultural development, are keenly aware that the development of the cultural industry is of great significance for making the country prosperous and strong and rejuvenating the nation, and have realized that the cultural industry plays a crucial role in enhancing Shenzhen's competitiveness as a city.

Shenzhen attaches importance to developing the cultural industry: First, Shenzhen has a high level of theoretical self-consciousness and has theoretically overturned the traditional view of developing the cultural industry only for the purpose of economic development by taking the development of the cultural industry as the means for improving the national influence and safeguarding national cultural sovereignty; so this certainly enhances the sense of mission and responsibility for developing the cultural industry. Second, Shenzhen links the development of the cultural industry with the functions and missions of the Shenzhen Special Economic Zone, and is determined to increase the level of development of the cultural industry so that it makes due contributions to promoting Chinese culture to the outside world and enhancing the national cultural soft power and cultural competitiveness. We believe that if other areas or cities across China can learn from Shenzhen's experience and attach great importance to developing the cultural industry like Shenzhen, China's road to building a culturally powerful country will be wider and smoother.

(II) Investing in the Construction of Cultural Industry Hubs and Parks in Order to Boost the Agglomeration Effect and Scale Effect

China's cultural industry developed late, its history is short, the number of cultural enterprises is relatively small and its scale effect is not sufficient. Therefore, it is particularly important to build cultural industry bases and cultural industry parks, in order to produce scale and agglomeration effects. In this regard, Shenzhen offers a successful experience for the rest of the country. At present, Shenzhen is home to more than 50 cultural industry bases and cultural industry parks, covering animation, games, design, digital design and publication distribution. The Overseas Chinese Town, the Dafen Oil Painting Village, the Artron Enterprise Group, Tencent and Shenzhen Curio World have been rated as demonstration bases of the national cultural industry. The Overseas Chinese Town has also been named the demonstration park of the national cultural industry. These industry parks and industry bases bring together thousands of enterprises, providing the important conditions for cultivating the leading cultural enterprises.

Shenzhen's cultural industry bases and cultural industry parks aim at nurturing a number of competitive industrial players, and guiding the cultural enterprises to develop into group-based and large-scale ones. In order to achieve this goal, Shenzhen has become the first in China to adopt the legislative means to issue the *Regulations of Shenzhen City for the Promotion of the Development of the Cultural Industry* and the *Plan of Shenzhen City for Revitalization and Development of the Creative Cultural Industry*, and a series of supporting policy measures have been introduced to provide the vigorous policy guarantee for developing the cultural industry.

(III) Finding Innovative Ways to Developing the Cultural Industry and Creating Distinctive Forms of an Emerging Sectors

Amid its rapid development, Shenzhen's cultural industry has also given birth to four new modes, including culture + technology, culture + finance, culture + tourism and culture + creativity, setting a good example for the rest of the country.

Shenzhen is the national cultural and technological integration demonstration base. Cultural and technological integration gives rise to the "culture + technology" developmental mode, which is a bright spot in the development of the cultural industry. According to incomplete statistics, by 2010, there were 6477 cultural technological enterprises in Shenzhen, accounting for about 70.37% of Shenzhen's cultural enterprises, and more than seven enterprises had been listed at home and abroad. Culture + technology has become a breakthrough in the high-end development of

Shenzhen's cultural industry and has generated a number of famous backbone enterprises with high competitive power at home and abroad, such as Tencent, Szdomain, Fantawild Holdings, Artron, A8 Music, Xinlei and GDC. With a combination of technological innovations and creative cultural elements, the cultural technological enterprises multiply the value of cultural products, and the effect of creating wealth is very apparent. Tencent became the first domestic internet enterprise with a revenue of more than 10 billion yuan. Fantawild Holdings Inc. has seen a sixfold growth of its total profit. Artron has delivered a turnover and profit at a growth rate of 70%. Culture + technology has created new advantages, new markets and new competitive power for Shenzhen's cultural industry, and it has become the new mode which influences the development of the national cultural industry.

Besides the new culture + technology mode, the people in Shenzhen's cultural industry have also sought out a new path in combining culture with finance to develop the culture + finance developmental mode. The China (Shenzhen) International Cultural Expo serves as a promotion and trading platform for Shenzhen's cultural products, even those from the rest of the country; it has built connections between the financial capital and cultural enterprises, between social capital and cultural enterprises, between the capital market and cultural enterprises; this is considered the first attempt to combine culture with finance in Shenzhen. The Shenzhen Culture Assets and Equity Exchange, put into operation in 2009, is a never-ending Cultural Expo; it further reflects the basic philosophy that "culture is connected with capital, trading creates value" and is building a national culture + finance professional service platform. In 2011, the China Culture Industrial Investment Fund—Shenzhen participated in its preparations—was established in Shenzhen, expanding the stage for the connection between culture and finance and broadening the new path for investments in and financing for the cultural industry.

The culture + tourism developmental mode was the first mode to take shape in Shenzhen. The theme parks built by the Shenzhen Overseas Chinese Town Group, including Splendid China, Folk Culture Village, Window of the World, Happy Valley and Overseas Chinese Town East, represent the new form of connection between culture and tourism and the new path for developing the cultural industry. With many years of operation and development, Overseas Chinese Town Theme Parks have become the largest group of theme parks with the largest number of tourists and the highest amount of tourism revenue. Overseas Chinese Town Group pays attention to innovating on the cultural significance of tourism and converts Chinese and foreign historical cultural resources into resources for tourism, and it has integrated cultural enterprises such as Shenzhen Song & Dance Troupe Performance Arts Co., Ltd. to stimulate the consumption of tourist culture with characteristic artistic performances. The large original humanistic performances, including Across the Century, Oriental Costume Show, Golden Mask Dynasty, Brilliance through the Ages, Epic Romance, Great Joy, and Mystery are the important tourism products of Overseas Chinese Town Theme Parks. Overseas Chinese Town's business model of combining culture with tourism has covered seven provinces and municipalities, greatly expanding Shenzhen's cultural influence and cultural radiation.

Creativeness is the soul and leading factor in the development of the cultural industry. A good idea can make a cultural enterprise even drive the industrial development of a city and a region. The cultural creativeness awarded Shenzhen the honorary title of the City of Design by the United Nations Educational, Scientific and Cultural Organization. For a long time, in Shenzhen, the new development model of the cultural industry—culture + creativity—has been taken as the important measure for upgrading the cultural industry, and full scope has been given to the roles of cultural creativeness and technological innovations in supporting and leading the development of the cultural industry, so it has given birth to a new developmental mode under which equal emphasis is placed on the cultural industry's growth rate, quality and performance, and its development is driven by both cultural creativeness and technological innovations. At present, Shenzhen is home to a number of creative industry parks such as Tianmian City-of-Design Creative Industry Park and Dafen Oil Painting Village, and high-level cultural creative works, including the animated cartoon Boonie Bears. In its future development, with the City of Design as the most authoritative and most convenient platform for cooperation and exchange in the international creative field, Shenzhen will lead the rapid development of the creative cultural industry and really become the front-runner in the development of the national cultural industry.

7.3.5 Building Creative "Cultural Visions" that Can Serve as Example for the Whole Country

In April, 2014, on the eve of the tenth China (Shenzhen) International Cultural Expo, Shenzhen put forward ten visions for Shenzhen's cultural development, attracting much attention from the media and the academic circles. Yu Ping, a cultural scholar and Director of the Culture and Technology Department, in an interview said: "In more than 30 years, great achievements have been made in Shenzhen's cultural construction, Shenzhen's cultural construction path and philosophy have drawn national attention, while the ten visions are exactly Shenzhen's more leading-edge line of thinking at the forefront of the cultural development; Shenzhen relies on cultural visions rather than cultural accumulation to develop its appeal and cohesive power."[15]

(I) **The Cultural Significance of Shenzhen's Visions for Cultural Development**

Shenzhen's visions for cultural development can be expressed in the following ten statements, with matching keywords:

Vision One: Making Shenzhen Philosophy the essential spirit of the times (keyword: ideas);

Vision Two: Let everybody feel the warmth of an inclusive city (keyword: inclusiveness);

---

[15]Yu Ping, Ten Grand Visions Contain Shenzhen's New Notions, *Shenzhen Special Economic Zone Daily*, May 5, 2014, Page A4.

Vision Three: Letting the media serve as the guardian and spokesperson of positive energy
(keyword: public opinion);

Vision Four: Providing every resident with easy access to culture (keyword: rights);

Vision Five: A strong cultural industry guaranteeing the correct direction for advanced culture
(keyword: industry);

Vision Six: Letting civilization grow in the sunshine of the rule of law (keyword: rule of law);

Vision Seven: Asserting the country's cultural sovereignty to protect the interests of the nation and its cities
(keyword: sovereignty);

Vision Eight: Making the city a friendly place for those who pursue culture and learning (keyword: talents);

Vision Nine: Putting scholarship at the top of urban culture (keyword: school of thought).

Vision Ten: Let innovative, smart and rigorous urban culture facilitate the rejuvenation of the Chinese culture (keyword: goal).

Overall, these ten visions involve various levels, including ideas, public opinion, rights, industry, sovereignty, talents, academics, rule of law and goal. They can be considered to panoramically display Shenzhen's future urban culture. Their bright spot and innovative significance lie in focusing on the people in urban cultural development, taking Shenzhen's cultural development as a means for carrying forward the national cultural sovereignty and boosting the rejuvenation of Chinese culture, giving prominence to the urban practical and urban model significance of Shenzhen's cultural development in the general pattern of China's cultural development. This shows that Shenzhen once again comes out in front across the country as the vanguard of cultural construction.

(II) This Set of Ten Objectives Bring Together Developmental Philosophy and Cultural Blueprint into an Organic Whole

These ten visions appear to be only ten slogans, but these slogans embody the cultural developmental philosophy of the policy-makers and depict the prospect and blueprint for cultural development. Professor Andrew Brown from the University of Cambridge said, in a book, that a politician needs slogans because slogans can show the prospect and bring hope to the people.

We regard these ten visions as the cultural developmental philosophies because they shed light on the future developmental philosophies for Shenzhen's culture. Vision One makes Shenzhen become the place for generating and growing the ideas of the times and the source of the spirit of the times. Vision Two advocates continued efforts to foster, with the inclusive character of an immigrant culture, a diversified healthy cultural ecological environment. Vision Three is dedicated to building an open, responsible and conscientious online public opinion environment under the rule of law, and the governance-assisting and people-friendly mainstream media which hold high the banner of the reform and opening up. Vision Four aims at fully realizing the citizens' rights in cultural enjoyment, cultural participation, cultural creation and protection of creative achievements. Vision Five is designed to upgrade the cultural industry, cultivate the new forms of business within the cultural industry and foster a vibrant cultural market. Vision Six focuses on actively building an environment immersed in the culture of the rule of law and cultivating the civilized citizens, communities and cities with the spirit of the rule of law and national virtues. Vision Seven centers on carrying forward the national cultural sovereignty, engaging in international cultural exchanges as an international first-class city, securing a say in cultural exchanges and displaying the distinctive features of urban culture. Vision Eight aims at developing a cultural talent platform and a "shelter" for cultural practitioners to turn Shenzhen into a talent highland full of talents, humanistic excellence and ideas. Vision Nine focuses on gradually shaping Shenzhen's school of thought characterized by a global horizon, a national stand, spirit of the times and the Shenzhen expression in urban cultural development. Vision Ten stresses efforts to make the best use of the crucial period of the development of urban culture so as to inject powerful cultural genes and develop the innovative, smart and power-oriented urban mainstream culture.[16] The above connotative expressions of these ten visions fully demonstrate the comprehensive philosophy for an all-round and high-standard development of urban culture, high theoretical and intellectual levels, distinctive foresight and vanguard character.

We deem these ten visions as the cultural blueprint because they fully depict an "ideal city" of culture. In this city, citizens enjoy full cultural rights, freely participate in cultural creation, get access to cultural achievements; the urban public opinion environment is under the rule of law, while openness, equity, conscience and responsibility become the consensus of the media; a galaxy of cultural elites get together and stand out with an innovative spirit; citizens respect and accommodate each other and live in harmony; the cultural industry flourishes and the cultural market is brisk; the academic culture is at the crest of urban culture, and Shenzhen's school of thought with distinctive characteristics comes into being; urban mainstream culture is full of a spirit of the times characterized by reform and innovation, and shows a new form characterized by innovation, wisdom and power; people from other areas flock to Shenzhen to learn new thoughts and ideas, and accept and spread them across the country.

We can imagine that if the cultural blueprint shown in Shenzhen's ten visions becomes reality, it will certainly become a "cultural sample" with an enormous influence and it will exert an immeasurable impact on the construction and development of China's contemporary culture. The cultural contributions from the Shenzhen Special Economic Zone will be recorded in the annals of history.

[16]Wang Jingsheng, Ten Grand Visions for Shenzhen's Cultural Development, *Culture Shenzhen*, 2014 (4).

Postscript

This book, *Special Economic Zones and China's Development Path* is the Major Program (10AJL001) undertaken by me under the National Social Science Fund. Most of the research fellows involved in the program participated in writing the book *China's Economic Zones: Design, Implementation, and Impact*. The book *China's Economic Zones: Design, Implementation, and Impact* is also published by the Social Sciences Academic Press (China); it was listed by the Publicity Department of the Central Committee of the Communist Party of China and the State General Administration of Press and Publication (currently the State Administration of Press, Publication, Radio, Film and Television) as one of the 35 recommended books for the 30th anniversary of China's reform and opening up; it was designated as the Chinese Academic Translation Program (11WJL001) under the National Social Science Fund in 2011 and was published in English and globally distributed by the British Path International; it was awarded the first prize of excellent achievements in philosophy and social science by Guangdong Province in 2011.

It took four and a half years to complete this book. Its overall framework was revised several times; adjustments, additions and deletions involving particular research fellows were conducted in response to the changes in its overall framework. The achievement, currently available to you, is defective to some extent and should be further improved and substantiated, but it is the result of our hard work, great efforts and devotion. As scholars, the pursuit of academic excellence is our responsibility and interest. As scholars living in the special economic zones, our research on the special economic zones and China's Development Path is not only a complex, but also an unshirkable, mission. With the promotion of an interest, and the excitation of a sense of responsibility and mission, the members in the Team of China's Development Path have worked in a united, cooperative and harmonious way, and have made progress side by side, have shared wisdom, grown and reaped together amidst explorations and thinking.

© Social Sciences Academic Press and Springer Nature Singapore Pte Ltd. 2018
Y. Tao and Z. Lu, *Special Economic Zones and China's Development Path*,
Research Series on the Chinese Dream and China's Development Path,
https://doi.org/10.1007/978-981-10-3220-2

In fact, an academic team is a community of thoughts. Debates make it vibrant, brainstorming more rational, explorations more cohesive. First of all, I thank Professor Lu Zhiguo, doctoral supervisor and Deputy Director of the College of Economics of Shenzhen University; he is my old partner—the book *China's Economic Zones: Design, Implementation, and Impact* is the result of our friendly cooperation. Professor Lu Zhiguo is a learned scholar in Western economic theory and one of few well-known teachers granted the classroom teaching award in Shenzhen University. He is responsible for finalizing the entire manuscript and conducting routine coordination relating to this research subject. He has made tremendous efforts and unique contributions to this book, *Special Economic Zones and China's Development Path*. He also wrote the first and second sections of the first chapter.

The third section of the first chapter was completed by Dr. Mao Liang. He is a young talent who graduated from Peking University and works in a down-to-earth manner. The second and third chapters were completed by associate professor Luo Haiping; he received a doctorate degree from the China Center for Special Economic Zone Research, Shenzhen University—the Humanities & Social Science Research Base under the Ministry of Education, and then joined Nanchang University as an new talent; he dedicated himself to researching the issues concerning the special economic zones as a doctoral candidate; after graduation, he published a number of academic papers on the special economic zones and China's Development Path; he is a diligent scholar with an active intellect, a great passion for and creativity in academic research. The fourth chapter was completed by Professor Zhang Kai, doctoral supervisor and Director of the International Business School of Shenzhen University; he is an academically excellent scholar; as an outstanding young scholar at Shenzhen University. He is one of the first group of overseas returnees under the Peacock Program of Shenzhen University for attracting overseas high-level talents and also one of the first group of winners under the Outstanding Young Teacher Cultivation Program of Shenzhen University for encouraging the development and growth of young scholars. The fifth chapter was jointly completed by associate professor Wu Fenglan and Dr. Gao Chuanlun. Associate professor Wu Fenglan is my first doctoral students; she participated in writing the book *China's Economic Zones: Design, Implementation, and Impact*; in the eight years after her Ph.D graduation, she has steadily grown in the academic field; she is steadfast and meticulous in her academic pursuit, which is her praiseworthy character as a scholar. Gao Chuanlun is a doctoral candidate currently under my supervision; he is smart and insatiable of learning, well-read, and has an active intellect; I believe his participation in writing this book, *Special Economic Zones and China's Development Path*, will certainly be valuable for him to receive the training concerning the method of historical research and to develop a spirit of down-to-earth scholarly research. The sixth chapter was completed by Professor Li Meng; he obtained a doctoral degree from Nagoya University; being honest, he has a profound knowledge in econometrics, works earnestly, rigorously conducts scholarly research; he is one of the few people awarded the honor and funding under the Liyuan Scholar Program of Shenzhen University for supporting and encouraging top-notch talents. The seventh chapter was completed by Mr. Wu Junzhong; Professor Wu Junzhong is former Director of the Department of Social Sciences of Shenzhen University and also a famous scholar of great attainments in cultural research; he participated in a feasibility study, discussion and research about the culture-based development of Shenzhen and the culture development and prosperity of the special economic zone; he is an old scholar who has witnessed Shenzhen's growth and development; he is a real and influential senior cultural figure. Professor Wu Junzhong originally retired and spent time writing books and propounding ideas. However, when we requested Mr. Wu Junzhong to help complete the research and writing involving cultural contributions from the special economic zones to China's modernization, he delightfully agreed to our request. Professor Wu is a resourceful senior scholar with rigorous scholarship and a respectable easy-going man. His strong sense of responsibility and mission, his academic devotion and scholarly meticulousness deeply move us. We hereby extend our heartfelt thanks and respects to Professor Wu Junzhong.

Finally, we thank the well-known economist Mr. Wei Xinghua for his care for and guidance of the research team. His wisdom, scholarly conviction, strength and spirit have enormously benefited us all. We thank Ms. Zhou Li, Deputy Editor-in-Chief of the Social Sciences Academic Press (China), for her unfailing support. The first book of our research team—*China's Economic Zones: Design, Implementation, and Impact*—was completed with her help and support and under her guidance. We thank Ms. Li Yanling, President of the International Branch of the Social Sciences Academic Press (China), for her help. We thank the editors in charge of this book Ms. Gao Jing and Ms. Yan Linke for their hard work and admirable professional spirit. We have gained friendship and trust while making academic improvements and enriching our thoughts. I believe that this is a wealth for all of us.

I hope that our research achievement can benefit those who are interested in it, and our thoughts can inspire the research fellows engaged in relevant issues, and our views can be responded to with rational criticism and an exchange of ideas. Both sharing and tempering in sharing is enjoyable and rewarding.

Deputy Secretary of the Party Committee, Secretary of the Discipline Inspection Commission of Shenzhen University,

Director, Professor, China Center for Special Economic Zone Research, Shenzhen University

—Humanities & Social Science Research Based under the Ministry of Education

Tao Yitao

Sangtai Danhuafu Residential Compound

January 5, 2016.

The manufacturer's authorised representative in the EU is Springer Nature Customer Service Centre GmbH, Europaplatz 3, 69115 Heidelberg, Germany. If you have any concerns regarding our products, please contact ProductSafety@springernature.com

Printed and bound by CPI Group (UK) Ltd, Croydon, CR0 4YY
30/09/2026
02225440-0011